T0290478

Cultural Heritage Care and Management

Cultural Heritage Care and Management

Theory and Practice

Cecilia Lizama Salvatore

ROWMAN & LITTLEFIELD
Lanham • Boulder • New York • London

Published by Rowman & Littlefield
A wholly owned subsidary of The Rowman & Littlefield Publishing Group, Inc.
4501 Forbes Boulevard, Suite 200, Lanham, Maryland 20706
www.rowman.com

Unit A, Whitacre Mews, 26-34 Stannary Street, London SE11 4AB

British Library Cataloguing in Publication Information Available

Library of Congress Cataloging-in-Publication Data Available

ISBN 978-1-4422-7217-0 (cloth : alk. paper)
ISBN 978-1-5381-1091-1 (pbk. : alk. paper)
ISBN 978-1-4422-7218-7 (electronic)

∞™ The paper used in this publication meets the minimum requirements of
American National Standard for Information Sciences—Permanence of Paper
for Printed Library Materials, ANSI/NISO Z39.48-1992.

Printed in the United States of America

Contents

List of Figures

Preface

Current books on cultural heritage management may focus on modern issues such as digital cultural heritage, digital preservation, and theorizing digital culture. Or they may focus with great depth on cultural heritage within the context of a specific discipline, such as on heritage as archaeology, on heritage tourism, on heritage and cultural institutions, such as archives and museums, and on the intersection of cultural heritage and ethics and/or the law. Not one discipline can claim jurisdiction of the broad realm and diverse prospects of cultural heritage management. Yet, while this presents diverse opportunities, problems can ensue when people begin to engage in specific aspects of cultural heritage management without a holistic understanding of cultural heritage. A problem can ensue, for example, when one goes forward focusing on the process of digitizing cultural heritage without acknowledging or knowing that this will affect different cultures in diverse ways.

Cultural Heritage Care and Management: Theory and Practice serves to provide a holistic approach to the management of cultural heritage. Breaking ground, it pays particular attention to the diversity in the world's cultural heritage and to the diverse effects of cultural heritage management on cultural communities. It posits the notion that it is critical that when caring for a community's cultural heritage, one has sufficient knowledge of the history and culture of that community, what makes "cultural heritage" in that community, and how the implementation of modern heritage management tools and technology will affect the culture and the community.

The collection in this book had its genesis in the editor's teaching of archives and cultural heritage to graduate students in a school of library and information management. A curriculum on graduate archival or museum studies education is guided by archival and museum studies professional associations. The curriculum stresses the principles, theories, and practices of the professions. The editor, however, quickly realized that it was important that students learning about these principles, theories, and practices also gain further understanding of the diversity of cultures and communities, and of the diverse cultural heritage components and the values placed on them. After all, an indigenous community may place more value on indigenous rituals and the preservation of these rituals than on a manuscript written by a scholar from the country that colonized the community.

This collection provides (1) undergraduate students who have been studying cultural heritage resources and management with a synthesis of the topic and (2) graduate students, especially those coming with different undergraduate backgrounds, with a foundational and holistic introduction to cultural heritage management. The collection is also intended for other college students and faculty who are simply curious about the diverse dimensions of cultural heritage management.

Archival practitioners, scholars, and educators recognize the increasing development of what are often called "community archives"—that is, institutions, collections, and resources that emerge, essentially, from the ground up and which are usually developed by a community within a larger, dominant, and ruling community.[1] These community archives are developed by those who often feel that they are far removed from the mission and activities of mainstream archives and other cultural heritage institutions and who now wish to have control of the way in which records reflect their identity and collective memory. In our global society, when we need to learn more about each other and interact with each other, it is more compelling than ever to give cultural heritage diversity grand efficacy and sanctity. Diverse communities, particularly underrepresented communities, want a place in the cultural heritage management discourse.

Advanced technology and technical systems have aided in the processes of cultural heritage management. The implementation of these technology and systems, however, is not "one size fits all." Ethical, social, cultural, and political issues have always accompanied cultural heritage management, and these issues have become even more complex in the high technology environment.

Cultural Heritage Care and Management: Theory and Practice is a rich resource that provides an introduction to the diverse components of cultural heritage and seeks to explicate the technological components of cultural heritage management and the issues that emerge in working with them. The chapters in this collection are written by experts representing cultures and communities from different regions of the world.

Chapter 1 begins with an exploration of the components of cultural heritage. The wide exploration sets the stage for the other chapters that confront the various issues that emerge when dealing with these components. The other chapters focus on cultural heritage in traditional and indigenous communities across the globe, including the United States, the Pacific (New Zealand, Guam, the Commonwealth of the Northern Mariana Islands, and the Federated States of Micronesia), Europe (France, Italy, and Spain), Eastern Europe (Romania), the Middle East (Syria), and South Africa. Regrettably, not all regions of the world are covered—a fact that demonstrates the intense scope of cultural heritage management. Simultaneously, this facilitates the need for another volume in the future.

Chapter 2 focuses on the care and access of traditional cultural expressions (TCE). The World Intellectual Property Organization (WIPO) points out that traditional cultural expressions are "part of the identity and heritage of a traditional or indigenous community" and "are passed down from generation to generation."[2] They "may include music, dance, art, designs, names, signs and symbols, performances, ceremonies, architectural forms, handicrafts and narratives, or many other artistic or cultural expressions." In this chapter, indigenous communities and marginalized communities are given a place within the broader cultural heritage management discourse.

The notion of dance and performance as forming cultural heritage or TCE is explored further in chapter 3. The author frames the discussion with dance and performance in the Federated States of Micronesia in the Pacific Islands and, delightfully, with a description of a colorful festival of the arts in the Pacific Islands.

The concepts of intangible cultural heritage (ICH) and TCE were not always part of the strong foundation of cultural heritage discourse. We learn about this in the story of the treatment of folklore. The UNESCO 1972 Convention Concerning the Protection of the World Cultural and Natural Heritage focused on physical entities and the built environment. It was not until its meeting in 1989 that UNESCO adopted a resolution on the "safeguarding of traditional culture and folklore."[3] Chapter 4 describes the story of public folklore in heritage studies and discourse, focusing on public folklore in the United States.

As stated earlier, ethical, social, cultural, and political issues have always accompanied cultural heritage management, and these issues have become even more complex in the high technology environment. To be sure, we need to be familiar with the dimensions of cultural heritage law to understand the complex legal and ethical issues that emerge in cultural heritage management. The legal approaches to the protection of cultural heritage are described in chapter 5.

The focus of chapter 6 is on the role of textiles in cultural heritage in Syria and thus adds further to the understanding of cultural heritage in that region of the world. Chapter 8 and chapter 9 add to the discussion of cultural issues and social issues related to cultural heritage management by focusing on cultural heritage in Romania.

UNESCO lists "oral traditions and expressions including language as a vehicle of the intangible cultural heritage" and includes oral traditions and expressions (and language) as one of the domains to be protected in its 2003 Convention for the Safeguarding of the Intangible Cultural Heritage.[4] On the island of Guam and on the islands of the Commonwealth of the Northern Mariana Islands (which include Saipan, Tinian, and Rota), the indigenous Chamorro language was subverted by colonial domination from countries such as Spain, Germany, Japan, and the United States. Chapter 7 describes the story of the Chamorro language and the modern efforts to revitalize it.

The last series of chapters focus on specific tools, technology, and methods that are applicable to cultural heritage management. There are diverse functions and processes in cultural heritage management, diverse types of cultural heritage components, diverse cultural heritage media and format, and diverse types of institutions. Chapter 10 gives a broad introduction to the tools and technology that could be applied in cultural heritage management.

As we are dealing with the digital information landscape, we are compelled to understand what this means to cultural heritage management. One area that we must pay particular attention to is the protection of digital cultural heritage. In chapter 11, the field and activity of digital curation are discussed, which help us understand the process of curating digital cultural heritage materials. As Yakel points out, digital curators are the newest type of information professionals, and digital curation is becoming the umbrella term for digital preservation, electronic records, and digital asset management.[5]

Recognizing the imperative to develop policies and resources for the care and protection of the world cultural heritage, organizations, groups, and individuals were actively documenting this heritage and its diverse components. And while documentation could be a noble act, it could also fuel intense debate. This is illustrated in chapter 12, on the juxtaposition of documentation and the "creation of audiovisual archives" with the call to return digital recordings to their origins. The author brings up the notion of cultural heritage "repatriation," a subject that is mired in controversy. The notion of cultural heritage repatriation reminds us of the complexity of ethics, morality, and the law around cultural heritage management. To be sure, communities, especially traditional communities, must have a voice in projects and efforts that seek to protect and preserve their heritage. An example of community-engaged archiving is described in chapter 13.

Arguably one method for protecting a cultural heritage object is the inclusion of that object on UNESCO's World Heritage List. But including an object on the list is not an easy task and is not without controversy.[6] The World Heritage List and the implications of it as an information system are discussed in chapter 14.

When one is studying or learning about cultural heritage through a book, article, or catalog, it will be more satisfying if images are provided on the cultural heritage site or component. In chapter 15, an even more advanced approach—a geo-referencing of heritage in bibliographies and library materials—is posited. With advancing information technology, why not? Similarly, in chapter 16, the description and visualization of cultural heritage is discussed. The authors discuss metadata specifications, such as the common standard, Dublin Core, and suggest their concept of "VECH" or "Visual Environment for Cultural Heritage" for a more rich approach to handling cultural heritage. And in chapter 17, the importance of communities playing a central part in cataloging and designating attributions to their cultural heritage, with Nicaragua and Morocco as the framework, is discussed. As is posited in chapter 18, the community participative approach is essential to understanding cultural heritage in a community. The focus of the chapter is on the community in the Dolomites in Italy.

To be sure, the complex nature of cultural heritage management cannot be confronted entirely in one collection. There are more cultures to discover, more subjects to discuss, and more issues to resolve. The editor set out to make the point that the discourse on cultural heritage management cannot be reduced to focusing only the latest tools and technology or on the different dimensions of the digital record. If, after reading this book, students, teachers, scholars, and researchers embrace the holistic, yet diverse nature of cultural heritage management, and wish to learn even more about them, then a primary objective for compiling these papers has been achieved.

NOTES

1. Andrew Flinn, "Independent Community Archives and Community-Generated Content: 'Writing, Saving and Sharing our Histories,'" *Convergence: The International Journal of Research into New Media Technologies,* 16, no. 1 (February 2010): 39–51.

2. http://www.wipo.int/tk/en/folklore/.

3. UNESCO, "Recommendation on the Safeguarding of Traditional Culture and Folklore," in *Records of the General Conference Twenty-fifth Session*, Paris, 17 October to 16 November 1989, accessed November 15, 2016.

4. UNESCO, "The Convention for the Safeguarding of Intangible Cultural Heritage," accessed November 15, 2016, http://www.unesco.org/culture/ich/en/convention.

5. Elizabeth Yakel, "Digital curation." *OCLC Systems & Services: International Digital Library Perspectives* 23, 4 (2007): 335–40.

6. See, for example: Bruno S. Frey and Lasse Steiner, "World Heritage List: Does It Make Sense?" *International Journal of Cultural Policy* 17, 5 (November 2011): 555–73.

Acknowledgments

Brian Diettrich: This chapter has benefited from discussion with friends, colleagues, and institutions in the Federated States of Micronesia and the wider Micronesian region over many years. Past research projects have been supported by the Wenner-Gren Foundation, the University of Hawai'i at Mānoa, Victoria University of Wellington, the New Zealand School of Music, and the College of Micronesia, both Chuuk and National campuses. My sincere thanks to Cecilia L. Salvatore for inviting me into this project.

Maria Aranzazu Respaldiza and Monica Wachowicz: This research was funded by the España Virtual CENIT project of the CDTI in the program through 2010 Ingenio CNIG in collaboration with Universidad Politécnica de Madrid: special thanks to Prof. Dr. Miguel Ángel Manso-Callejo and Prof. Dr. Antonio Vázquez Hoehne.

Tasha Vorderstrasse: The author would like to thank Dr. Fiona Rose Greenland and Dr. Oya Topçuoğlu for their assistance. This article is an outgrowth of the author's work on the University of Chicago Oriental Institute project Modeling the Antiquities Trade in Iraq and Syria (MANTIS).

Part I

**CULTURAL HERITAGE MANAGEMENT:
ESTABLISHING BACKGROUND**

Cultural Heritage Components

Cecilia Lizama Salvatore and John T. Lizama

INTRODUCTION

We have long accepted that globalization affects our lives and our communities in both positive and not so positive (or perhaps even negative) ways. From a cultural heritage stance, we know that globalization has facilitated the processes whereby communities learn more about each other's cultural heritage through physical and virtual interaction. Consequential to this is the debate that globalization insinuates hybridization and interferes with our unique identities and our diversity.[1] It is perhaps this that is prompting communities to act on documenting, organizing, and cataloging, and making accessible their cultural heritage, all with a keen eye toward its preservation—in other words, to manage their cultural heritage. In this chapter, we describe the components of cultural heritage and introduce ways in which they can be managed. In the global milieu, the components of cultural heritage are diverse and run the gamut from those that have been deemed a priority for heritage preservation by mainstream cultural heritage institutions to those that are lesser known and named, but are nonetheless given priority by lesser known communities, such as indigenous communities. In describing the diverse cultural heritage components, we are mindful that antecedent to understanding the processes of documenting, organizing, providing access to, and preserving cultural heritage—i.e., the processes of cultural heritage management—is understanding just what constitutes cultural heritage.

THE COMPONENTS OF CULTURAL HERITAGE

Intangible and Tangible Cultural Heritage

We looked hard for where we would find the common definition of cultural heritage. It is the very purpose of this book, in fact, to be mindful of the complexity of cultural heritage and cultural heritage components and of the diverse, global notions of what constitutes cultural heritage, as well as our own respect of global communities with their own diverse perspectives. Ultimately, we yield to the United Nations Educational, Scientific, and Cultural Organization (UNESCO) to assist us in defining cultural heritage components, because of their global and international stance. In that regard, UNESCO defines cultural heritage as both tangible and intangible.[2] Tangible cultural heritage includes movable items such as paintings, sculptures, coins, and manuscripts, and immovable items such as monuments and archaeological sites. It also includes underwater cultural heritage such as shipwrecks, underwater ruins, and cities. By its very nature—that is, its physical properties—tangible cultural heritage is visible and easy to detect and discern. And as Foote points out, the durability of tangible cultural heritage "defines them as communicational resources that can be used to transmit information beyond the bounds of interpersonal contact."[3]

Tangible Cultural Heritage

Movable Tangible Cultural Heritage—Paintings, Sculptures, Coins, and Manuscripts

When one speaks of cultural heritage, paintings and sculptures quickly come to mind.[4] In a very real sense, their mobility and intriguing nature, as well as their visual attractiveness, make these materials readily accessible and available in museums and other cultural heritage institutions. Additionally, they are favored as collectibles by individuals as well as institutions. There is, as well, a plethora of material on the management of the cultural heritage component of paintings, sculptures, coins, and manuscripts—from their history and meaning to disputes about them, and more.[5] We are all familiar with at least one of the well-known and well-documented paintings, sculptures, coins, and manuscripts—for instance, the *Mona Lisa*. But there are also lesser-known paintings, sculptures, coins, and manuscripts. Take the rai stones or stone money of the islands of Yap in the Federated States of Micronesia. The Yapese risked their lives moving around with the heavy, circular stone money, as they used them for all sorts of social transactions, such as a dowry, gift, or in exchange for food.

Figure 1.1. **"Presentation of Yapese stone money for FSM (Federated States of Micronesia) inauguration."**
Trust Territory of the Pacific Islands Archives/Photograph Collection. The work of the Department of Interior, and thus, is in the public domain.

Most rai had a pedigree and were passed down from generation to generation.[6] While modern currency has replaced the rai, it remains central to the cultural heritage of the Yapese islanders and illustrates their ingenuity in taking something that seemed futile and turning it into something of value.

Immovable Tangible Cultural Heritage—Land, Landscape, Architectural Sites, and Monuments

UNESCO has taken on a special role in protecting land, landscape, architectural sites, monuments, and geological formations. At its General Conference of the United Nations Educational, Scientific and Cultural Organization meeting in Paris in 1972, it set the stage for a global initiative to protect the world's natural and cultural heritage sites. Working with states and communities, it set out to identify sites that would be inscribed on the World Heritage Sites list. UNESCO would support the protection of these sites from an established World Heritage fund.[7]

In 1994, a new global strategy was established—the Global Strategy for a Representative, Balanced and Credible World Heritage List, the aim of which is "to ensure that the List [World Heritage List] reflects the world's cultural and natural diversity of outstanding universal value."[8] This strategy is a response to a study that showed the imbalance in the inscription of sites. "Europe, historic towns and religious monuments, Christianity, historical periods and 'elitist' architecture (in relation to vernacular) were all over-represented on the World Heritage List; whereas, all living cultures, and especially 'traditional cultures,' were underrepresented." Since the establishment of the new global strategy, more and more sites from these underrepresented countries and communities have been added to the list.

Intangible Cultural Heritage

The debate over the World Heritage Sites list aside, there is much more to immovable cultural heritage, particularly in marginalized and indigenous communities, that dictates discussion that is beyond the scope of this chapter. Understanding the role of land as heritage in these communities can help us understand why some communities mourn for and protest the changes to their heritage landscape, even if these changes are touted as beneficial to economic development. Furthermore, it can help us understand why Western law cannot be expected to easily resolve land ownership disputes. One of us presided over legal cases that involve land ownership and land as heritage and thus can attest to this.

As stated earlier, tangible cultural heritage is easy to detect and discern; on the other hand, intangible cultural heritage is more complex. In its 2003 General Conference, UNESCO adopted the Convention for the Safeguarding of Intangible Cultural Heritage and identified five major domains into which the convention would categorize intangible heritage. UNESCO maintained that these domains were more than just identifiable; UNESCO besieges us to manage—hence, *safeguard*—them and the components that comprise them. These five major domains include: (1) oral traditions and expressions; (2) performing arts, widely defined; (3) social practices, rituals, and festive events; (4) knowledge and practices concerning nature and the universe; and (5) traditional craftsmanship.[9]

Intangible Cultural Heritage—UNESCO Domain: Oral Traditions and Expressions

Passed on by word of mouth, oral traditions and expressions are intangible cultural heritage that are threatened by urbanization and industrialization, as well as modern forms of communication and dissemination. Oral traditions and expressions are used to pass on knowledge, cultural and social values, and collective memory, and they include "proverbs, riddles, stories, children's songs, legends, myths, songs and epic poems, spells, prayers, psalms, songs, dramatic representations, etc." They "transmit knowledge, cultural and social values, and a collective memory. They are essential to keep cultures alive."[10] At a presentation at the Library of Congress, Chandra Reedy further described UNESCO's five major domains. She provided the *Olonkho*, the heroic epic arts of the Yakut in the easternmost region of the Russian Federation as an example of the domain of oral traditions and expressions.[11] The epic tales are narrated by members of the community who are proficient in acting, singing, and improvisation. The epic tales express beliefs, customs and legends about ancient warriors and legends about deities, spirits and animals, and address contemporary events such as the disintegration of nomadic society.

Janice M. Del Negro is a modern storyteller who has written about the folktale and the art of storytelling. She describes the folktale as stories passed orally from generation to generation, but may also be captured and documented, and storytelling as the oral presentation of narrative to listeners without text or props.[12]

Aghan Odero Agan explains further the place of storytelling in cultural heritage. He writes, "It is in stories and storytelling that the ways in which human beings lived and interacted with the changing landscapes, and even mindscapes, were preserved, well before the advent of the printed word. Thus, it is no coincidence that the art of storytelling is a crosscutting cultural heritage, identifiable with every human grouping."[13] He further writes, "In many instances, Africa has been defined and publicized by its numerous physical cultural sites and countless artefacts in many museums around the world. However, there is still much to be learned about the continent through its under-exploited intangible heritage found in oral traditions, wrapped up in tales, riddles, proverbs, tongue-twisters, chants."[14]

Intangible Cultural Heritage—UNESCO Domain: Performing Arts, Widely Defined

Performing arts range from vocal and instrumental music, dance and theater to pantomime, sung verse and beyond to the instruments, objects, artifacts, and spaces associated with them. The domain of performing arts may be found in other intangible cultural heritage domains, such as in the domain of social practices, rituals, and festive events.[15] Consider the *Sinulog*, the exuberant dancing in the streets by Filipinos from Cebu City in the Philippines during the Sinulog Festival. The dance, from the Cebuano word *sulog* or water current, is a dance in which dancers move back and forth with the beat of drums to mimic the flow of the water current. The Sinulog Festival originated in Cebu City to celebrate the Cebuanos' conversion to Roman Catholicism, and is held on the third Sunday of January. The Sinulog Festival is even held elsewhere, where there is a community of immigrants from Cebu City.[16]

Performing arts are being actively documented, generally—i.e., plays are being performed, music is being recorded, and dance is being preserved. Consider the work of the Dance Heritage Coalition in documenting and preserving dance in the United States and the work of Diehl+Ritter, through its website "tanzholds.de," in preserving dance in Germany.[17] In our era of globalization and technological advances, performing arts have become more popular and commercialized. Performing arts that are endangered, remain, however. Again, at the Library of Congress, Reedy gives the example of Vedic chanting. While there used to be 1,000 Vedic recitation branches, there are now no more than thirteen. The Vedas are "an ancient corpus of poetry, philosophy, myths and rituals that date back over 3,500 years transmitted orally in the Vedic language, which is derived from classical Sanskrit. To ensure that the sound of each word would be retained unaltered, the practitioners, who are Brahman priests, are taught from childhood a set of complex recitation techniques based on tonal accents."[18]

Intangible Cultural Heritage—Social Practices, Rituals, and Festive Events

Whether traditional or modern, social practices, rituals, and festive events structure our lives, and in a very real sense, illustrate our worldview. The events may involve a small or large group of people and are tied to a special time or place. Worldwide, sports events and attendance of these events have become a ritual and studied across diverse disciplines.[19] On the other hand, the royal ancestral ritual in the Jongmyo Shrine in Seoul, South Korea, is part of South Korea's cultural heritage that UNESCO seeks to preserve. As Reedy explains, the ancestral ritual is

> a Confucian ritual dedicated to the ancestors of the Joseon dynasty of the 14th to 19th Centuries. It incorporates song, dance, music and food and wine offerings and is practiced once a year. It's a unique example of a Confucian ritual no longer celebrated in China but inspired by classical Chinese texts on a cult of ancestors and filial piety. Endangerment within this domain is centered on the fact that these types of activities depend on broad participation of a community and modern society's migration and a splintering of a society may lead to a loss of heritage, economic changes make them difficult to support and increasing participation of tourists in events may bring a reduction to short highlights instead of a full event.[20]

Goldsmith describes beauty pageants as cultural markers and as serving as a country's or community's identity during a specific time.[21] Consider the Miss America beauty contest in the United States. It started in Atlantic City in 1921 to boost tourism, but the contestants were soon touched by the glamour of Hollywood, and during the Second World War, were ostensible in their patriotism.

Likewise, in her description of the Miss Universe Pageant of 1928, Grout gives a good example of how festivals and pageants serve as cultural markers. During that time in their history, the United States and France were at war; nevertheless both countries permitted their contestants to come together for the Miss Universe Pageant. By the completion of the pageant, the two countries were exchanging damning words about what constituted favorable characteristics in a woman.[22]

Intangible Cultural Heritage—Knowledge and Practices Concerning Nature and the Universe

The domain of "knowledge and practices concerning nature and the universe" includes "numerous areas such as traditional ecological wisdom, indigenous knowledge, knowledge about local fauna and flora, traditional healing systems, rituals, beliefs, initiatory rites, cosmologies, shamanism, possession rites, social organisations, festivals, languages and visual arts."[23] These knowledge and practices are particularly central to the cultural heritage of native and indigenous communities, and are inherently under serious threat from the impact of globalization—from climate change and urbanization to the change in the natural environment, as well as the impact of natural disasters.

Reedy provides the Vanuatu sand drawings as an example of this knowledge concerning nature and the universe.[24] With one finger, the Vanuatuans draw directly on the ground in sand, volcanic ash, or clay. The sand drawings are more than an artistic expression; they are a multifunctional writing system that serves as a means of communication among speakers of about eighty language groups. The drawings communicate and transmit rituals, myths, and information about local histories, systems, and patterns. The practice of sand drawings are also endangered as a result of globalization.

Indigenous navigation is central to the cultural heritage of the people of the Pacific Islands. The exogenous groups who came to colonize these islands throughout their long history were quite impressed by the ability of their people to sail their hand-built small crafts and proas across the Pacific Ocean waters with speed and accuracy.[25] In Micronesia, the indigenous people also create "stick charts" to map out the location of the many islands in the vast ocean.[26]

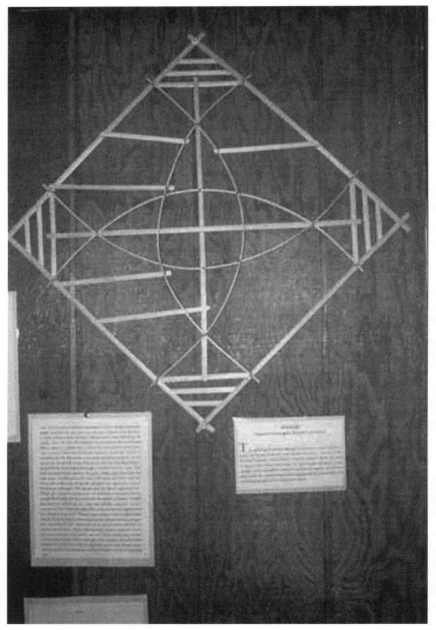

Figure 1.2. A Marshallese stick chart on display at the Majuro Museum.
Angela K. Kepler via Creative Commons.

Indigenous or celestial navigation is knowledge concerning nature and the universe because it is instinctive. The "stick charts" that are used are made of coconut fiber and shells, and are memorized by the navigators before they set on their journey out to sea. At sea, they rely on their knowledge of and rapport with the sea. This knowledge is intangible and is learned from experience and, in particular, diligent mentorship by a master navigator.

Intangible Cultural Heritage—Traditional Craftsmanship

It is commonplace for many communities to flaunt the work of their traditional craftsmen and craftswomen as a maneuver to highlight their cultural heritage. For instance, communities in China flaunt the adept talents and creations of paper-cutting artisans. Paper-cutting artisans were traditionally women farmers.[27] As a craft from China, paper-cutting has a long history in the country and has been attributed to the tradition or ritual of worshipping, evocation, and sacrificing. It is one of the most popular folk decoration arts in the country.[28]

In the African continent, African masks are created for different individuals and for different purposes. These masks symbolize the vastness of the African continent and the diversity in and complexity of African history. They continue to intrigue scholars and researchers.

UNESCO has identified three thematic areas of action, one of which is the theme, "Protecting our Heritage and Fostering Creativity." One of the foci of this theme is the component of arts and crafts. UNESCO assists communities in "unlocking the potential of the creative economy through the support for local initiatives related to arts, crafts and artistic creation and by working with artists groups and associations."[29]

Food and Foodways—Tangible/Intangible Cultural Heritage

Food symbolizes the culture of a community, and foodways tell us more about the relationship between food and culture. Specifically, foodways include the customs and traditions relating to food and its preparation.[30] This is recognized by UNESCO and so, it continues to recognize different types of food and foodways and establish initiatives that safeguard the foodways of a community. One such project is the initiative to safeguard traditional foodways in Kenya.[31] Recognizing that the foodways and food traditions of Kenya are at risk, the initiative aims to safeguard the foodways of two communities in Kenya by raising awareness of and safeguarding the endangered diversity of their traditional foodways and related knowledge about nature.

Bonnekessen explores further the relationship between food and culture.[32] She writes, "In short, food becomes a lens through which we may explore the stratified realities of a society, its ideas about worth, about class, sex/gender, race, religion, and even nationality and humanity."[33] This we know to be true. In the United States, for example, we associate meat with men and perhaps even masculinity and plant-based food with the feminine entity. In her study of college students, Tuomainen suggests that food habits are one of the last cultural traits that communities are willing to let go when they move outside their community. She found in her study of Ghanians in England that the lack of availability of ingredients and resources and their uncertainty about their place in their new community swayed them away from their foodways; however, this changed and they began to make food from their own cuisine when they regained their confidence as to their identity and after they sought to make ethnic ingredients more available.[34]

MANAGING THE CULTURAL HERITAGE COMPONENTS

Introduction

There are vast dimensions of cultural heritage management that we cannot cover exhaustively in this chapter. Thus, we provide here a glimpse of some of these dimensions. We posit that in order to effectively manage cultural heritage resources, one must look at the lifecycle of the cultural heritage resource or record itself—from its creation, quickly followed by its selection and acquisition, to its organization and cataloging and classification (and thus its accessibility) and to its preservation. Thus, we describe here some of the dimensions within the framework of the lifecycle of the cultural heritage resource or record. One of the authors of this chapter teaches in the area of archives and cultural heritage management and has come to appreciate the value in looking at the lifecycle of the resource or record. In looking at the lifecycle, and more specifically, each phase of the lifecycle, one inevitably pays particular attention to the issues that emerge at each phase and must be adept to confront them. Cultural heritage resources and materials are many and diverse, and the knowledge and skills necessary to manage them are not one size fits all. Documenting a movable tangible cultural heritage object, for example, entails identifying the standards and structure to catalog and classify it, conducting research on the history of the object, and so on; on the other hand, documenting an intangible cultural heritage object such as an oral expression entails first identifying the tools to record the expression, then identifying the standards and structure to catalog and classify it, and so forth.

The Creation and Documentation of Cultural Heritage

The creation of a cultural heritage resource or record occurs in what we would call an *organic* or *auxiliary* fashion. When it occurs organically, it occurs in the process of members of a community or culture living their lives. Consider the event of a country's high official being inaugurated. Say it was decided some years ago that the inauguration of the country's high official would always be documented and recorded as it makes explicit the history of the country. And say a traditional ceremony accompanies the inauguration. In recording or documenting the event, the community will be recording or documenting its culture as well. Furthermore, the recording that is made is immediately ingested as part of the community's cultural heritage.

On the other hand, let us say that one day someone decides to document the relationship between food and culture. She works with one community to arrange the recording of food production and of stories related to food and food production in the community. In this example, while the event itself—food production—is organic, the decision to document it and thus create a cultural heritage resource or record is auxiliary.

Issues for Consideration

The organic and auxiliary nature of a cultural heritage resource illustrates a critical issue in the initial phase of its lifecycle. On the one hand, the creation of certain cultural heritage resources happens organically and is easily ingested. On the other hand, a resource is created or documented when we decide that we cannot miss documenting certain resources or the resources of certain communities. We run the risk of neglecting the preservation of the heritage of other communities—such as communities that do not have the resources (such as the recording tools and equipment) to document their heritage at the front end of the lifecycle.

We run the risk of excluding these communities—or at the very least marginalizing these communities—in the wide realm of social memory.

The exclusion of some voices in societal and cultural memory has been a sustained debate in the archives and cultural heritage management community. Seminal to this debate in the United States is Howard Zinn's call for archivists to be proactive in collecting and archiving historical records to ensure that the voice of the underrepresented is heard as well as the voice of those in power.[35] Of late, the voice of those who have felt marginalized in the wide realm of societal memory and who feel that their voices need to be heard have, in fact, been outspoken.

The advent of technology adds another layer to the discussion thread about who is left out of societal memory. Even modern institutions have not fully grasped the arena of born digital records—for example, the extent to which born digital records are created and ingested. While this is a much more complex issue than we have space to discuss in the chapter, it is sufficient to point out the following: born digital records are being created at an increasing speed with the increasing availability of advanced technology (e.g., records are being created via social media tools like Instagram and Twitter) and it is not easy to keep with them. As we work diligently to ingest and preserve these records, we must address these questions:

1. Are we equipped with adequate knowledge about ingesting and preserving digital records, and
2. Are we allowing time to also look for records created by communities who do not have all the modern information and communication tools?

The Selection and Acquisition of Cultural Heritage Resources

The selection and acquisition of cultural heritage resources for ingestion is often based on the mission of the community, organization, or institution that has set out to acquire these resources. Thus, it is likely that the mission of a cultural heritage institution in a city is to select and acquire records and resources related to its history and culture. Similarly, the mission of a university is to select and acquire records and resources related to the history of the university and related to the individuals affiliated, at one time, with the university (e.g., alumni, faculty, board members).

Issues for Consideration

In the selection and acquisition of cultural heritages resources and records, it is important, once again, that there is a balance between mainstream cultural heritage resources and records and the resources and records of underrepresented and marginalized groups and communities. Consider the cultural heritage center in a city to which immigrants are moving at a rapid rate. The immigrants are poised to comprise the majority ethnic group in the community. A long-time staff member at the cultural heritage center might be compelled to select and acquire only resources and records related to the long-time residents out of concern that their culture is disappearing. On the other hand, the mission of the cultural heritage center of the community is to document, select and acquire, organize, and preserve records and resources related to the community and all members of the community.

Another issue points directly to the process and activity of acquisition—the taking control of the resources or records by a steward organization or institution, or perhaps an individual. It is important that those involved in the creation of the resource understand what happens when another party acquires the resource. It is important that they understand if they are giving custodial control of the resources or giving full intellectual control. Custodial control refers to keeping the records under the care and protection of the institution; on the other hand, intellectual control means that you turn over the resources and records to the institution to do whatever they want to do with it. Communities must be informed of likely consequences when they turn over full intellectual control of their cultural heritage resources—for example, do they know that their material could be digitized and made accessible online and used in different ways? Records and resources have different meanings in a community. When these records and resources are digitized and made widely accessible, what meaning will they exude when they might be out of their original context?

The World Intellectual Property Organization (WIPO) has given space to the discussion of traditional cultural expressions or TCEs—similar to many of the components that we have described in this chapter.[36] WIPO points out that TCEs should be protected by "existing systems, such as copyright and related rights, geographical indications, appellations of origin and trademarks. For example, contemporary adaptations of folklore are copyrightable, while performances of traditional songs and music may come under the WIPO Performances and Phonograms Treaty and Beijing Treaty on Audiovisual Performances."

The Organization (or Cataloging and Classification) of Cultural Heritage

Cultural heritage resources and records are organized so that they could be retrieved easily at a later time. It is ineffectual to select and acquire diverse materials and put them away only to be unable to go back and retrieve them and make sense of them. It is ineffectual to arrange and organize resources in a database in a nonstandardized fashion that users would not know where to begin in trying to access and retrieve them. The organization of records and resources includes the cataloging and classification of these records and resources, following accepted cataloging and classification rules and standards. Institutions in the United States, for instance, are likely to implement the Library of Congress Subject Headings. And when institutions follow the same rules and standards, they can more easily share their records and resources with each other.

Issues for Consideration

Rules and standards have been developed by mainstream and powerful institutions or organizations, and even states and governments. In this chapter, we have described the cultural heritage components of diverse communities from around the world. It is important that these components are cataloged and classified as accurately as possible. Some organizations and communities are tackling the issue of accurate and appropriate classification of TCEs as well as Traditional Knowledge or TKs. The WIPO is doing its part in this.[37] Communities in India are doing the same thing.[38] For instance, they are developing classification systems for their Indian Systems of Medicine, the Siddha, relating to meditation and enlightenment, and so forth.

Accessing and Exhibiting Cultural Heritage

When a community's cultural heritage is organized, cataloged, and classified with appropriate rules and standards, as well as with consideration to the community itself, it is less likely that it will draw much criticism. Nevertheless, the stage in which the cultural heritage resource or record is made accessible and, particularly, exhibited has drawn much criticism, and even controversy. Various associations, organizations, and governments, such as the Canadian government and the United States' American Alliance of Museums, have put out a description of the core competencies of the modern museum curator or specialist. Among the core competencies are programming and evaluation skills, user or customer relations, subject specialization or specialized knowledge of the subject of the exhibition, and technology skills.[39] To be sure, one must be adept in developing a program that will accurately represent the cultural heritage of a community outside of its ordinary context, and one must work with the community, as well as visitors, to assess and evaluate the effectiveness of the exhibition and presentation of the cultural heritage resources. More importantly, one must be knowledgeable of the cultural heritage and must know when to confer with members of the community of the cultural heritage. Finally, in the modern world, one must be able to effectively use advanced tools and technology to maximize the effectiveness of the exhibition and access.

Issues for Consideration

The literature on how access and exhibitions have garnered controversy and criticism is extensive. Consider the feminists' protest of the Jack the Ripper Museum and the exhibition of the Elgin Marbles at the British Museum (that they be returned to Greece) in London alone. Two pivotal issues that emerge in providing access to and exhibiting cultural heritage resources and records are (1) copyright and (2) intellectual property, and non-maleficence. The Berne Convention for the Protection of Literary and Artistic Works, which was adopted in 1886, has been a tool that has guided the access, use, and reuse of literary and artistic works in much of the Western world, even though the United States did not immediately sign on to it.[40] It was not until 1989 that the United States signed on to it. The Berne Convention provides guidance in many areas, but more importantly on issues related to the translation, the adaptation, the reproduction, and the performance of cultural heritage literary and artistic works. The WIPO, which was established in 1967, is a significant addition to the Berne Convention, as it also focused on patents, trademarks, and designs.[41]

In providing access to cultural heritage, particularly the heritage of traditional or underrepresented communities, we must try to ensure non-maleficence (i.e., that harm is not done on the communities). To be sure, harm is done when those who provide access and those who gain access to a community's cultural heritage infringe on the intellectual property rights of that community. However, harm may be done as well when we do not try to understand a community and its cultural heritage and we display a cultural heritage resource in a negative or opposing context.

The Preservation of Cultural Heritage

At the beginning of this chapter, we noted the role that globalization has on cultural heritage management. Elsewhere, we noted that technology added another layer to the discourse on cultural heritage management. To be sure, globalization has instigated cultural heritage preservation projects and activities. As communities are changing and cultural heritage seems to be disappearing, individuals, groups, and institutions have stepped forward to preserve it. Technology can be useful as a tool for documenting, and thus, preserving, cultural heritage. Consider the tools for oral history. Not too long ago, we could audio-record an interview about a particular cultural or historical event and place the audio-recording in a safe place for preservation. Now we can also video-record the interview, the activity of recording can be mobile, and the recording can be transcribed and uploaded on the Internet so that it can be accessed from any computer.

Issues for Consideration

Two paramount issues in the preservation stage of the lifecycle of a resource or record are (1) the sustainability of the preservation tool and product and (2) the time, money, and effort that are required to carry out the preservation activity. The tool or technology that is used in the preservation of cultural heritage resources is as useful as the longevity of the tool or technology itself. As noted earlier, we can now video-record oral interviews as well as cultural events. But what do we do about the audiocassette tapes that were used to record oral interviews over twenty years ago? Do we still have the equipment, the cassette players, to retrieve the oral interviews? And if we wish to migrate them to newer and advanced technology, do we have the time, money, and effort to do that? And what happens when the newer technology is replaced by even newer technology? The challenge for many communities is not just to effectively document their cultural heritage, but to effectively preserve the documentation.

CONCLUSION

Locally, nationally, and internationally, communities are seeking to manage and preserve their cultural heritage. Antecedent to cultural heritage management is understanding what constitutes cultural heritage. In writing this chapter, we wanted to underscore that point. We hope that the description of the diverse components of cultural heritage is sufficient. And we hope that by grasping these diverse components, readers will pay particular attention to their management and to the issues that emerge in doing so. Other authors have written about the vast dimensions of cultural heritage management, and we encourage readers to turn to these authors.

NOTES

1. Pham Duy Duc, "Cultural Diversity under Conditions of Globalization," *Nature, Society & Thought* 19, no. 1 (2006): 97–207; Asha Mukherjee, "Culture, Tradition and Globalisation: Some Philosophical Questions," *Social Alternatives* 35, no. 1 (2016): 53–56.

2. UNESCO. Illicit Trafficking of Cultural Property. http://www.unesco.org/new/en/culture/themes/illicit-trafficking-of-cultural-property/unesco-database-of-national-cultural-heritage-laws/frequently-asked-questions/definition-of-the-cultural-heritage/#topPage; UNESCO. What is Intangible Cultural Heritage? http://www.unesco.org/culture/ich/en/1com.

3. Kenneth E. Foote, "To Remember and Forget: Archives, Memory, and Culture," *American Archivist* 53 (1990): 379.

4. Khan Academy. What Is Cultural Heritage? https://www.khanacademy.org/humanities/art-history-basics/beginners-art-history/a/what-is-cultural-heritage.

5. Mark Dike DeLancey, "Collecting, Collections, and Cultural Heritage in the Cameroon Grassfield," *African Arts* 49, no. 2 (Summer 2016): 1–4; Derek Fincham, "Justice and the Cultural Heritage Movement: Using Environmental Justice to Appraise Art and Antiquities Disputes," *Virginia Journal of Social Policy & the Law* 20, no. 1 (Fall 2012): 43–95.

6. Scott M. Fitzpatrick, "Banking on Stone Money," *Archaeology* 57, no. 2 (Mar/Apr 2004): 18–23.

7. UNESCO. Convention Concerning the Protection of the World Cultural and Natural Heritage. http://whc.unesco.org/en/conventiontext/.

8. UNESCO. Global Strategy. http://whc.unesco.org/en/globalstrategy/.

9. UNESCO. The Convention for the Safeguarding of Intangible Cultural Heritage. http://www .unesco.org/new/en/santiago/culture/intangible-heritage/convention-intangible-cultural-heritage/.

10. UNESCO. "Traditions and Oral Expressions, Including Language, as Vehicle of the Intangible Cultural Heritage." http://www.unesco.org/culture/ich/es/tradiciones-y-expresiones-orales-00053.

11. Chandra Reedy. Preservation of Intangible Cultural Heritage. https://www.loc.gov/today/cyberlc/ feature_wdesc.php?rec=4509.

12. Janice M. Del Negro, *Folktales Aloud: Practical Advice for Playful Storytelling* (Chicago: American Library Association, 2013).

13. Aghan Odero Agan, "Storytelling as a Means of Disseminating Knowledge in Museums: The Example of Sigana Moto Moto," *Museum International* 58, no. 1–2 (2006): 76.

14. Ibid., 77.

15. UNESCO. Performing Arts (such as traditional music, dance and theater). http://www.unesco.org/ culture/ich/en/performing-arts-00054.

16. Enrique G. Oracion, "The Sinulog Festival of Overseas Filipino Workers in Hong Kong: Meanings and Contexts," *Asian Anthropology* 11, no. 1 (2012): 107–127.

17. Dance Heritage Coalition. http://www.danceheritage.org/; Tanzfonds Heritage. http://tanzfonds .de/en/home/.

18. Reedy.

19. Lee Philip McGinnis, James W. Gentry, and Julia McQuillan, "Ritual-Based Behavior That Reinforces Hegemonic Masculinity in Golf: Variations in Women Golfers' Responses," *Life Sciences* 31, no. 1 (Jan/Feb 2009): 19–36; Marci D. Cottingham, "Interaction Ritual Theory and Sports Fans: Emotions, Symbols, and Solidarity," *Sociology of Sport Journal* 29, no. 2 (Jun 2012): 168–185.

20. Reedy.

21. Rosie Goldsmith, "And the Winner is . . . ," *New Statesman*, 134, no. 4762 (10/17/2005): 34–35.

22. Holly Grout, "Between Venus and Mercury: The 1920s Beauty Contest in France and America," *French, Politics, Culture and Society* 31, no. 1 (Spring 2013): 47–68.

23. UNESCO. Knowledge and Practices Concerning Nature and the Universe. http://www.unesco. org/culture/ich/en/knowledge-concerning-nature-00056.

24. Reedy.

25. Todd Ames, "Maritime Culture in the Western Pacific: A Touch of Tradition," *Pacific Asia Inquiry*, 4, no. 1 (Fall 2013): 94–108.

26. Cari Romm, "How Sticks and Shell Charts Became a Sophisticated System for Navigation," January 26, 2015. http://www.smithsonianmag.com/smithsonian-institution/how-sticks-and-shell-charts -became-sophisticated-system-navigation-180954018/.

27. Jing Xiaoeli, "Preserving a Tradition," *Beijing Review* 50, no. 41 (10/11/2007): 38–39.

28. Cultural China. Paper-cut. http://traditions.cultural-china.com/en/16Traditions145.html.

29. UNESCO. Protecting Our Heritage and Fostering Creativity. http://www.unesco.org/new/en/juba/ thematic-areas-of-action/protecting-our-heritage-and-fostering-creativity/.

30. Collins English Dictionary. https://www.collinsdictionary.com/us/dictionary/english/foodways.

31. UNESCO. Safeguarding Traditional Foodways of Two Communities in Kenya. http://www.unesco .org/culture/ich/en/projects/safeguarding-traditional-foodways-of-two-communities-in-kenya-00176.

32. Barbara Bonnekessen, "Food Is Good to Teach: An Exploration of the Cultural Meanings of Food," *Food, Culture & Society* 13, no. 2 (June 2010): 280–295.

33. Bonnekessen, 280.

34. Helena Margaret Tuomainen, "Ethnic Identity, (Post) Colonialism and Foodways: Ghanaians in London," *Food, Culture & Society* 12, no. 4 (December 2009): 525–554.

35. Howard Zinn, "Secrecy, Archives, and the Public Interest," *Midwestern Archivist* 2, no. 2 (1977): 14–27.

36. World Intellectual Property Organization (WIPO). Traditional Cultural Expressions. http://www.wipo.int/tk/en/folklore/.

37. WIPO. Topic 3—The TK Resource Classification (TKRC): Classification Methodologies of Traditional Knowledge (TK). http://www.wipo.int/meetings/en/doc_details.jsp?doc_id=162785.

38. Traditional Knowledge Resource Classification (TKRC). http://www.tkdl.res.in/tkdl/LangDefault/common/TKRC.asp?GL=Eng; Fulvio Mazzocchi, "Western Science and Traditional Knowledge: Despite Their Variations, Different Forms of Knowledge Can Learn from Each Other," *EMBO Reports* 7.5 (2006): 463–466. *PMC*. Web. March 13, 2017. In addition, traditional or indigenous knowledge has been rediscovered as a model for a healthy interaction with, and use of, the environment, and as a rich source to be tapped into in order to gain new perspectives about the relationship between humans and nature.

39. Government of Canada. Museum Knowledge Workers for the 21st Century. http://canada.pch.gc.ca/eng/1443703972188/1453817039039; American Alliance of Museums. Curator Core Competencies. http://www.aam-us.org/docs/default-source/professional-networks/curator-core-competencies.pdf?sfvrsn=2.

40. WIPO. Berne Convention for the Protection of Literary and Artistic Works. http://www.wipo.int/treaties/en/ip/berne/.

41. WIPOL Inside WIPO. http://www.wipo.int/about-wipo/en/.

2

Beyond Stewardship and Consultation

Use, Care, and Protection of Indigenous Cultural Heritage

Loriene Roy and Ciaran Trace

INTRODUCTION

Libraries, archives, and museums (LAMS) have within their collections tangible evidence of tribal beliefs, communications, histories, and artistic expressions. These expressions are present in a range of formats from images in photographs or videos, to stories and life histories captured in audio recordings, records, and print transcripts, to cultural objects such as baskets, clothing, ledger art, and armaments, to retold cultural stories published as literature for children and youth, and to contemporary literature. In the United States, attention to the handling of indigenous cultural material in museums increased with the passage of NAGPRA, the Native American Graves Protection and Reparations Act, in 1990.[1] Even with legislation affecting collections in some cultural heritage institutions, the relationships between tribal communities, their cultural heritage, and cultural heritage institutions are uncertain—sometimes supportive, sometimes antagonistic, largely disconnected.

This chapter discusses the multiple roles and voices of both the LAM professional communities and the originating tribal communities in the access and care of traditional cultural expressions (TCE). This conversation about connecting with traditional communities is of great consequence for the daily practices of librarians and archivists and is significant in terms of how we prepare students for their future LAM careers. The organizational structure of the chapter is centered on the Five W's (who, what, when, where, why) and one H (how), adding a brief discussion also of the concept of No. The chapter also introduces promising new developments, such as the Mukurtu content management system, that can provide a technological bridge for balancing community traditions and cultural institution policies. We also discuss why stewardship is an insufficient role for LAMs in that it brings a cultural bias to a process that should, but does not always, include negotiation and power sharing with the source communities of traditional cultural knowledge.

WHO: THE SOURCE COMMUNITIES AND LAM INSTITUTIONS AND WORKERS

Those involved in this conversation and stewardship process include the indigenous peoples and their cultural expressions as well as those working in LAM institutions.

When focusing on cultural heritage manifestations, indigenous people can be regarded as the communities of origin or as the source communities.[2] This consideration supports the Native value of community over time—that is, those who have a right or connection with an object include not only those who originally created the object but also their genealogical descendants. The concept of source community also reflects aspects of indigenous worldview, especially as it relates to time. This notion of time is reflected in the Maori phrase, "me hoki whakamuri, kia ahu whakamua, ka neke"—our future lies in the past.[3]

A discussion of who is indigenous is found in an online book, *Library Services to Indigenous Populations: Case Studies*, published in June 2013. The essay considers the rationale behind the need to define indigenous peoples and how indigenous peoples define themselves. It provides responses to the commonly asked questions "Are there any indigenous people?" and "Isn't everyone indigenous?," considers the dilemma of those who are not indigenous but want to self-identify as Native, and the debate around blood quantum or the requirement of prescribed genetic/genealogic lines to indigenous identity. In Aotearoa/New Zealand, this brings up the notion of biculturalism—with recognition of the Maori as the original peoples and, actually, all others as more recent arrivals.[4] In Hawai'i the distinction between indigenous people and others is seen in discussions of settler populations arriving on the islands after the Native Hawai'ian peoples.[5] In the end, the notion of who is indigenous can be stated simply, "indigenous communities know who their people are."[6]

The information fields have strong professional organizations that have helped define their domain areas, provide practical information for their workers, and respond to key issues affecting their work and presence. These national and international organizations often play a primary role in introducing their members to discussions surrounding TCE as they play out within the sphere of collecting and the provision of services.

At the international level, these organizations include the International Federation of Library Associations and Institutions (IFLA). IFLA presidents and members have encouraged their association to explore its role in supporting indigenous knowledge across the globe. The results can be seen in the passage of a statement in 2006 acknowledging the intrinsic value and importance of indigenous traditional knowledge and in conference presentations on indigenous issues at IFLA presidential meetings, and annual and regional conferences.[7] In December 2008, the Professional Committee of IFLA approved the formation of a Special Interest Group on Indigenous Matters, located under the umbrella of the IFLA Library Services to Multicultural Populations Section.[8] These SIG members were involved in the revision of the guidelines on training LIS professionals that incorporated indigenous ways as the eleventh core element in an LIS curriculum.[9]

At the national level, general organizations that provide one or more platforms on indigenous matters include the American Library Association (ALA), the Society of American Archivists (SAA), and the Library and Information Association of New Zealand/Aotearoa (LIANZA).[10]

In the United States, the American Library Association (ALA) is the professional body for librarianship. ALA expresses its commitment to the key action area of diversity primarily through its organizational structure. ALA is governed by a council of some 180 members, made up of 100 at-large councilors elected by the ALA membership, 11 representatives of the 11 divisions of ALA, others representing the Round Tables with the largest memberships, and around 50 chapter councilors elected by state library associations. Sixteen council committees, including the Committee on Diversity, report to this council. Established in 1981, the fifteen-member Committee on Diversity is charged with wide-ranging tasks, from providing a forum for research on diversity issues to recruitment of a diverse workforce.[11] Diversity within the field is also reflected in the history and activities of the five U.S. national ethnic library associations affiliated with ALA: the American Indian Library Association (AILA), the Asian/Pacific American Library Association (APALA), the Black Caucus of ALA, the Chinese Americans Library Association (CALA), and REFORMA: the National Association to Promote Library Services to Latinos and the Spanish-Speaking.[12]

There are also national associations outside the United States that are more specifically focused on indigenous issues including Te Ropu Whakahau (Maori in libraries and information management) in Aotearoa/New Zealand, and the Aboriginal and Torres Strait Islander Library and Information Resource Network (ATSILIRN) in Australia.[13]

Several organizations within the United States and internationally also exist largely to plan gatherings of those interested in indigenous cultural heritage settings and their work. Federally funded national conferences on tribal libraries, archives, and museums were launched in the United States starting in 2002 with financial support from the U.S. Institute of Museum and Library Services (IMLS). These conferences led to the establishment of the Association of Tribal Archives, Libraries, and Museums (ATALM) in January 2011. Other such organizations include the Tribal College Librarians Professional Development Institute, and the International Indigenous Librarians Forum (IILF).[14] IILF has taken place every other year since 1999 in locations including Aotearoa/New Zealand, Sweden, the United States, Canada, Australia, and Norway.

Professional development for tribal college librarians is available through the annual Tribal College Librarians Professional Development Institute usually held on the campus of Montana State University in Bozeman, Montana, in the United States.[15] Issues of interest encompass the practicalities of day-to-day operations of tribal college libraries, including acquisitions and use of resources such as medical databases, and updates on local activities such as construction projects and management case studies. Such events bring indigenous peoples involved in culturally based heritage environments in direct contact with library workers, propelling discussions of commonalities and differences in serving Native patrons as well as discussions about existing as a Native person within institutional workplaces.

While national and international organizations play a role in introducing their members to discussions surrounding TCE, this conversation is still in its infancy. Regardless of their education and connections with key organizations, McCarthy found that many professionals nonetheless "lack a critical analysis of biculturalism and other aspects of their work in terms of culture, identity and institutional structure."[16] All things considered, the wisest path indicates that both Native and non-Native library workers still have much to learn from each other. This learning must be an ongoing process, and one that takes place in multiple venues, both within and outside of the professional organizational context.

WHAT: THE OBJECTS/TRADITIONAL CULTURAL EXPRESSIONS

In the midst of the originating/source community and the cultural heritage institution are the products, cultural images, records, and writings by and about the Native peoples. Source communities and holding institutions view the material/content/object differently. To the non-indigenous this may be a container or "an inert artifact"; to the indigenous community the material or object is a "taonga or living object ancestor."[17] Non-indigenous LAM workers might strive for clear and tight definitions of what traditional cultural expressions are. Indigenous peoples may be reluctant to do so since probing questions might infringe on privacy, and disclosure might be subject to cultural taboos.

The way of life for the source communities is reflected in many activities and in the resultant tangible creations. These expressions are regarded by the Maori, or indigenous peoples of Aotearoa/New Zealand, as taonga tuku iho or treasures handed down:

> A taonga can be any item, object or thing that represents the ancestral identity of a Maori king group (whanau, hapu or iwi) in relation to particular lands and resources. Taonga can be tangible like a cloak, a greenstone or a war canoe, or they can be intangible like the knowledge used to be able to carve, recite genealogy or sing a lament . . . They are seen as the spiritual personification of particular ancestors, either as direct images or through association. Descendants experience this wairua (ancestral spirit) as ihi (presence), wehi (awe) and wana (authority). Thus taonga are time travelers that bridge the generations, enabling descendants to ritually meet their ancestors face to face.[18]

These taonga or objects and/or cultural content lie in the center of the discussion of stewardship and consultation. Once traditional knowledge is removed from its cultural setting, then it is vulnerable and susceptible to change. Objects have their own extant histories and also have a history layered on them after their arrival in a cultural repository. These histories summon many questions. Were they stolen? Did they receive preservation treatments? Were they processed? In the process of being accessioned into a cultural heritage institution, objects acquire descriptions in accordance with professional practice but such processing/cataloging may neglect the fact that the object itself has needs. When removed from their places and communities of origin, objects become dislocated, isolated, and without context. Such practices may also alienate the source communities, failing to tell the full story of their histories and significance. Even if cultural materials do not reside near their communities of origin, their source communities have "spiritual ownership."[19]

Materials may also acquire new layers of experience if they live apart from their originating community. Sometimes this new life alters their physical structure—such as the use of pesticide in treating some objects for insect damage.[20] As Nakata points out, the result of this process of alteration should be to open up professional practice to increased examination and scrutiny:

> When it employs methods and instruments of Western science, which involve fragmentation across categories of information, isolation and ex situ storage in regional, national and international archives and networks then it begins to lay itself open to the same criticisms as "Western science," which has largely failed in development contexts. It becomes not embedded in local meanings and contexts but separated from its original context—and entity to be studied, worked on, developed, integrated, transferred, and ultimately changed to fit another.[21]

WHEN: THE TIMING OF STEWARDSHIP AND CONSULTATION

For museum and archives personnel, the interim answer to envisioning their work with tribal communities has been to define their work as stewardship. Stewardship brings with it the connotation that a steward is acting as a surrogate for another in the process. Stewardship not only describes one role for personnel in those cultural heritage institutions but it also promotes a set of attitudes: The two key elements of the stewardship concept are the ability to care for, manage, or control persons or things and accountability for the proper exercise of that ability. A steward exercises power and authority but does not have license to do so in a self-serving or careless manner.[22]

For the LAM community, the act of stewardship is often achieved through a process of consultation. Consultation is not only a conversation that takes place between LAM personnel and Native community members, it is also a process of collaboration and relationship building. The First Archivists Circle explains the purpose for consultation: "Collecting institutions and Native communities are encouraged to build relationships to ensure the respectful care and use of archival material."[23] However, true inclusion of Native voices and opinions takes place throughout a decision-making process and not after LAM personnel have already made their decisions. One reason for the necessity of such inclusion is that to source communities, negotiation in and of itself becomes reminiscent of treaty scenarios whereby Native peoples, once again, are presented with loss as the only result or outcome.

When professional organizations consider their roles as stewards of indigenous heritage materials, they often see consultation as the extent of involvement of indigenous communities in this work, whereas tribal members see consultation as a first step. This speaks to fundamental differences in motivations: in a study of museums in Aotearoa/New Zealand in 1995, researchers found that the notion of partnership was viewed differently by Maori, the indigenous peoples of Aotearoa/New Zealand and by non-Maori Pakeha, individuals of European descent. Maori felt partnership should focus on power sharing, while Pakeha felt it focused on social inclusion.[24] Nordstrand, Hopi exhibit planner for the U.S. National Park Service, notes that, "If the goal is to build a long-lasting relationship with the community, a more involved collaborative process should be developed."[25] While LAM workers may see such community building as difficult if not impossible, Alcoff considers it a failure if "the possibility of dialogue is left unexplored or inadequately pursued by more privileged persons."[26]

We hold that those working in cultural heritage institutions, including libraries, should step outside of an exalted view of their stewardship roles. While this role is based on professional education and training, it is not superior to the knowledge, practice, traditional use, and cultural views of access of the originating or source communities—the indigenous peoples themselves. The answer to when stewardship and consultation should take place is both early and forever, including the steps that need to be taken to start conversation and its ongoing continuance.

WHERE: SITUATING STEWARDSHIP AND CONSULTATION

Where is a question that considers the place of stewardship and of contact. LAM physical spaces house and provide access to a range of cultural expressions, some more tangible than others. Even for LAMs not under tribal management, they can serve to reunite people, bringing them into contact with cultural material that is no longer in their midst, some forgotten, some not known. The LAM may also be seen as a distant location where material is held without context, cold, without the story that accompanies it.

It is here that the actions of stewardship and consultation also take place. It is here where the powers of those involved meet and are felt. Discussion of space should also include a consideration of how LAM institutions might be viewed by cultural communities. This includes in-house policies that may be felt as rules, borders, boundaries, hierarchy, and red tape. These are the spaces of "rigorously applied professional standards and long-term conventions."[27]

Consultation space is the place to build the relationship with the tribal community. Questions arising concerning this space include whether or how to make it an indigenous workspace. Must it be on indigenous land? Isn't all land indigenous? Is this space wherever indigenous materials are located? Museums offer a physical space that includes the "contact zone," a concept described by Mary Louis Pratt as: "the space in which peoples geographically and historically separated come into contact with each other and establish ongoing relations, usually involving conditions of coercion, racial inequality and intractable conflict."[28]

Considering setting brings up new questions. For example, can you take an existing setting and adapt it to meet the requirements of indigenous protocol? Or, do you construct new settings that are indigenous in nature from the beginning? Perhaps settings are placed on a continuum of development that reflects a range of indigenous identity, similar to Durie's continuum of biculturalism. Thus, settings where indigenous cultural heritage may be found include unmodified mainstream institutions, institutions that incorporate indigenous perspectives, those that actively involve indigenous communities, those existing alongside indigenous cultural heritage institutions, and independent institutions organized and managed independently by indigenous peoples.[29]

HOW: CARING FOR, SPEAKING FOR, SPEAKING WITH CULTURAL EXPRESSIONS

Indigenous community members and LAM workers may view their roles in handling traditional cultural expressions differently. They might also consider the other's interpretation of their role as foreign, obsolete, offensive, or unforgiving. These differences acknowledge a contested ground with concern over use and ownership resulting in an impasse. The impasse is expressed sometimes in silences or in tone that is felt to be adversarial or disruptive. For indigenous members, contact with cultural material is similar to a relationship they might have with another living person. They might interpret the LAM workers' activities as directed toward molding the object, cloaking it with the policies, with the purpose of protecting it from use. How can conversations start anew or be revisited with respect and progress toward actions that are beneficial?

All matters under the question of "how" are sometimes grouped in professional parlance under the topic of consultation within the umbrella of stewardship. Thus, consultation can be seen as layers of communication, thought, and decision making. To the LAM practitioner, the orientation is to focus on the object with concerns about its physical makeup and how it responds to other physical characteristics of the environment into which it is placed. The object becomes part of an exhibition or display:

> In these displays nature was partly a wonder, a curio to be pondered, a wild if alluring paradise that had to be tamed and controlled, and also a library of specimens, a system waiting to be catalogued and measured as a step in the process of colonization.[30]

LAM workers consider the traditional cultural expression as similar to other materials and content in their collections. This is the action of incorporating the cultural expression into learned practice that involves the broad areas of:

Governance, management, and planning
Care of collections and taonga
Public programmes, including exhibitions
Customer service
Relationships with communities.[31]

To LAM professionals, their role as stewards speaks to their interpretation of their service as guardians of the object and their responsibility to their present and future patrons. Their institutions are the living expression of these combined service points to the extent that they may demonstrate actions of social responsibility. However, stewardship is a promotion of an unequal distribution of power. The focus is on care and not on the equality of ownership (everything from decision making and policy setting to everyday use and access). Instead, stewardship can be seen as a continuum, where the ultimate goal is one of shared policy setting between the originating community and the holder of the cultural knowledge. Where an organization is placed on the continuum is based on a number of factors or features: an organizational structure that includes indigenous representation, creation of an environment that welcomes indigenous patrons, and services designed in collaboration with those audiences.

To Native people, care of the cultural expression is based on protocol or the daily etiquette of living right. The originating community approaches the object or content from the perspective that the material or object is alive. This evokes the necessity of an introduction. This introduction, or protocol, is more than a recitation but is instead a process and a type of procedure. In native circles, protocol is also custom. Answering the question "who are your people?" is not an exercise to satisfy curiosity but may delineate lines of connectedness; it provides a historical perspective, indicates whether communication is even permissible in some cases, and provides the context of a future relationship. The object is shown respect, much as a person might be shown respect. In some cases, the object is treated in a specific way because it is special or has a unique history.

The indigenous perspective of the object considers its context—the object's story, and its meaning, including aspects of its spirituality. Many objects are in and of themselves considered alive. They have had unique roles when they were with the people, and they are records of those histories. Since their histories extend beyond their physical construction and appearance, their significance is layered with meanings.

For Native people, the more appropriate role is that of "cultural guardianship," or what the Maori call kaitiakitanga.

> The act of guardianship, kaitiakitanga, requires clear lines of accountability to whanau, hapu or iwi [family, tribe, or subtribe] and is more frequently associated with obligation than authority. Transfer of the ownership of a resource away from tribal ownership does not release tangata whenua [the indigenous people] from exercising a protective role . . . although it does make the task more difficult since others will also have an interest.[32]

Thus, there are two or more sides to considering ownership and access of tribal cultural manifestations. And, like other aspects of Native life—such as land and their representation and images in popular media—the larger, non-Native voice has exerted its way. The discussion often dissolves into a situation that views Native people as being selfish, positioned in opposition to the "greater good." In other words, "indigenous claims of cultural ownership [are weighed] against the broader society's need for open communication."[33]

While the LAM perspective and the indigenous ways of life might appear to be at odds with one another, they also share the common desire to take care of cultural materials. Whether care is exhibited as storage or as use in cultural ceremonies, both actions support the survival of cultural expressions. And for that indigenous peoples are thankful.

Both LAM professionals and indigenous peoples seek examples of successful dialogue and action when it comes to care and access of traditional cultural expressions. While individual cases of success or failure are useful in understanding lessons learned, larger scale options are desirable. As McCarthy says, "too often independent outcomes are sought by multiple groups when collective or mainstream solutions are more feasible and sustainable."[34] NAGPRA, the

Native American Graves and Reparations Act of 1990, has shown that such dialogue is possible. NAGPRA has "given American Indians considerable clout with museums in matters lying beyond the law's limited scope. More than anything, NAGPRA promoted the creation of new institutional arrangements—joint-use committees, review panels, and repatriation offices—that have redefined relationships between museums and indigenous communities. Consultation has become an element of everyday practice in museums and archives whose holdings include American Indian materials."[35]

One recent tool that holds great promise in expediting and facilitating these discussions and actions is Mukurtu. Cultural anthropologist/ethnographer Dr. Kimberly Christen was working in Australia with the Warumungu staff of the Nyinkka Nyunyu Art and Culture Center when she noticed a distinct problem with existing content-based management systems available for documenting digital archival collections. She noted that they did not provide "granular levels of access for various types of users, nor a way to customize protocols for access based on cultural parameters."[36] This observation led to the development and subsequent application of the Mukurtu content management system, providing indigenous peoples and their LAM collaborators with, for the first time, the option to mirror indigenous traditional protocol in making content available digitally. Mukurtu applications have involved the building of digital collections, especially the repatriation of objects once removed from source communities and now returning as surrogates in digital form.

Mukurtu allows tribal members to define user communities, and in doing so, it allows varying levels or layers of access. Some content may be open to anyone who views a site while other content may have restrictions set by the source communities. Restrictions may also be placed on the source community. As Brown notes, "the collective nature of culture does not mean that its elements are uniformly distributed. Information is nearly everywhere held differentially along lines of age, gender, social class, kinship, and occupation . . . knowledge may be compartmentalized along lines of age and gender or unevenly shared between ritual experts and lay persons."[37] Thus, the community might set access by gender—with only women allowed to view "women's work" and men allowed to view other content. Certain content may be available only during certain times of the year or during certain time of one's life. Expert or special knowledge may be needed to access some content while other content may be restricted to those who share a specific connection, such as a clan affiliation. These decisions come about through relationship building and the resultant sharing or yielding of power, and are manifest in a co-curation of collections. Mukurtu is also an instrument of advocacy since it permits and welcomes the inclusion of Native language content in script and in audio.

Mukurtu is a tool that offers and provides an approach to making the indigenous view of access and openness tangible.[38] Mukurtu allows archives workers to "to undo . . . privileging practices and, in their place, to establish a set of standards that allows for multiple voices, layered context, diverse forms of metadata, and the expansion of the archival record."[39]

WHY: CONCERN FOR CULTURAL EXPRESSIONS

Why is the probing question.

LAM professionals have inherited legacy materials. While the objects or information are unique and often are cultural treasures, LAM workers employ approaches to their care that are often representative of how indigenous peoples have been mistreated over time. Objects have uncertain histories for how they have arrived in LAMs: some were gifted, donated, sold, or stolen. Objects have been removed from their originating context and they have acquired new layers of experience and interpretation. Some physical objects were altered—with ownership stamps added and treatments applied to reduce real or possible damage. Written accounts may reflect tribal beliefs but their accounting may have been misinterpreted or taken by non-tribal people; stories may, thus, be available without their associated access protocols. And indigenous peoples have been, or might feel, that they are prevented from contact with the knowledge, whether by distance or by the LAM procedures for access.

As a result, the humans involved often become entrenched: LAM professionals behind their professional values and codes, and indigenous peoples behind their hurt feelings and tribal knowledge.

Why, then, speaks to the essential questions, starting with why collect, why organize, why share traditional knowledge and its expressions? From the cultural heritage professional, the why is addressed in professional codes of ethics and practice.

From the indigenous person's point of view, the why is a question that is often accompanied by pain. Why take, or steal, our material? Why close it off from tribal members? Why describe it in ways that are offensive? Why be resistant to including us? Why speak in a demeaning fashion to us? Why do you think you are right?

"Why" brings many more probing questions. Do LAM personnel and policies illustrate majority culture response/recognition of Native culture? Is the Native view on TCE and the role of LAMS a growing verbalization that reflects the indigenous path toward self-determination? Can a heritage setting recognize that there is more than one way of doing things, one that reflects the philosophies of indigenous peoples? Is partnership possible?

SUMMARY: GOING BEYOND CONSULTATION AND STEWARDSHIP

Conversations on indigenous cultural heritage touch on the needs, interests, desires, and potential rewards or damages to a range of audiences.

For both indigenous source communities and LAM professionals, discussion about traditional cultural expressions involves an awareness, an assertion, an awakening during a convergence of thinking, an emergence of tools, and a conversation about change. We talk about the materials, thinking, expressions, lifestyles of indigenous peoples and the institutions that might collect, hold, arrange, organize, display, and share the materials or their descriptions.

Becoming aware of the who, what, when, where, how, and why of working with traditional cultural expressions is a step toward acknowledging that Native peoples have a right to determine what happens with their cultural expressions. It is opening oneself to listening to indigenous peoples' voices, voices that are allowing themselves to say "no" to mismanagement of resources, "no" to misinterpretation of their heritage, "no" to prying into their cultural privacy. The right to cultural privacy is "the right of possessors of a culture—especially possessors of a native culture—to shield themselves from unwanted scrutiny."[40]

Saying "no" gives Native peoples agency to reduce the distance between cultural expressions and their communities of origin. As they have gained economic strength and returned to their cultural lives, indigenous peoples have reclaimed not only their language but also other aspects of their cultures. These actions of control are statements of strength, asserting that they still remain, they stand tall, and that these actions are ones that contribute to strengthening a cultural presence now and into the future.

The non-Native response to "no" is often based on apprehension and fear. There is fear that materials will not be cared for in the same manner. LAM professionals have kept the materials alive to this point and for that indigenous communities are grateful. There is fear that access restrictions will be added—that Native peoples, once they again own what they first created, will now impose barriers to the use of the objects. This is thought to be akin to censorship, in direct opposition of librarianship's firmly held belief in intellectual freedom. However, as Brown points out, "no appeals to free speech will settle the moral debate occasioned by thoughtless and disrespectful use of a people's iconography."[41]

The reality is that the professional role may be limited to one of considering a future user much like oneself while ignoring the originators of the knowledge. LAM professionals may not willingly want to step away from the table, away from the role of steward, even if requested to do so by Native people.

Listening and following "no" may feel to LAM professionals that they are relinquishing control. The desire to exert control is part of the professional education of LAM workers who learn the processes and philosophies of organizing knowledge. It is important to understand that a European, Western mind-set persists and infiltrates the professional fields. Librarianship, for example, was born as a profession in 1876 with the establishment of the American Library Association, a time when U.S. federal policy considered tribal people those who were to be conquered, whose time was coming to an end. Cultural institutions may be perceived as reflections of government policies of assimilation. They may be interpreted as miniatures of the reservation system—where tangible expressions are removed from their communities and sites of origin and reintroduced on display or hidden as remnants of a romantic past. Even the professional tasks of description and documenting may involve a non-indigenous interpretation of the indigenous past while ignoring the indigenous present and future.

These discussions call on institutions and professionals working in them to not only acknowledge the presence of source communities and their connections to objects/expressions in their care, but also to understand that the institutions have options in how they proceed to care for this content. This is a "change from [exerting] sole institutional control to [embracing] kaitiakitanga, customary guardianship."[42]

That is not to say that feelings will not arise in these discussions, feelings that are normal and which must be recognized. These range from resentment, "anxious goodwill," shock, cynicism, exclusion, "awkwardship, tension, and confusion," pressured. But it is only through moving in new directions that the potential lies for gratitude, "learning, exchange, and genuine personal growth."[43]

Beyond stewardship calls on LAM professionals to provide an environment where indigenous peoples feel comfortable. This extends from the staff, to the signage, to the protocols of greeting and services. It is akin to advocacy. Can the non-indigenous professionals permit indigenous people to have control, their say over "the destiny of their significant cultural property" while, in return, accept the gift of inviting indigenous people to "place upon a peculiarly European institution their own particular feel?"[44] These are the actions of actively connecting source communities with their cultural expressions and not waiting for the source community to wander in.

Kreps refers to this listening as a process of liberating culture:

> Liberating culture is not only about giving back or restoring a people's right to or control over the management of cultural heritage. It is also about liberating our thinking from the Eurocentric view of what constitutes a museum, artifact and museological practice so that we might better recognize

alternative forms. The liberation of culture allows for emergence of a new museological discourse in which points of reference are no longer solely determined and defined by the west. This "new inclusiveness" acknowledges that those who have been marginalized as "the others" are central to the creation of new museological paradigms.[45]

Through liberating culture, LAMs may be transformed. This transformation converts their settings from places that hold, separate, and isolate cultural knowledge to living places that serve as extensions of the vibrancy of living peoples. Can those places that hold indigenous knowledge be transformed from "a death house, a sad repository of plunder and grief, a cave of relics; but instead [to] a place of joy and laughter and memory; a haven of inspiration and hope; the silently sleeping seeds of life itself"?[46] Some LAM institutions are clearing the way. Like many activities involving humans, it starts with conversations centered on the TCE.

NOTES

1. Native American Graves Protection and Repatriation Act of 1990 § 2, 25 U.S.C. § 3001 (1990).

2. Peers, Laura and Alison K. Brown, eds., *Museums and Source Communities: A Routledge Reader* (London: Routledge, 2003).

3. Heikell, Vicki-Anne, "Our Future Lies in the Past: Me Hoki Whakamuri, Kia Ahu Whakamua, Ka Neke," *International Preservation News* 61 (December 2013), 12.

4. Szekely, Chris, "Bicultural Librarianship in New Zealand." In Szekely, Chris, ed., *Issues and Initiatives in Indigenous Librarianship: Some International Perspectives* (Wellington: Te Ropu Whakahau; National Library of New Zealand/Te Puna Matauranga o Aotearoa, 1999), 5–12.

5. Fujikane, Candace and Jonathan Y. Okamura, eds., *Asian Settler Colonialism: From Local Governance to the Habits of Everyday Life in Hawai'i'* (Honolulu: University of Hawai'i Press, 2008).

6. Roy, Loriene, "Who is Indigenous?" In Roy, Loriene and Antonia Frydman, eds., *Library Services to Indigenous Populations: Case Studies* (available at http://www.ifla.org/publications/library-services -to-indigenous-populations-case-studies. Accessed on 8 June 2013), 10.

7. IFLA. *IFLA Statement on Indigenous Traditional Knowledge.* 2002. Available at: www.ifla.org/ en/publications/ifla-statement-on-indigenous-traditional-knowledge. Accessed on 23 March 2014.

8. IFLA. *Special Interest Group on Indigenous Matters.* Available at: http://www.ifla.org/indige nous-matters. Accessed on 23 March 2014.

9. IFLA. *Education and Training Section. Guidelines for Professional Library/Information Educational Programs.* 2012. Available at: http://www.ifla.org/publications/guidelines-for-professional -libraryinformation-educational-programs-2012. Accessed on 23 March 2014.

10. ALA. Available at: ALA.org. Accessed on 23 March 2014; Society of American Archivists. Available at: http://www2.archivists.org/. Accessed on 23 March 2014; LIANZA. Available at: http://www .lianza.org.nz/. Accessed on 23 March 2014.

11. ALA. Committee on Diversity (COD). "Charge." Available at: http://www.ala.org/groups/com mittees/ala/ala-minconcul. Accessed on 23 March 2014.

12. AILA. Available at: http://ailanet.org/. Accessed on 23 March 2014; APALA. Available at: http:// www.apalaweb.org/. Accessed on 23 March 2014; Black Caucus of ALA. Available at: http://www.bcala .org/. Accessed on 23 March 2014; CALA. Available at: http://cala-web.org/. Accessed on 23 March 2014; REFORMA. Available at: http://www.reforma.org/. Accessed on 23 March 2014.

13. Te Ropu Whakahau. Available at: http://www.trw.org.nz/. Accessed on 23 March 2014; ATSIL-IRN. Available at: http://aiatsis.gov.au/atsilirn/index.php. Accessed on 23 March 2014.

14. ATALM. Available at: atalm.org. Accessed on 23 March 2014; IILF 2013. Available at: http:// ailanet.org/activities/iilf-2013/. Accessed on 23 March 2014.

15. Tribal College Librarians Professional Development Institute. Available at: http://www.lib.mon tana.edu/tcli/. Accessed on 23 March 2014.

16. McCarthy, Conal, Museums and Maori: Heritage Professionals, Indigenous Collections,Current Practice (Wellington: Te Papa Press, 2011).

17. McCarthy, 60.

18. Paul Tapsell in McCarthy, Conal, *Museums and Maori: Heritage Professionals, Indigenous Collections, Current Practice* (Wellington: Te Papa Press, 2011), 169.

19. McCarthy, 60.

20. Odegaard, Nancy, "The Issue of Pesticide Contamination." In Ogden, Sherelyn, ed., *Caring for American Indian Objects: A Practical and Cultural Guide* (St. Paul, MN: Minnesota Historical Society, 2004), 69–81.

21. Nakata, Martin, "Indigenous Knowledge and the Cultural Interface: Underlying Issues at the Intersection of Knowledge and Information Systems," paper given at the 68th IFLA Council and General Conference, Glasgow, Scotland, August 18–24, 2002.

22. Bakken, Peter W., "Stewardship." *Encyclopedia of Environmental Ethics and Philosophy*. Ed. J. Baird Callicott and Robert Frodeman. Vol. 2 (Detroit: Macmillan Reference USA, 2009), 282–284. Gale Virtual Reference Library. Web. 23 Mar. 2014.

23. First Archivists Circle. "Protocols for Native Archival Materials." 2007. Available at: http://www2.nau.edu/libnap-p/protocols.html. Accessed on 23 March 2014.

24. McCarthy, 103.

25. Nordstrand, Pollyanna, "The Voice of the Museum: Developing Displays," In Ogden, Sherelyn, ed., *Caring for American Indian Objects: A Practical and Cultural Guide* (St. Paul, MN: Minnesota Historical Society, 2004), 13.

26. Alcoff, Linda, "The Problem of Speaking for Others." *Cultural Critique* (Winter 1992), 5–32, 30.

27. McCarthy, 69.

28. Mary Louis Pratt in Clifford, James Routes: *Travel and Translation in the Late Twentieth Century* (Cambridge, MA: Harvard University Press, 1997), 192.

29. McCarthy, 147–148.

30. McCarthy, 2011, 30.

31. Museum of New Zealand/Te Papa Tongarewa. *New Zealand Museums Standards Scheme*. Available at http://www.tepapa.govt.nz/nationalservices/howwehelp/pages/nzmuseumsstandardsscheme.aspx. Accessed on 3 April 2014.

32. Durie, Mason, *Te Mana, Te Kawanatanga: The Politics of Maori Self-Determination* (Melbourne, Australia: Oxford University Press, 1998), 23.

33. Brown, Michael F., *Who Owns Native Culture?* (Cambridge, MA: Harvard University Press, 2003), xii.

34. McCarthy, 236.

35. Brown, 247.

36. Christen, Kimberly, "Opening Archives: Respectful Repatriation," *The American Archivist* 74 (Spring/Summer 2011), 186.

37. Brown, 28, 183.

38. Brown, 42.

39. Christen, 198.

40. Brown, 27–28.

41. Brown, 94.

42. McCarthy, 168.

43. McCarthy, 83.

44. McCarthy, 65.

45. Kreps, Christina F., *Liberating Culture: Cross-Cultural Perspectives on Museums, Curation and Heritage Preservation* (London: Routledge, 2003), 145–146.

46. Te Awekotuku cited in McCarthy, 66.

3

Ephemerality and Permanence

Situating Performance as Intangible Cultural Heritage

Brian Diettrich

Parallel rows of glistening bodies moved in time, adorned with scented garlands (*mwara-mwar*) and fragrant coconut oil (*marekeiso*). Women gracefully performed *dokia*, seated dances in which they struck small resonant sticks (*lepin tuhke*) on a length of wood across their laps and against those of dancers at their sides. Men simultaneously danced *wehn*, rhythmic steps to right and left with vigorous hand and arm movements, and followed by *kepir*, a dance of twirled wooden paddles (*padil en kepir*). The combined voices of both men and women traced the contour of the chanted poetry and expressed themes of place and the cultural past. The dancers were from the northern chiefdom of Kiti on the island of Pohnpei, and their performance took place on Guam in May 2016 for the twelfth Festival of Pacific Arts, a quadrennial celebration of Pacific Island arts and cultures. The Pohnpeian delegation to the festival gave special prominence to *koulin kahlek*, a multisensorial genre that simultaneously combines music, dance, poetry, woven and floral attire, and aromatic aesthetics in a unified presentation. Organized both for special events at home and for festive occasions abroad, presentations of *koulin kahlek* are a means of communicating and affirming culture, land, and people. Performances such as these are powerful forms of human expression, and they are also significant vehicles for cultural heritage.

I begin this chapter with a festival presentation from Pohnpei as a means to initiate an exploration of performances within the frameworks of heritage, and particularly with the domain of intangible cultural heritage. Examining performance with all of its component elements suggests challenges for the "work" and ideology of heritage, and this in turn prompts us to query the meaning and significance of heritage for performance. What critical perspectives does the production of heritage bring to practices such as music and dance? What cultural issues are embedded in heritage frameworks for performance, and how does understanding these allow us to consider more deeply the full range of human cultural practices, past and present? I suggest in this chapter that heritage discourse enacts a kind of translation for performance in which issues of cultural ephemerality and permanence are amplified. Considering the relationship between heritage and performance underscores a number of debates about culture and preservation that have emerged under the rubric of heritage. Cultural value and hierarchy play significant roles in addressing separate types of performance as well as what qualifies as heritage (and what does not), and these questions raise the ubiquitous and contested labels of "traditional" and "contemporary" (Mallon 2010). The Pohnepian *koulin kahlek* performance

Figure 3.1.   Performance of Pohnpeian Koulin Kahlek at the Twelfth Festival of Pacific Arts, Guam.
Photo by B. Diettrich, 2016.

might be conveniently labeled as "traditional," for example, but such a branding overlooks the contemporary festival contexts of the performance, or the innovations enacted by Pohnpeians over time in music, movement, ensemble, and attire. Moreover, any consideration of performance as heritage must account for the "work" of cultural policies that promulgate or inhibit practices, and that in turn intersect with local, national, and transnational institutions. According to Henry, "understanding the performative dimensions of cultural heritage is crucial for comprehending the how grassroots social movements in Oceania creatively work the political space between nation and state" (2011:191). These factors underline questions about "heritage for whom" and "heritage by whom," and which are revealed in performances at events like the Festival of Pacific Arts, in which local priorities and national policy play out in regional and international dialogue and debate.

Throughout this chapter, I address these issues and queries with case examples from the Pacific Islands and particularly from the Federated States of Micronesia (FSM), where I have undertaken research on music and dance since 2000. The FSM is a nation comprised of more than 600 islands in the northwest Pacific, and consists of four states from west to east: Yap, Chuuk, Pohnpei, and Kosrae. Comprised of both high islands and atolls, the FSM is a diverse nation, culturally, linguistically, and also in performance. Music and dance include time-honored practices handed down from ancestors and often kept within families and lineages, but also practices created during the complex colonial interactions of the region and a proliferation of new practices that draw on global popular culture, particularly reggae and contemporary dance forms.[1] Today a significant and growing community of FSM citizens resides outside of the home islands, in the region on Guam or in Hawai'i, or in the continental United States. In these diverse locations performance remains closely linked with cultural heritage.

This chapter examines performance through a focus on music and dance in the FSM as a means to address ideas and questions about cultural heritage globally. In the first part of this chapter, I explore how media and technology have played a crucial large role in the legacies of reproduction and archiving of performance as heritage, and particularly with regard to music. Next I examine the significance of performance for community in the Pacific, and I focus on one village event from Chuuk State. Afterward, I discuss the importance of national and transnational policy questions regarding heritage and performance. This chapter is framed as an introduction to some of the issues and challenges in the relationship between heritage and performance, and which has been the focus of a large body of interdisciplinary scholarship.

PERFORMANCE, REPRODUCTION, AND REPATRIATION

The concept of performance encapsulates a wide range of meanings, ideas, and applications. According to Hellier-Tinoco, performance is a "framed event, an enactment out of tradition, and a discrete object of attention in which the framing is inherently part of the event itself" (2011:37). Within this framed event, performance may involve practices such as music, sung and recited poetry, structured movement of the body, sounding/moving objects, aromatic decorations, and also the tactile experience of wearing appropriate attire, manipulating instruments, and performing on the earth or a stage. The time element is crucial to understanding performance, and the resulting ephemerality and intangibility of cultural practices emphasize the process of creation, recreation, and transformation across specific temporal contexts. Writing about this transient aspect of performance, Phelan famously stated: "Performance cannot be saved, recorded, documented, or otherwise participate in the circulation of representations of representations: once it does so it becomes something other than performance" (Phelan 1993:146; see also Kirshenblatt-Gimblett 2004). According to Phelan, a fundamental quality of performance is its disappearance, what she refers to as its "nonreproductive" trait (ibid.:148). This perspective is at odds with any agenda of preservation, but it also raises a number of questions about how we engage with performance in society, especially in present-day contexts that are saturated with the reproduction of images, sounds, and experiences. In contrast to Phelan, Pigliasco effectively argues that the disappearance of performance need not be its defining feature, and argues that we should therefore be mindful of "the diachronic, dialogic aspect intrinsic to any traditional cultural expression" (2011:331).[2] In the discourse about performance as heritage anxieties about permanence and ephemerality continue to hold central attention, both within indigenous communities and globally.

The translation of music, dance, and other practices into new forms of presentation—media such as photography, sound recordings, and film—comprises significant legacies of performance as heritage. Since the late nineteenth century new, evolving technologies have recorded and transmitted the intangible aspects of culture to tangible forms, and indigenous peoples and their practices have been a central focus of this attention (Sterne 2003, Hochman 2014). In the early decades of the development of ethnomusicology, for example, research was attuned and prioritized toward continual documentation, collection, and archiving of the music of others (and sometimes dances), and especially through audio forms (Myers 1992). Today this work and the resulting audio repositories of cultural knowledge offer new opportunities for heritage work, through repatriation, revival, and new creation, processes that are also documented and reproduced into new forms.

The Pacific was a significant early frontier in the ethnological preservation of cultural practices through media reproduction. The earliest audio recordings for Micronesia, for example, were made by Furness on the island of Yap in 1903, who wrote of his interest to "obtain permanent records of their songs and incantations" (Smith 1998:994; Furness 1910:69). Only four years later, Augustin Krämer made recordings in Yap and Chuuk in 1907, and returned for further work in 1910 (Ziegler 2006). Audio reproduction and audio preservation have always intersected closely with colonial enterprises, and this relationship played out through a number of administrative expeditions in Micronesia. While Spain did not take a strong research focus in the region, perhaps from its limited colonial presence but also its preoccupation with violent subjugation on some islands, the German administration was significantly different. Although brief, the German period (1899–1914) coincided with the growth of museum collections internationally and this was evident through the work of the Hamburg Expedition, which undertook research and collection across the region in 1909 and 1910 (Berg 1988, Petersen 2007). Music and dance were not focuses of the German work, but the ethnographers produced extensive chapters on the performing arts in the resulting twenty monographs on Micronesia. German researchers also made approximately eighty-six wax cylinder recordings, and a series of short moving images from Chuuk—some of the earliest films of Pacific dance (Weinstein 2010). The focus of these German reproductions was to record the oldest traditional practices that were assumed to be "vanishing" due to modernization and missionization, ideas that surrounded experiences with indigenous people globally. This colonial salvage work emphasized preservation for posterity, a theme that would repeat itself through Micronesia's later colonial engagements.

The Japanese mandate of Micronesia brought new projects of documentation and preservation to the performing arts. Pioneering music researcher Hisao Tanabe, for example, visited in 1934 and made recordings on acetate disks (Tanabe 1968, 1978). Muranushi followed him in 1936 and made dictaphone recordings as part of the Bishop Museum's expedition to Micronesia (Tatar 1985). After the United States gained military control of the region following World War II, new American researchers came with continued and extensive work in preservation. Work focused on performance followed later in the 1960s, for example in the work of Edwin Burrows (1963) and Barbara B. Smith (Diettrich and Smith 2005). Through both the Japanese and the American periods, researchers have continued to build an international archive of cultural heritage that has taken intangible elements of culture and transformed them into new tangible forms of media, often storied in international or private collections. Recent decades has brought renewed questions about access to these valuable materials as well as new work toward making these materials available, in contemporary digital formats and in repatriation projects.

REPATRIATION

Today a significant focus of heritage work is the management of media reproductions of music and dance by local and international institutions. My own work in this regard has engaged closely with the repatriation of sound recordings to communities in Micronesia, especially in the FSM, but additionally in Palau and the Marshall Islands (Diettrich 2018). Most recently, I worked with ethnomusicologist Barbara B. Smith to return recordings she made in Micronesia in 1963. Smith initiated the project to repatriate the recordings to appropriate institutions in Micronesia where the wider community could access them. I assisted with both the technical work of transferring the recordings to digital formats and also the liaising with institutions in Micronesia. Considering the repatriation of the 1963 recordings by Smith offers a brief window into the process of repatriation and the significance of historical sound recordings as cultural heritage.

The original recordings of the Barbara B. Smith collection consist of thirty magnetic reel recordings made between September 1963 and January 1964. The collection includes examples from Palau, Yap, Ulithi, Chuuk, Pohnpei, Kosrae, and the Marshall Islands. At the time the recordings were made, Smith taught in the music department of the University of Hawai'i at Manoa, and where a number of young Micronesians had come to Honolulu for study. At the instigation of some of those students, Smith traveled to Micronesia to record some of the oldest and most significant genres of music. The resulting audio recordings comprise the largest series from Micronesia immediately after World War II. The corpus of recording includes music and dances that reach back at least to the early twentieth century such as chant, historical instrumental music, and the use of old forms of language, as well as new examples that were contemporary in 1963 but are rare today, such as string band music (Diettrich 2007a). The collection is of significant historical and cultural heritage value to the performing arts of Micronesia, as attested by listeners when introduced to the historical recordings. The repatriation of sound recordings is more than simply a transfer of media, however, and as I have explored elsewhere (Diettrich 2017), the resounding of voices in past audio recordings can have important implications for listening experiences and the ability to hear and engage with the past voices of relatives and ancestors.

Considering the full process of repatriation for recordings such as those from Smith involves both research and technical work, including: (1) setting the aims of the repatriation project, (2) transferring the original recordings to digital format and editing the final versions, (3) preparing a detailed inventory of the recordings (drawn from original field notes and drafted in consolidation with cultural experts), (4) arranging of the legal transfer of the recordings to appropriate institutions, (5) returning and organizing the recording collection in the "home" community, and finally (6) long-term archiving of the original recordings at an appropriate institution. Smith and I completed most of the technical work on this project by 2005, and the Palau part of the project was completed in that year with the Palau National Museum. However, it was not until 2015 that we were able to deposit digital copies of the recordings for the FSM and the Marshall Islands, in part due to ongoing questions about the best and most appropriate local archive willing to accept the recordings. Finding the best local archives can be a challenge in some Pacific nations, due to insufficient support for archival facilities. In the FSM, digital copies of the Smith collection are housed at the Pacific Archives of the College of Micronesia, National Campus on Pohnpei, and in the Marshall Islands at the library of the College of the Marshall Islands on Majuro. The repatriation of the 1963 historical recordings to Micronesia has added to the cultural resources of the region and has already inspired discussions and new performances, similar to other projects of repatriation (Campbell 2012, Hilder 2012, Kahunde 2012). This is a reminder of Kirshenblatt-Gimblett's statement (1995) that "heritage produces something new in the present that has recourse to the past" (1995:369–370). Considering repatriation and the process of resounding historical voices highlights how performances can move fluidly from intangible to tangible form and back again into renewed experiences for local communities.

PERFORMANCE AND COMMUNITY

Performance is an active part of communities in which individuals and groups create, maintain, and reproduce heritage as part of public events. Studying such events brings an understanding of the relationships between community, performance, and heritage. In the FSM today there are a number of public, community events that emphasize heritage presentation, as listed in table 3.1. While most are directed toward local audiences from the FSM, Yap Day has increasingly become an important international tourist event. In addition to the listed events, educational institutions at secondary and tertiary levels in the FSM hold annual "culture day" events, in which students undertake performances and other activities connected to indigenous culture. At these events students decide on particular traditional music and dance repertory, sometimes with new choreography and musical arrangements, and create appropriate attire. Culture day activities remain an important means for young people to engage with performance heritage, and due to the cultural diversity in the FSM, students also learn from each other. The most expansive of these events occurs at the College of Micronesia-FSM, and which I have described in detail elsewhere (Diettrich 2015). Still another series of events for the performative display of heritage are government inaugurations in Chuuk State.

In Chuuk, municipal, state, and national government events play an important role in bringing communities together. Such events make connections between past and present, and as such they often include displays of especially valued music and dance, as well as new compositions and choreographies. At the state level in Chuuk the highest of these events is the inauguration of a governor. Because Chuuk State is widely dispersed with forty-one islands—some of which lie an overnight sea voyage from the state center—many islands hold their own election celebrations in which the governor (or in some cases the lieutenant governor) and other officials make a visit. These celebratory arrivals offer an opportunity for each municipal area to engage with the state government about current political issues, as well as to request funding. Due to transportation complications (by fieldtrip ship for the outer islands), the need for fund-raising, and the sheer number of distinct island communities, some islands end up holding their inauguration one or two years *after* a governor is officially elected by the state. In most inaugurations, an island's villages come together for a major welcome feast, while using the occasion to focus attention on various island projects and concerns. Music and dance play fundamental and polysemous roles throughout inauguration events including welcoming, paying respect, entertaining, and in raising sometimes thorny issues in a public forum. In 2006 and 2007 I attended a number of these events in Chuuk Lagoon and its outer islands for the inauguration of Governor Wesly Simina, who was elected in April 2005. One especially vibrant inauguration was held by the island of Feefen in Inaka Village in January 2006 and included

Table 3.1   Celebratory Days in the FSM with Significant Community Performances

Event	Official Date
Yap Day	1 March
Cultural and Traditions Day	31 March
College of Micronesia Founding Day	1 April
Liberation Day (Kosrae)	8 September
Liberation Day (Pohnpei)	11 September
FSM Independence Day	3 November
Christmas Day	25 December

a state visit by the governor. I attended the event to document the performances together with colleagues from the College of Micronesia, Media Studies department. A brief examination of the Feefen inauguration and especially one particular performance provides a window into the role performance heritage at local events.

At inaugurations and other community events heritage and tradition take numerous forms. After the formal arrivals on Feefen, the inauguration ceremony officially began with an *afanafan* (formal speech) by a male elder and traditional leader. Initiating an event with the respect afforded traditional leaders occurs throughout many contemporary political events in Chuuk. This introductory speech included a short excerpt of *itang*, a genre of rhythmic recitation that uses its own esoteric and opaque language. *Itang* is a significant and rarely heard performance medium of political and cultural lore, and it is a highly guarded performative and linguistic heritage of Chuuk (Diettrich 2017). Considering performance as heritage does not only entail presentations that are inclusive of the broader public, but also the understanding and transmission of *itang*, for example, still largely follows traditional Chuukese hierarchy of separate lineages and clans, and although publicly sounded, it is not democratically transmitted.[3] In this way the construction of some heritage in Chuuk follows a largely local understanding of performance that emphasizes stewardship according to ancestral descent and within its cultural contexts (Nason and Peter 2009). As part of a public event at the Feefen inauguration, the performance of *itang* by a traditional leader marked the importance of the occasion and offered a symbol of cultural and political respect to the government visitors.

In addition to the introductory protocol, speeches, and the feast for visiting government officials, many villages from Feefen presented songs and/or dances. Many of the performances consisted of *kéénún etiwetiw* (welcoming songs) and a number of them showed an enthusiasm for rap, hip-hop, and other contemporary styles. Toward the end of the celebration, in contrast, a small group of men and women sat in a circle on the ground under a makeshift tent in the performance space. Some of the performers wore a few strands of young palm leaf skirts over their clothes, while everyone donned *mwaramwar* (garlands) on the head or around the neck with some prepared from a knotted towel. As the performers arranged themselves, the audience moved in close and formed a wall of observers completely around the circle of performers. In addition, elderly men and women were part of the performance group, and the inclusion of elders, especially in dance, is rare in Chuukese performance practice given the emphasis on youth. The addition of elder performers brought further distinction to the performance that was to follow. Considered together, all of these visual signals marked the performance as cultural by significant (*éwúche*) from the others presented that day. With the rhythmic clapping of hands and slapping of thighs, the group began a performance of *éwúwénú*, social sitting dances iconic of Chuuk's intangible heritage.

The genre called *éwúwénú* refers to a sequence of chants and songs accompanied by choreographed seated dance, focused on hand and arm gestures and rhythmic body percussion. Chuukese refer to the combined performances of poetry, chant, song, and gesture by the single name *éwúwénú*, though some of the chants that comprise *éwúwénú* are called *engi*, traditional chants about love and romance. Historically the *éwúwénú* dance was performed as a means of village or island-wide socializing, particularly during the off-season for breadfruit. The social aspect of the dance included the pursuit of romance, as the chant texts and contextual information from elders today indicate. While formerly a more regular part of annual social activities, today performances of *éwúwénú* are reserved only for special occasions, and their infrequency marks their heritage value. The cultural knowledge about *éwúwénú* is associated with specific areas and clans in Chuuk, including on the high lagoon island of Feefen.

The inauguration performance in 2006 consisted of a sequence of exclamatory chant, song, and love chant, each punctuated by distinct body percussion and gesture, and with a total of seven individual sections linked together into one coherent performance. The poetry of each section ranged widely from traditional welcomes, to lyrics about romantic love drawn from *engi* (love chants); the last section of the *éwúwénú* moved seamlessly into state government politics and lawmaking as newly composed lyrics spoke about taxes and a recent political issue. The performance was thus as equally relevant to current island political frameworks as it was an expression of Chuukese performance tradition. While clearly a time-honored genre of performance that has been perpetuated on Feefen, the *éwúwénú* performance linked closely with social concerns of the present and was a means of polysemic communication for the people of Feefen and the wider Chuukese community. Performance occasions like the 2006 Feefen performance of *éwúwénú* represent a means by which communities maintain performative heritage, but also how performance is at the center of social engagement. Finally, while performance traditions like *éwúwénú* have elements of continuity to them in poetry, music, and dance, they are also far from fossilized presentations or replicas of past art forms. Performances are dynamic elements of heritage that are also part of the current lifeways of communities. The dynamic quality of performance is significant to the sustainability of performance genres as heritage work considers the cultural futures of music and dance practices (Titon 2009). The next and final section of this chapter addresses some of these concerns in the work of heritage policy for the Pacific.

Figure 3.2.   Performance of Éwúwénú at Inaka Village, Feefen Island, Chuuk.
Photo by B. Diettrich, 2006.

PERFORMANCE AND CULTURAL POLICY

A significant realm of intangible heritage in the Pacific and internationally involves cultural policy.[4] Policy may range from areas of institutional support on one end of the spectrum to law on the other, and it may involve local, state/national, or international bodies. Policy directives can be complex and even contradictory, and all the more so when the subject involves intangible practices such as music and dance. The Pacific has seen an increasing interest in local and national policies toward the protection of intangible heritage, and especially in the face of high-profile cases of contestation, for example with traditional Solomon Islands music in the *Deep Forest* dispute (Zemp 1996), with Hawaiian hula in tourism contexts (Desmond 1997), with the commodification of Fijian firewalking (Pigliasco 2010), in the recent representation and copyright protection of the Māori *haka* "Ka Mate" (Gray and Scott 2012), or in recent issues of representation and appropriation in the 2016 Disney film *Moana* (Diaz 2016).[5] An increasing focus of scholarship has addressed heritage as cultural and intellectual property but this framework is often at odds with the indigenous relational approaches to cultural ownership (Nason and Peter 2009, Pigliasco 2011), as well as the thorny problem of cultural appropriation across national boundaries. Nevertheless, the emerging attention given to intellectual property in indigenous cultural practices is of growing concern in heritage debates in the Pacific.

Still another issue is the relationship between cultural policies of Pacific nations and colonialism. The policies and laws of nations that seek to manage heritage are often derived from or facilitated through current or former colonial laws that are in some cases incompatible with indigenous law and traditions. Heritage policy in the Federated States of Micronesia, for example, has been largely drawn from the United States and set up under the U.S. administration of the islands. The FSM formerly encompassed part of the Trust Territory of the Pacific Islands (TTPI) immediately after World War II, and this area was administered first by the U.S. Navy and afterward by the U.S. Department of the Interior. In the 1960s the United States included its Micronesian colonies under its policies of historical preservation. For example, the passing of the National Historical Preservation Act of 1966 was significant toward still powerful notions of "preservation" in the FSM. The frameworks of heritage laws in the FSM from this period were focused on physical sites and places, and the urgency of preservation did not encompass intangible heritage. Perhaps more importantly, the ideas of needing to "preserve" culture and traditions have played and continue to play a significant role in how heritage is considered and practiced in Micronesia, and including from its former focus on tangible sites. In 1974 individual Historic Preservation Offices were created in Micronesia and following this, the FSM National Preservation Act of 1979 stated: "It is the policy of the FSM to protect and preserve the diverse cultural heritages of the people of Micronesia and, in furtherance of that policy, to assist in the identification and maintenance of those areas, sites, and objects of historical significance within the FSM."[6]

The general American direction of heritage in Micronesia could be seen in the ways that important historical sites in the FSM were added to the U.S. National Register of Historical Places, thus assigning a mark of heritage was also a means of U.S. colonial possession (Hanlon 2011). Moreover, the American framework that saw only tangible sites as recognized heritage further denied local Micronesian notions of heritage and value, such as in oral and performance practices. The ramifications of these colonial shadows and policies in Micronesia have only begun to be studied and understood, but the colonial interfaces with heritage suggest a renewed imperative to decolonize heritage practices and priorities internationally.

Over the past fifteen years the FSM, along with other Pacific nations, has been in the process of transforming its heritage policies in part to better align with a number of international and transnational models (Serrano 2013). For example a number of initiatives have come through the Pacific Islands Forum and UNESCO that seek to move heritage into frameworks comparable to local frameworks. Recently, the *Pacific World Heritage Action Plan 2016–2020*, for example, notes that "indigeneity is inseparable from heritage" and that "heritage is holistic, embracing all life, both tangible and intangible, and is understood through our cultural traditions" (1). Still, performance in the Pacific region remains woefully underrepresented in most transnational heritage proclamations and monuments. At the time of writing, the Tongan genre *lakalaka*, "dances and sung speeches of Tonga," remains the only representative performance genre for the Pacific region in the "Representative List of the Intangible Cultural Heritage of Humanity."[7] It remains to be seen how a closer integration with these transnational frameworks by Pacific nations might positively advocate for local perspectives and practices of intangible heritage.

Within the FSM, sites of heritage remain a focus of energy for preservation, but growing efforts have begun to refocus heritage toward ideas inclusive of performance. In 2007 the FSM created the Office of National Archives, Culture, and Historic Preservation, which has played an increasing role in the documentation of intangible heritage at the national level. Following this, in 2010 the Mori administration of the FSM passed the proclamation of the "Micronesia Culture and Traditions Day," which gave more federal recognition to performance traditions within the communities. Mori said of the newly designated day: "Every nation requires a national holiday to reflect upon its cultural and traditional heritage and uniqueness and the Federated States of Micronesia is no exception" (FSM Information Services, 2010). In addition to this proclamation, a 2011 cultural mapping project offered a holistic view of heritage as both tangible and intangible (Kim 2011). Most recently, in 2012 the FSM ratified the 2003 UNESCO Convention for the Safeguarding of Intangible Cultural Heritage. The FSM ratification focused on practices of navigation (which includes performance) and stated: "being rich in cultural heritage, the FSM has some of the last remaining traditional navigators in the Pacific within the outer islands of Yap and Chuuk, whose knowledge in canoe building and navigation are in danger of extinction if not properly preserved" (FSM, Seventeenth Congress 2012). As the FSM moves toward greater engagement with transnational heritage policies, the international attention toward cultural expressions such as performance will likely continue to raise awareness about this cultural area of the Pacific.

REFLECTION

In her article "Theorizing Heritage," Kirshenblatt-Gimblett noted that "whereas we have tended to focus on that which counts as heritage, much remains to be done on the instruments for producing heritage" (1995:379). In this chapter I have examined some of these "instruments" with regard to performance as heritage, and I have focused on media, contexts, and policies that comprise significant cultural landscapes in the Pacific. I have suggested that the relationship between performance and heritage is founded in part with anxieties about ephemerality and permanence in cultural practices, and that these ideas are central to understanding the cultural work of heritage management in areas such as music and dance. Much emphasis on performance historically has focused on preservation, especially through its reproduction as media, such as in sound and film. The legacies of this work and the renewed interest in international archives of performance have offered new projects of relocating, reviving, and innovating performance as heritage. From the perspective of communities in the Pacific, performances offer connections to the more distant past and are primary areas of participatory and sustainable practices. I have suggested that heritage frameworks would benefit from an increased and nuanced understanding of local, indigenous ideas of conceiving and safeguarding performance practices within community frameworks, and especially as Pacific nations continue to adopt into transnational agreements regarding intangible heritage. The broad area of cultural heritage policy has become an emergent area of interest for the Pacific, at the same time that heritage protection and appropriation remain widely contested and discussed. Returning to Kirshenblatt-Gimblett, the case of the Pacific suggests that a greater understanding of the translating and transformation between heritage and performance might bring an increasing awareness to the cultural frictions, values, and priorities of communities and of practices that lie at the intersection of both pasts and presents. A greater attention to the emergence of intangible cultural heritage offers new perspectives for Pacific futures.

NOTES

1. The people who comprise the FSM today experienced separate administrations of Spain (1886–1899), Germany (1899–1914), Japan (1914–1945), and the United States (1945–1979).
2. See Pigliasco (2011) for a useful overview of intangible cultural heritage and lawmaking.
3. See Falgout (1992) for a similar discussion of this issue on the island of Pohnpei.
4. A fuller discussion of heritage policy in the FSM is found in Diettrich (2015).
5. The upcoming Avatar film sequel that has been apparently inspired by Micronesian navigation is the latest example in a legacy of cultural appropriation and will likely spark similar contestation (*Huffingtonpost* 2012).
6. See "Code of the Federated States of Micronesia": http://fsmlaw.org/fsm/code/index.htm.
7. See the inscription page on the UNESCO website: http://www.unesco.org/culture/ich/en/RL/lakalaka-dances-and-sung-speeches-of-tonga-00072.

BIBLIOGRAPHY

Berg, Mark L. "The Wandering Life Among Unreliable Islanders: The Hamburg Südsee Expedition in Micronesia." *The Journal of Pacific History* 23, no. 1 (1988): 95–101.

Burrows, Edwin Grant. *Flower in My Ear: Arts and Ethos of Ifaluk Atoll*. Seattle: University of Washington Press, 1963.

Campbell, Genevieve. "'Ngariwanajirri, the Tiwi 'Strong Kids Song': Using Repatriated Song Recordings in a Contemporary Music Project." *Yearbook for Traditional Music* 44 (2012): 1–23.

Desmond, Jane. "Invoking 'The Native': Body Politics in Contemporary Hawaiian Tourist Shows." *The Drama Review* 41, no. 4 (1997): 83–109.

Diaz, Vince. "Disney Craps a Cute Grass Skirt: Unpacking Insidious Colonial Power and Indigenous Enabling in Disney's 'Moana.'" *The Hawaii Independent*, 29 September. Online: http://hawaiiindependent.net/story/disney-craps-cute-grass-skirt; accessed 1 October 2016.

Diettrich, Brian. "Listening Encounters: Sound Recordings and Cultural Meaning from Chuuk State, Micronesia." In *Oceanic Music Encounters: Essays in Honour of Mervyn McLean*, edited by Richard Moyle, pp. 47–58. University of Auckland, Department of Anthropology, 2007a.

Diettrich, Brian. "Across All Micronesia and Beyond: Innovation and Connections in Chuukese Popular Music and Contemporary Recordings." *The World of Music* 49, no. 1 (2007b): 65–81.

Diettrich, Brian. "Performing Arts as Cultural Heritage in the Federated States of Micronesia." *International Journal of Heritage Studies* 21, no. 7 (2015): 660–673.

Diettrich, Brian [in press]. "Returning Voices: Repatriation and the Emergence of Shared Listening Experiences." In *The Oxford Handbook of Musical Repatriation*, edited by Frank Gunderson and Bret Woods. New York: Oxford University Press, 2018.

Diettrich, Brian. "Chanting Diplomacy: Music, Conflict, and Social Cohesion in Micronesia." In *A Distinctive Voice in the Antipodes: Essays in Honour of Stephen A. Wild*, edited by Kirsty Gillespie, Sally Treloyn, and Don Niles, 195–218. Canberra: Australian National University, 2017.

Diettrich, Brian, Jane Freeman Moulin, and Michael Webb. *Music in Pacific Island Cultures: Experiencing Music, Expressing Culture*. Global Music Series, edited by Bonnie Wade and Patricia Campbell. New York: Oxford University Press, 2011.

Diettrich, Brian and Barbara B. Smith. *Catalogue of Field Recordings Made in Yap, Ulithi, Pohnpei, and Chuuk in 1963 by Barbara B. Smith*. University of Hawai'i at Mānoa, Pacific Collection, 2005.

Falgout, Suzanne. "Hierarchy vs. Democracy: Two Strategies for the Management of Knowledge in Pohnpei." *Anthropology & Education Quarterly* 23, no. 1 (1992): 30–43.

Federated States of Micronesia Information Services. "New National Holiday for Culture and Traditions in FSM." Press Release 0310-38. Palikir, Pohnpei, 25 March, 2010.

Federated States of Micronesia, Seventeenth Congress. A Resolution to Ratify the United Nations Educational, Scientific, and Cultural Organization Convention. Palikir, Pohnpei, 9 November, 2012.

Federated States of Micronesia, Standing Committee Report 16-71. Micronesia Culture and Traditions Day. Palikir, Pohnpei, 12 February, 2010.

Furness, William Henry. *The Island of Stone Money: Yap of the Carolines*. Philadelphia: J. B. Lippincott, 1910.

Gray, Earl and Raymond Scott. "Rights of Attribution for Ka Mate Haka." *Journal of Intellectual Property Law & Practice* 8, no. 3 (2012): 200–202.

Hanlon, David. "Nan Madol on Pohnpei." In *Made in Oceania: Social Movements, Cultural Heritage and the State in the Pacific*, edited by Edvard Hviding and Knut M. Rio, 121–140. Wantage: Sean Kingston Publishing, 2011.

Hellier-Tinoco, Ruth. *Embodying Mexico: Tourism, Nationalism, and Performance*. New York: Oxford University Press, 2011.

Henry, Rosita. "Dancing Diplomacy: Performance and the Politics of Protocol in Australia." In *Made in Oceania: Social Movements, Cultural Heritage and the State in the Pacific*, edited by Edvard Hviding and Knut M. Rio, pp. 179–194. Wantage: Sean Kingston Publishing, 2011.

Hilder, Thomas R. "Repatriation, Revival and Transmission: The Politics of a Sámi Musical Heritage." *Ethnomusicology Forum* 21, no. 2 (2012): 161–179.

Hochman, Brian. *Savage Preservation: The Ethnographic Origins of Modern Media Technology*. Minneapolis: University of Minnesota Press, 2014.

Huffingtonpost [online]. "Avatar" Sequels: James Cameron Inspired By Micronesians. 30 March 2012. http://www.huffingtonpost.com/2012/03/30/avatar-sequels-james-cameron_n_1392665.html. Accessed 24 September 2016.

Kahunde, Samuel. "Repatriating Archival Sound Recordings to Revive Traditions: The Role of the Klaus Wachsmann Recordings in the Revival of the Royal Music of Bunyoro-Kitara, Uganda." *Ethnomusicology Forum* 21, no. 2 (2012):197–219.

Kim, Myjolynne, Marie. *Into the Deep: Launching Culture and Policy in the Federated States of Micronesia*. Secretariat of the Pacific Community on behalf of the Federated States of Micronesia Office of National Archives, Culture and Historic Preservation. Pohnpei: FSM, 2011.

Kirshenblatt-Gimblett, Barbara. "Theorizing Heritage." *Ethnomusicology* 39, no. 3 (1995): 367–380.

Kirshenblatt-Gimblett, Barbara. "Intangible Heritage as Metacultural Production." *Museum International* 56, no. 1–2 (2004): 52–64.

Mallon, Sean. "Against Tradition." *The Contemporary Pacific* 22, no. 2 (2010): 362–381.

Myers, Helen. *Ethnomusicology: An Introduction*. New York: W. W. Norton & Company, 1992.

Nason, James, Joakim Peter. "Keeping Rong from Wrong: The Identification and Protection of Traditional Intellectual Property in Chuuk, Federated States of Micronesia." *International Journal of Cultural Property* 16 (2009): 273–290.

Pacific World Heritage Action Plan 2016–2020. 2015. United Nations Educational, Scientific, and Cultural Organization.

Petersen, Glenn. "Hambruch's Colonial Narrative: Pohnpei, German Culture Theory, and the Hamburg Expedition Ethnography of 1908–1910." *The Journal of Pacific History* 42, no. 3 (2007): 317–330.

Phelan, Peggy. *Unmarked: the Politics of Performance.* New York: Routledge, 1993.

Pigliasco, Guido Carlo. "We Branded Ourselves Long Ago: Intangible Cultural Property and Commodification of Fijian Firewalking." *Oceania* 80, no. 2 (2010): 161–181.

Pigliasco, Guido Carlo. "Are the Grassroots Growing? Intangible Cultural-Heritage Lawmaking in Fiji and Oceania." In *Made in Oceania: Social Movements, Cultural Heritage and the State in the Pacific*, edited by Edvard Hviding and Knut M. Rio, 321–337. Wantage, UK: Sean Kingston Publishing, 2011.

Serrano, Katharina. "Intangible Cultural Heritage in The Pacific Islands: Why Europe Should Listen In." *Pacific Studies* 36, no. ½ (2013): 77–93.

Smith, Barbara. B. "Micronesia" [Recordings of Oceanic Music]. In *The Garland Encyclopedia of World Music*, Volume 9: Australia and the Pacific Islands, edited by Adrienne L. Kaeppler and Jacob Love, pp. 993–994. New York: Routledge, 1998.

Sterne, Jonathan. *The Audible Past: Cultural Origins of Sound Production.* Durham, NC: Duke University Press, 2003.

Tanabe, Hisao. *Nan'yo, Taiwan, Okinawa Ongaku Kikô.* Tokyo: Ongaku no Tomosha, 1968.

Tanabe, Hisao. *The Music of Micronesia, the Kao-Shan Tribes of Taiwan, and Sakhalin.* Recorded by Hisao Tanabe in Micronesia in 1934; sleeve notes and editing by Hideo Tanabe. Toshiba TW-80011. LP. 1978.

Tatar, Elizabeth, ed. *Call of the Morning Bird: Chants and Songs of Palau, Yap, and Ponape.* Honolulu: Bernice Pauahi Bishop Museum, 1985.

Titon, Jeff Todd. "Music and Sustainability: An Ecological Viewpoint." *The World of Music* 51, no. 1 (2009): 119–137.

Weinstein, Valerie. "Archiving the Ephemeral: Dance in Ethnographic Films from the Hamburg South Seas Expedition 1908–1910." *Seminar: A Journal of Germanic Studies* 46, no. 3 (2010): 223–239.

Zemp, Hugo. "The/An Ethnomusicologist and the Record Business" *Yearbook for Traditional Music* 28 (1996): 36–56.

Ziegler, Susanne. Textdokumentation und Klangbeispiele, CD-ROM Beilage zum Katalog. *Die Wachszylinder des Berliner Phonogramm-Archivs.* Berlin: Ethnologisches Museum, Staatliche Museen zu Berlin, 2006.

4

Cultural Heritage and Public Folklore

Tales of Tradition

Gregory Hansen

Locally, nationally, and internationally, those interested in heritage have moved beyond thinking of heritage in terms of a legacy of the elite that is preserved in a nation's archaeological treasures, crown jewels, and the patrimony of the built environment. Along with thinking of heritage as it is preserved in high-style historic buildings, villages, and neighborhoods, we recognize the importance of incorporating intangible cultural heritage (ICH) into ways we think about heritage resources. In this respect, our thinking has expanded away from valuing heritage as constructions in the built environment as we seek to recognize how heritage is an emergent process that is connected to wider systems of meaning. In this process, ICH is pulled out of the margins. While it may have been seen as a resource that contributes to local color, writers like Laurajane Smith argue for the centrality of ICH within contemporary heritage discourse (Smith 2006, 106–113). An interest in the intangible may embellish the appeal of archaeological resources, and the *bricks-and-mortar* concepts of heritage, but the meaning of material culture is grounded in intangible connections that people share, negotiate, and often contest. These connections are made manifest in the cultural creativity of diverse people, and they include the fine arts, literary creations, and other cultural expressions that constitute a broader concept of heritage resources. As historic preservationists, archaeologists, museum curators, and other heritage professionals continue to engage with the value of the intangible within wider heritage discourses, they are continuing to recognize the importance of folklife as cultural heritage. In the United States and around the world, folk and vernacular expressive forms are becoming more integrated into the heritage movement.

The international expansion of critical heritage studies has sparked an interest in American public folklore. Although various nations have long histories of incorporating folklife into their policies and programs, there are unique developments in American folklore studies that can provide resources for expanding our ideas of ICH. The charter document for the coalescence of contemporary public sector folklore was the passage of Public Law 94-201. The U.S. Congress passed this legislation as the "American Folklife Preservation Act" during America's bicentennial in 1976. The legislation authorized the establishment of the American Folklife Center within the Library of Congress, and it also created charter documents for conceptualizing folklife, folklore, and folk arts within the National Endowment for the Arts and other governmental agencies (Jabbour 2003, 430). The public sector folklore movement expanded from this national base into arts and humanities councils across the nation, and the majority of American states now support folklife programs through similar legislation. One of the most tangible elements of this process is an oft-cited definition of folklife. In this formulation, "folklife" is cast as an inclusive term that includes and subsumes concepts such as "folklore," "folk art," "folk music," and "vernacular architecture":

> American folklife is the traditional, expressive, shared culture of various groups in the United States: familial, ethnic, occupational, religious, and regional. Expressive culture includes a wide range of creative and symbolic forms, such as custom, belief, technical skill, language, drama, ritual, architecture, music, play, dance, drama, pageantry, and handicraft. Generally these expressions are learned orally, by imitation, or in performance, and are maintained or perpetuated without formal instruction or institutional direction. (Bartis 2001, 1)

This definition is a charter for legislation in American states that has authorized state and local public sector folklore programs. It has also contributed to ways that UNESCO incorporates folklore and folklife into its constructions of ICH (Kurin 1997, 194).

Because this configuration of folklife is well established within public folklore, it can serve as a starting point for connecting American folklore to wider ideas about folklore across the globe. The definition works well within its framework as a legal document even though its specific points have been critiqued within scholarship (Kirshenblatt-Gimblett 1992, 36). Many of these specific critiques are outside of the scope of this article, but a further exploration of this articulation of folklore provides a useful way to connect the concept of "tradition" to wider ideas about heritage. Since the inception of contemporary approaches to public folklife programs, folklorists have continued to explore the various meanings of "tradition." Their discussion of the rich and oftentimes divergent ideas about what constitutes tradition is remarkably resonant with ways that we conceptualize heritage. Exploring how tradition is conceptualized within folklore scholarship opens up a range of interests in how we characterize heritage.

The place of "tradition" as a central element within folklore was well established soon after William John Thoms wrote of "folk-lore" as "good Anglo compound" in 1846. Thoms's original definition of folklore didn't include "tradition" in his articulation as he posited the term as a replacement for "popular antiquities" (Boyer 1997, 53). In essence, Thoms argued that folklore constitutes a body of older items and activities that those in the mass population preserve, relic-like, in their social life. Thoms connected this process of preservation to tradition, but folklorists made the connections" and "tradition" more explicit by the end of the nineteenth century. In *Explaining Traditions: Folk Behavior in Modern Culture*, Simon Bronner writes how Victorian authors such as Edwin Sidney Hartland posited the academic field of folklore as the "science of Tradition" in his 1904 publication *Folklore: What Is It and What Is the Good of It?* (Bronner 2011, 75). In the twentieth century, there were nuanced ways of conceptualizing folklore as tradition, and today most folklorists recognize that folklorists continue to engage with an understanding of relationships between tradition and folklore.

A provocative element of this engagement was launched by Dan Ben-Amos 125 years after William John Thoms (re)coined the term "folk-lore." In "Toward a Definition of Folklore in Context," Ben-Amos purposely excised "tradition" from his formulation of folklore when he defined "folklore" as *artistic communication in small groups* (Ben-Amos 1971, 13). The integration of a new definition into the nascent performance-centered approaches had its advantages. Ben-Amos's caveat that the discipline can't survive if predicated on a disappearing subject is worth heeding. This idea of folklore has some intellectual currency today, but most public folklore discourse includes a more specific formulation of folklore that includes "tradition," as offered in PL 94-201. Despite some value in Ben-Amos's redefinition, there are also numerous problems in his articulation (Bronner 2011, 69). For example, Ben-Amos's definition doesn't encompass material folk culture in a useful manner. There is artistry in craft, but much of the handiwork of material folk culture is motivated by utilitarian needs rather than aesthetic desires. Furthermore, people don't construct vernacular dwellings for the prime purpose of communication. Neither is much of their use of vernacular architecture focused on communication. Ben-Amos's definition also is of limited use when we look at occupational folklife. Robert McCarl's useful distinction between ceremonial and substantive occupational folklore, for example, is a good case in point (McCarl 1978, 8–9). McCarl argues that the ceremonial traditions in occupational folklife, such as a topping out ceremony, often incorporate highly aestheticized symbolic values. He also explains that the bulk of occupational folklife, however, is centered around the utilitarian tricks of the trade and inside knowledge that form substantive occupational traditions within a specific work community. There may be an art, for example, to separating marketable shrimp out of a pile of bycatch, but most shrimpers view it as a nasty, tedious job. The emphasis on aestheticizing work, as Raymond Williams argues, can even obscure—rather than clarify—central elements of the political-economy of the workplace (Williams 1958, 154–158).

Ben-Amos's definition also does not work well when used to characterize some of the time-honored genres of folklore that are integral to the wider discourse on ICH. A community's folk beliefs may be articulated with an aesthetic appeal, but focusing on their stylization once again obscures what likely is a deeper meaning within this genre. There are also some dangerous folk beliefs, and placing an aesthetic gloss over beliefs that are highly irrational, dangerous, or even oppressive blunts the critical edge that also is integral to the study of folklore. Even genres that are characterized as "verbal arts" are not necessarily understood as "artistic communication" by their practitioners. Tom Mould's exegesis of Choctaw and Mormon religious narratives, for example, challenges the centrality of aesthetics in studying narrative (Mould 2011, 137). Mould found that defining some stories as "art" misrepresents the way that their tellers wish to express the meaning of their narration. Other verbal arts may not be particularly artistic, and it is important to further explore differences between what is stylized, what is aesthetic, and what is richly artistic.

Finally, the concept of "small group" as a criterion for folklore was problematic even when Ben-Amos first formulated his ideas. Many forms of folklore are created and sustained in large group contexts. Rock 'n' roll audiences, for example, herald the on-stage arrival of rock bands with lighters at concerts in large venues, and sports fans cheer their teams in unison in stadiums around the world. These rituals are all elements of contemporary folk expression that also have long-established precedents within public spectacle. With the new research on folklore and the Internet, the criterion of small groupness becomes even more untenable, especially when the idea of a folk group is restricted to the older constructs of face-to-face interaction (Blank 2009). It is curious that in the global community that explores communication within the World Wide Web, folklore has emerged as a vibrant element of contemporary culture. While excising "tradition" from folklore was seen as a modern way to update our ideas about folklore, even in cyberspace we see the persistence of tradition.

The idea of folklore in PL 94-201 was formulated by public folklorists, with a strong influence from Archie Green, about the time that Ben-Amos published his influential 1971 article (Green 2001). Curiously, thirteen years after this publication, Ben-Amos wrote another article that revisits the idea of tradition. His commentary on the "Seven Strands of Tradition" is an engaging and influential contribution to our understanding of folklore (Ben-Amos 1984). Recent scholarship has reclaimed the idea of tradition in folklore—a range of scholars have added more strands to Ben-Amos's treatise on tradition (Bronner 2011; Cashman, Mould, and Shukla 2011). Taken apart or woven together, they have the potential to contribute to a better understanding of how folklore is resonant with the wider heritage movement.

Just as folklore and tradition can be conceptualized in various ways, there is a growing literature on ways to conceptualize heritage. It is useful, however, to consider ways that the articulation of definitions within official policy helps to anchor the dialogue in common concerns. In the same way that "folklife" is codified in legislation, "heritage" also is defined in official decrees. Consider, for example, how the 2005 Council of Europe Framework Convention on the Value of Cultural Heritage for Society provides a definition of "heritage" within its charter document: "Cultural heritage is a group of resources inherited from the past which people identify, independently of ownership, as a reflection and expression of their constantly evolving values, beliefs, knowledge and traditions" (Council of Europe 2005: Section I, Article 2(a)). Here, the conceptualization of "cultural heritage" is cognate with numerous articulations of "tradition." Despite some differences between this perspective on heritage versus the conceptualization of folklife in the American Folklife Preservation Act, it is clear that both articulations emphasize the place of tradition within folklife and heritage. Both definitions highlight the importance of belief and knowledge as well as the importance of expressive culture within their conceptualization. They explicitly differ in characterizing whether or not cultural traditions are owned by members various social groups, but both share an implicit argument that the symbolic value of these resources is essential to ways that people imbue them with meaning. There may be ways to formulate cohesive definitions of "heritage" and "tradition" that unify both concepts, but it is perhaps more useful to follow Ben-Amos's approach of sketching out ways that the terms are used in a scholarly inquiry. In each strand, "tradition" can be used nearly synonymously with "heritage." His original aim was less to unravel each strand under critical scrutiny and more to demonstrate how different ideas about tradition index different interests in folklore. The same approach also provides ways to articulate reasons why people are interested in heritage.

Ben-Amos gives us the first strand of tradition—or heritage—as "lore." This second half of Thoms's "good Anglo compound" emphasizes the idea that tradition comprised a body of knowledge or learning (Ben-Amos 1984, 102). Early formulations of folklore stressed the idea that this lore survives in the present as a relic from the past. The implicit idea was that this lore would soon lose its place in the world due to the inevitable march of progress. Today, folklorists may work to document, preserve, and revitalize older traditions as they work within programs that emphasize the conservation of culture (Hufford 1994). Likewise, heritage often is portrayed as a remnant of the past. Its value often is connected to the scarcity of heritage resources, and much of the impetus for the heritage movement is rooted in a desire to preserve its legacy.

Ben-Amos articulates the idea of tradition as item and inventory in his second strand. Here, he looks at "tradition as an artistic canon" (Ben-Amos 1984, 105). Whereas lore may be seen as an abstract form of traditional knowledge, the idea of tradition as canon is more specific. The distinctive items of lore that comprise folklore are subsumed together as a collective resource. Individual items acquire a greater significance when they are seen as components of a larger system of cultural expression. When various individual elements of tradition, such as a folk musician's individual tunes, become codified into a more cohesive totality, they acquire new meanings that emphasize the importance of collective knowledge. The musician's fiddle tunes now become a repertoire, and this resource is then connected to the wider canon of traditional musical expression that connects the individual to wider communities. The establishment of regionally distinctive styles, for example, depends upon individual musicians who are recognized for their contributions to maintaining—and contributing—to a specific heritage of musical tradition. As Samantha Breslin demonstrates, this process often involves a process of immigration, diffusion, and the formation of an artistic canon that is derived from acknowledging the master musicians' influence on a local community's aesthetic values (Breslin 2012, 158). In Breslin's study of Irish roots within Newfoundland, she delineates how Canadian fiddlers construct a regional music tradition by adopting tunes and styles from musicians who are recognized as masters of a musical heritage. Specific repertoires of tunes from Ireland's regional styles are played in St. John's as manifestations of the more general heritage of Ireland's rich and diverse fiddling tradition. Collectively, the tunes comprise a dynamic canon of artistic resources that characterize not only the heritage of the Irish fiddling but they also are significant heritage resources within the little tradition of a more localized expressive culture of this Canadian maritime province.

"Tradition as a process" is evident in typical contexts of teaching traditions to younger generations as arts are passed down over time. This third strand focuses on ways that tradition is a way of teaching and learning (Ben-Amos 1984, 116). Tradition, here, is a legacy of the past. Consequently, its preservation in the future depends on a willingness to teach and learn the old way within the present. Whereas heritage often is seen abstractly as the handing down of a legacy from the past, the nature of folk tradition is more particular. Public Law 94-201 includes specific language about the process within which folklore typically is learned. Folklore is different from other aspects of culture and heritage because a folk tradition often is perpetuated through informal means of instruction. Richard Dorson termed this element of folklore as "unofficial culture" to emphasize that there are different communities of practice that support folklife (Dorson 1978, 23). Folklorists generally are more interested in the traditions that are learned outside of formal educational institutions. Rather, they explore how informal learning takes place within communities that continue to preserve older forms of cultural expression while also adapting these traditions to contemporary life (Bowman and Hamer 2011). Heritage, here, is a bit broader in its scope, for a nation's heritage includes the fine arts, high-style cultural expression as well as mass culture. The boundaries between folk culture, popular culture, and elite culture may be blurry, but of these elements may be foregrounded as heritage. Folklorists, however, remind us to also look at the traditions that are rarely enshrined as the canonical knowledge of formal education.

Ben-Amos's fourth strand is a bit more abstract. He explains that tradition can be seen as "mass" (Ben-Amos 1984, 117). In concrete terms, regarding tradition as mass can refer to ways that tradition, as a whole, is understood in relation to its potential to symbolize wider aspects of cultural identity. We use this sense of tradition, for example, when we speak of tradition as a representation of the character of a group of people. An effort to establish a nation's literary tradition is an especially salient way that tradition can imbue the works of various writers with meaning. This argument that folklore is important to the cultural traditions of a nation spins around this idea of tradition. Ben-Amos explains that the sense that individuals are "tradition-bearers" also is connected to this concept of tradition. The connections between heritage and tradition, here, are clear. Much of the argument for historic preservation and cultural conservation employs the trope of safeguarding a people's heritage. The argument has strong rhetorical appeal when heritage is symbolized as a treasure trove to safeguard rather than as a list of discrete activities unified as "tradition."

It is tempting to go beyond thinking of tradition as a metaphor and literalizing it into an actual existing phenomenon that Ben-Amos terms "mass." Early ideas about tradition, in fact, regarded it as a superorganic entity (Bauman and Briggs 2003, 176). Thinkers such as Johann Gottfried Herder firmed up a foundation for thinking of tradition as a living repository of artistic and spiritual resources that is embodied in the soul of the nation (Wilson 1973, 832). Folklorists have critiqued both the reification of folklore within these formulations of tradition, and the related idea of culture as a superorganic force has long been dismissed in anthropological theory (Sapir 1917). Nevertheless, common parlance often supports a reified view of tradition, and it is challenging to unite disparate cultural expressions as manifestations of tradition without objectifying an abstract idea. The same challenges show up in heritage discourse. Heritage is often posited as an inheritance and a legacy of the past. In this discourse there often are implicit—even explicit—assumptions that heritage is a real thing that exists independent of individual acts of expressive culture. Talking about tradition and heritage without using figurative language is challenging. When we turn tradition and heritage into icons, indexes, and symbols, the concern is that we may believe that abstractions are real. Ian Russell's critique of the roots and branches approach to heritage is one of the more eloquent challenges to the reification of tradition and heritage (Russell 2010, 31). He explores the negative potential of reifying heritage, especially when it is cast as a basis for a people's identity. He challenges representations of heritage as a living manifestation that grows from a tradition that is rooted deeply in history. While the roots and branches imagery may contribute to a sense of unity within disparate societies, Russell demonstrates how this arboreal model can support exclusionary ideologies and dangerous cultural politics. He suggests, instead, a newer model useful for fostering more positive and inclusive heritage values. Russell's metaphor for looking at heritage in a more inclusive way is to consider it as a system of interrelationships of meaning. Here, tradition is one star within a massive constellation of meanings that contribute to the global system of expression that allow individual societies to express in the present the deep values that are derived from their significant pasts (Russell 2010, 35).

The fifth strand also is directly connected to concerns with thinking of tradition as mass. Rather than thinking of tradition as a collective entity that stands alone, "tradition" has been equated with "culture" (Ben-Amos 1984, 119). Citing Melville Herskovits, Ben-Amos notes how there is a long history in which tradition and culture have been used as synonyms. Most contemporary scholars would reject the idea that all aspects of culture can be described as "traditional," but they also would recognize that tradition is an important component of most cultural processes. Within Public Law 94-201, for example, the idea of tradition is connected to learning specific kinds of cultural expression. Within this legislative verbiage, what is traditional within culture is that which exists outside of the mechanisms for teaching high culture and popular culture. Although folklorists have expanded the idea of tradition by recognizing how there are traditions within the fine arts, few label paintings by Jackson Pollack as "traditional." The same bracketing of some aspects of culture as "traditional" also shows up in a range of other fields. For example, folklorists would easily label a home remedy as an aspect of "traditional medical practices" whereas they wouldn't be apt to describe neurosurgery in the same way.

The idea of heritage as culture is important. Throughout time, we have tended to think of heritage more as history than as culture. The focus on preserving heritage as an inheritance from the past is resonance with the idea of preserving tradition as folkways inherited from the past. These two formulations tend to emphasize the historical qualities of artifacts rather than the contemporary cultural processes that make heritage resources meaningful in the present. James Abrams discusses challenges in thinking of heritage more as a relic of the past than as a contemporary cultural process in his important essay "Lost Frames of Reference" (Abrams

1994, 25). Using examples from Pennsylvania's heritage movements, Abrams explains that heritage discourse is a response to concerns within the contemporary social dynamics. By resituating heritage away from a preservationist agenda, he explores how heritage sites are literally constructed as contemporary forms of cultural expression. Abrams explores problems with thinking of heritage as the past, but emphasizing how it is an interpretation of the past in the present. An important aspect of heritage studies is the exploration of reasons why these divergent heritages are cultural constructions based on history. Thus, if we were to recast Henry Glassie's aphorism that "there is one past but many histories" (Glassie 1982, 650) we can then recognize *there is one past but many heritages*.

Ben-Amos's sixth strand also is highly abstract. He shows that tradition can be seen as *langue*, or the abstract system of interrelationships that make the performance of creative expression possible and meaningful (Ben-Amos 1984, 121). Ferdinand de Saussure's distinction between *langue* and *parole* remains influential. He posits *langue* as the essential element of language. In Saussure's theory, *parole* is the actual speech act, *langue* is the system that allows us to understand individual sounds or written notations (Saussure [1916]/2011, 9–15). Kay Cothran applies this idea of *langue* to the idea of tradition. In this respect, her idea of tradition is that it consists of "the rules by means of which a given context is made sensible, by means of which further contexts are made possible" (Cothran 1979, 445). Cothran's idea of tradition as a dynamic, interpretive system has proven to be useful. Henry Glassie develops the idea by asserting that tradition serves as a mediator between history and culture (Glassie 1995, 399). By characterizing tradition as a "swing term" that connects the past to the present, he emphasizes the dynamic quality of tradition to serve as a schematic device for understanding how the past is meaningful in the present. This process, Glassie asserts, is evident not only when we use tradition to understand contemporary cultural expression but also when we use tradition as a resource for our own cultural creativity.

Tradition, here, is a dynamic system for enriching our understanding of what is meaningful within contemporary life. This argument is resonant with a new discourse on heritage. George Smith, Phyllis Mauch Messenger, and Hilary Soderland critique the static approach of objectifying heritage as objects to be possessed (Smith, Messenger, and Soderland 2010, 15). Instead, they provide ways to recenter heritage discourse by focusing on the values that make heritage a more meaningful resource in contemporary culture. They shift into the deeper, systematic level by bringing the idea of "heritage values" into the discourse. In this perspective, the "quintessence of heritage values could be defined in terms of freedom and responsibility as expressed in mores of duty, honor, personal responsibility, fairness, inclusiveness, stewardship, social obligations, and an extensive array of similar ideals" (Smith, Messenger, and Soderland 2010, 16). Further defining and fostering these values is a complex task, and inquiries into values often leads to spirited, if even contentious, discourse. Proponents of the heritage values approach, however, recognize that dialogue and debate are integral to various movements designed to answer a question that Peter Howard sees as integral to the heritage movement. Namely, "What is it that people want to save?" (Howard 2006, 484). An in-depth understanding of these values also helps enrich our understanding of why we wish to preserve heritage resources. When we view heritage as *langue*, heritage emerges a system that makes the preservation of historic and cultural resources meaningful.

Folklorists have created a seventh strand that is the opposite of tradition as reaction to tradition as *langue*. Whereas *langue* is an abstraction in which the essential aspects of language consist of that which is devoid of its speech sounds or orthographic representations, *parole* is the actual expression of speaking or writing. Noam Chomsky recast the *langue/parole* distinction by positing a similar dichotomy between competence and performance (Chomsky 1982, 89). Chomsky's linguistic theory makes subtle distinctions between *parole* and performance, but the focus on linguistic competence remains the center of his generative grammar as well as other theories derived from Saussure's foundation for structuralism. Folklorists, most notably Dell Hymes, have further recast Saussurean perspectives by foregrounding performance-centered approaches to studying culture. Instead of seeing performance as utterance and output, Dell Hymes argues that performance is an achievement (Hymes 1975, 352). Performance theory and the broader formulations of the ethnography of communication have refined theoretical ideas about the nature of performance, and folklorists have developed sophisticated ways to demonstrate how performance involves highly elaborate and systematic resources that merge the creation of texts with their social and communicative contexts. In his landmark presidential address to the American Folklore Society, Hymes recasts the idea of tradition and places it into the wider performance studies paradigm. By showing how tradition is rooted less in time and more in social life, Hymes emphasizes the idea of tradition as an emergent process (Hymes 1975, 353). Using the Chinook Indian narrative "The Sun's Myth (The Sun's Nature)," he demonstrates how speakers (and listeners) create traditional discourse in response to contemporary rhetorical and social contexts. Thus, tradition becomes an accomplishment that is evident when one takes responsibility for being "on stage," thereby presenting verbal art under circumstances that open the performer up to evaluation (Hymes 1975, 352). This idea of tradition as performance is further developed in Henry Glassie's eloquent prose when he defines *tradition* as the "creation of the future out of the past" (Glassie 1995, 395). We perform traditionally in the present, when we create and respond to cultural expression in ways that use resources from the past for forging our future. Following Hymes, Glassie asks us to consider tradition as an event.

The idea of performing tradition is central to contemporary ideas about heritage. Examining how heritage is placed on display yields a useful resource for its study. Rather than working with nebulous concepts about what constitutes a people's heritage, researchers using performance theory can document and interpret heritage by studying how its resources are staged in events or placed on display in exhibits (Kurin 1997, 13). Both the performance and the curation of heritage can be systematized within performance theory. These types of displays of heritage also provide important resources for understanding heritage as a form of cultural representation that emphasizes self-representation. The parallel between *tradition as performance* and *heritage as performance* is directly evident in the writing of Peter Aronsson and Lizette Gradén. In their introduction to *Performing Nordic Heritage*, they explain how they unify their fine compilation of articles using a performance-centered approach. "We approach heritage not merely as remnant of the past, but as a particular cultural practice that uses the past to produce heritage in the present" (Aronsson and Gradén 2013, 12). In thinking of tradition and heritage as performance, researchers gain new opportunities to analyze, interpret, and articulate the key component of the competence that emerges in performance. Focusing on heritage as a mode of cultural expression provides insight into central terms that are relevant to values that comprise the community's system of cultural competence. We can study, for example, why ideas about accuracy, inclusion, and authenticity are highly charged concepts within heritage discourse when we ascertain what's at stake when tradition and heritage are performed.

In the thirty years that have followed Ben-Amos's original publication of the "Seven Strands of Tradition," folklorists, anthropologists, historians, and other scholars have continued to explore the nature and meaning of tradition. Simon Bronner gives an insightful treatment of ways to understand tradition in relation to a variety of other concepts, including implicit ideas about progress and science as well as a range of ideological constructs (Bronner 2011, 40–48). The scope of his discussion and the work of other writers such as Edward Shils deserve more consideration in relation to contemporary heritage discourse (Shils 1981). Within the academic discourse, scholars can learn from the advocacy work of folklorists working in the public sector (Jabbour 2003, 423). Their advocacy work in inscribing tradition into Public Law 94-201 has established a workable formulation of folklore and folklife within the broader historic preservation and cultural conservation aegis (Green 2001).

There are also other areas where the scholarship on tradition has direct connections to heritage. "Tradition" often is used in economic terms. A "traditional economy" often refers to economies that are small scale, and often based on subsistence farming, reciprocity, and communal social systems (Shils 1981, 303). The idea of grounding economy more in use-value rather than in capitalistic exchange connects several of Ben-Amos's strands of tradition. When portrayed as heritage, these livelihoods often are cast as integral components of the roots of a region's culture. Tradition can be seen as spectacle. By its nature, a spectacle is a performance. Spectacles that specifically showcase a people's traditions can provides important resources for heritage studies (Ray 2003, 10). Since the publication of scholarship by Hobsbawm and Ranger, it's been trendy to conceptualize tradition as an invention (Hobsbawm and Ranger 1983). This approach is clearly resonant with studies that look at ways that heritage is constructed in response to social, cultural, and political circumstances, and there's a growing literature on implications for understanding heritage as an invention. James Abrams looks at this invention of heritage in his discussion of Pennsylvania heritage sites. One of the more remarkable examples that he provides is the Eckley Miner's Village, near Hazleton. The remnants of the settlement would most likely have been demolished had it not be used as a movie site. In 1968, Hollywood reconstructed what was left of the town for *The Molly Maguires* (Abrams 1994, 31–33). After the Paramount Studies completed production, the site was eventually donated to the State of Pennsylvania as an open-air museum. The movie saved the town, but the site was preserved more as an antiquated movie set rather than as an accurate representation of what the town actually looked like during the operation of the coal industry. Aspects of Eckley's history are preserved and presented to the public, but the Hollywood vision pervades the imagery.

Sue Tuohy expands and develops the idea of an invented tradition by writing how traditions are also complicit with Benedict Anderson's idea of the imagined community (Anderson 1991; Tuohy 1988). An *imagined tradition* is real, but the power of the imagination supersedes what actually can be documented and verified. Tuohy's insights into the nature and dynamics of the imagined tradition have important implications for exploring implications of an *imagined heritage*. The power to create an imagined heritage is an important theme in heritage discourse. Laurajane Smith asserts that the preservation of the built environment as heritage cannot be separated from the intangible cultural heritage that makes these buildings valuable (Smith 2006, 56). She and other writers explore how this process of imagining these connections can both distort and enhance our understandings of historical sites.

There are areas, however, where parallels between heritage and tradition—as conceptualized in the field of folklore—do not necessarily share the same connections. The terms are not necessarily synonymous. For example, heritage does not always work well as a replacement term in each of Ben-Amos's seven strands. Nevertheless, the parallels between ways we conceptualize *tradition* and *heritage* are important. Looking at folklorists' diverse perspectives on tradition can shed new light on ways to envision heritage. The differences and similarities in definitions all point to salient ways for understanding heritage discourse. Heritage discourse, in turn, can contribute to new perspectives in folklore. The traditions that constitute a people's folklife are major components of intangible cultural heritage. The work of public folklorists in codifying folklore into cultural protection policy that safeguards folklife around the globe provides essential resources for furthering our international heritage discourse.

REFERENCES

Abrams, J. "Lost Frames of Reference: Sightings of History and Memory in Pennsylvania's Documentary Landscape." In M. Hufford (ed) *Conserving Culture: A New Discourse on Heritage*, A publication of the American Folklore Society. Washington, DC: American Folklife Center/Library of Congress, 1994.

Anderson, B. *Imagined Communities: Reflections on the Origin and Spread of Nationalism* (revised and expanded edition). London: Verso, 1991.

Aronsson, P. and Gradén, L. (eds). *Performing Nordic Heritage: Everyday Practices and Institutional Culture*. Surrey, England: Ashgate, 2013.

Bartis, P. *Folklife and Fieldwork: An Introduction to Field Techniques* (revised edition). Washington, DC: American Folklife Center/Library of Congress, 2002.

Bauman, R. and Briggs, C. *Voices of Modernity: Language Ideologies and the Politics of Inequality.* Cambridge: Cambridge University Press, 2003.

Ben-Amos, D. "Toward a Definition of Folklore in Context." *Journal of American Folklore* 84, no. 331 (1971): 3–15.

———. "The Seven Strands of *Tradition:* Varieties in Its Meaning in American Folklore Studies." *Journal of Folklore Research* 21 (1984): 97–131.

Blank, T. (ed). *Folklore and the Internet: Vernacular Expression in a Digital World.* Logan: Utah State University Press, 2009.

Bowman, P. and Hamer, L. (eds). *Through the Schoolhouse Door: Folklore, Community, Curriculum.* Logan: Utah State University Press, 2011.

Boyer, T. "The Forsaken Founder, William John Thoms: From Antiquities to Folklore," *The Folklore Historian* 14 (1997): 61.

Breslin, S. "Putting Down Roots: Playing Irish and Newfoundland Music in St. John's." In I. Russell and C. Goertzen (eds) *Routes and Roots: Fiddle and Dance Studies from around the North Atlantic 4,* Aberdeen: Elphinstone Institute/University of Aberdeen, 2012.

Bronner, S. *Explaining Traditions: Folk Behavior in Modern Culture.* Lexington: University of Kentucky Press, 2011.

Cashman, R., Mould, T., and Shukla, P. (eds). *The Individual and Tradition: Folkloristic Perspectives.* Bloomington: Indiana University Press, 2011.

Chomsky, N. *Some Concepts and Consequences of the Theory of Government and Binding.* Cambridge: Massachusetts Institute of Technology Press, 1982.

Cothran, Kay. "Participation in Tradition." In Jan H. Brunvand, (ed) *Readings in American Folklore.* New York: Norton, 1979.

Cothran, Kay. "Participation in Tradition," *Keystone Folklore* 18 (1973): 7–13.

Council of Europe. "Faro Framework Convention on the Value of Cultural Heritage for Society." Electronic document, http://conventions.coe.int/Treaty/EN/Treaties/Html/199.htm, accessed November 12, 2017.

Dorson, Richard M. "Folklore in the Modern World." In Richard M. Dorson, (ed) *Folklore in the Modern World.* The Hague: Mouton Publishers, 1978.

Glassie, H. *Passing the Time in Ballymenone: Culture and History of an Ulster Community.* Philadelphia: University of Pennsylvania Press, 1982.

———. "Tradition." *Journal of American Folklore* 108 (1995): 395–412.

Green, A. *Torching the Fink Books and Other Essays on Vernacular Culture.* Chapel Hill: University of North Carolina Press, 2001.

Hobsbawm, E. and Ranger, T. (eds). *The Invention of Tradition.* Cambridge: Cambridge University Press, 1983.

Hufford, M. (ed). *Conserving Culture: A New Discourse on Heritage.* American Folklore Society. Washington, DC: American Folklife Center/Library of Congress, 1994.

Hymes, D. "Folklore's Nature and the Sun's Myth." *Journal of American Folklore* 88 (1975): 345–369.

Jabbour, A. "Folklife, Intangible Heritage, and Historic Preservation." In R. Stipe (ed) *A Richer Heritage: Historic Preservation in the Twenty-First Century.* Chapel Hill: University of North Carolina Press, 2003.

Kirshenblatt-Gimblett, B. "Mistaken Dichotomies." In R. Baron and N. Spitzer (eds) *Public Folklore.* Washington, DC: Smithsonian Institution Press, 1992.

Kurin, R. *Reflections of a Culture Broker: A View from the Smithsonian,* Washington DC: Smithsonian Institution Press, 1997.

McCarl, R. "Occupational Folklife: A Theoretical Hypothesis." In R. Byington (ed) *Working Americans: Contemporary Approaches to Occupational Folklife.* The California Folklore Society, Los Angeles: University of California, 1978.

Mould, T. "A Backdoor into Performance." In R. Cashman, T. Mould, and P. Shukla. *The Individual and Tradition: Folkloristic Perspectives.* Bloomington: Indiana University Press, 2011.

Ray, C. (ed). *Southern Heritage on Display: Public Ritual and Ethnic Diversity within Southern Regionalism.* Tuscaloosa: University of Alabama Press, 2003.

Russell, I. "Heritage, Identities, and Roots: A Critique of Arborescent Models of Heritage and Meaning." In G. Smith, P. Messenger, and H. and Solderland (eds) *Heritage Values in Contemporary Society.* Walnut Creek, CA: Left Coast Press, Inc., 2010.

Sapir, E. "Do We Need a *Superorganic?*" *American Anthropologist* 19 (1917): 441–447.

Saussure, Ferdinand de. *Course in General Linguistics,* Perry Meisel and Haun Saussy (eds) and Wade Baskin (tr). New York: Columbia University Press, [1916]/2011.

Shils, E. *Tradition.* Chicago: University of Chicago Press, 1981.

Smith, G., Messenger, P., and Solderland, H. (eds). *Heritage Values in Contemporary Society.* Walnut Creek, CA: Left Coast Press, Inc., 2010.

Smith, L. *Uses of Heritage.* London: Routledge, 2006.

Tuohy, S. Imagining the Chinese Tradition: The Case of Hua'er Songs, Festivals, and Scholarship. PhD dissertation, Bloomington: Indiana University, 1988.

Williams, R. *Culture and Society: 1780–1950* (reprint edition, 1983). New York: Columbia University Press, 1958.

Wilson, W. (1973). "Herder, Folklore and Romantic Nationalism." *Journal of Popular Culture* 6, no. 4 (1973): 819–835.

5

Legal Approaches to the Protection of Cultural Heritage

Patty Gerstenblith

The major threats to cultural heritage come in the twin forms of destruction during military conflict and looting of sites and collections. Both in antiquity and in contemporary times, we see these destructive activities often going hand-in-hand (Miles 2008, 33–104). While the Roman authors Cicero and Polybius provide antecedents for the protection of cultural heritage, these ideas appeared first in modern history in the writings of the international legal theorist Emmerich de Vattel in the mid-eighteenth century (Miles 2008, 300–2). The Hague Conventions and Regulations of 1899 and 1907, which were influenced by the first written code of military conduct known as the Lieber Code, drafted for the Union Army in 1863 during the American Civil War, engrained concepts of protection into international law.

It was only with the end of the Second World War and the ruin that the Nazi forces wreaked upon Europe from both a humanitarian and cultural perspective that the international community approached international humanitarian law from a comprehensive perspective. The late 1940s saw the large-scale development of international humanitarian law principles, embodied primarily in the Convention on Genocide and the four Geneva Conventions. The subject of cultural property protection was separated into its own distinct convention, the 1954 Hague Convention on the Protection of Cultural Property during Armed Conflict. In the decades that followed, the incentive provided by the international art market to theft of art works and the looting of archaeological and ethnological objects led to promulgation of several international conventions, in particular the 1970 UNESCO Convention on the Means of Prohibiting and Preventing the Illicit Import, Export and Transfer of Ownership of Cultural Property, with the goals of restraining some of the more detrimental aspects of the market and to encouragement of nations to undertake more effective measures to protect their cultural heritage. This chapter will examine, first, the legal principles that protect cultural property during armed conflict; second, the legal principles that attempt to regulate the international market; and finally, it will briefly consider the law that pertains to the domestic cultural heritage of the United States.

ARMED CONFLICT: THE 1954 HAGUE CONVENTION AND ITS TWO PROTOCOLS

The 1954 Hague Convention was the first international legal instrument devoted exclusively to the subject of cultural property (or cultural heritage).[1] The Hague Convention defines cultural property as:

movable or immovable property of great importance to the cultural heritage of every people, such as monuments of architecture, art or history, whether religious or secular; archaeological sites; groups of buildings which, as a whole, are of historical or artistic interest; works of art; manuscripts, books and other objects of artistic, historical or archaeological interest; as well as scientific collections and important collections of books or archives.

Article 1(a). The Convention also includes in its definition buildings "whose main and effective purpose is to preserve or exhibit the movable cultural property" (Article 1(b)) and "centers containing a large amount of cultural property" (Article 1 (c)).

The two core provisions of the Convention require the safeguarding of and respect for cultural property (Article 2). Safeguarding encompasses positive actions that a nation should take during peacetime to protect its own cultural property in case of armed conflict (Article 3). This duty involves such actions as disaster preparedness and documenting of cultural property that fits the Hague Convention definition. The Convention permits the marking of cultural property with a distinctive emblem known as the "blue shield," but this is not required for the property to receive protection.

The second core responsibility is respect for cultural property (Article 4). This encompasses refraining from the use of cultural property in ways that would expose it to destruction or damage during armed conflict and by refraining "from any act of hostility directed against such property" (Article 4(1)). However, these obligations are excused in cases where "military necessity imperatively requires . . . a waiver" (Article 4 (2)), a term that the Convention does not define. Article 4(3) prohibits the theft, pillage, or misappropriation of cultural property. This provision had received relatively little attention before the looting of the Iraq Museum in Baghdad in April 2003 during the U.S. invasion. It is not clear whether this imposes an obligation on a military to prevent looting by those who are not part of its military force.

Article 7 calls on the States Parties to take particular measures within their militaries. The first is to introduce provisions into the regulations and instructions for the military to ensure observance of the Convention and "to foster in the members of their armed forces a spirit of respect for the culture and cultural property of all peoples" (Article 7(1)). This brings together broader themes—considerations of culture and considerations of cultural property. In other words, the Convention addresses primarily the tangible aspects of culture, but it incorporates concern for the culture of all peoples (that is, intangible aspects), as well. The second part of Article 7 calls on States "to plan or establish in peacetime, within their armed forces, services or specialist personnel whose purpose will be to secure respect for cultural property and to cooperate with the civilian authorities responsible for safeguarding it" (Article 7(2)).

The First Protocol to the Convention was also adopted in 1954 and applies exclusively to moveable cultural objects. The Protocol prohibits the removal of such objects from occupied territory and imposes on Parties to the Protocol the obligation to return illegally removed cultural objects to their country of origin. It also establishes a rubric by which one State may deposit cultural property in another State for safekeeping during armed conflict, with the objects returned at the end of hostilities.

As methods of warfare evolved and our understanding of the means and necessity for protecting cultural property also changed, the international community recognized the need to update the Convention. This became even more apparent during the Balkan Wars of the 1990s when cultural heritage, particularly religious structures but also the historic city of Dubrovnik and the Ottoman period Bridge at Mostar, became targets of the warring factions. To update the international legal instruments, the Second Protocol was completed in 1999 and came into force in 2004 (Toman 2009; van Woudenberg and Lijnzaad 2010). Among the key contributions of the Second Protocol is its clarification and limitation of what constitutes "military necessity" (Article 6), changing the Convention's definition of a military objective from a static one, based on the cultural property's location, into a dynamic one, based on its function. Thus, the military necessity waiver applies to situations in which "cultural property has, by its function, been made into a military objective" and "there is no feasible alternative available to obtain a similar military advantage to that offered by directing an act of hostility against that objective" (Article 6a).

Article 7 introduces the concept of proportionality, known from other international humanitarian legal instruments, by imposing the obligation to avoid or minimize incidental damage to cultural property and to "refrain from deciding to launch any attack which may be expected to cause incidental damage . . . which would be excessive in relation to the concrete and direct military advantage anticipated." Articles 10–14 provide for the granting of enhanced protection to more significant cultural property that meets specific criteria. Article 15 requires the creation of criminal sanctions for serious violations of the Convention and the Protocols and establishes command responsibility by "extending criminal responsibility to persons other than those who directly commit the act." Article 16 requires States that are party to the Protocol to establish criminal offenses under their domestic law and to extend jurisdiction to non-nationals for certain offenses. Finally, Article 9 addresses in greater detail the responsibilities of an occupying power to safeguard cultural property during occupation and incorporates a principle of noninterference in the cultural heritage of occupied territory.

After fifty-five years, the United States finally ratified the 1954 Hague Convention in 2009, but it has not acted on either the First or Second Protocol. As of the end of 2016, there are 127 States Parties to the main Convention, 104 to the First Protocol, and 69 to the Second Protocol. All major military powers, with the exception of the United Kingdom, have ratified the main Convention. The United Kingdom has been moving over the course of 2016 toward ratification and implementation of all three instruments. While many provisions of the main Convention are considered to have become a part of customary international law, there is less agreement as to whether the provisions of the two protocols have achieved similar status.

It was recognized, at least from the early 1990s, that States needed to make greater efforts to prepare during peacetime for the protection of cultural property in case of armed conflict (Boylan 1993, 71–72). In 1996, several international cultural organizations joined to form the International Committee of the Blue Shield (ICBS) (Cole 2008, 66–67), which is now known simply as Blue Shield, taking its name from the distinctive emblem adopted by the Hague Convention to mark protected cultural property. Article 27(3) of the Second Protocol designates the ICBS as an advisory body to the Committee for the Protection of Cultural Property in the Event of Armed Conflict. The Blue Shield movement includes twenty-three national committees, which have as their primary goal the ratification of the 1954 Hague Convention and its Protocols and working with the various militaries to foster compliance with these legal instruments. Among their functions is the formulation of "no strike" lists or cultural inventories that identify and provide the locations of cultural sites, monuments, and repositories. These lists are an essential part of military planning so that direct damage to such sites can be avoided or at least minimized and States can thereby fulfill their legal obligations.

At the end of the Balkan conflict, the International Criminal Tribunal for the former Yugoslavia was established to prosecute those involved in the commission of war crimes. Several military leaders were charged and convicted particularly for the intentional destruction of religious structures. In addition, the shelling of the World Heritage Site of Dubrovnik and the destruction of the Ottoman period Bridge at Mostar formed the basis for prosecutions (Gerstenblith 2016,

370–72). In 1999, the Rome Statute, which established the International Criminal Court (ICC), was adopted. Article 8(2)(b)(ix) (applying to international armed conflict) and Article 8(2)(e) (iv) (applying to non-international armed conflict) identify the intentional destruction of cultural heritage as a war crime. The ICC carried out the first prosecution for destruction of cultural heritage without inclusion of other war crimes or crimes against humanity in 2015–2016 when it prosecuted Ahmad Al Faqi Al Mahdi for the intentional destruction of nine mausolea and the Sidi Yahia mosque in Timbuktu, Mali, in 2012, under the control of Al Qaeda–linked groups. The ongoing destruction of cultural heritage in the Middle East and North Africa, particularly in Iraq, Syria, Egypt, Yemen, and Libya, is too extensive to cover in this chapter and has been discussed at great length elsewhere (Gerstenblith 2016, 354–61).

CONTROLLING INTERNATIONAL TRADE IN ART AND CULTURAL HERITAGE

In the post–Second World War period, the appetite of the international art market for works of art and cultural objects grew commensurately with the increase in wealth of the European and North American countries. This demand provided an economic incentive to thefts from public and private collections, looting of archaeological sites to obtain undocumented artifacts, and illegal export. At the same time, with the end of colonialism in much of the world, particularly Africa and Asia, the new countries sought legal means to conserve at home what remained of their heritage, after so much had been lost to the colonial powers. These activities led to the development of an international legal regime to restrain the more detrimental aspects of the market and to the formulation of specialized legal doctrines to respond, in particular, to the detriment caused by the looting of archaeological sites.

International Legal Instruments

Sparked in particular by the work of Professor Clemency Coggins (1969), who brought world attention to the destruction of Maya architectural and monumental sculptural remains in Central America, the world community under the leadership of UNESCO drafted a new international convention to confront the illegal trade in art works, antiquities, and ethnographic objects. These efforts culminated in the 1970 UNESCO Convention on the Means of Prohibiting and Preventing the Illicit Import, Export and Transfer of Ownership of Cultural Property ("the 1970 UNESCO Convention" or "the Convention"). The Convention currently has 131 States Parties.

The goal of this convention is to regulate the international trade in cultural property, to encourage nations to regulate their domestic trade in cultural objects and to protect their cultural property in situ, and to provide an international mechanism for recognition of different countries' export controls with respect to cultural objects. The 1970 UNESCO Convention, in Article 1, defines cultural property as "property which, on religious or secular grounds, is specifically designated by each State as being of importance for archaeology, prehistory, history, literature, art or science" and which belongs to one of eleven enumerated categories, including paintings, drawings, original works of sculpture, rare manuscripts and incunabula, coins more than one hundred years old, ethnological objects, products of archaeological excavations (both regular and clandestine) or of archaeological discoveries, and "elements of artistic or historical monuments or archaeological sites which have been dismembered."

To most ratifying States, the core provision of the Convention is Article 3, which states that "[t]he import, export and transfer of ownership of cultural property effected contrary to the provisions adopted under this Convention by the States Parties thereto, shall be illicit." According to Patrick O'Keefe, who authored the definitive commentary on the Convention, this provision means that States Parties shall not permit the import of property whose export from another State Party was illegal (O'Keefe 2007, 41–44). In contrast, the United States implements primarily Articles 7(b) and 9, rather than Article 3. The former calls on States Parties to prohibit the import of stolen cultural property that had been documented as part of the inventory of a museum or a religious or secular public monument or similar institution. Article 9 provides a mechanism by which a State Party may call upon other States Parties for assistance in cases where its "cultural patrimony is in jeopardy from pillage of archaeological and ethnological materials." Such assistance includes controlling exports, imports, and international commerce in the materials affected.

In 1995, another international convention, the UNIDROIT Convention on Stolen or Illegally Exported Cultural Objects, was finalized (Prott 1997). While the 1970 UNESCO Convention is a product of public international law and operates on a State-to-State basis, the UNIDROIT Convention functions within a private law framework and was devised to appeal more to the civil law nations than the 1970 UNESCO Convention did. The UNIDROIT Convention utilizes the same definition of cultural property as that in the UNESCO Convention. Perhaps its most innovative aspect is that in Article 3(2), the Convention equates illegal excavation with theft when this is consistent with local law: "a cultural object which has been unlawfully excavated or lawfully excavated but unlawfully retained shall be considered stolen, when consistent with the law of the State where the excavation took place."

The UNIDROIT Convention provides that stolen and illegally exported objects should, in most circumstances, be returned to the original owner or, in cases of illegal export, the State of origin and that fair and reasonable compensation must be paid to a good faith purchaser of stolen or illegally exported cultural objects. To be eligible for compensation, the purchaser must have "neither [known] nor ought reasonably to have known that the object was stolen and can prove that it exercised due diligence when acquiring the object" (Article 4(1)). Article 4(4) provides that:

> In determining whether the possessor exercised due diligence, regard shall be had to all the circumstances of the acquisition, including the character of the parties, the price paid, whether the possessor consulted any reasonably accessible register of stolen cultural objects, and any other relevant information and documentation which it could reasonably have obtained, and whether the possessor consulted accessible agencies or took any other step that a reasonable person would have taken in the circumstances.

Particularly in the realm of antiquities, certain factors should be taken as indicating likelihood of theft or illegal export. These include origin in areas known to have been massively looted, such as Iraq, Syria, and Afghanistan; the presence of soil, mud, or straw on the object; and certain classes of antiquities, such as Cycladic figurines and South Italian Red Figure vases, of which as much as 90 percent of the known objects have been shown to be recently looted.

While the United States Senate gave its unanimous consent to ratification of the 1970 UNESCO Convention in 1972 and enacted implementing legislation in 1983, it took close to thirty years before other major market countries demonstrated interest in the 1970 UNESCO Convention. That situation began to change in the late 1990s and early 2000s. As some market nations examined both the 1970 UNESCO Convention and the 1995 UNIDROIT Convention in the late 1990s, they realized that, because the UNIDROIT Convention allows for little derogation from its provisions under only certain limited circumstances, the 1970 UNESCO Convention allowed for greater flexibility in the convention's implementation. This arguably led to a series of ratifications of the UNESCO Convention. In 1998, France joined the 1970

UNESCO Convention, and the United Kingdom and Japan did so in 2002. These were soon joined by Sweden, Denmark, Switzerland, and Germany. The most recent European countries to join the Convention are Belgium, the Netherlands, Luxembourg, and Austria.

Depending on how a country views a particular convention, it may need to enact implementing legislation to give the convention domestic legal effect. The extent to which a convention is legally binding within a nation then depends on the parameters of this domestic legislation. While the UNIDROIT Convention severely limits a ratifying State's ability to modify its terms, the major market countries that have ratified the 1970 UNESCO Convention have taken very different approaches to its implementation and with arguably very different degrees of success.

"Across-the-Board" Import Restrictions

Most States Parties implement Article 3 by granting reciprocal recognition to the export restrictions of other States when the export restrictions are promulgated as part of their implementation of the 1970 UNESCO Convention. Examples of market States that follow this implementation method are Australia, Canada, and Germany. Germany amended its implementing legislation in 2016 to adopt this method of reciprocal recognition of export controls, largely in response to the crisis of widespread looting of archaeological sites in Middle Eastern countries, particularly Syria. Under this legislation, an importer must present documentation that the cultural property was legally exported if it left another State Party to the 1970 UNESCO Convention after 2007, the date of Germany's ratification of the Convention. In the absence of documentation that establishes otherwise, it is presumed that the cultural property was unlawfully exported from the relevant State Party after 2007.

Implementing Article 3 through Bilateral Agreements

Switzerland is the only State Party that implements Article 3 but requires other States Parties to enter into supplementary bilateral agreements. Despite a superficial resemblance to the United States' system of bilateral agreements, in that import restrictions are based on categories of types of cultural objects rather than on specific objects, the Swiss model differs in several important respects. Because they implement Article 3, the Swiss bilateral agreements are not limited to archaeological and ethnological materials but, rather, apply to all types of cultural property. They are of potentially unlimited duration, are directly negotiated by the Swiss Ministry of Culture, and do not need to be renewed. Most of the Swiss agreements are truly bilateral in nature in that they call for recognition of Swiss regulations on the export of cultural property and each agreement has two designated lists of protected cultural properties—one list of Swiss cultural property and the second list for the cultural property of the State with which Switzerland has the agreement. Switzerland has agreements in force with Italy (2008), Greece (2011), Colombia (2011), Egypt (2011), China (2014), Cyprus (2014), and Peru (2016). The Federal Council can take additional measures for a limited amount of time under Article 9 of the Convention when a "State's cultural heritage [is] jeopardized by exceptional events" and did so with respect to Syria's cultural heritage.

The 1995 UNIDROIT Convention and Hybrid Approaches

Several market nations have ratified both the 1970 UNESCO Convention and the 1995 UNIDROIT Convention on Stolen or Illegally Exported Cultural Objects. These nations typically adopt implementing measures pursuant to both Conventions. These measures emphasize compliance with the UNIDROIT Convention, which is mandatory in its requirements for implementation.

Some nations have ratified only the 1970 UNESCO Convention and yet have incorporated some particular principle or measure that is found in the UNIDROIT Convention. The Netherlands is an example of this hybrid approach. While implementing Article 3 of the 1970 UNESCO Convention by prohibiting the import of cultural property that has been illegally exported or unlawfully appropriated, the legislation defines unlawful appropriation to include unlawful excavation at archaeological sites. This approach incorporates the UNIDROIT Convention's Article 3(2) equation of unlawful excavation at an archaeological site with theft.

The United Kingdom has taken something of a hybrid approach as well, incorporating the misappropriation definition from Article 3(2) of the UNIDROIT Convention into its criminal legislation, the Dealing in Cultural Objects (Offences) Act 2003. This Act created a new offence for dealing in "tainted cultural objects." One commits this offense if he or she "dishonestly deals in a cultural object that is tainted, knowing or believing that the object is tainted" (Section 1, Subsection 1). A "tainted object" is one that is removed contrary to law from "a building or structure of historical, architectural or archaeological interest" or from an excavation (Subsection 4), regardless of whether the removal took place in the United Kingdom or in another country or whether the law violated is a domestic or foreign law (Section 2, Subsection 3).

Specific Designation

When Japan ratified the 1970 UNESCO Convention in 2002, it required that objects whose recovery is sought to have been recorded or inventoried before they were stolen or illegally exported. This requirement is particularly problematic for regulating the trade in previously undocumented objects (O'Keefe 2007, 202). This provision effectively implements only Article 7(b) of the Convention by prohibiting import of "specified foreign cultural property," which is defined as "cultural property that has been stolen from an institution stipulated in Article 7(b)(i) of the Convention." Japan's implementation therefore seems entirely inadequate to deal with the problems of looted and therefore undocumented archaeological and ethnographic objects, as well as with the realities of difficulties in providing lists of objects stolen from museums and other public collections (O'Keefe 2007, 124–28; Lee 2012, 12–13).

This approach places a significant burden on a nation attempting to recover illegally removed archaeological objects that were previously undocumented and ethnographic objects, which, by their nature as part of an indigenous community, may also not be inventoried. Cultural objects that are part of a more traditional collection, such as a museum, church, or private collection, may not be inventoried for lack of capacity.

Implementation of Article 9

The United States enacted its implementing legislation, the Convention on Cultural Property Implementation Act (CPIA) (19 U.S.C. §§ 2601–2613), in 1983. It directly implements only two provisions of the UNESCO Convention, Article 7(b) and Article 9, although it references other sections of the Convention, by adopting the Article 1 definition of cultural property and referring to the obligations under the Convention of other States Parties outlined in Articles 5 and 6. Although the United States was the first significant market nation to ratify the Convention, this method is seriously flawed, especially in light of the steps that other States Parties have taken in recent years.

The United States' implementation of Article 9 is complex and imposes significant burdens on the requesting State Party. The CPIA provides a mechanism by which the United States can enter into bilateral agreements (or Memoranda of Understanding) with other States Parties for the imposition of import restrictions on designated categories of archaeological or ethnological materials. A State Party must first submit a request to the United States for a bilateral agreement with supporting documentation concerning the criteria required by the CPIA before an agreement can be negotiated. In the close to thirty-five years that the CPIA has been in effect, the United States has entered into bilateral agreements with only seventeen nations: Belize, Bolivia, Bulgaria, Cambodia, Canada (which was not renewed in 2002), China, Colombia, Cyprus, Egypt, El Salvador, Greece, Guatemala, Honduras, Italy, Mali, Nicaragua, and Peru. A bilateral agreement may not last more than five years, but it may be renewed an indefinite number of times. The agreement sets out the list of designated categories of materials whose import is to be restricted and includes provisions that create a path for mutual cooperation in the realm of cultural heritage protection, the provision of technical assistance, and certain aspects that are specific to the particular country involved.

A scheme that relies on agreements with individual nations raises certain difficulties. The boundaries of modern nations and ancient cultures, even indigenous communities, do not necessarily coincide. The Inca culture in South America, the Maya culture of Central America, and the Roman culture of the Mediterranean and Europe are but a few examples of ancient cultures that span more than one modern nation's borders. While import restrictions that operated on a cultural, rather than modern nation-state, basis might be more effective, international conventions are State-to-State agreements and function on that basis. A second shortcoming of this system is that in order to initiate the process, a State must submit a request for an agreement through diplomatic channels. In situations of emergency conditions or where the United States and the other State are not on good diplomatic terms, it may be difficult or impossible to submit a request. The situations in Iraq in 2003 and Syria today illustrate these obstacles. In both cases, Congress had to pass special legislation to change the normal CPIA requirements by eliminating the need for a request, applying the import restrictions to broader categories of cultural materials, and by allowing the import restrictions to last for a longer period of time.

Theft and Stolen Property: Foreign National Ownership of Archaeological Objects

Theft occurs when a rightful owner is deprived of possession of a cultural object without permission. This includes removal from a private collection or a public one (such as a museum, library, archive, or religious institution). In addition to well-developed legal principles that apply to recovery of and prosecution for the handling of stolen property, the law has developed a particular doctrine to deal with the removal of archaeological objects directly from the ground. The looting of archaeological sites has increased significantly since the middle of the twentieth century even as the increasing application of scientific methodologies, including controlled retrieval with the full stratigraphic context intact, means that greater quantities of information could be recovered from the proper excavation of sites. The looting of sites harms all of us through losses to our knowledge and understanding of the past.

Beginning in the mid-nineteenth century, many nations that are rich in archaeological resources enacted laws that vest ownership of undiscovered archaeological objects in the nation. These laws serve the dual purposes of preventing unfettered export of antiquities and of protecting archaeological sites in which antiquities are buried. Vesting laws create ownership rights that are recognized even when such antiquities are removed from their country of discovery and are traded in foreign nations. When ownership of an antiquity is vested in a nation, one who removes the antiquity without permission is a thief and the antiquities are stolen property. This enables both punishment of the looter and recovery of possession of the antiquity from either the looter or a subsequent purchaser. This, in turn, reduces the economic value of looted antiquities by making them unsalable, thus deterring the initial theft. Some of the earliest such laws were adopted in Greece, Egypt, and Turkey, but they are now common throughout the Mediterranean, Central and South America, and parts of Asia.

A series of judicial decisions in the United States, including the federal criminal prosecutions in *United States v. McClain*, 545 F.2d 988 (5th Cir. 1977); 593 F.2d 658 (5th Cir. 1979), and in *United States v. Schultz*, 333 F.3d 393 (2d Cir. 2003), established that archaeological objects removed in violation of a nation's vesting statute retain their characterization as stolen property, even after they are brought to the United States. This triggers the availability of various legal actions, including private replevin, civil forfeiture, and criminal prosecution, as well as the basis for negotiated settlement of foreign national claims, depending on the relevant factual circumstances. This doctrine is now accepted in the federal appellate circuits that most often confront market issues related to antiquities, including the Second, Ninth, Fifth, and Eleventh circuits.

The decisions in *United States v. McClain* and *United States v. Schultz* establish the criteria required for recognition of a foreign national ownership law of archaeological remains. Based on these holdings, one can deduce that there are four elements that must be satisfied before an archaeological object will be recognized as owned pursuant to a foreign national ownership law: (1) the vesting law must be clearly an ownership law on its face; (2) the nation's ownership rights must be enforced domestically and not only upon illegal export; (3) the object must have been found within the country claiming ownership; and (4) the object must have been located within the country at the time the law was enacted.

The purpose of the first requirement is that the vesting must be clear and unambiguous so as to give notice to U.S. citizens who might be adversely affected by these laws, particularly in a criminal prosecution (*Schultz*, 178 F. Supp. 2d at 447; *McClain*, 545 F.2d at 997-1002). The purpose of the second requirement is to distinguish national ownership from export controls because export controls are not enforced by another nation absent a specific agreement to do so. The third requirement ensures that the national ownership law is not given extraterritorial effect and the fourth requirement ensures that the national ownership law is not given retroactive effect.

The British courts have aligned with those in the United States by recognizing Iran's right to sue to recover antiquities looted from graves in the Jiroft region and later acquired by the London dealer, Barakat (*Government of the Islamic Republic of Iran v. The Barakat Galleries Ltd*, Court of Appeal [Civil Division], EWCA Civ 1374 [2007]). While not definitively concluding that Iran had a national ownership law, the court held that Iran had a superior right of possession, which gave it standing to sue for return of the antiquities.

DOMESTIC CULTURAL HERITAGE OF THE UNITED STATES

This chapter will turn now to discuss more briefly some of the legal issues related to the domestic cultural heritage of the United States. These issues can be divided into those related specifically to the protection of archaeological sites and resources and those related more broadly to Native American heritage.

Archaeological Heritage

The first attempt at the federal level to protect archaeological heritage came with enactment of the Antiquities Act of 1906, 16 U.S.C. §§ 431–433. The Antiquities Act provides that the president may set aside as national monuments "historic landmarks, historic and prehistoric structures, and other objects of historic or scientific interest" located on lands owned or controlled by the federal government (including Indian tribal land, forest reserves, and military reservations) and penalizes the destruction, damage, excavation, appropriation, or injury of any historic or prehistoric ruin, monument, or object of antiquity. In 1974, the Ninth Circuit Court of Appeals held that the criminal provisions of the Act were unconstitutional because the legislation failed to define adequately terms such as "ruin," "monument," and "object of antiquity." The Act thus violated due process by failing to give the person of ordinary intelligence a reasonable opportunity to know what the Act prohibited (*United States v. Diaz*, 499 F.2d 113, 115 [9th Cir. 1974]).

In part in response to the *Diaz* decision, the Archaeological Resources Protection Act (ARPA) was enacted in 1979. ARPA vests ownership of archaeological resources found on federally owned and Indian tribal lands, with exceptions now provided in the Native American Graves Protection and Repatriation Act, in the federal government and requires that anyone who wishes to excavate or remove archaeological resources from such lands first obtain permission from the federal government (16 U.S.C. § 470cc; § 470ee(a)). ARPA also prohibits trafficking in archaeological resources removed from public or Indian lands without a permit or otherwise in violation of any federal law and trafficking in interstate and foreign commerce of any archaeological resources taken or held in violation of federal, state or local law (16 U.S.C. § 470ee(b) and (c)). While subsection (b) refers specifically to artifacts from federal or Indian lands, subsection (c) refers to artifacts illegally trafficked in interstate or foreign commerce. This opens the possibility for the application of ARPA to cases involving artifacts from private and state lands as well as from foreign countries. Finally, ARPA provides for both civil fines and criminal penalties (16 U.S.C. § 470ee(d) and § 470ff).

ARPA cured the defect of the Antiquities Act by providing a clear definition of "archaeological resource" as "any material remains of past human life or activities which are of archaeological interest, . . . [and] at least 100 years of age" (16 U.S.C. § 470bb(1)). The definition of "archaeological resource" is not limited to objects found on federal lands. Therefore, ARPA applies to crimes involving archaeological resources from private land within the United States and from foreign countries, in the right circumstances. In *United States v. Gerber*, 999 F.2d 1112 (7th Cir. 1993), the government successfully prosecuted a dealer for selling artifacts illegally removed from private land and then transferring them across state lines. In *United States v. Melnikas*, 929 F. Supp. 276 (S.D. Ohio 1996), the government prosecuted an Ohio book dealer for import and sale of manuscripts stolen from various European collections, including the Vatican. This prosecution is significant, in part, for the application of ARPA based on the definition of archaeological resource to include books and manuscripts (Marous and Marous 2006). In the case where the object originates in a foreign country, it must be characterized as stolen property, either in the traditional sense or as previously discussed in terms of archaeological objects subject to foreign national ownership, so that possession and other activities would be in violation of state laws relating to stolen property.

Native American Cultural Heritage

The Native American Graves Protection and Repatriation Act (NAGPRA) is a comprehensive approach to the disposition of Native American human remains and cultural items (25 U.S.C. §§ 3001–13). NAGPRA has three primary components. First, NAGPRA provides for the restitution of newly discovered human remains and associated burial items discovered on federally owned or controlled land to Native American tribes under certain circumstances. It provides a priority order of the ownership of Native American human remains and burial objects, including lineal descendants, the Indian tribe or Native Hawaiian organization on whose tribal land such objects or remains were discovered or to those with the "closest cultural affiliation" with the remains or objects (25 U.S.C. § 3002(a)).

Second, NAGPRA provides a mechanism for the restitution to Native American tribes of human remains, associated and unassociated burial goods, sacred objects, and objects of cultural patrimony that are in the collections of federal agencies and private museums and institutions that receive federal funding. Associated funerary objects are objects that were placed with individual human remains and the human remains and objects are in the possession or control of the same agency or museum, while unassociated funerary objects are those where the human remains with which they were originally buried are no longer in the possession or control of the agency or museum. Sacred objects are "specific ceremonial objects which are needed by traditional Native American religious leaders for the practice of traditional Native American religions by their present day adherents." Object of cultural patrimony means "an object having ongoing historical, traditional, or cultural importance central to the Native American group of culture itself . . . and which . . . cannot be alienated, appropriated, or conveyed by an individual . . . and such object shall have been considered inalienable by such Native American group at the time the object was separated from such group" (25 U.S.C. § 3001(3)). NAGPRA establishes a mechanism by which federal agencies and museums notify tribes through the publication of inventories or summaries of their Native American holdings and then procedures by which such items may be repatriated to the tribe or Native Hawaiian organization (25 U.S.C. §§ 3003–3004).

Finally, NAGPRA prohibits trafficking in Native American human remains without the right of possession as provided under NAGPRA and in cultural items that were obtained in violation of NAGPRA 18 U.S.C. § 1170 (a)-(b). In *United States v. Corrow*, which concerned objects of cultural patrimony obtained by a dealer from the family of a *hataali*, or Navajo religious singer, the Tenth Circuit held that the criminal provisions were not unconstitutionally vague 119 F.3d 796 (10th Cir. 1997). The Ninth Circuit came to the same conclusion in *United States v. Tidwell*, 191 F.3d 976 (9th Cir. 1999), which involved Hopi masks and other cultural items from the Pueblo of Acoma.

Beginning in 2013, several auctions of Native American cultural objects have been held in Paris. The Native American tribes consider these objects to be sacred, including Hopi *katsinam*, Navajo masks, and other tribal cultural objects. Virtually nothing is known as to when and how these objects were obtained by the consignor, in large part because the French courts have refused to delay the sales or require the auction houses to present evidence of the objects' provenance (or ownership history). Further, the courts held that U.S. law was not clear in prohibiting the sale of such objects outside of the United States (Nicolazzi, Chechi, and Renold 2015). In one case the proposed sale of a sacred Acoma Pueblo shield was halted because of specific evidence that the shield had been stolen (Schilling 2016).

Legislation was introduced in the U.S. Congress in 2016, the Safeguard Tribal Objects of Patrimony Act. Among other provisions, it would impose export restrictions on Native

American cultural objects that are obtained in violation of either ARPA or NAGPRA. If this legislation were to be enacted in a future Congress, it would be the first time that the United States has restricted the export of specifically cultural objects. However, while it might provide a basis for recovery of Native American cultural objects that are exported in the future, it would be of little assistance in the effort to recover objects that have already been removed from the United States. Despite many advances in the legal protection granted to cultural heritage, these Paris auctions illustrate the shortcomings of relying exclusively on the legal system to protect cultural heritage.

NOTE

1. The terms cultural property and cultural heritage are sometimes used interchangeably and the lack of clear definition and universally accepted terminology indicates the relatively recent nature of this field. Cultural property refers to both movable and immovable tangible property, while cultural heritage can include intangible elements, such as language, traditions, ritual practices, and folklore. Cultural heritage is today used more generally in international fora and legal instruments, while cultural property tends to be used in the United States, which emphasizes the ownership aspects that are inherent in the word "property." Heritage, on the other hand, emphasizes stewardship aspects and the obligation to preserve for the sake of future generations.

BIBLIOGRAPHY

Boylan, Patrick J. *Review of the Convention for the Protection of Cultural Property in the Event of Armed Conflict (The Hague Convention of 1954)*. UNESCO Doc. CLT93/WS/12 101, 53. 1993. Available at http://unesdoc.unesco.org/images/0010/001001/100159eo.pdf.
Chamberlain, Kevin. 2013. *War and Cultural Heritage.* Leicester: Institute of Art and Law, 2013.
Coggins, Clemency Chase. "Illicit Traffic of Pre-Columbian Antiquities," *Art Journal* (Fall 1969): 94–98.
Cole, Sue. "War, Cultural Property and the Blue Shield," in P. G. Stone and J. Farchakh Bajjaly (eds), *The Destruction of Cultural Heritage in Iraq* 65–71. Woodbridge, UK: Boydell Press, 2008.
Gerstenblith, Patty. "The Destruction of Cultural Heritage: A Crime Against Property or a Crime Against People?" *John Marshall Review of Intellectual Property Law* 15 (2016): 336–393.
Lee, Keun-Gwan. "An Overview of the Implementation of the 1970 Convention in Asia." 2012. Available at: http://www.unesco.org/new/fileadmin/MULTIMEDIA/HQ/CLT/pdf/Lee_en.pdf.
Marous, Sarah and J. Michael Marous. "ARPA in the International Context: Protecting the Articles of Faith," in Sherry Hutt, Marion P. Forsyth, and David Tarler (eds), *Presenting Archaeology in Court: Legal Strategies for Protecting Cultural Resources* 39–45. Oxford: AltaMira Press, 2006.
Miles, Margaret M. *Art as Plunder: The Ancient Origins of Debate about Cultural Property*. Cambridge: Cambridge University Press, 2008.
Nicolazzi, Laetitia, Alessandro Chechi, and Marc-André Renold. "Case Hopi Masks—Hope Tribe v. Néret-Minet and Estimations & Ventes aux Enchères," *ArThemis* (2015). Available at https://plone.unige.ch/art-adr/cases-affaires/hopi-masks-2013-hopi-tribe-v-neret-minet-and-estimations-ventes-aux-encheres/case-note-2013-hopi-masks-2013-hopi-tribe-v-neret-minet-and-estimations-ventes-aux-encheres.
O'Keefe, Patrick J. *Commentary on the UNESCO Convention, second ed.* Institute of Art and Law, 2007.
O'Keefe, Patrick J. "Using UNIDROIT to Avoid Cultural Heritage Disputes: Limitation Periods," in James A. R. Nafziger and Ann M. Nicgorski (eds), *Cultural Heritage Issues: The Legacy of Conquest, Colonization, and Commerce.* Leiden, Netherlands: Brill Academic Publishers, 2010, 389.

O'Keefe, Roger. *The Protection of Cultural Property in Armed Conflict.* Cambridge: Cambridge University Press, 2006.

Prosecutor v. Ahmad Al Faqi Al Mahdi, ICC-01/12-01/15, available at https://www.icc-cpi.int/en_menus/ icc/situations%20and%20cases/situations/icc0112/Pages/situation%20index.aspx.

Prott, Lyndel V. *Commentary on the UNIDROIT Convention.* 1995. Leicester: Institute of Art and Law, 1997.

Schilling, Vincent. "Paris Auction Update: Acoma Shield Pulled, Attendance Low Amid Protests," *Indian Country.* 2016. Available at http://indiancountrytodaymedianetwork.com/2016/05/31/paris -auction-update-acoma-shield-pulled-attendance-low-amid-protests-164657.

Toman, Jiří. *The Protection of Cultural Property in the Event of Armed Conflict.* Brookfield, CT: Dartmouth Publishing Co., 1996.

Toman, Jiří. *Cultural Property in War: Improvement in Protection: Commentary on the 1999 Second Protocol to the Hague Convention of 1954 for the Protection of Cultural Property in the Event of Armed Conflict.* Paris: UNESCO Publications, 2009.

van Woudenberg, Nout and Liesbeth, Lijnzaad (eds). *Protecting Cultural Property in Armed Conflict: An Insight into the 1999 Second Protocol to the Hague Convention of 1954 for the Protection of Cultural Property in the Event of Armed Conflict.* Leiden: Martinus Nijhoff Publ., 2010.

Part II

CULTURAL HERITAGE MANAGEMENT
IN TRADITIONAL CULTURES

6

Roman Textiles and Heritage in Syria

Tasha Vorderstrasse

INTRODUCTION

This chapter examines the importance of Roman textiles to our understanding of the threatened archaeological heritage of Syria. Since textiles are organic, they are best preserved in arid environments, meaning that Roman and medieval textiles are most often found in the Near East in Egypt and Nubia, with their desert climates, and with limited numbers of textiles being found in other countries in the wider region. Consequently, textiles are often overlooked when scholars examine the different types of archaeological objects that might have been looted from Syria. This chapter highlights the importance of textiles from Syria, examining the evidence from three sites: Palmyra, Dura Europos, and Halabiyya-Zenobia. The textiles from Dura Europos and Palmyra are largely contemporary to the Roman period, while most of the Halabiyya-Zenobia textiles date back to the Late Roman/Early Byzantine period. First, the importance of textiles in studies of archaeological heritage in general, particularly focusing on the evidence from Egypt and Nubia, is examined. Then, we will turn to the evidence from Syria and what it can tell us about textiles that might be found from Syria. The rarity of textiles in Near Eastern contexts outside of Egypt and Nubia means that many Near Eastern scholars have not previously dealt with them and therefore they make assumptions regarding textiles and modern day looting. They suggest that textiles would not be of interest to looters, which is not the case. It is clear that textiles are of considerable interest to looters and therefore must be considered when trying to reconstruct the places where objects are looted in Syria.

TEXTILES AND HERITAGE

While textiles constitute an important part of the archaeological record, many textiles are found outside scientific excavations. Peruvian textiles, for example, are well known for their excellent, preserved quality, making them very attractive to collectors and therefore targets for looters. There are many museums and private collectors with large collections of Paracas, Nasca, and Wari textiles that presumably come from Peru. Once the textiles are looted, much of the accompanying archaeological context is lost, including where they were actually found.[1] The problem then for scholars is trying to attribute those textiles back to their original archaeological context in the absence of other evidence. This problem and its challenges have been studied in South American contexts.[2] Archaeologists who have studied Peruvian textiles that have been extensively collected by museums and which lack an archaeological context have identified the difficulties in ascribing a provenance to textiles on the basis of style.[3] These studies point to the fact that textiles are an important part of collections of looted artifacts.

In the Near East, the largest numbers of textiles have come from Egypt and Nubia, and as a result, the largest number of looted textiles are found to come from there. The large collections of decorated "Coptic" textiles from Egypt starting in the nineteenth century suggest that these textiles are very desirable to collectors. Nevertheless, the interest by collectors in textiles has not been reflected in the archaeology of Egypt. Many archaeologists simply have never collected textiles from excavations, because those found in many of these sites were not considered "museum worthy" and therefore not something that archaeologists wanted to save. It has only been recently that more archaeologists have realized the importance of textiles. In studies of different types of textiles found in excavations, it has been concluded that Late Antique textiles from Egypt could be divided into two types: those that come from funerary contexts and those that come from domestic contexts. Those from the funerary contexts of burials and tombs tend to be fairly complete, while the smaller fragments usually come from domestic contexts such as rubbish dumps where they were deliberately thrown away.[4]

Most of the textiles preserved in museums and private collections do not have an archaeological context or come from early twentieth-century excavations that were not particularly scientific, and therefore the textiles were not preserved in a particularly scientific manner. This has led to the assumption that textiles are not particularly common in archaeological contexts and only the most attractive and well-preserved pieces tended to be kept.[5] Therefore, since textiles often lack archaeological context, their origin is often assumed. This of course becomes particularly problematic when one is trying to assign textiles to a particular region or site. In the case of Late Antique Egyptian textiles, the assignment of these textiles to Egypt is usually made on the style of the textiles. Based on the large amount of material from Egypt, this is not an unreasonable assumption. Nevertheless, studies of the at-Tar textiles from Iraq that date to the Late Antique period and Syrian textiles (see below) demonstrate that these styles may be far more widespread than previously assumed[6] and therefore Egypt should not necessarily be the default provenance. Further, as textiles from other regions can be transported large distances such as the Chinese, Central Asian, and Middle Eastern textiles that appear in Church treasuries in Western Europe (Stauffer 1991; Galliker 2014: 185), provenance is clearly a complicated issue.

Another difficulty is dating textiles because they have been removed from their accompanying archaeological context. In the absence of this information, textiles are frequently dated to a particular period on the basis of an art historical style. Radiocarbon dating of these textiles has demonstrated that in some cases the traditional art historical dating of certain types of textiles are actually incorrect.[7] Further complicating the matter is the frequent reuse of textiles because of their value, a phenomenon that has been documented in textile finds from different periods. Therefore, while radiocarbon dates are useful, they can only tell archaeologists about the date of the fabric, not necessarily of the garment. Sometimes even the date of the fabric and its decoration are different, as the textile continued to be used in different ways over time.[8] Further complicating this is the fact that nineteenth- and twentieth-century excavators, such as Antoine Gayet who worked at the site of Antinoe in Egypt, sold their finds in order to be able to fund new exhibitions and often staged mummies with textiles that did not belong with that particular body.[9]

When one looks at well-preserved Late Antique clothing from Egypt, they often consist of clothes such as tunics with embroidered bands or roundels that were stitched onto plain linen. Therefore, it was common practice to cut out the bands or roundels, which could then be easily displayed and the rest of the undecorated cloth would be discarded. This meant that the information about the original type of clothing was then lost, in addition to 90 percent the garment.[10] In other cases, however, preserving the entire garment is important, but one is left with the problem of how to display the object. In 1998, the Metropolitan Museum of Art bought a group of textiles that they believed came from the north Caucasus, specifically the site of Moscevaja Balka, which is well known for its textiles. Since the material was looted, it is unclear where or indeed when it was acquired.[11] The Metropolitan Museum of Art did not buy everything from this group of material, however, and a silk robe allegedly from the Tang period was auctioned from the same group of material in 2014 by Bonham's.[12] Again, no provenance was given. The Bonham's textile was heavily reconstructed in order to create a whole garment, which would presumably make it easier to display and be more attractive to buyers. This caftan and the Metropolitan Museum of Art caftan were reconstructed in 1995 after the initial auction of the pieces in 1994. Since this reconstruction was inaccurate, the Metropolitan Museum of Art removed it in 1996.[13] Still, even poorly preserved textiles can be of interest to museums if the fabric and design are interesting enough. A silk textile at the Metropolitan Museum of Art (08.109.1b), described as being decorated with textiles and griffins and dating to the early thirteenth century, is in extremely poor condition. Nevertheless, it was purchased by the Metropolitan Museum of Art in 1908, although it is not on view.

Therefore, it is clear that textiles are attractive items for individuals who collect ancient and medieval art. In Egypt, the best preserved textiles come from mortuary contexts, but many textiles have been altered, preserving only the parts that were decorated. Nevertheless, there have been attempts to reconstruct garments so they can be displayed in what collectors consider an attractive manner. Fragments of textiles are commonly sold at auction, as an examination of the terms "textile fragment," "Coptic textile," or "Roman textiles" in the auction consolidation website LiveAuctioneers (www.liveauctioneers.com) in October 2016 shows. Many of the textile fragments from the Near East do indeed appear to be Egyptian, keeping in mind the provenance problems outlined above. They are sometimes sold in frames but in other cases one simply buys loose fragments of textiles. In some instances, their descriptions have been invented in order to make them more attractive. A Late Roman textile sold for $1,500 at the Artemis Gallery on October 22, 2015, is an excellent example of this phenomenon. The textile is described as a "Rare Romano Egyptian Textile Panel—Gladiator."[14] This description is incorrect as this textile probably comes from a large hanging tapestry and the figure represents a statue standing on a column.[15] One can see the top of the column here but the rest of the depiction of the pillar on the textile has been cut away. There are also clear signs of cutting on the rest of the textile and this is even acknowledged in the description, which somewhat surprisingly states: "These decorative panels were often cut away from the linens used to wrap mummies by artifact collectors in the 19th and early 20th centuries."[16]

TEXTILES FROM SYRIA

In contrast to Egypt and Nubia, Syria is not known for its rich textile heritage, outside of a few key sites that will discussed here.[17] Textiles have not been preserved in Syria at a large number of sites, but the climate of some parts of eastern Syria has made the preservation of textiles possible at the Roman sites of Palmyra, Dura Europos, and Halabiyya-Zenobia.[18] While the archaeological finds of textiles have been largely restricted to the arid eastern region around the Euphrates on the border with Iraq, the recent find of textiles in a hoard of armor and weapons at the Damascus Citadel[19] suggests that textiles at archaeological sites could be more widespread than previously assumed. In many cases, however, the environment of many parts of Syria means that textile remains have disappeared, often leaving little or no trace behind. As Toll stated already in 1937, "Undoubtedly, if the conditions of the soil and of climate in Syria had been as favorable as those in Egypt, the number of textiles found in Syrian necropoleis would have been enormous."[20] In a tomb found at the Bronze Age royal palace at Qatna, for instance, excavators found traces of dye in areas of bronze staining in the tomb floor, suggesting that the textiles worn were dyed with royal purple. Microscopic examination of the material from the site identified millimeter-sized fragments of textiles, allowing them to identify plain weave textiles and one example of tapestry weave.[21] This demonstrates that careful scientific study of the ground in likely places may reveal traces of textiles, but the civil war in Syria has prevented further archaeological study in this direction.

Studies of the possible looted archaeological heritage from Syria have made assumptions about the likely types of objects that might appear on the market. These studies usually do not include textiles. The few scholars who have discussed textiles do not believe that they are looted from sites in Syria and sold on the market. Völling suggests that textiles do not survive in Syria in general due not to environmental factors, but rather because looters do not see them as valuable, unlike looters in Egypt. As a result, textiles are often intentionally destroyed by these looters.[22] This ignores the fact that there have been many archaeological excavations in Syria but few have actually discovered textiles. If they were common, one would expect them to be found more frequently. Daniels and Hanson look more specifically at the site of Dura Europos. After noting the presence of textiles and leather and texts written in various languages found there, Daniels and Hanson proceed to concentrate on coins from the site. Then, after stating that coin hoards were found in different parts of the city by the scientific excavations at the site, they posit that the purpose of looting Dura Europos is to uncover coin hoards and jewelry rather than objects such as textile fragments. They argue that textiles would be destroyed by the looters' efforts to uncover more precious items and that they do not have a market in any case.[23]

As the evidence has demonstrated above, textiles do have a ready market among collectors and have been systematically looted to meet that demand. This argues that looters learn how to uncover fragile items such as textiles and would be unlikely to intentionally destroy them or to discard them in favor of coins, many of which might be bronze issues that would only be worth a small amount. While it is true that coins are very marketable items and recent work has shown a surge in coins that may have a Syrian provenance since 2011,[24] that does not mean that textiles would not be looted as well from both archaeological sites and museums. Further, evidence for an increase in the appearance of Palmyrene funerary portraits has been documented since the outbreak of the civil war in 2011 as well as the looting of tombs.[25] Therefore, it is possible that textiles were found by the looters in these tombs and may subsequently appear on the market. There is also the possibility that the textiles have already appeared on the market but have not been recognized as Syrian due to their resemblance to textiles from Egypt.

Palmyra is probably the most famous site of textiles from Syria, due to the rich variety of textiles, including rare imports, that are documented there. It constitutes the bulk of what is known about textile fragments in Syria. Over 2,000 textile fragments have been found at the site.[26] As in Egypt, the textiles come from the mortuary contexts at Palmyra, namely the tower tombs, of which there are about 250, although most of them have not been excavated or published.[27] Each tomb belonged to a family or clan and could contain hundreds of burials (Stauffer 2013). The tower tombs seem to have created a micro-climate that allowed the preservation of a variety of different types of textiles, including objects of local production as well as imported silks.[28] These textiles covered bodies that had been mummified, but most of the mummies have been destroyed by looters,[29] meaning that textiles are not necessarily found in situ when they are discovered in the tombs by archaeologists. The textiles found in tower tomb 65, for instance, were discovered near the entrance of the tomb. This suggests that they were dropped there by tomb robbers.[30] Despite these problems, however, it has been possible to reconstruct the way that textiles covered the mummies, which has implications for the types of textiles that survived. The bodies of the dead were not actually dressed in clothing or shrouds but rather had been dried out and then wrapped in three textile layers. The innermost layer was made from very fine linen or wool that was fairly unworn and then this was followed by a second layer of less fine linen that was torn into broad strips. Pieces of large cloaks or tunics were used on the inner wrappings of the mummies, while the outer layer, which would have been visible, is where the strips of colored textiles such as silks or richly decorated wool were used.[31] One should not assume that all the mummies were wrapped in this way, however, since one example is attested of a mummy who was wrapped in rug made from wool. There were some other textiles and netting whose exact relationship to the mummy was not clear. The netting is made in the *sprang* technique, but the type of cloth used is not clear.[32] Radiocarbon dating of *sprang* hairnets from Egypt ranges from the mid-fourth through eighth centuries AD, with hairnets being made of wool and linen.[33]

While wool is the most common type of textile that has been found at Palmyra, linen, silk, and cotton fragments have also been found. The material famously includes imported Chinese silk damasks and brocades, some of which were decorated with Chinese characters. These silks closely resemble Chinese silks found in western China. Other silk textiles were produced locally using imported Chinese silks.[34] There are also cotton textiles that might have been produced locally, or possibly imported from India or Egypt.[35] The Palmyra textiles were studied in the most detail by Pfister (1934–1940), who noted similarities with the textiles of Palmyra and Egypt,[36] for example. Further, since the Chinese textiles resemble those found elsewhere (see above), it means that determining whether or not particular Chinese textiles might have come from Palmyra if they are unprovenanced, would be difficult. Nevertheless, textiles were made from strips of various sizes and they were reused from clothing,[37] which makes the Palmyrene textiles distinct from the Dura Europos textiles.

In contrast to Palmyra, the textiles of Dura Europos did not come from the necropolis located outside the city but rather from the city wall embankment and its towers, as well as four graves in the citadel. The fact that both Cumont's excavations and the later Yale University–French Academy excavations found textiles in the fortifications of the site[38] argues that the textiles were concentrated in particular areas thanks to climatic conditions which were clearly not present in the necropolis. The main publication of the textiles has been Pfister and Bellinger's study of the Yale textiles, which shows that we are currently missing a portion of the original textiles that were excavated. The editors of the textile publication note that the excavators left the textiles that had no patterns on them at the site of Dura, which numbered about one hundred.[39] Most of the pieces went to the Yale University Art Museum, while twenty-two were sent to the Trocadero Museum in Paris and were later transferred to the Museum Quai Branly.[40] In contrast to Palmyra, the textiles are not associated with mummies, for which there is no evidence from Dura Europos.

Most pieces are not that large, with the exception of two tunics, one fairly complete, both from the citadel necropolis[41] and a blanket or curtain that was used to wrap a corpse as a shroud. Indeed, most of the decorated textiles were probably used to wrap bodies rather than belonging to garments that were worn.[42] There was also a felt hat.[43] There are signs of reuse in the textiles and the majority of the pieces were wool, with one cotton fragment, two silk pieces, and some made from linen. They argued that the silk was made locally[44] and it has been suggested that the reason that no imported pieces of silk were found was that Dura Europos was off the Silk Road.[45] It is also possible however that the preservation of the textiles impacts what was found. While some textiles were found in graves, most were found in the habitation of the city and therefore likely to be different from the funerary textiles found at Palmyra because they show what was in use at the time,[46] not what was deliberately placed in a tomb. Nevertheless, one can see certain similarities in the textiles found at Dura Europos and Palmyra.[47] The way that the textiles were preserved argues that the looters would have only found textiles if they had excavated in certain parts of the city. If the looters did find such fragile objects, there is no reason they could not send them to market as is done in Egypt, provided the textiles were of sufficient quality and interest. Certainly some of the textiles found in the excavations were large or decorated and might be something that would be considered desirable on the part of collectors. The site of Dura Europos has been looted extensively since the outbreak of the Syrian conflict, meaning that it is likely that textiles have been found.

The site of Halabiya-Zenobia presents a different picture of the preservation of textiles and how certain single events can greatly impact that type of textiles discovered by archaeologists. The site of Halabiya-Zenobia had tower tombs, such as those seen at Palmyra, and there is anecdotal evidence that at least one of them contained a mummy of a similar type attested there.[48] Textiles were discovered during initial excavations in 1936 by Toll when he was working on the Dura Europos excavations. All the textiles that he found he dated to the sixth century, except for a silk piece that he thought was third century AD. He reported finding a grave with a silk textile in one tower tomb, as well as a wooden sarcophagus in another that was well preserved and containing a variety of different objects including silk fragments.[49] It is in the 1940s excavations that a large number of well-preserved textiles were discovered. The vast majority of the textiles came from one particular tower tomb, with one textile from another grave and two from the citadel.[50] While one might assume that the textiles came from bodies buried purposely in the tower tomb and therefore date to the Roman period,[51] the excavator suggested a different scenario. He stated that the textiles came from the bodies of women and children who had taken refuge from the Sasanian invasion at the site that occurred at the beginning of the seventh century. He argued then that the bodies were covered with a layer of bird guano and then collapsed from the tower, leading to the preservation of the textiles.[52] Although he does not give any reasons for why bird guano would preserve the mummies, both bird[53] and bat guano[54] has been observed as a preservative for natural mummies and presumably led to the preservation of the textiles. Indeed, at the similar site of Tall as-Sin, which is located about 60 km from Zenobia-Halabiyya, only small oxidized fragments of textiles were preserved that had come into contact with metal.[55] Toll's earlier work at the site also reported finding textiles and a large number of skulls in disarray in the same tower tomb.[56] Recent archaeological investigations of the site by Blétry have revealed a few more examples of textiles at the site, namely two large linen fragments that she believes were used as shrouds and presumably date to the Roman period.[57]

Toll's study was limited but he noted similarities between his textile and those from Egypt, but still felt the textiles were produced locally. In the well-preserved wooden sarcophagus he found fragments of silk that he believed had been imported from China, as had been observed at Palmyra. These fragments are extremely small.[58] His study was limited and the more numerous textiles from the 1940s excavations were once again studied by Pfister after an initial publication of material by Toll, who noted that most of the textiles were made out of linen, with some of silk and cotton.[59] Not surprisingly, given the good preservation at the site, there were a number of complete or nearly complete textiles, primarily children's tunics. Pfister suggested that the tunics were similar to earlier Syrian examples from Palmyra and Dura Europos as well as Egypt.[60] In addition, a pair of linen trousers was preserved[61] that is similar to other examples that are thought to be from Egypt and have been dated to the sixth or seventh century,[62] which would tend to support Pfister's date for the textiles. This date contradicts the original suggestion that trousers of this type actually date to the twelfth century.[63] While one might assume that there was no market for undecorated trousers, a pair with clear parallels to these was auctioned in 2007 by Christie's, as a part of a lot of a textile roundel and leather sandals, for $25,588. The trousers are described as being "Coptic linen," which reflects the fact that there are Egyptian parallels as well. Despite the similarities that Pfister observed with other textiles in Egypt and Syria, he noted that some of the textiles were still unique to the site.[64] One of the most unique pieces, which was a tunic with Greek embroidery on it,[65] was strangely not published by Pfister. There is no report of any earlier textiles such as the Chinese import observed by Toll. Blétry does not discuss her textile fragments in detail but it seems likely that they are contemporary with the construction of the tombs and therefore are from the same period as the Dura Europos and Palmyra textiles.

CONCLUSION

Despite the statements of some scholars studying the cultural heritage of Syria, textiles form an important part of its material remains, even if those from sites where scientific excavations have occurred are limited. It is clear that the textiles from Syria have clear connections with Egyptian textiles and this obviously has implications for textiles that are unprovenanced. It means that the textiles that are on the art market described as Egyptian could also come from Syria. The removal of the textiles from their archaeological context also causes considerable problems, not only because the provenance is lost and could be confused but also because the dating and understanding of these textiles is often lost. The textiles known from Syria come from controlled excavations, but given the issues described above, there could easily be more in the mass of textile fragments that are auctioned every year. Nevertheless, the examination of the textiles from Palmyra, Dura Europos, and Halabiyya gives us an idea of the types of materials that might be coming out of Syria and the differences between the textiles from these sites might make it one day possible to provenance looted Syrian textiles.

NOTES

1. Peters 2004; Yates 2014a; Yates 2014b; Yates 2015: 34, 36.
2. Dwyer 1979: 106; Paul 2007: 375–377.
3. Silverman 2002: 89–93.
4. Vogelsang-Eastwood 1990: 1; Thomas 2002; Thomas 2006; Thomas 2007: 137, 153; Schrenk 2010: 13.

5. Vogelsang-Eastwood 1990: 1; Calament 2004; Hoskins 2004: 130–132; Thomas 2007: 137; Andersson Strand et al. 2010: 152, 158; van Strydonck 2016: 13.

6. See Sakomoto 2001, who suggests that the textiles are actually imports.

7. van Strydonck et al. 2004: 231; van Strydonck et al. 2011: 241; van Strydonck 2016: 13.

8. Crowfoot 2011: 16; van Strydonck et al. 2011: 245, 257; Thomas 2012: 131; Hallmann 2015: 124–125, 131–133; van Strydonck 2016: 13.

9. Sowada et al. 2011; van Strydonck Vanden Berghe, Boudin, Quintelier 2011: 257; Richardin et al. 2013a: 74, 76; Richardin et al. 2013b: 351; van Strydonck 2016: 13.

10. Droß-Krüpe and Paetz gen. Schieck 2015: 222–223.

11. Knauer 2001.

12. Bonhams, *Asian Art*, 9 November 2015, Lot 415.

13. Kajitani 2001: 91–92, Figs. 19–20.

14. https://new.liveauctioneers.com/item/41519161_rare-romano-egyptian-textile-panel-gladiator.

15. Vorderstrasse 2015: 189–190.

16. *Ibid.*

17. For an overview see Thomas 2007: 154. See also Gleba 2011: 6–7.

18. For these textiles in the Damascus Museum see Yokohari 1972.

19. Nicolle 2011.

20. Toll 1937: 18.

21. James et al. 2011: 1109–1113.

22. Völling 2016: 544–545.

23. Daniels and Hanson 2015: 90–91.

24. Wartenberg 2015, esp. 4.

25. Raja 2016: 36–38, 42–44, No. 15.

26. Schmidt-Colinet 1995: 47.

27. Schmidt-Colinet 1995: 47; Schmidt Colinet et al. 2000: 1; de Jong 2007: 74.

28. Droß-Krüpe and Paetz gen. Schieck 2015: 222.

29. Schmidt-Colinet et al. 2000: 4; de Jong 2007: 196.

30. Żuchowska 2014: 143–144.

31. Pfister 1934: 8–9; Schmidt-Colinet 2000: 56–57; Stauffer 2012.

32. Gawlikowski 1992: 114; Maik 1994: 17–18.

33. De Moor et al. 2014: 105.

34. Schmidt-Colinet 1995: 47; Stauffer 1996: 425–427; Schmidt-Colinet et al. 2000; Żuchowska 2013a: 133, 143, 146–147; Żuchowska 2013b: 383; Żuchowska 2014: 143, Table 1; Żuchowska 2016.

35. Schmidt-Colinet 1995: 47; Żuchowska 2013b: 383. The Palmyra textiles were studied in the most detail by Pfister 1934–1940.

36. Pfister 1934: 24, 60; Pfister 1951: 9, no. 1.

37. Shamir 2007: 123.

38. Cumont 1926: 251–252, Pl. XCII.1–2, XCIII.1; Pfister and Bellinger 1945: 1; Matheson 1992: 126, 128.

39. Rostovtzeff et al. 1951: vii; Baird 2006: 54, no. 260.

40. Granger Taylor 2012: 72, no. 58.

41. Pfister and Bellinger 1945: 17, Cat. Nos. 1–2.

42. *Ibid.*: 6, 34, 116.

43. *Ibid*: 58.

44. *Ibid.*: 1.

45. Droß-Krüpe and Paetz gen. Schieck 2015: 222.

46. Granger Taylor 2006: 128.

47. Pfister and Bellinger 1945: 6, 14–15.

48. Sartre-Fauriat 2000: 237.

49. Toll 1937: 11, 16–17; Pfister 1951: 50–51; Blétry 2015: 450.

50. Pfister 1951: 1–4.
51. See Blétry 2012 for the dating of the tombs themselves.
52. Pfister 1951: 49; Lauffray 1991: 213.
53. Moshenka 2014.
54. Aufderheide 2003: 60, 89–91.
55. Montero Fenollos and al-Shbib 2008: 190, 254, 297, 315, Figs. LII.2, LIV.1.
56. Toll 1937: 17–18.
57. Blétry 2015: 450, figs. 517 and 566.
58. Toll 1937: 19–21.
59. Pfister 1951: 4.

Pfister 1951: 12–13. See also Vogelsang-Eastwood 1994: 90, fig. 151 who notes the similarities betw60. een one tunic from Akhmim.

61. Pfister 1951: 21.
62. Benazeth 2011, 29: figs. 17–18.
63. Rutschowskaya 1990: 58, no. 40.
64. Pfister 1951: 49.
65. Lauffray 1981; Lauffray 1991: 213, no. 12.

BIBLIOGRAPHY

Andersson Strand, Eva, Karin M. Frei, Margarita Gleba, Ulla Mannering, Marie-Louise Nosch, and Irene Skals. "Old Textiles—New Possibilities." *European Journal of Archaeology* 13 (2010): 149–173.

Aufderheide, Arthur C. *The Scientific Study of Mummies.* Cambridge: Cambridge University Press, 2003.

Baird, Jennifer. Housing and Households at Dura-Europos: A Study in Identity on Rome's Eastern Frontier. Unpublished PhD Thesis, University of Leicester, 2006.

Bénazeth, Dominique. Accessoires vestimentaires dans la collection de textiles coptes du musée du Louvre. In *Dress accessories of the 1st millennium AD from Egypt*, eds. Antoine De Moor and Cäcilia Fluck, 12–33. Tielt: Lannoo, 2011.

Bletry, Sylvie. "Les nécropoles de Halabiya-Zénobia." *Syria* 89 (2012): 305–330. *Zenobia-Halabiya: Habitat urbain et nécropoles. Cinq années de recherches de la mission syro-française (2006–2010).* Cuadernos Mésopotamie 6. Université de la Corogne: Ferrol a Coruna, 2015.

Calament, Florence. "L'apport historique des découverte d'Antinoé au costume dit de 'cavalier sasanide.'" In *Riding Costume in Egypt: Origin and Appearance*, eds. Cäcilia Fluck and Gillian Vogelsang-Eastwood, 37–72. Leiden: Brill, 2004.

Crowfoot, Elisabeth G., with Donald King and Michael Ryder. *Qasr Ibrim: The Textiles from the Cathedral Cemetery.* Excavation Memoirs 96. London: Egypt Exploration Society, 2011.

Cumont, Franz. Fouilles de Doura-Europos (1922–1923). *Bibliothèque archéologique et historique* 9. Paris: Paul Geuthner, 1926.

Daniels, Brian I. and Katharyn Hanson. "Archaeological Site Looting in Syria and Iraq: A Review of the Evidence." In *Countering the Illicit Traffic in Cultural Goods: The Global Challenge of Protecting the World's Heritage*, ed. France Desmarais, 83–94. Paris: ICOM, 2015.

de Jong, Lidewijde. Becoming A Roman Province: An Analysis of Funerary Practices in Roman Syria in the Context of Empire. Unpublished PhD dissertation, Stanford University, 2007.

Droß-Krüpe, Kerstin and Annette Paetz gen. Schieck, "Unravelling the Tangled Threads of Ancient Embroidery: A Compilation of Written Sources and Archaeologically Preserved Textiles." In *Greek and Roman Textiles and Dress: An interdisciplinary Anthology*, ed. Mary Harlow and Marie-Louise Nosch, 207–235. Ancient Textile Series 19. Oxford: Oxbow Books, 2015.

Dwyer, Jane P. "The Chronology and Iconography of Paracas-Style Textiles." In *Junius B. Bird Pre-Columbian Textile Conference*, ed. Ann P. Rowe and Elizabeth Benson, 105–128. Washington, DC: Textile Museum, 1979.

Galliker, Julia L. Middle Byzantine Silk in Context: Integrating the Textual and Material Evidence. Unpublished PhD thesis, University of Birmingham, 2014.

Gawlikowski, Michał. "Palmyra 1992." *Polish Archaeology in the Mediterranean* 4 (1992): 111–118.

Gleba, Margarita. "Textiles Studies: Sources and Methods." *KUBABA* 2 (2011): 1–26.

Granger Taylor, Hero. "Textiles from Khirbet Qazone and the Cave of Letters: Two Burial Sites Near the Dead Sea: Similarities and Differences in Find Spots and Textile Types." In *Textiles in Situ: Their Find Spots in Egypt and Neighbouring Countries in the First Millennium CE*, ed. Sabine Schrenk, 113–131. Riggisberger Berichte 13. Riggisberg: Abegg-Stiftung, 2006.

———. "Fragments of Linen from Masada, Israel—the Remnants of Pteryges?—and Related Finds in Weft-and Warp-twining including Several Slings." In *Wearing the Cloak: Dressing the Soldier in Roman Times*, ed. Marie-Louise Nosch, 56–84. Ancient Textile Series Vol. 10. Oxford: Oxbow Books, 2012.

———. *Halabiyya-Zenobia: place forte du limes orientale et la Haute-Mesopotamie au VIe siecle. Tome II: L'architecture publique, religieuse, privee et funeraire.* Bibliothèque archéologiq et historique 138. Paris: Libraire Orientaliste Paul Geuthner, 1991.

Hallmann, Aleksandra. "More Items of Funerary Linen from the Deir el-Bahari Assemblages." *Polish Archaeology in the Mediterranean* 24 (2015): 113–136.

Hoskins, Nancy Arthur. "A Green Riding Coat Fragment in the Henry Art Gallery, Seattle." In *Riding Costume in Egypt: Origin and Appearance*, ed. Cäcilia Fluck and Gillian Vogelsang-Eastwood, 129–136. Leiden: Brill, 2004.

James, Matthew A., Nicole Reifarth, Anna J. Mukherjee, Matthew P. Crump, Paul J. Gates, Peter Sandor, Francesca Robertson, Peter Pfälzner, and Richard P. Evershed. "High Prestige Royal Purple Dyed Textiles from the Bronze Age Royal Tomb at Qatna, Syria." *Antiquity* 332 (2009): 1109–1118.

Kajitani Nobuko. "A Man's Caftan and Leggings from the North Caucasus of the Eighth to Tenth Century: A Conservator's Report." *Metropolitan Museum Journal* 36 (2001): 85–124.

Knauer, Elfriede R. 2001. "A Man's Caftan and Leggings from the North Caucasus of the Eighth to Tenth Century: A Genealogical Study." *Metropolitan Museum Journal* 36 (2001): 124–154.

Lauffray, Jean. "Zenobia Halabiye, ville fortresses sur les bords de l'Euphrate." *Archéologia* 150 (1981): 20–29.

Maik, Jerzy. "The New Textile Finds from Palmyra." *Archaeological Textiles Newsletter* 18–19 (1994): 11–13.

Matheson, Susan. "The Tenth Season at Dura Europos: 1936–1937." *Syria* 69 (1992): 121–140.

Montero Fenollos, Juan Luis, and Shaker al-Shbib. *La necropolis bizantina de Tall as-Sin (Deir ez-Zor, Siria).* Biblioteca del Próximo Oriente Antiguo 4. Madrid: Consejo Superior de Investigaciones Cientificas, 2008.

De Moor, Antoine, Cäcilia Fluck, Mark von Strydonck, and Mathieu Boudin. "Radiocarbon Dating of Linen Hairnets in Sprang Technique." *British Museum Studies in Ancient Egypt and Sudan* 21 (2014): 103–120.

Moshenka, Gabriel. "Thomas 'Mummy' Pettigrew and the Study of Egypt in Nineteenth-Century Britain." In *Histories of Egyptology: Interdisciplinary Measures*, ed. William Carruthers, 201–214. Abindon: Routledge, 2014.

Nicolle, David. *Late Mamlūk Military Equipment.* Damascus: IFPO, 2011.

Paul, Anne. "Diversity and Virtuosity in Early Nasca Fabrics." *Andean Past* 8 (2007): 375–406.

Peters, Ann. "Textile Theft in Ica, Peru: A Threat to Heritage and Its Conservation." *Culture without Context* 15 (2004): 4–6.

Pfister, Rodolphe. *Textiles de Palmyre découverts par le Service des antiquités du Haut-commissariat de la République française dans la nécropole de Palmyre.* 3 volumes. Paris: Les Éditions d'art et d'histoire, 1934–1940.

———. *Textiles de Halabiyeh.* Bibliothèque archéologique et historique 48. Paris: Institut français d'archéologie de Beyrouth, 1951.

Pfister, Rodolphe and Louisa Bellinger. *The Excavations at Dura Europos Final Report IV, Part 2. The Textiles.* New Haven, CT: Yale University Press, 1945.

Raja, Rubina. "The History and Current Situation of World Heritage Sites in Syria." In *Cultural Heritage at Risk: War of Museums in War and Conflict*, ed. Kurt Almqvist and Louise Belfrage, 27–48. Stockholm: Axel and Margaret Ax:son Johnson Foundation, 2016.

Richardin, Pascale, Magali Coudert, Nathalie Gandolfo, and Julien Vincent. "Datation par le radiocarbone: étude chronologique des momies et de leur matériel funéraire." In *Collections égyptiennes d'Anttinoé (Momies, tissus, céramiques et autres antiques) - Envois de l'Etat et dépôts du musée du Louvre (1895–1925)*, ed. Yannick Lintz and Magali Coubert, 74-81. Paris: Musée du Louvre. I, 2013a.

———. "Radiocarbon Dating of Mummified Human Remains: Application to a Series of Coptic Mummies from the Louvre Museum." *Radiocarbon* 55: 345–352.

Rostovtzeff, Michael I., Alfred R. Bellinger, Frank E. Brown, Nicholas P. Toll, and C. Bradford Welles. "Preface." In *The Excavations at Dura Europos Final Report IV, Part 2. The Textiles.*, Rodolphe Pfister and Louisa Bellinger, vii. New Haven, CT: Yale University Press, 1951.

Rutschowscaya, Marie-Helene. *Tissus Coptes*. Paris: Editions Adam Biro, 1990.

Sakamoto Kazuko. "A Re-Consideration of the Human Figure Emblems Excavated in the at-Tar Caves in Iraq." In *The Roman Textile Industry and Its Influence: A Birthday Tribute to John Peter Wild*, ed. Penelope Walton Rogers, Lise Bender Jørgensen, and Antoinette Rast-Eicher, 56–64. Oxford: Oxbow, 2001.

Sartre-Fauriat, Annie. *Des tombeaux et des morts: Monuments funeraires, société et culture en Syrie du Sud du 1er s. av. J.—C. au VIIe s. apr. J.-C. Volume II: Synthese.* Bibliothèque archéologique et historique 158: 2. Beirut: Institut français d'archéologie du Proche-Orient, 2000.

Schmidt-Colinet, Andreas. "The Textiles from Palmyra." *Aram* 7 (1995): 47–51.

Schmidt-Colinet, Andreas, Annemarie Stauffer, and Khaled Al 'Asad. *Die Textilien aus Palmyra: Neue und alte Funde.* Damaszener Forschungen 8. Mainz: P. von Zabern, 2000.

Schrenk, Sabine. "Introduction." In *Textiles in Situ: Their Find Spots in Egypt and Neighbouring Countries in the First Millennium CE*, ed. Sabine Schrenk, 9–16. Riggisberger Berichte 13. Riggisberg: Abegg-Stiftung, 2006.

Shamir, Orit. "Textiles from the 1st Century CE in Jerusalem: A Preliminary Report." In *Ancient Textiles: Production, Craft, and Society*, ed. Carole Gillis and Marie-Louise Nosch, 120–125. Ancient Textiles Series 1. Oxford: Oxbow Books, 2007.

Silverman, Helaine. "Differentiating Paracas Necropolis and Early Nasca Textiles." In *Andean Archaeology II: Art, Landscape, and Society*, ed. William H. Isbell and Helaine Silverman, 71–105. New York: Kluwer Academic/Plenum Publishers, 2002.

Sowada, Karin, Geraldine E. Jacobsen, Fiona Bertuch, Tim Palmer, and Andrew Jenkinson. "Who's That Lying in My Coffin? An Imposter Exposed by 14C Dating." *Radiocarbon* 53 (2011): 221–228.

Stauffer, Annemarie. *Die mittelalterlichen Textilien von St. Servatius in Maastricht.* Bern: Abegg Stiftung, 1991.

———. "Dressing the Dead at Palmyra in the Second and Third Centuries AD." In *Dressing the Dead in Classical Antiquity*, ed. Maureen Carroll and John Peter Wild, 89–98. Stroud: Amberly, 2012.

———. "Textiles from Palmyra: Local Production and the Import and Imitation of Chinese Silk Weavings." *Annales archéologiques arabes syriennes* 42 (1996): 425-430.

van Strydonck, Mark. "Radiocarbon Dating." *Topics in Current Chemistry* 374 (April 2016): 13.

van Strydonck, Mark, Antoine De Moor, and Dominique Bénazeth. "14C dating Compared to Art Historical Dating of Roman and Coptic Textiles from Egypt." *Radiocarbon* 46 (2004): 231–244.

van Strydonck Mark, Ina Vanden Berghe, Mathieu Boudin, and Kim. Quintelier. "Euphemia: A Multidisciplinary Quest for the Origin and Authenticity of a Mummy's Clothes and Accessories." In *Dress Accessories of the 1st Millennium AD from Egypt*, ed. Antoine De Moor and Cäcilia Fluck, 236–257. Lannoo: Tielt, 2011.

Thomas, Thelma K. *Fabric of Everyday Life: Historic Textiles from Karanis, Egypt.* Online exhibition (2002). http://www.lsa.umich.edu/kelsey/galleries/Exhibits/textiles/index.html. Accessed July 7, 2016.

————. "Reevaluating Textiles from Karanis." In *Textiles in Situ: Their Find Spots in Egypt and Neighbouring Countries in the First Millennium CE*, ed. Sabine Schrenk, 135–148. Riggisberger Berichte 13. Riggisberg: Abegg-Stiftung, 2006.

————. "Coptic and Byzantine Textiles found in Egypt: Corpora, Collections, and Scholarly Perspectives." In *Egypt in the Byzantine World, 300–700*, ed. Roger Bagnall, 137–162. Cambridge: Cambridge University Press, 2007.

————. "'Ornaments of Excellence' from 'the Miserable Gains of Commerce': Luxury Art and Byzantine Culture." In *Byzantium and Islam, 7th to 9th Century: Age of Transition*, ed. Helen C. Evans with Brandie Ratliff, 124–133. New York: Metropolitan Museum of Art, 2012.

Toll, Nicholas. "The Necropolis of Halebie – Zenobia." *Annaly Instituta imeni N. P. Kondakova* 9 (1937): 11–22.

Vogelsang-Eastwood, Gillian. *Resist-Dyed Textiles from Quseir al-Qadim Egypt*. Paris: A. E. D. T. A, 1990.

————. *Die Kleider des Pharaos: Die Verwendung von Stoffen im Alten Ägypten*. Kestner-Museum/ Batavian Lion: Hannover and Amsterdam, 1995.

Völling, Elisabeth. "Textiles as Cultural Heritage in Fieldwork and Repositories." In *Proceedings of the International Congress on the Archaeology of the Ancient Near East Volume 1: Traveling Images-Transfer and Transformation of Visual Ideas, Dealing with the Past: Finds, Booty, Gift, Collections at Risk: Sustainable Strategies for Managing Near Eastern Archaeological Collections*, ed. Rolf S. Stucky, Oskar Kaelin, Hans-Peter Mathys, and Andrew S. Jamieson, 543–550. Wisebaden: Harrossowitz, 2016.

Vorderstrasse, Tasha. "Tapestry Panel." In *A Cosmpolitan City: Muslims, Christians, and Jews in Old Cairo*, ed. Tasha Vorderstrasse and Tanya Treptow, 189–190. Oriental Institute Museum Publications 38. Chicago: The Oriental Institute, 2015.

Ute Wartenberg Kagan. "Collecting Coins and the Conflict in Syria." https://eca.state.gov/files/bureau/ wartenbergsyria-coincollecting.pdf. Accessed November 9, 2016.

Yates, Donna. "Paracas Textiles." In *Trafficking Culture Encyclopedia*, 2014a. http://traffickingculture .org/encyclopedia/case-studies/paracas-textiles/.

————. "Sacking the Necropolis: How 100 Peruvian Mummy Textiles Ended Up in Sweden." 2014b. http://www.anonymousswisscollector.com/2014/06/paracas-past-looting-and-trafficking-of-mummy -bundle-textiles-from-peru.html.

————. "Illicit Cultural Property from Latin America: Looting, Trafficking, and Sale." In *Countering Illicit Traffic in Cultural Goods: The Global Challenge of Protecting the World's Heritage*, ed. France Desmarais, 33–56. Paris: ICOM, 2015.

Yokohari Kazouko. "Textiles au Musée national de Damas." *Annales archéologiques de Syrie* 24 (1974): 39–46.

Żuchowska, Marta. "From China to Palmyra: The Value of Silk." *Światowit* 21 (2013a): 133–154.

————. "Palmyra and the Far Eastern Trade." *Studia Palmyreńskie* 12 (2013b): 381–387.

————. "'Grape Picking' Silk from Palmyra. Han Dynasty Chinese Textile with Hellenistic Decoration." *Światowit* XII (2014): 143–162.

————. "Palmyra and the Chinese Silk Trade." In *Palmyrena: City, Hinterland and Caravan Trade between Orient and Occident: Proceedings Held in Athens, December 1–3, 2012*, ed. Jørgen C. Meyer, Eivand H. Seland, and Nils Anfinset, 29–38. Archaeopress: Oxford, 2016.

7

Chamorro Language Revitalization in the CNMI and Guam

Elizabeth Rechebei and Sandra Chung

Chamorro, which is spoken in the Mariana Islands, has the largest number of speakers of any indigenous language of Micronesia, but has also been called one of Micronesia's most endangered languages. Over the last hundred years, as the Mariana Islands came under the administrative control of the United States—first Guam in 1898, and then the Northern Mariana Islands in 1947—the language has gradually lost ground to English. This marginalization is accelerating. Between 2000 and 2010, according to data from the U.S. census, the Chamorro population in the Mariana Islands remained relatively stable (72,127 in 2000 and 72,283 in 2010), but the number of speakers of Chamorro fell from 44,887 to 37,646. Language decline is most pronounced among younger generations: even in the Northern Mariana Islands, most children below the age of eighteen now use only English at home.

In response, a number of indigenous efforts has been mounted to maintain and preserve the Chamorro language. These initiatives have arisen separately in Guam and in the Northern Mariana Islands, which are separate political entities: Guam is an unincorporated U.S. territory, while the remaining Mariana Islands form the U.S. Commonwealth of the Northern Mariana Islands (henceforth the CNMI). Some initiatives, but not all, have had the support of government and the public schools. What unites them is the overarching desire to document as much of the language as possible and keep it alive for future generations of speakers. This chapter surveys these initiatives and attempts to place them in historical and sociopolitical perspective.[1] Although we have tried to cover Guam as well as the CNMI, our discussion focuses more on the CNMI, since we are more familiar with the situation there.

BACKGROUND

Foreign domination of the Mariana Islands began in the mid-seventeenth century, some two hundred years before the colonization of other islands of Micronesia. The Spanish colonial period, which lasted until 1898, had a profound effect on indigenous Chamorro culture. Traditional organizational structures, religious beliefs, kinship systems, music, dress, practices such as fishing, canoe-building, and storytelling, and even personal names were replaced by Spanish colonial counterparts. The Chamorro language was one of the few aspects of material culture to survive. It survived, in part, by incorporating large numbers of words borrowed from Spanish (Borja, Borja, and Chung 2006, 113–120; Rodríguez-Ponga 2009).

Early language documentation of Chamorro went hand in hand with foreign domination of the Mariana Islands and its people. The first grammars and dictionaries of Chamorro were written by priests or colonial administrators who aimed to create tools that would enable Chamorros to learn the colonial language.

The first grammar of Chamorro was written by Father Diego Luis de Sanvitores, the Jesuit priest who established the first Spanish colony in the Mariana Islands in 1668. Sanvitores wrote his grammar, *Lingua Mariana*, on the voyage from Mexico to Guam, based on information from a Tagalog who had lived for many years in the Mariana Islands. The grammar was written in Latin, partly to enable Chamorros to learn the catechism directly in Latin rather than through the medium of Spanish (Winkler 2015, 263–264). Much later in the Spanish colonial period, in 1865, a "Chamorro grammar" and a Spanish–Chamorro dictionary were written by Father Aniceto Ibáñez del Carmen, an Augustinian Recollect from Spain who was vicar principal and curate of the Hagåtña parish and a fluent speaker of Chamorro. Although Ibáñez del Carmen's works provide much information about Chamorro, they were intended to serve as pedagogical materials for Chamorro students learning Spanish, so the language whose structure they describe is not Chamorro but Spanish (Stolz 2011, 184; Zimmermann 2011, 168).

In 1898, after the Spanish–American War, Spain ceded Guam to the United States and then sold the Northern Mariana Islands to Germany. The new colonial administrations worked quickly to publish their own descriptions of the Chamorro language. On the American side, Edwin William Safford, who was deputy to the first naval governor of Guam, wrote an excellent Chamorro grammar, which appeared as a series of journal articles in 1903–1905 and was then reprinted as a book. Edward von Preissig, a U.S. Navy paymaster, wrote a dictionary and grammar of Chamorro that was published by the U.S. Government Printing Office in 1918. On the German side, Georg Fritz, the first district administrator of the Northern Mariana Islands, published a Chamorro grammar in 1903 and a Chamorro dictionary in 1904. These works had various scholarly and pedagogical aims. Safford expressed the hope that his grammar "may be of service to students of comparative philology" (Safford 1903, 289). On the other hand, von Preissig began the English–Chamorro section of his dictionary by saying, "The author realizes that the greatest usefulness of his work will not be in . . . aiding Americans in the acquisition of . . . the Chamorro tongue, but rather in the actual help toward a more thorough appreciation of the English language by the Chamorro children" (von Preissig 1918, 2). Von Preissig's dictionary evidently did not succeed in this. In 1922, in reaction to the fact that Chamorro was still the dominant language in Guam, the naval governor instituted a "no Chamorro" rule in the schools and ordered all copies of the dictionary to be collected and burned. After World War I, when the Northern Mariana Islands came under Japanese mandate, a similar "no Chamorro" rule was imposed by the Japanese administration. Later, in the 1970s, students in one private school in the Northern Marianas were penalized for speaking Chamorro with a fine of a nickel; however, the public school taught the Chamorro alphabet. Today, Chamorro is required in the public schools but not in the private schools.

The first major work on Chamorro to be completed outside the colonial power structure was *Die Chamoro Sprache* (1940), which is still the most detailed Chamorro grammar to date. Its author, H. Costenoble, is identified by Stolz et al. 2011 as Hermann Costenoble (1893–1942), one of nine children in the first family of German homesteaders to settle in the Northern Mariana Islands. The Costenoble family arrived in Saipan in 1903 and relocated to Guam a year later. Hermann, who learned to speak Chamorro as a child on Guam, completed the first draft of his grammar between 1915 and 1919, after he had left the Mariana Islands but when he "still remembered the language vividly" (Stolz et al. 2011, 233). Arguably, his grammar is the first description of Chamorro to be written by a native speaker of the language.

The thirty-five years between 1940 and 1975 brought profound changes to the political, educational, and language situation of the Mariana Islands. After World War II, Guam emerged from the control of the U.S. Navy to become an unincorporated U.S. territory with a civilian government. The Northern Mariana Islands passed from Japanese control to U.N. trusteeship, and ultimately began negotiations with the United States that would lead to commonwealth status. In 1968, the U.S. Congress passed the Bilingual Education Act, which recognized linguistic minority rights in the schools and provided funding for bilingual education programs. Finally, although the Chamorro language was still robust in the Northern Mariana Islands, it had become vulnerable in Guam, where most Chamorro parents were speaking English at home to their children. These developments had an impact on the documentation of Chamorro. Increasingly, the goal of documentation efforts was to teach the structure of Chamorro to Chamorro students in the schools and thereby contribute to the language's maintenance and preservation. Central to these efforts was the work of the late Donald M. Topping and his Chamorro collaborators, the late Dr. Bernadita C. Dungca (from Guam) and the late Pedro M. Ogo (from Rota).

Originally from West Virginia, Topping taught at the Territorial College of Guam from 1956 to 1962. After completing the PhD with a dissertation on Chamorro structure and teaching of English, he joined the linguistics faculty at the University of Hawaii. As Language Coordinator for the UH Peace Corps Training Center from 1963 to 1966, he collaborated with Ogo to develop Peace Corps language lessons for Chamorro; these lessons were published in book form as *Spoken Chamorro* (1969). As Principal Investigator for the Pacific Languages Development Project, which was funded from 1970 to 1974 by the Trust Territory of the Pacific and the University of Hawaii, Topping supervised the development of grammars, bilingual dictionaries, and standard orthographies for all the major languages of Micronesia. He himself collaborated with Ogo and later with Dungca to produce a grammar and dictionary of Chamorro. These works, which are linguistically more sophisticated than previous descriptions, were also the first to recognize Chamorros as equal partners in the documentation of their language. The *Chamorro Reference Grammar* (1973) was coauthored by Topping and Dungca; the *Chamorro-English Dictionary* (1975) was coauthored by Topping, Ogo, and Dungca. At roughly the same time, in Guam, Dr. Katherine B. Aguon published *Let's Chat in Chamorro* (1971), a short introduction to conversational Chamorro. And in 1978, a group of teachers and consultants in the Guam Department of Education began their own effort to draft a Chamorro dictionary. Although their work was abandoned in 1982, it formed the basis for a grassroots dictionary completed and published much later.

Two larger trends emerge from this brief historical summary. First, in the twentieth century the ultimate goal of language documentation efforts shifted away from assimilation to the ruling culture and toward preservation of the indigenous culture. Second, native speakers of Chamorro became more centrally involved in these efforts and received greater recognition for them.

CULTURAL IDENTITY AND LANGUAGE DECLINE

Despite the fact that Guam and the CNMI are now self-governing, the themes of cultural change and language decline have continued into the twenty-first century. There are some differences. Change toward the dominant American culture is not enforced by law, but rather achieved through the subtle, pervasive pressures of mass marketing, television, and the Internet; many of the cultural practices that are now disappearing were first introduced during the Spanish colonial period. Nonetheless, the changes have been significant. Catholicism, which has long been a dominant force in almost every aspect of Chamorro life, has become less important to some younger Chamorros. Traditional values, such as respect (*rispetu*) and family (*familia*), are arguably eroding. The traditional women's dress, the mestisa, which had been introduced from the Philippines in the nineteenth century and was worn on special occasions in the first half of the twentieth century, is now rarely seen. Linguistic change is also at work: shifts in authority and organizational structures in communities come with new words, mostly borrowed from English. Kinship terms borrowed from Spanish, such as *nietu* "grandson" and *nieta* "granddaughter," are giving way to newer terms borrowed from English, such as *gran* "grandchild." The Spanish number system that replaced the indigenous number system during the Spanish colonial period is now being replaced with the English number system. During the Spanish administration, indigenous given names were replaced with Spanish names of saints, and indigenous surnames largely disappeared, although some—such as Hocog, Manglona, Taisakan, Taitingfong—still exist, especially in Guam and Rota. Today, most young Chamorros do not have Spanish given names, such as Carmen, Dolores, Ramon—and their associated Chamorro nicknames, Ammi', Ling, Bo—but rather names of American celebrities, cartoon characters, and others seen on television, such as Brianna, Alvin, and so on. Interestingly, names given to the different generations of Chamorros tend to reflect the dominant cultural influences in the Marianas. Most recently there has been a resurgence, albeit small, of Chamorro names such as Atdåo, Pulan, and Tåsi being given to children as their first names.

The Chamorro language itself continues to lose ground to English. Although Chamorro has been an official language in Guam since 1972 and in the CNMI since 1985, in reality the language of public settings and official documents is English. Most public discussion in government, schools, churches, and other organizations is in English; informal talk among younger people is in English, with the addition of occasional slang words in Chamorro and the common greeting *håfa dai*. There are English-language newspapers, but no Chamorro-language newspapers, although editorials and opinion pieces in Chamorro are published from time to time. Fluency in Chamorro is not required or encouraged for jobs in government and commerce. The number of Chamorros in the Mariana Islands continues to fall, due to immigration from elsewhere and outmigration of Chamorros to the continental United States. Most importantly, Chamorro parents are speaking English rather than Chamorro in the home. For some young people, Chamorro words and phrases—such as *fottin gå'ga'*, which can be translated very roughly "animal force"—have become important symbols of Chamorro cultural identity, but most of these young people do not speak the language fluently or at all.

These are some of the tragic changes that are affecting the language and culture of Chamorros today. One can only imagine what may have been going through the minds of the Chamorros who understand the subtle decline of the language and its consequences for Chamorro self-identity. In his MA thesis (2014), Kenneth G. Kuper correlates the decline of the Chamorro language in Guam with the emerging movement to revive and strengthen Chamorro identity and culture. He also identifies language subjugation as a powerful, effective means of control that has continued since the Spanish period. To date, no one we know of has conducted comprehensive research on the multiple impacts of Chamorro language decline or resurgence on Chamorros' sense of identity.

INDIGENOUS EFFORTS IN GUAM

Given that the Chamorro language first came into sustained contact with English on Guam, it is unsurprising that it first began to decline on Guam—perhaps as early as 1940, and certainly in the immediate aftermath of World War II. Guam is also where indigenous efforts to document and maintain the language first took hold.

The educator and legislator Dr. Katherine B. Aguon was an early leader in these efforts. Beginning in 1971, she published a number of books on conversational Chamorro, many of which combine language instruction with information about food, music, dress, and other aspects of Chamorro culture. Perhaps her most extensive work to date is *Chamorro: A Complete Course of Study* (2007), which offers a year-long sequence of Chamorro language lessons.

Under Aguon's leadership, a team of Chamorros in Guam undertook to revive the grassroots dictionary project that had been initiated in 1978 and then set aside in 1982. The work to restore and complete the original materials led to the publication in 2009 of *The Official Chamorro-English Dictionary / Ufisiåt Na Diksionårion Chamorro-Engles* (henceforth, the *Ufisiåt*), with Aguon as the lead editor and Teresita C. Flores and Lourdes T. Leon Guerrero as assistant editors.

In broad outline, the *Ufisiåt* bears some resemblance to the *Chamorro-English Dictionary* (henceforth, the *CED*), which was coauthored by Topping, Ogo, and Dungca thirty-four years earlier. Both dictionaries contain over 9,000 Chamorro entries with English definitions and other information, including parts of speech and Chamorro sentences illustrating usage. Both dictionaries employ some version of the standardized Chamorro orthography developed originally in 1971 by the Marianas Orthography Committee and lightly revised in Guam in 1983. That spelling system is still the official Chamorro orthography in Guam, but has been replaced by a different orthography in the CNMI (see below).

In other respects, the *CED* and the *Ufisiåt* are very different works. The *CED* was compiled by a trio consisting of trained linguists (Topping and Dungca) and speakers of two different dialects of Chamorro (Dungca and Ogo), supported by a significant academic infrastructure. So it is not surprising that the *CED* has the completeness and systematicity often associated with academic dictionaries. The bulk of the *CED* consists of Chamorro entries with English definitions, but a reverse English–Chamorro finder list is also provided. Entries were compiled from a range of sources, including earlier dictionaries of Chamorro (Topping, Ogo, and Dungca 1975, xiii). The entries include words used throughout the Mariana Islands as well as words specific to the dialects of Guam, Rota, or Saipan. Names of flora and fauna are given extensive coverage, and their definitions include both common names and scientific names. Chamorro nicknames are also covered systematically. Although the *CED* employs an idiosyncratic system of parts of speech, the classification of words according to this system is highly consistent.

The *Ufisiåt*, which was published by Guam's Department of Chamorro Affairs, is a grassroots dictionary compiled by community members whose goal was to preserve the language they spoke for future generations. The focus is on the Chamorro spoken in Guam, so some words are identified as archaic even though they are in common use in the CNMI (see e.g. the *Ufisiåt*'s entries for *apigige'* "a kind of pudding," *åsson* "lie down," *dokdok* "a wild seeded breadfruit," *esalao* "call, shout"). The traditional system of parts of speech is employed, but words and phrases are occasionally classified in surprising ways; for example, the phrase *pot fabot* "please" is classified as a verb. A concerted effort is made to identify word origins. This is more successful for borrowings than for indigenous words, some of which are labeled "origin unknown" even when they are descended from one of the linguistic ancestors of Chamorro (e.g., *funas* "erase," which is descended from Proto-Malayo-Polynesian **punas*; see Blust and Trussel 2015).

The *Ufisiåt* is not the only documentation initiative to emerge in Guam in recent years. There has also been a surge in electronic resources. Several websites developed in Guam, or by Guamanians in the continental United States, provide electronic dictionaries and other resources for language learning. The *Chamorro Online Dictionary* is a web-based dictionary that can be viewed online or downloaded in .pdf format; its sources include the *CED* and von Preissig's dictionary. *Learning Chamorro* is a far more ambitious website that offers a dictionary with over 9,000 entries, a suite of language lessons, audio dialogues with word-by-word analysis, sections on grammar, and examples of Chamorro written materials. Many of the dictionary entries are credited to the *CED*; the suite of language lessons is based mostly on Topping and Ogo's *Spoken Chamorro*. In the world of mobile phone applications, two different Chamorro dictionaries are available as Android apps on Google Play. All these resources have apparently been developed independently from one another, a fact that speaks both to the intense local interest in preserving the language and to the decentralized character of grassroots initiatives.

This is an impressive range of materials. One reasonable next step would be to begin to coordinate and synthesize them. Dr. Faye Untalan has begun this process in the area of language instruction. With funding from the Administration for Native Americans, she is working to develop a standardized college-level curriculum for beginning language instruction in Chamorro for use in Hawaii, Guam, and the CNMI.

Another major initiative is the Hurao Academy, a Chamorro immersion program that was started by Ann Marie Arceo in 2005. Funded by the Administration for Native Americans, the Hurao Academy offered after-school and summer programs as well as adult evening programs, and development of materials to support the program. Other groups in Guam, mostly in the performing arts, are involved in the perpetuation of Chamorro culture and language.

At the policy level, the Guam Department of Education has mandated and expanded the study of Chamorro language and culture (see Public Law 31-45).

INDIGENOUS EFFORTS IN THE CNMI

Indigenous efforts to document and maintain Chamorro began later in the CNMI.

Among the many events that served to raise awareness of the decline of the Chamorro language were the Chamorro Conferences held in Guam in 2006, in Rota in 2007, and in Saipan in 2008. These conferences brought together educators, government officials, activists, and others from throughout the Mariana Islands to discuss indigenous issues that crossed political boundaries. Language use and language preservation were major topics of discussion. Indeed, at the 2008 Chamorro Conference, a concerted effort was made to hold as many public discussions as possible in Chamorro rather than in English.

At roughly the same time, the CNMI saw a surge in the publication of books written in Chamorro, above and beyond the relatively brief religious tracts, educational materials, and children's books that had previously constituted the language's written literature. On the religious side, Bishop Tomas A. Camacho, assisted by a number of other fluent Chamorro speakers, completed and published a Chamorro translation of the New Testament in 2007. On the secular side, the brothers Joaquin F. Borja and Manuel F. Borja wrote a monolingual book of Chamorro poems, stories, and essays, *Estreyas Mariånas*, which was published with funding from the Administration for Native Americans in 2006. The Chamorro stories, poems, and essays written by the legendary author and poet Tun Juan A. Sanchez were published by the NMI Council for the Humanities in 2009. That same year, with funding from the Administration for Native Americans to the Traditional Medicine and Culture Association, Manuel F. Borja and Jose S. Roppul published a massive trilingual encyclopedia of native medicine in the CNMI, with oral histories of traditional healers and information about medicinal plants in Carolinian, Chamorro, and English. Finally, Chamorro translations were published of a number of works originally written in English, including children's books from the Motheread program, an analysis of the Covenant, a book of World War II memories, and a book on cultural sites in the CNMI. Taken together, these works give a glimpse of what can be accomplished if the Chamorro language is maintained and preserved.

In 2008, the two of us—a Chamorro educator (Rechebei) and a trained linguist (Chung)—received funding from the National Science Foundation for a project to upgrade the documentation of the Chamorro language. A key part of the project was the revision of the *CED*. We had planned to work with a small group of fluent speakers of Chamorro to create entries for words not already in the *CED*, remove redundant entries, provide more traditional parts of speech, and increase the number and complexity of the Chamorro sentences illustrating usage. But the work took an unexpected turn: many more community members than we had anticipated wanted to be actively involved in the revision. We introduced more infrastructure so that everyone who wanted to participate could be included. After the death in 2009 of Dr. Rita H. Inos, the original head of the revision, three editors were identified: Manuel F. Borja, Elizabeth D. Rechebei (both from Saipan), and Tita A. Hocog (from Rota). Six working groups were formed to revise and augment the *CED* entries: four on Saipan, one on Tinian, and one on Rota. Additional thematic groups investigated the vocabulary associated with different cultural practices, such as fishing, traditional medicine, and weddings. Elders served as consultants. In the end, some thirty Chamorros were active members of the working groups, and more than seventy others participated in one way or another in the first stage of the revision process (see Chung and Rechebei 2014). The project turned into a community-wide effort, with data collected at every opportunity, including family gatherings, funerals, at shopping centers, restaurants, and even via telephone calls. One editor has a wide network of Chamorro speakers in Guam and Rota readily available via cell phone.

Work on the dictionary led to spelling reform. At our initial planning meetings, it became clear that almost all participants were dissatisfied with the official Chamorro orthography, which they found hard to use. This was the orthography that had originally been developed in 1971, lightly revised in Guam in 1983, and used in most written materials published since, including the *CED* and the *Ufisiåt*.

Two core principles of orthography design can be summed up as slogans. According to "one sound, one symbol," each distinctive sound of the language should be spelled the same way in all words in which it appears. According to "one word, one spelling" each word should be spelled the same way in all its forms. Only some languages have sound systems that allow both of these principles to be satisfied. English, for instance, has a sound system that brings the two principles into conflict, and so does Chamorro. English orthography famously satisfies "one word, one spelling" but permits multiple spellings for the same distinctive sound. The 1971 Chamorro orthography is similar; in that orthography, the vowel /u/ is spelled *u* in *åsu* "smoke" but *o* in *hasso* "think, remember" and *påtgon* "child."

To address their dissatisfaction, working group members joined forces with the CNMI's Chamorro/Carolinian Language Policy Commission and the NMI Council for the Humanities to hold an orthography workshop in Saipan in 2009. The participants quickly arrived at a proposal for a new orthography with a different design. This new orthography satisfies "one sound, one symbol" but allows a word to be spelled differently in its different forms. The vowel /u/, for instance, is now spelled *u* in *åsu* "smoke," *hassu* "think," and *påtgun* "child." But although "child" is spelled *påtgun*, "my child" is spelled *patgon-hu*, because the second vowel in this form of the word is not /u/ but rather /o/.

The new orthography became the CNMI's official Chamorro orthography in 2010, and is being used in the dictionary revision. Fluent speakers, language learners, and teachers report that this orthography is far easier to use—a clear positive. On the other hand, the fact that the 1971 orthography is still the official orthography in Guam will make it harder to develop a uniform set of Chamorro language materials that can be used throughout the Mariana Islands.

Multiple orthographies also create a roadblock for dictionary users, who must know exactly how to spell a word in the dictionary's orthography in order to locate the entry for it. In 2011, we began working with graduate students at the University of California, Santa Cruz, on an online version of the revised dictionary that could get around this roadblock. Boris Harizanov developed a search engine and parser that takes the user's online input and searches for potentially matching entries in the revised dictionary. His suite of programs neutralizes the differences between the two official orthographies, can locate the root in an inflected or derived word, and does not require an exact match in order to display a potentially relevant entry. The result is that users of the online version can locate a Chamorro word successfully without knowing exactly how to spell it. A different version of Harizanov's search engine and parser has since been developed by Karl DeVries. Both versions have the potential to make the revised dictionary accessible to a wide audience in the Mariana Islands and elsewhere.

The revised dictionary, which contains more than 10,000 entries, has been in the editing phase since 2012, and will take several more years to complete.

LOSS OF ELDERS AND THEIR MEMORIES OF THE LANGUAGE

During the early stages of work on the dictionary revision, workgroup members from Saipan, Tinian, and Rota realized the urgent need to reach out to Chamorro elders for information about words unfamiliar to the groups. A number of elders were interviewed who had forgotten some words, struggled to recall them, or were unsure of their meanings. These experiences brought an immense sense of loss not only to the working groups but also to the elders themselves. Those who could still recall the meanings of words were overjoyed that their knowledge would be included in the revised dictionary; they asked, for obvious reasons, that the revision be completed as soon as possible. Those who could not recall the words but knew that they exist shed tears of sadness. Since 2008, when the revision began, some participants—both elders and working group members—have passed on. The passing of each Chamorro speaker is a great loss, because of their knowledge and experiences of the language and culture—information which in many cases has not been documented. However, as many Chamorros understand today, the revival and strengthening of the Chamorro language is both a real challenge and very possible.

OTHER EFFORTS TO PROMOTE THE USE OF THE CHAMORRO LANGUAGE

The Chamorro language and culture are being kept alive not only in the Mariana Islands but also in the continental United States, where many Chamorros now reside. This is particularly evident in San Diego and other communities in California, and in the states of Oregon, Washington, and Idaho, where Chamorro populations can be found. Annual events promoting Chamorro culture through songs, dances, arts and crafts, and food are special opportunities for Chamorros to gather and celebrate their ethnicity and at the same time share with the wider community. Chamorro language competitions among students from Guam and the CNMI are also regular events, beginning with local preparatory competitions and leading up to the Marianas-wide event held in Guam. The Internet provides another outlet for Chamorro language and culture, with online dictionaries, language lessons, blogs in Chamorro or about Chamorro culture, and photos and videos of Chamorro events. Still other online materials include comedies, narratives, and mini-movies that are a mixture of English and Chamorro presentations. Cultural groups in the Marianas, including school clubs, regularly perform during important events and entertain dignitaries and tourists. In the CNMI, October is Cultural Heritage month, and Chamorro culture is showcased in its many forms. Both older and younger generations participate in these events. The federally funded Aging Center, Sagan Manåmku', is a valuable resource as well. Students, scholars, and others who are interested in the history of Chamorros and their language frequently visit the center to conduct interviews and simply to enjoy the company of elders.

Both Guam and the CNMI have government agencies that promote Chamorro culture and language. In the CNMI, these include the Chamorro/Carolinian Language Policy Commission, the Office of Indigenous Affairs, and the Historic Preservation Office. Over and above this, another creative avenue for the teaching of Chamorro language and culture is through community projects. Federal grants from the Administration for Native Americans have supported a number of projects over the years. In Guam, these include the Hurao Academy and the Authentic Chamorro Dance and Traditions Project. In the CNMI, they include the Children of Our Homeland Project at the Public Library, the Traditional Medicine and Culture Project, and an elementary school project on generational knowledge transmission. More recently, the CNMI's Public School System received federal funding to support and enhance the teaching of Chamorro and Carolinian language and culture.

In the CNMI, formal language instruction in Chamorro is conducted in the elementary grades, mostly in the public schools. Chamorro language is a required subject in the elementary grades. A bill currently under consideration in the CNMI Legislature would require mandatory Chamorro language classes for high school graduation. The Motheread/Fatheread Program sponsored by the NMI Council for the Humanities has added Chamorro language instruction to its curriculum for all, including non-Chamorros. The Humanities Council has been at the forefront in promoting Chamorro language and culture through conferences, workshops, and sponsorship of the dictionary revision effort. The public school system has developed a process for certifying Chamorro language instructors and continues to develop materials and relevant resources. However, there is still a dire need for more materials in Chamorro. One critical resource is the anticipated revised *Chamorro–English Dictionary*, which will be supported by a forthcoming grammar by Sandra Chung.

Many other activities to promote Chamorro language and culture can be found on the Internet. The Internet and social media are among the most effective methods for disseminating information, especially for younger generations, who are mostly not proficient in the language but now have ready access to electronic resources and can use this to project more creative ways of using the language. At the same time, issues of accuracy and misinterpretation may arise. These may not be so serious as to outweigh the benefits of mass dissemination of information about Chamorro.

There is a lack of qualified individuals who can teach Chamorro, both in the CNMI and in Guam, where Chamorro is required in the schools. The language documentation materials that we have just surveyed are important not only for students but also for the professional development of Chamorro teachers.

RECOMMENDATIONS FOR THE FUTURE

One of the most important outcomes of the ongoing efforts to preserve and promote the Chamorro language will be to leverage them so that they all support one another. While resources are extremely limited, pockets of communities have been quite active recently in developing creative ways of supporting the language. The most critical need at this point is to engage the most fluent speakers, who are the oldest Chamorros, and to involve the younger generation in the process. In traditional Chamorro society, elders were the center of attention, esteemed for their knowledge, wisdom, accomplishments, and social status. Today, they are frequently left alone and silent at family or community events. The CNMI's federally funded Aging Center (Sagan Manåmku') serves different language and cultural groups and therefore, the language used is English. Young people are more effectively engaged by social media than by conversations in Chamorro. Entertainment is mostly from outside the culture and in English. Possibly the only time that young people explore the Chamorro language is when they are doing school assignments.

A center where Chamorro elders can share their knowledge and be consulted is one way to nurture and engage the most fluent speakers of the language. Community activities that could reach out to younger speakers could be developed. Written materials, videos, and lectures could be presented. Art and performances, such as performances of traditional songs (Chamorrita), are other avenues that could entertain and, at the same time, teach the culture and the language. Food has always been an important aspect of Chamorro culture. The history of food preparation, the role of different community members in food preparation, and all the cultural practices involved could be of great interest not only to Chamorros but others.

Policies to require the teaching and use of the Chamorro language could also be supported. In the CNMI, the public school system does have programs for this, but they could be improved. Private schools do not teach Chamorro. The CNMI legislature is currently considering a law to require Chamorro language classes for high school graduation. Interestingly, the public school system has expressed concerns and is not in full support. One issue is the multiethnic, multicultural character of the Mariana Islands, where Chamorro students and Chamorro teachers are rapidly becoming a minority. Another issue concerns the training and certification of Chamorro language teachers, which is still at an early stage.

CONCLUSION

What we have surveyed here in terms of resources and efforts to preserve the Chamorro language, incomplete though it may be, speaks to the importance of consolidating individual community initiatives and providing them with a larger infrastructure.

NOTE

1. For reasons of space, the discussion in the text is limited to documentary works addressed to a wide audience, and does not include academic works written primarily for linguists.

BIBLIOGRAPHY

Aguon, Katherine B. *Let's Chat in Chamorro*. Agana: Guam Business and Professional Women's Club, 1971.

Aguon, Katherine B. *Chamorro: A Complete Course of Study*. Hagåtña: Katherine B. Aguon, 2007.

Aguon, Katherine B., Teresita C. Flores, and Lourdes T. Leon Guerrero, eds. *The Official Chamorro-English Dictionary / Ufisiåt Na Diksionårion Chamorro-Engles*. Hagåtña: Department of Chamorro Affairs. 2009.

Blust, Robert, and Stephen Trussel. *The Austronesian Comparative Dictionary, Web Edition*. http://www.trussel2.com/acd/.

Borja, Joaquin F., Manuel F. Borja, and Sandra Chung. *Estreyas Mariånas: Chamorro*. Saipan: Estreyas Mariånas Publications, 2006.

Borja, Manuel F., and Jose S. Roppul. *Directory of Traditional Healers and Medicinal Plants in the Commonwealth of the Northern Mariana Islands*. Saipan: Inetnon Åmot Natibu yan Kuttura, 2009.

Chamorro Online Dictionary. http://www.chamoru.info/dictionary/.

Chung, Sandra, and Elizabeth D. Rechebei. "Community Engagement in the Revised *Chamorro-English Dictionary*." *Dictionaries* 35 (2014): 308–317.

Costenoble, H. *Die Chamoro Sprache*. The Hague: Nijhoff, 1940.

Fritz, Georg. "Chamorro Grammatik." *Mitteilungen des Seminars für Orientalische Sprachen an der Friedrich-Wilhelms-Universität* 6 (1903):1–27.

Fritz, Georg. *Chamorro-Wörterbuch*. Berlin: Georg Reimer, 1904.

Ibáñez del Carmen, Aniceto. *Gramática chamorra*. Manila: Ramirez y Giraudier, 1865.

Ibáñez del Carmen, Aniceto. *Diccionario español-chamorro*. Manila: Ramirez y Giraudier, 1865.

Kuper, Kenneth G. Na'la'la' i Hila'-ta, Na'matatnga i Taotao-ta: Chamorro Language as Liberation from Colonization. MA thesis, University of Hawaii, Manoa, 2014.

Learning Chamorro. http://www.learningchamorro.com/.

Nuebo Testamento / The Chamorro New Testament. Saipan: Diocese of Chalan Kanoa, 2007.

Preissig, Edward R. von. *Dictionary and Grammar of the Chamorro Language of the Island of Guam*. Washington, DC: Government Printing Office, 1918.

Rodríguez-Ponga, Rafael. *Del español al chamorro: Lenguas en contacto en el Pacífico*. Madrid: Gondo, 2009.

Safford, William Edwin. "The Chamorro Language of Guam." *American Anthropologist* 5 (1903–1905): 289–311, 508–529; 6: 95–117, 501–534; 7: 305–319.

Sanchez, Tun. Joan Aguon. *Estoria-Hu*. Micronesian Authors Initiative No. 3. Saipan: NMI Council for the Humanities, 2009.

Sanvitores, Diego Luis de. *Lingua Mariana*. Micro-Bibliotheca Anthropos 14. Posieux/Fribourg: Anthropos Institute, 1954[1668].

Stolz, Thomas. "The *Gramática chamorra*." In *Philippine and Chamorro Linguistics Before the Advent of Structuralism*, edited by Lawrence A. Reid, Emilio Ridruejo, and Thomas Stolz, 183–200. Berlin: Akademie Verlag, 2011.

Stolz, Thomas, Christina Schneemann, Barbara Dewein, and Sandra Chung. "The Mysterious H: Who Was the Author of Die Chamoro Sprache?" In *Philippine and Chamorro Linguistics Before the Advent of Structuralism*, edited by Lawrence A. Reid, Emilio Ridruejo, and Thomas Stolz, 227–242. Berlin: Akademie Verlag, 2011.

Topping, Donald M., and Pedro M. Ogo. *Spoken Chamorro*. Honolulu: University of Hawaii Press, 1969.

Topping, Donald M., and Bernadita C. Dungca. *Chamorro Reference Grammar*. Honolulu: University of Hawaii Press, 1973.

Topping, Donald M., Pedro M. Ogo, and Bernadita C. Dungca. *Chamorro-English Dictionary*. Honolulu: University of Hawaii Press, 1975.

Winkler, Pierre. "The Chamorro Verb According to Diego Luis de Sanvitores (1627–1672)." *Historiographia Linguistica* 42 (2015): 261–313.

Zimmerman, Klaus. "The *Diccionario español-chamorro* (1865) by Padre Fray Aniceto Ibáñez del Cármen: A Historiographical Characterization of a Pedagogic-Lexicographic Discourse Type in Late Colonial Austronesia." In *Philippine and Chamorro Linguistics Before the Advent of Structuralism*, edited by Lawrence A. Reid, Emilio Ridruejo, and Thomas Stolz, 163–182. Berlin: Akademie Verlag, 2011.

8

The Trilogy of Cultural Heritage

Preserving Intangible Heritage in an Ethnographical Museum

Alexandru Chiselev

FROM *BEING* AND *BECOMING* TO *KNOWING*

The modern ethnological and anthropological trends define the concept of heritage as a set of *artifacts* (results of human action as tangible answers to human needs, characterized by certain materials, know-how, origin, function, and value) and *mentifacts* (spiritual productions as a result of interpretation systems and mentalities) with a collective dimension, with multiple meanings, and that are generationally transmitted. Material and immaterial components specific to a cultural community (traditional or modern, rural or urban) represent the ethnographical heritage. In a synthetic sense, ethnographic heritage is a system with a material component (immobile / built and mobile) and an immaterial component. Its unity and the unity of its subsystems are easily observed when interventions are made within a subsystem and the effects of these interventions on other subsystems emerge. There is reciprocal interaction among subsystems.

The immobile ethnographic heritage includes in Romania—besides elements of vernacular architecture—some components with cultural, religious or municipal characters (e.g., churches, mosques, museums, cultural centers, pubs, grocery stores, shops, statues, parks, etc.), perhaps depicting a certain historical period and an ethnic imprint of the population and which are integrated into the natural and anthropogenic landscape.

The mobile ethnographic heritage includes, in legal terms in Romania, only cultural goods classified into the National Register, under two categories: Thesaurus and Fund. But strategically, cultural goods existing within a territory (such as in field, in households, in churches, etc.), also called *virtual ethnographic heritage* and which generate potential goods for museums should also be considered.

A special attention must be given to the notion of *contemporary heritage*. There are three main areas of this:

- folk art objects that are preserved using traditional techniques and styles (e.g., textiles, pottery, wooden objects);
- artisan objects with folk inspiration (e.g., interior decorations, wire-knits and knittings, and iron crafts);
- objects of modern decorative art (e.g., arras, macramé, small furniture).[1]

Craftsmen are keepers and transmitters of the knowledge and skills related to this art. The best craftsmen are included in the category of *Living Thesaurus*. In contemporary Romania, the young generation is strongly encouraged to preserve their heritage. Children learn from museums, youth centers, and NGOs that focus on crafts, such as painted icons, Easter Eggs, rugs, carved objects, Christmas masks, and so on.

The general sense of the term *intangible ethnographic heritage* is an ensemble of practices, representations, expressions, knowledge, skills that communities, groups, and individuals recognize as part of their cultural heritage, transmitted and recreated continuously. Contemporary ethnologists include into this heritage five categories of resources:

- individual keepers of knowledge (so-called *living treasures*: craftsmen, singers, dancers, and, why not, people who still know old incantations against Evil Eye and other techniques connected to ethnoiatry[2] inclusively to cure cancers, etc.);
- enterprises that use knowledge and know-how (e.g., a job as a baker, vintner, grocer);
- organizations—associations or informal groups (cultural associations, folk ensembles, groups of carol singers—*Colindat*,[3] groups of *Căluşari*[4]);
- expressions (custom, holiday or festival, ritual, game, or verbal forms) and cultural spaces (public places concentrating cultural traditional).

Heritage through its many facets is dynamic in time and variable in space, self-regulated by the interaction of the subsystems, being a result of the action of multiple factors, grouped in different frames. *The natural environment generates, the historical context models, the socio-economic framework defines, and the cultural cadre preserves and reinvents.*

FROM *KNOWING* TO *RECOGNIZING* THE VALUE

The ethnographic heritage that is depicted in a museum is gathered through systematic research (laboratory and field) and its value is highlighted through exhibitions, catalogs, articles, studies, national registers, and so forth.

- The *Ethnographic and Folk Art Museum* in Tulcea and the houses from Enisala, Babadag, and Cerna carry a double meaning: on the one hand, they show parts of the cultural built heritage (Historical Monuments List), and on the other hand, they are a way to preserve other types of heritage (material and immaterial). Thus they are, at the same time, object and subject of heritage issues. The *Ethnographic and Folk Art Museum* (the former centre of National Bank—Tulcea subsidiary), built in the interwar period of 1924–1927, is one of the most emblematic public edifices from Tulcea, constituting a valuable example of architecture with national forms. The heritage of the museum reflects, by the diversity of the collections, a unique cultural model generated by the coexistence between Romanians and other ethnic or ethno-cultural groups (Aromanians, Meglenoromanians, Ukrainians, Russian-Lippovans, Bulgarians, Turks, Crimean and Nogay Tatars, Greeks, Italians, Germans, etc.). These objects constitute an invaluable ethnographic fund, decoded in the collections of Folk Art (Textiles, Costumes, Jewelry, Easter Eggs), Ethnography (Wooden objects, Crafts, Occupations), Photo—document (Old Photos, Old Acts), and Industrial Heritage.
- The pavilion exhibition from the courtyard of the museum contextualizes objects used in the traditional occupations, crafts, and transport in Northern Dobruja (southeast part

of Romania), and by extension, on the entire Romanian territory (agriculture, viticulture, apiculture, stonework, wood manufacture, pottery and blacksmith, overland and water transport).

- The Peasant Household preserved in situ in Enisala is located in the center of homonym locality, and represents a synthesis of traditional architecture from Northern Dobruja (Razim Lake area) from the early twentieth century.
- The architectural ensemble includes a house with a pantry and some typical annexes like summer kitchen and oven for baking bread, stables, granary, sheds, and fountain. The planimetry of the house is traditional, with a central porch hall and two rooms.
- The annexes were reconstructed (a form of museification of cultural heritage) and became now exhibition spaces with tools for agriculture, beekeeping, fishing, cooperage, blacksmith, pottery, textile industry.
- The interior display reveals a great variety and the aesthetic valences of traditional textiles, with ornamental compositions, stylized patterns with suggestive names (*little trees, nut* or *tomato, girls, horse and horseman*).
- *The Oriental Art Exhibition* from Babadag is organized into Panaghia House, located near Ali-Gazi-Pasha Mosque, and built in the architectural style of the old Babadag. The exposed heritage includes pieces of folk art belonging to the Turks and Tatars from Dobruja (textiles, embroidery, clothing, jewelry, and copper vessels for ritual or quotidian use) and also pieces of oriental art made in manufactories and or in industrial spaces.
- The typical oriental ornamental patterns such as cypress, hyacinth, pomegranate fruit, complemented with gold and silver metallic thread, generates chromatic and decorative compositions with a great aesthetic value.
- *The Memorial House of the poet Panait Cerna*, originally the home of a craftsman from the middle of the nineteenth century, is located in the center of Cerna Village, near the church. The memorial exhibition organized in three halls presents the biographical data of the poet, reproductions after photographs, documents, civil status and education acts, poetic works, critical references.
- In other exhibition spaces was reconstituted the traditional peasant interior within this area. The outdoor exhibition presents the traditional agricultural tools, one of the main occupations practiced in this area.

FROM *RECOGNIZING* TO *APPLYING* AND *ENHANCING THE VALUE*

The ethnographic heritage in a museum is preserved, being displayed into the main exhibition (Multiculturality from Dobruja) or the temporary ones (e.g.: *Black Magic vs. White Magic; Once upon a time—It was a big wedding in the village; The egg, the cross and the saint bread—Easter Traditions, Fairytales—save an imaginary world*). Museums conduct activities such as conservation and restoration of cultural goods, reconstitution of aspects that cannot be found in contemporary times, representation of intangible heritage, and finding the best technical solutions for exhibiting certain pieces.

We can say that the exhibition is the materialization of an idea and the expression of one belief in *something* (tangible or not). It can be said that the exhibition is a mix between art and technology, based on an idea and ending with the visual image of the idea conceived for one specific space. For this reason the person who realizes an exhibition can be named *exhibition author.*

Recent theories of exhibition realizations do not consider the visitor as just a neutral, passive subject, with a one-way process of reception capability (i.e., the museum emits and the visitor simply receives the message or topic or words). On the contrary, the visitor is active subject, and when all meanings are exhausted, he discovers new meanings of exhibition conventions.[5]

In the contemporary world, at theoretical level, the exhibitions are resultants of the following perspectives:[6] artifact display,[7] communicator of ideas, visitor activity, and the environment created. In reality, these four elements have different impacts depending on the exhibition theme and type of exhibition.

In the following table, I present the characteristics of the four perspectives based on the type of exhibition: the descriptive-educational exhibition, the exhibition of discovery, exhibition, the conceptual exhibition, or the experimental exhibition.[8]

Type of Exhibition	Artifact Display	Way to Communicate the Ideas	Visitor Activity	Environment Created
A type Descriptive—educational	Object speaks for itself, Objects are ordered in contexts	Clear, concise, synthetic	Average: Listen, play, learn	Specifically, reconstruct a moment or space; open
B type of discovery	Hidden display; The object must be found	Allow to be gradually discovered	High: The A type + Search, discover, know, learn	Labyrinth, hiding elements
C type Conceptual	Objects realize compositions; objects lose their notion	Leaves space for interpretation; diffuse	Subtle: Reflect, meditate	Unique, combining elements
D type Experimental	Object goes into the background;	Mix of other types	The C type	Original, surreal, fantastic, spectacular

The *descriptive-educational exhibition* respects the conventional museum technique rules, defining concrete ideas in a logical sequence of objects with known functions, doubled with technique methods in the background (general lighting, photos and text, reconstitution, etc.). The object is selected for representativeness and value (aesthetic, contextual[9]). The exhibition display is clear and the visitor receives an average amount of information, with the possibility of filtration through his or her own prism. This has impact on the individual and/or group visitor.

In the *exhibition of discovery* approach, the display mode is segmental, modular, and unconventional. The object or the context of the exhibition is hidden in a labyrinthine tunneling structure, with the possibility of browsing in an unique and unrepeatable way of the route (the public can choose the visiting variant, depending on motivation). At this exhibition type, the museum technique component helps to discover gradually the idea expressed by an object or complex of objects, which retains the forefront in the exhibition reception. The impact of this exhibition is realized when it is visited by small groups or individuals.

Various themes can be adapted to various museum technique components, giving way to the following subtypes of these exhibitions:

- The *Labyrinth* type of exhibition is when space is segmented by modular or panel structures
- The *Tunnel / Cave* type of exhibition is when there are tunneling structures of equal or variable heights

- The *Stairs* type of exhibition shows upward or downward, flat portions, plus labyrinth or tunnel structures
- The *Cube type*[10] of exhibition is when the labyrinthine structures are mobile. It is also when *escape* from the exhibition space happens after following an algorithm.

The *conceptual* or *metaphoric exhibition* display is inspired by current conceptual art,[11] which moves the emphasis from aesthetic pleasure to the debate of ideas between the public and the exhibition itself. In this context the concept substitutes the object. The abstract can be expressed through complex interrelated objects with a dynamic more or less normal, coupled by a solid museum technique component. Life, death, fear, dream, fantasy, fatigue, pleasure can become visual, even palpable. In this way, the abstract can be touched, seen, or smelled, and can cause a complex and unpredictable reception of the exhibition.

In the case of the *experimental exhibition*, there are many forms of expression and a mix of conventional and unconventional techniques. The environment looms large and the object is removed in a second reception. The idea is supported by static and / or dynamic visual tools. Auditing and performing become a phenomenon.

The role of the museum in society and its way of correlation to the heritage that is managed and to the needs of the target audience are dynamic and depend on sociocultural changes. Profound social changes can lead to the dynamism of museum action by focusing on the public audience. The result is the diversification of what museums offer, depending on the age, sociocultural, and professional characteristics of the target audience. As a result, the museum becomes a truly interactive educational center that responds to a diverse audience and the lifestyle and learning ability, cultural training, and social perspectives of its members.

The return of visitors in the museum depends on personal (emotional) connections created in a relatively short time. The museum education process is customized according to the target structure and implemented in the form of modular programs, structured by age and visitor habits, such as how the visitor organizes his or her visit.

The *Ethnographic and Folk Art Museum* in Tulcea develops educational activities during the school year in partnership with educational institutions. These activities include:

- *Pedagogical workshops*, in which students express their creativity making art objects inspired by ethnographic heritage (e.g., painted eggs, icons, toys, fabrics, clothing accessories);
- *Thematic lessons*, with ethnographic and folklore issues, such as the traditional costume and emblem of cultural identity; good wishing in Romanian carols; cultural identity in a globalized world; March revival of nature; calendar habits from multi-ethnic perspectives; and the popular creation of different ethnic groups of Easter symbols and meaning;
- *Pedagogical exhibitions*, in which students exhibit the works made in educational workshops;
- *Little Ethnographer Awards* given at the end of each school year. The museum offers awards and diplomas to teams of students for their participation in different activities. This is a festive event attended by students, parents, teachers, and museum staff.

NOTES

1. Alexandru Chiselev, conference title: *Rural sustainable development and ethnographic heritage from Northern Dobruja*, "Culture and Civilization at Lower Danube" Symposium, Călăraşi, Romania, 2008.

2. Fitotherapeutic, hydrotherapeutic, homeopathic, diathermic, aromatherapeutic, psychotherapeutic (therapeutic charm or incantation), folk orthopedic surgery, etc.

3. Inscribed in 2013 on the Representative List of the Intangible Cultural Heritage of Humanity.

4. Inscribed in 2008 on the Representative List of the Intangible Cultural Heritage of Humanity.

5. In the sense that the museum did not recreate or don't want to achieve 100 percent reality, all the presented contexts becoming a conventional accommodation of reality, using objects that may lose functionality in certain situations and even the essence.

6. Smithsonian Institution, *Exhibition concept models*, July 2002.

7. An artifact may be defined as an object that has been intentionally made or produced for a certain purpose.

8. Alexandru Chiselev, conference title: *From descriptive to experimental in the temporary exhibitions of E.F.A.M.*, "Culture and Civilization at Lower Danube" Symposium, Călărași, Romania, 2011.

9. For example, a ragged shirt is valuable if it becomes a piece of clothing to represent a witch.

10. Model inspired from the homonymous movie, directed by Vincenzo Natali in 1997.

11. Conceptual art is art in which the concept(s) or idea(s) involved in the work take precedence over traditional aesthetic and material concerns.

Preserving the Gastronomical Heritage in a Multiethnic Region

Tulcea County, Dobruja Region, Romania as a Case Study

Juliana Titov

Together with traditional clothing and costume, architecture, and myths and beliefs, alimentary culture is a crucial cultural tradition. One who works with a cultural tradition must have adequate knowledge and understanding of that cultural tradition. He must conduct enough research to be able to explain the changes and the points of permanence, the characteristic elements, the exotic or picturesque, and he must know what represents marks of convergence and intercultural communication.

The knowledge of the past and present of a gastronomic heritage gives us the methods for preserving it for the future, in correlation with the principles of sustainable development. The museum has the essential role of researching the gastronomical heritage of a cultural community, monitoring its current transformations, and recommending and applying best practices. The museum has this role in the multiethnic region of Romania.

The research of the gastronomical heritage of Dobruja in the southeast part of Romania involves the decoding of the interaction among native Romanians—the so-called *dicieni*,[1] Moldavians, and Transylvanian shepherds with other populations, such as the Bulgarians, the Russian-Lippovans, the Ukrainians, the Greeks, the Turks, the Tatars, the Italians—in other words, cultures that have stayed in Romania for a period of time or that have settled in Romania.

Studies of gastronomical heritage start with studies of the basic elements of nutrition and food and generally include the context of preparation (e.g., the occasion for the preparation; the actants; and the system of requirements, restrictions and prohibitions determined by religious, magical, and ritual thinking), of consumption (the temporal festive scenery—at a family or community gathering, as well as daily consumption, and the order of serving, etc.), and of the symbolic accessories that accompany the food and foodways.

The traditional alimentary system is the result of the interdependence between local resources and the occupations of inhabitants. Considering that every era has brought new elements, the research of the construction of alimentary identity becomes difficult. The food traditions do not remain unchanged; they are shaped by the passage of time, especially through contact between cultures. In the history of humanity, food and foodways were determined by the natural environment, the socioeconomic structure of a community, the religious and spiritual concepts embraced by the community, and the collective mind-set of the community. The alimentary act focused on the physiologic and metabolic dimension, as bio-energetic support; it evolved according to geographic and cultural contexts, generating their specific meanings and connotations. Communities provide individual codes and cultural patterns that vary according to economic and social factors, in different historical periods.

"The alimentary code seemed to be a dialect of culture, with identifying rules of human groups, from the same typology of distinction between *I, You* and the *Other*."[2] Beyond this, the alimentary code had a strong influence on the various segments of culture and human behavior. *The alimentary code* has the ability to portray the identity and global image of sociohumanity in temporal sequence. At the same time, it has the perspective of selecting the participating groups and even individuals as leaders. Because of this, the study of alimentation is a particular interest in the history of worldviews and ways of thinking. It is sufficient to see an inhabitant from Dobruja at one holiday meal to know the culture he belongs to (city, village, ethnicity) and the level of civilization of his particular culture, religion, or social group.

Unlike other elements of cultural heritage, alimentation and food and foodways put the individual in a position of quotidian manifestation, and in the most characteristic moments of his life (birth, marriage, death), as an individual member of his family or as a member of a group. It is difficult to talk about gastronomical identity as a rigorously defined cultural model, but we can naturally talk about *identity elements* in the food and foodways of a people or a nation. In time, culinary differences between cultures, between countries, and even between areas of the same country were crystallized.

The alimentary act, in all its complexity, becomes a particularly evident identity component that defined the socioeconomic status. While the eating of simple aliments such as vegetable soup, boiled or baked potatoes, and so on, was the mark of a lower socioeconomic level, the long elaborated food, such as cabbage rolls, stuffed pike, rose jam, was the symbol of prestige, wealth, social elitism. In this way, food and foodways highlighted differences between the poor peasants who used rapidly prepared aliments (preferably soups) and the rest of the population who preferred the processing of raw aliments for obtaining a variety of dishes with exquisite taste and with a special attention to the presentation of the meal.

The alimentary system of Dobruja, as well as the whole Romanian alimentary system, has emerged as the relationship between local resources—occupations of inhabitants and the lifestyle characteristic to this multiethnic area. We cannot talk about the gastronomical heritage of an area without considering the reconciliation of *permanence* with *change*, of *conservatism* with *modernity*; the fact that a culture can maintain some type of identity while assimilating over time new values, practices, and symbols, adapting them in a process of reinterpretation and synthesis to specific models inherited from tradition. We can observe layers of influences, adaptations, and changes of raw materials, of processing procedures, habits, tastes, which concurred to the long process of structuring the current food system.

The festive and partially quotidian food divides Dobruja into two: the fish area and the meat, dairy, and vegetables area. This fact does not exclude the variety because in Danube Delta, like in the continental area, we can find sour soups, stews, and mixed fillers, especially for the Christian groups in special days ("dispensations in Lent time," patrons of church). If people from Danube Delta proved ingenious in what we called "the ethno-gastronomic style," inventing and reinventing always other fish recipes, the farmers and herdsmen from Dobruja disposed from multitude of resources that they turned into supplies.

The Dobrujan village and the main occupants, in correlation with topography, divided the area into a "world of fish" (Danube Delta, Lake Razelm), an "agrarian world" (Danube Valley), and a "pastoral world" (Măcin Mountains and Casimcei Plateau). We can distinguish some common features:

- *the natural composition of food*, in the almost primitive sense of "raw" (for fruits and seeds) and of "cooked" (for milk, vegetables, meat, fish);
- *limited assortments* of products, such as those already mentioned;
- *conservatism* (but not primitivism) in purchasing (directly from the household or in the immediate vicinity) and cooking (in the rustic kitchen), in which pottery and other utensils (made in wooden, simple, or with artistic patterns) were used.

The unique character of the area is a result of the heterogeneous structure of the population that, with a contribution of varied cultural traditions of each ethnic group, contributes to building a highly complex alimentary system. Furthermore, we can speak about an alimentary system based on raw aliments that result from agriculture, livestock, fishing, viticulture, horticulture, and apiculture. The main staple was and is the cereal culture, notably wheat, rye, millet, and later, corn. The livestock completed the feed resources with dairy and meat products, such as: pig, with the exception of Muslims who are prohibited from eating it; sheep and goat, which are rarely or never consumed by Ukrainians and Russian-Lippovans; cattle, which is consumed by all ethnic groups; horse, except for the Turks, Tatars, and sometimes, the Aromanians; poultry, which are supplemented by fish; frogs, preferred by Italians from Greci Village; venison; fruits and vegetables; and honey.

Eating of fish (i.e., freshwater, such as carp, Gibel carp, pike, perch, catfish, tench, roach, etc., and saltwater, such as mackerel, saurel, frog fish, anchovy, sprat, sterlet, Russian sturgeon, beluga, grey mullet, shark, brill) in large quantities and almost daily is distinguishable of the populations from Danube Delta (Romanians, Ukrainians, Russian-Lippovans). Hunting is today restricted by legislation, but in the past it completed the diet for all populations (wild boar, hare, waders, mallards). Furthermore, consumed by all population were the fruits (apple, pear, plum, apricot, quince, nuts), vegetables (tomatoes, cucumbers, peppers, eggplants, potatoes), and honey (eekeeplinden, acacia, sunflower, mere plants). The Bulgarian vegetable cultivators and Romanian bers were quite famous in the region.

By the late nineteenth through the beginning of the twentieth centuries, a number of elements of food heritage emerged and today serve as *identity mark* for each of the ethnic groups, even if they commonly are based on the same raw products; the difference is in the way and time of baking and the ceremonial process that is involved. In that sense:

- The *Romanians* have the *martyrs*, which are made with leaven dough and honey on March 9 and *Dobrujan pie*, which is eaten in the New Year's Night (with coins and epistles inside, to know who will have good luck next year), in the *Cheese Shrove Sunday* (two Sundays before the Great Lent) or at a wedding ceremony (the Tuesday after the wedding was named; the bride must demonstrate to guests that she knows how to stretch a thin flaky crust). They have *sărmăluțe* (pickled cabbage rolls with pork meat), frequently eaten at festive meals and *drob, pasca, red eggs, Easter cake*, which are eaten at Easter time.[4]
- The *Aromanians* have pie (*pita de veardză*—pie with nettles, *pita di praș*—pie with leek, *pita di știr*—pie with *Artiplex hortensis*, *pita di spanac*—pie with spinach, *pita di curcubetă*—pie with pumpkin). They have recipes with milk from sheep or goat (*culastra, mârcatu*—yogurt, etc.), dishes with sheep meat (*cucurudu, câvârmă, pâstârmă*, suet), and ritual baking (*tigăni*—a type of donuts given to the new mother).[5]
- The *Russians—Lippovans* have simple soups with vegetables (*șci, pahliobka*, Russian borsch) and different baked goods (*vareniki, pirajki, ladâciki, cnâși, pișka* ș.a.).[6]

- The *Ukrainians* have fish and foods with fish (soup, spitted carp, boiled fish with potatoes) and ritual baking (*şisca molodoi*—bride's round bread).[7]
- The *Turks* have barley bread, recipes with sheep / horse / bund meat (*şuberek, ghiudem, kurban*), and sweets (*baclavale, revani*).[8]
- The *Tatars* have soup with millet and recipes with sheep / horse / bund meat (*ghiudem, kurban*).[9]
- The *Italians* have pasta dishes (*pasta asciutta, penne al ragu di verdure*) and different baked goods (*panettone, fritelle di riso*).[10]
- The *Greeks* have recipes with lamb / sheep meat (e.g. *curban*), pies (*karido pitam, spanaco pitam),* and ritual baking (*kori*—the cake of girl).[11]

Regardless of ethnic group, in the traditional life the alimentation is characterized by a clear distinction of content and quality in *daily* and *festive* occasions. Furthermore, the religious and spiritual conceptions of community impose some culinary rules in the context of *fasting* and *holidays*.

Very important to the gastronomic heritage of each ethnic group is the calendar of holidays. Romanians and Aromanians are keepers of New style orthodox beliefs, while the Ukrainians and Greeks from the countryside respect the Old Style Calendar (Julian Calendar) and the Russian—Lippovans are Old Believers (Russian Old Rite). Finally, the Italians from Greci Village are Catholics and the Turks and Tatars follow the rules of the Islamic calendar.

The religious requirements generated specificities that over centuries of living together, established into points of convergence. The preference for aliments with symbolic values in the important moments of human life (e.g., bread, fish, wine), the severe compliance of fasting, the provision of gifts and food offerings (e.g., alms to the tomb in the *Day of the Dead*) that were observed of Romanians only in the past but is now observed of all populations in the study such as the Turks and Tatars, and the prohibiting of eating without a prey now give a zonal cultural identity of the Dobrujan gastronomic heritage.

NOTES

1. Constantin Giurescu, *News about the Romanian population of Dobrogea in medieval and modern maps* (original title: *Ştiri despre populaţia românească a Dobrogei în hărţi medievale şi moderne*), Constanţa, Archeologic Museum, page 5.

2. Petru Ursache, *Gastrosophia or the living cuisine* (original title: *Gastrosofia sau bucătăria vie*), Bucharest, Eikon Publishing, 2014, page 61.

3. Interviewed person: Otilia Meragiu, born in 1947; interview December 2012, Greci Village.

4. Interviewed persons: Florica Arion, born in 1953; Ioana Şuerică, born in 1951; interview March 2013, Luncaviţa Village.

5. Interviewed persons: Zoiţa Şamata, born in 1952; Dumitru Steriuş, born in 1959; interview July 2013, Stejaru Village.

6. Interviewed persons: Fedosia Maroz, born in 1961; Olga Niculai, born in 1962; Maricela Feodorov, born in 1953, interview July 2013, Slava Cercheză Village; Pelaghia Ivanov, born in 1953; interview December 2011, Sarichioi Village.

7. Interviewed persons: Grigore Condrat, born in 1948; Verginica Condrat, born in 1951; Parasca Gavrilă, born in 1956, interview December 2011, Dunavăţu de Jos Village.

8. Interviewed persons: Nizami Safie, born in 1941; Arif Pachizea, born in 1925, Arif Elvinaz, born in 1962; interview February 2012, Ciucurova Village.

9. Interviewed persons: Geanbai Nedin, born in 1951, Adilsah Reian, born in 1960; interview March 2012, Tulcea.

10. Interviewed persons: Lucica Vals, born in 1943, Silvia Palan, born in 1940, interview June 2011, Greci Village.

11. Interviewed persons: Ioana Dascalu, born in 1957; Sultana Pintilie, born in 1960, Gabriela Pintilie, born in 1952; interview June 2013, Izvoarele Village.

Part III

TECHNOLOGY'S ROLE IN CULTURAL
HERITAGE MANAGEMENT TODAY

The Tools and Technology in Cultural Heritage Management

Cecilia Lizama Salvatore

INTRODUCTION

In organization theory, Scott defined technology as "the means, activities, and knowledge used to transform materials into organizational outputs."[1] Thus, at a university, the chalk and chalkboard, as well as the instructor, comprised the technology used to transform course material into outputs that will result in student learning. As we know today, we generally use the screen projector, the computer, online course content materials, the asynchronous and synchronous classroom, and the online course content management programs and applications or apps. In a real sense, we are using advanced or high technology to supplement or in place of the old chalk and chalkboard.

This definition of technology in organization theory makes the point that ultimately technology is only as useful as the manner in which it fulfills the functions of and activities and processes in the institution or organization. More importantly, it draws our attention towards technology as it fulfills functions and facilitates and expedites activities and processes. In this chapter, I describe the tools and technology in cultural heritage management paying particular attention to the activities and processes of cultural heritage institutions and the functions and knowledge in these institutions.

Historically, archives have preserved materials that were "created or received by a person, family, or organization, public or private, in the conduct of their affairs and preserved because of the enduring value contained in the information they contain or as evidence of the functions and responsibilities of their creator, especially those materials maintained using the principles of provenance, original order, and collective control."[2] Today, archives also actively collect records, rather than wait to receive them; they actively document history and heritage. Similarly, a museum is an institution that "acquires, conserves, researches, communicates and exhibits the tangible and intangible heritage of humanity and its environment for the purposes of education, study and enjoyment."[3] Thus, the tools and technology used in cultural heritage institutions should assist staff in documenting, organizing and describing, preserving and conserving, and making accessible and displaying cultural heritage components; they should enable users to interact in some way with these components.

To be sure, technology has changed in cultural heritage management. Rapid advances in the development of information and communications technologies (ICT) and web and mobile technologies have boosted the development of tools and technology that are applicable to the management of cultural heritage resources and have increased initiatives and projects that are dedicated to using these tools and technology.

In describing cultural heritage management tools and technology, it is sometimes necessary to mention industry and brand names. I remind the reader that brand and industry names constantly change, however the focus, ultimately, is on the capabilities and functionality of the tools to transform inputs into organizational or institutional outputs.

In addition, mention of industry and brand names are limited to my local and regional knowledge. And finally, I am mindful that there are so many more tools and much more technology than I can be aware of or that I have space to describe in this chapter.

I specifically describe here tools and technology as they are applicable and are meaningful to:

1. The internal, administrator, and back-end activities and functions of the institution or organization (i.e., the functions and activities of documenting, collecting, organizing and describing, and making accessible cultural heritage resources).
2. User access and interactive, and front-end capabilities (i.e., the ways in which, through cultural heritage institutions' functions, activities, and processes, users and other stakeholders are able to access and engage with cultural heritage records).

TOOLS FOR INTERNAL, ADMINISTRATIVE, AND FRONT-END ACTIVITIES AND FUNCTIONS

General Spreadsheets, Relational Databases, and Open Software Tools

Smaller institutions or collections primarily want a relatively inexpensive tool with which they can maintain some sort of control and an inventory of their records and resources, with perhaps minimal capability to manipulate and arrange this inventory. Lacking the staff, time, and required resources to manage their records and collections, a robust program is out of their reach. In a very real sense, they need new technology so that they can move beyond the manual technology of an accession notebook and a file cabinet. In this scenario, a spreadsheet or relational database could serve a small cultural heritage institution or collection adequately. In fact, a spreadsheet program such as MS Excel or a relational database application, such as Filemaker Pro, has served these types of institutions. These tools have enabled them to manipulate, sort, and filter data. Furthermore, they are affordable because, for example, MS Excel comes with the Microsoft Office suite of products granting a sort of economies of scale, and Filemaker Pro provides an educational discount and costs less than $500, which includes technical and customer support.

A relational database can also do more than assist in documenting cultural heritage. For example, one story that has been described to me was of a folklorist using the database application for shared fieldwork and archives. The folklorist and her partner folklorist used Filemaker Pro for twenty-five years, accessing and editing the database from separate designated computers. The database allows up to five access points and allows remote web access as well. In addition to sharing fieldwork data, the poster has used the tool to track membership and donation records, conduct basic accounting, and import and export to a spreadsheet to share with contractors and partners.

Relational databases have been used in imaginative ways, such as to display quantitative and qualitative information about forced migration in a particular region of the world. Jessop found that GIS technology had much potential when applied to humanities data. In his research, he explored ways to use spatial data from a geodatabase and visualize further data, and from that developed a digital collection of a cultural heritage.[4]

Spreadsheets and relational databases are not designed specifically for cultural heritage institutions. There are similar technological tools that are built for other purposes, but provide the capacity—especially when combined with other programs—to highlight certain functions of and processes in cultural heritage institutions. These tools are selected because of their robust capacity and affordability. The Building Information Modeling (BIM) is a prime example.

Elsewhere, Salvatore and Lizama described the diverse components of cultural heritage. These diverse components illustrate the tangible and intangible nature of cultural heritage.[5] Tangible cultural heritage components include land, monument, and structure. The BIM software is open source software that is used by designers, architects, conservators, engineers, and so on to digitally visualize the functional and physical characteristics of structures. It is used to visualize the progress in the development of structural models and to support building functions such as structural analysis and specification management. Logothetis and Stylianidia described how BIM open source software could also be used to model and reconstruct cultural heritage buildings and other structures and monuments.[6] Megahed explained that with BIM technology the reconstruction and restoration of historic and cultural heritage structures can be aided through 3D modeling.[7]

While spreadsheets and relational database programs can work for small institutions, there are integrated management tools and systems that are designed to provide integrated support for the workflow and the diverse functions within a cultural heritage institution. These are systems that are designed to access, catalog, and classify or arrange and describe, manage a collection, and allow for adequate search and retrieval of records and resources. They provide support for the archival workflow of appraisal, accessioning, arrangement and description, publication of finding aids, collection management, and preservation. They also integrate nomenclature, controlled vocabulary, and processing standards that are adopted by cultural heritage institutions. Before I describe these systems, I will describe what is meant by standards, controlled vocabulary, and nomenclature, focusing specifically on metadata standards, cultural heritage controlled vocabulary, and museum nomenclature.

Metadata, Controlled Vocabulary, and Nomenclature

I describe here metadata, controlled vocabularies, and nomenclature in order to provide meaning to further discussion about tools and technology in cultural heritage institutions. It should be noted, however, that there is much more to these topics that the reader can find elsewhere.

Literally defined, metadata is data about data. In the early days of the web, metadata schema was developed to take care of resource discovery on the web. There are now metadata standards for diverse purposes. There are *descriptive metadata, technical metadata, preservation metadata, structural metadata, rights metadata*, and *markup languages.*[8]

The Dublin Core metadata schema, a descriptive metadata schema, emerged in 1995 from a workshop in Dublin, Ohio, where invited participants gathered to address the need for a more stable list of structured terms or schema that could be used across the globe to describe a wide range of resources. The original "Dublin Core" was a core vocabulary of fifteen elements for use in describing a wide range of resources, including simple and generic resources. These fifteen elements, now used to describe many types of information object or asset, include *contributor, coverage, creator, date, description, format, identifier, language, publisher, relation, rights, source, subject, title*, and *type*. The Dublin Core metadata standard is maintained by the Dublin Core Metadata Initiative (DCMI), and has been expanded since it was first introduced to include up-to-date metadata terms, such as vocabulary encoding schemes and encoding syntax schemes.[9]

The Dublin Core metadata schema is widely disseminated and remains very popular among archivists and librarians for the standard description of digital objects, resources, and collections. But as Gill explained, metadata "has [also] been increasingly adopted and co-opted by more diverse communities" and "its definition has grown in scope to include almost anything that describes anything else."[10] A digital camera, for example, embeds a specific type of metadata in digital images.

Other metadata and related standards have since been developed by groups, institutes, and consortia. The United States Library of Congress is a good resource for many of these standards and provides a description of many of them, including:

> The VRA Core, the "data standard and XML schema for the description of works of visual culture as well as the images that document them";
> METS (Metadata Encoding & Transmission Standard), which is the "structure for encoding descriptive, administrative, and structural metadata";
> and the most recent, BIBFRAME (Bibliographic Framework Initiative), which "serves as a general model for expressing and connecting bibliographic data," and more.[11]

In Great Britain, the Digital Curation Centre (DCC) also provides information on metadata standards, such as metadata standards that are supported by diverse academic disciplinary communities.[12] For example, in physical science, the International Virtual Observatory Alliance Technical Specifications is "a set of specifications, including metadata standards, that enables the integration of many astronomical archives into an international virtual observatory."[13] And in social science and the humanities, the Data Documentation Initiative (DDI) is "an international standard for describing data from the social, behavioral, and economic sciences. Expressed in XML, the DDI metadata specification supports the entire research data life cycle."[14]

For archivists throughout the world, the International Council on Archives (ICA) has "united archival institutions and practitioners across the globe to advocate for good archival management and the physical protection of recorded heritage, to produce reputable standards and best practices, and to encourage dialogue, exchange, and transmission of this knowledge and expertise across national borders."[15] For example, it developed ISAD(G): General International Standard Archival Description which provides, in fourteen languages, general rules for archival description in order to promote accessibility of archival materials.[16] The ISAD(G): General International Standard Archival Description has informed Describing Archives: A Content Standard (DACS), the United States' standard for describing archives, personal papers, and manuscripts.[17] DACS is a *content* metadata standard.

Another metadata standard used by archivists, not just in the United States but elsewhere as well, is EAD or Encoded Archival Description. In archives, where access to records, materials, and collections is commonly provided on a finding aid, the *structural* metadata, EAD, is useful as it is "non-proprietary de facto standard for the encoding of finding aids for use in a networked (online) environment."[18] The finding aid describes records and collections in archives and assists users in understanding the materials in the archives, while it also maintains the repository's physical and intellectual control over the materials. The finding aid shows the hierarchical nature of records and collections—for example, items in a folder, in a series, or in a record group. As a structural metadata, EAD is able to show this hierarchy and the relationships within it.

In working with cultural heritage objects and resources, it makes sense to have controlled vocabulary that could be used to describe, catalog, and classify these objects and resources and thus provide consistent and effective access points. A widely used vocabulary is the Library of Congress Subject Headings (LCSH), the "only subject headings list accepted as a worldwide standard."[19] The American Folklore Society, on the other hand, continues to develop the *AFS Ethnographic Thesaurus*, which "can be used to improve access to information about folklore, ethnomusicology, ethnology, and related fields."[20]

The Getty Research Institute developed several vocabularies that "contain structured terminology for art, architecture, decorative arts, archival materials, visual surrogates, conservation, and bibliographic materials."[21] Two Getty vocabularies are the *Art & Architecture Thesaurus (AAT)* and the *Cultural Objects Name Authority (CONA)*. The *AAT* is a "structured vocabulary, including terms, descriptions, and other metadata for generic concepts related to art, architecture, conservation, archaeology, and other cultural heritage," and *CONA* "compiles titles, attributions, depicted subjects, and other metadata about works of art, architecture, and other cultural heritage, both extant and historical, linked to museum collections, special collections, archives, libraries, scholarly research, and other resources."[22]

In the United States, museum nomenclature was developed by Robert Chenhall, with the American Association for State and Local History (AASLH), in the late 1970s.[23] Since then, the nomenclature has been updated and expanded by the AASLH. At the time of this writing, *Nomenclature 4.0 for Museum Cataloging* is being used by museum catalogers.[24] At the international level, the International Council of Museums' (ICOM) International Committee for Documentation is developing *Lightweight Information Describing Objects (LIDO)*, "a format for contributing collection information for resource discovery."[25]

In a discussion about standards and vocabulary, the development of the "uncontrolled vocabulary," the folksonomy, cannot be ignored. A folksonomy is "built when many people use a shared system to label online content such as web pages or images with descriptive terms and names, known as tags."[26] "The folksonomy aspect of 'uncontrolled' tags comes into play when all the tags applied to a specific resource by multiple users are aggregated and ranked. For example, if one person tags an image with the term 'impressionist' it doesn't carry a great deal of weight in terms of searching. But if hundreds of users use this term, and it is the most frequently applied tag for a particular image or other online resource, it is a pretty safe bet that the resource is about or related to Impressionist art."[27]

Integrated Management Systems

In her widely referenced report, Lisa Spiro identified the characteristics and features of archival management software and programs that are the main decision points for selection and rejection by archivists. Spiro interviewed users and reviewed the literature and previous studies in order to create matrices that archivists could use to make comparisons of the different archival management software and programs.[28] To be sure, the report makes explicit the complexity as well as the robustness of cultural heritage technology.

While Spiro's report is not very current, it has brought up general points that are still relevant and that we cannot overlook. For example, the desired features of an archival management software or program are still relevant. Archivists still desire the following features:[29]

- *Integrated:* Whether the archivist could enter data in one database, rather than in multiple databases, in order to generate multiple outputs, such as an EAD finding aid, an accession list, and so forth.
- *Legacy data:* Whether data previously created and projects already completed, such as the creation of EAD finding aids, could be seamlessly imported to a new archival management system.
- *Easy exporting of data:* It is critical that data in obsolete technology is not lost and could be cleanly and easily exported when the institution is migrating to new technology.
- *Web publishing capabilities:* Whether, through a web-publishing component of the archival management program, the archivist can publish the archives' finding aids on the web. Web-publishing capabilities enable the archivist to provide wider access to the finding aids and collections, even though she might not have had formal training in web design and publication.
- *Simple yet powerful:* A program is not too complex and easy to use when it provides a template that integrates processing standards and can also quickly generate EAD at the click of a button.
- *Rigorous, standards-based:* Whether the software or program conforms to archival standards, such as DACS and EAD, thus reducing the chance for errors and inconsistencies.
- *Provides collection management feature:* Ideally, an archival management system should also enable the archivist to maintain and manage her collection, such as keeping track of statistical data.
- *Portable:* Whether it provides the capability to support data entry or work offsite or through mobile technology.
- *Aids in setting priorities for processing:* "Some archival management systems enable archives to record which collections are higher priorities, thus allowing archivists to plan processing more effectively."[30]

The features and characteristics that are main decision points in selecting and acquiring existing archival management software or program are still relevant as well. Spiro listed the following features and characteristics:

- *Automating the processing and description of collections through the archival management system versus generating EAD by hand and managing collections through other software*

   Does the system enable staff to create a valid EAD finding aid by simply entering information in the system and with not having advanced knowledge of EAD and XML markup language? An archival management program like Archon, for example, both generates and publishes EAD finding aids.
- *Open source versus commercial*

   Is the system open source or commercial? Open source—that is, free—may not necessarily be favorable. Open source often means that formal user support is not available or, at least, not readily available. Archon, for example, is open source, but support is available primarily through FAQ and forum on its website. On the other hand, Cuadra Star is a commercial program that is not affordable to many cultural heritage institutions, especially small to midsize institutions, but it provides not only support via its website, but via telephone, e-mail, teleconferencing, and web conferencing many hours of the day.

- *Hosted by company or local institution*

    With some archival institutions lacking the in-house infrastructure to maintain an archival management system, it is important to know whether the archival management system provides the option of hosting the software for institutions. "In addition to hosting, many companies will assist customers in importing legacy data into the software. Generally, customers who pay a company to host their data reported that there were few technical problems and that the company's servers rarely went down."[31]A commercial product is more likely to provide hosting services; Cuadra Star does that, for example.

- *Cost*

    Naturally, cost is a critical factor; either you can or you cannot afford to purchase the product. And the cost for archival management software ranges from free (open source) to hundreds of thousands of dollars. Spiro reminded us that open source does not always mean free. Consider, for example, Collective Access, an open source software with the unique and desirable features of being customizable and having "robust support for multimedia, including images, audio, video, and text."[32] It may be that an institution does not have the technical staff that can customize the program and maximize its potential. The institution, therefore, is compelled to hire staff to specifically carry out these functions.

- *Sustainability and reliability and maturity*

    As Spiro points out, software comes and goes. An archivist is rightly concerned about the sustainability of the archival management software it is considering for purchase. It will be a good idea to inquire if the software is working on a sustainability plan.

Archon and Archivists' Toolkit are two open source programs that were enthusiastically endorsed by the Society of American Archivists when they were launched. They were programs that were developed in the United States and that adhere rigidly to archival functions and workflow. Since 2009, however, when representatives of New York University, the University of Illinois Urbana–Champaign, the University of California San Diego, and the Andrew W. Mellon Foundation agreed to integrate Archon and Archivists' Toolkit into a single application, there were concerns about the sustainability of these two archival software programs. The Mellon Foundation provided generous funding for the development of this single application, which is now ArchivesSpace. In September 2013, the Mellon-funded development project concluded, version 1.0 of ArchivesSpace was released, and enrollment of general members began. Additionally, the developers and managers of Archivists' Toolkit and Archon stopped providing any kind of user support or bug fixing to their programs.[33]

ArchivesSpace is described as an open source program, but membership in the ArchivesSpace community is encouraged. Membership costs money. Membership levels vary and, thus, costs to install and implement the program vary. Membership helps in the sustainability of ArchivesSpace, and as of this writing, the program continues to grow and improve as the "next-generation web-based archives information management system, designed by archivists and supported by diverse archival repositories."[34] Furthermore, there are still institutions that had launched Archon and Archivists' Toolkit who continue to use them because of their inability to join the ArchivesSpace membership community.

- *Quality of customer support*

    What kind of support will the archivist receive after acquiring the archival content management program? As stated earlier, software that does not cost anything tends to come

with no or very minimal direct customer support. Customer support would likely come from a forum made up of others who have acquired the software, not from a help desk at the company headquarters.
- *Support for archival standards*

    Does the archival management software adhere to archival standards and best practices? Adherence to standards such as EAD and DACS ensures interoperability.
- *Web-based versus desktop client*

    Web-based software allows anyone with web access to contribute records to the distributed cataloging. This may be favorable to an archivist, while another archivist may be concerned about the security and reliability of her records and collections on the web.
- *Support for publishing finding aids online versus generating EAD for export*

    It has been years since the publication of Spiro's report, and by now archival management software and programs should automatically allow and support the publishing of finding aids online. Thus, once information is entered into these programs, they can be immediately searchable online. Most of the programs known by archivists—such as ArchivesSpace, Collective Access, Archon, Cuadra Star, Eloquent Archives—provide this support.
- *Support for linking to digital objects*

    An archival management software or program should not only provide access to collections and finding aids, but also to digital objects or surrogates, such as audio files, video, images, and so on. Since the publication of Spiro's report, this kind of access is expected of archival management software and programs.
- *Support for collection management and the capability to manage reports, statistics, and projects*

    Some archivists would like their archival management software to do more than provide access to finding aids, objects, and collections. They want it to provide support for collection management, such as appraisal and creating deeds of gift labels, and support for tracking statistics, creating statistical reports. Many of the archival management programs, especially the commercial products, such as Cuadra Star and Eloquent Archives, provide this service.

In her report, Spiro focused on archival collections and thus on the needs of archival records and materials and on the archival workflow. Museum curators and managers have different needs, on the other hand. Whereas records in archives are commonly not removed from the archives or from their location, objects, images, and other materials in museums can move from place to place, such as when they are selected to be exhibited in another location or when they are loaned to another institution. An integrated management system for a museum should also include templates that are not required by most archivists, such as a template that describes an exhibit and thus asks for information about the title of the exhibit and the name of the curator. Finally, a museum software or program should also use museum lexicon and nomenclature.

An informal survey of small historical society collections and small museums in the United States reveal that PastPerfect was a favored integrated management system because of its low cost, availability of technical support, and its dashboard, pages, and interface that support museum workflow. These institutions did not have access to highly trained technical staff, and for the relatively low cost of under $1,000, they could have an integrated system plus an off-site user and technical support system for the installation, implementation, and maintenance of the system. Museum standards and the AASLH's nomenclature are embedded in PastPerfect. Thus, staff in small cultural heritage institutions can use the program for functions such as cataloging of items, objects, and collections without having obtained advanced formal training. Staff can also use the program to track inventory, document exhibits, maintain contact and donor lists, and manage development and campaign initiatives.[35]

Museums exhibit cultural heritage components and educate and even entertain users and visitors, and there are museum programs and software that more effectively facilitate these functions. Zoos, aquariums, and children's museums, for example, have implemented programs, such as the Explorer Systems Museum Software, which enhance their functions, services, and initiatives. Additionally, the Explorer Systems Museum Software manages additional services that are provided such as birthday parties, camps, gift shop, and fund-raising.[36]

Managers of larger or more robust museum collections would do well with higher-end management programs. Examples of robust programs include Argus, which is offered by the same company that offers Cuadra Star for archives, and Eloquent Museums, which is offered by the same company that offers Eloquent Archives. These programs are favored by well-recognized museums worldwide. In Chicago, Illinois, alone, for example, Emu, a product of Axiell, is the museum collections management program used at the Chicago Museum of Science and Industry, the Field Museum of Natural History, and the University of Chicago Oriental Institute. Similar to the robust archival management software and programs, these museum software programs are flexible web-based collections management system platforms that enhance curation and cataloging. But in addition, they expand outreach and access benefiting both in-person and virtual visitors.[37]

The availability of very high-end museum software programs makes it easy to engage in access and outreach initiatives. The Council on Library and Information Resources (CLIR) in the United States, for example, is "working with The Antiquities Coalition and other institutions in the United States and abroad to explore the feasibility and technical prototyping of a Digital Library of the Middle East (DLME). The DLME would create a digitally based, internationally shared inventory of cultural artifacts that includes detailed descriptions and images, and confirms objects' ownership and legal status. This information would help determine whether an item of cultural or historical significance offered for sale or being transferred was acquired illegally."[38]

This very noteworthy initiative is made possible by a partnership between CLIR and Axiell that was forged in December 2016. Through this initiative, "large-scale digitization and cataloging of museum, library, and archival physical objects—as well as artifacts from archeological sites—will be supported throughout the Middle East to enrich the scope of cultural materials online. Images and descriptions from the DLME will be made publicly available, to the extent permitted by copyright, to encourage greater understanding of the region's cultural legacy."[39]

ACCESS AND USE

In the modern environment, archives and museums are compelled to find innovative and creative ways to reach out to their users, visitors, audience, and other stakeholders. In the archives profession two of the core domains that schools in archives programs in the United States should teach are: (1) Reference and Access, and (2) Outreach, Instruction, and Advocacy. In the domain of "Reference and Access," archives students should know about "the policies and procedures designed to serve the information needs of various user groups, based on institutional mandates and constituencies, the nature of the materials, relevant laws and ethical considerations, user needs, and appropriate technologies. Instruction in this area should also include the study of user behavior, discovery and access techniques and technologies, user-based evaluation techniques, and the interaction between archivist and user." In the domain of "Outreach, Instruction, and Advocacy," archives students should know about the "theories and practices used to identify archival constituencies and their needs and to develop programs that promote increased use, understanding of archival materials and methods, resources, visibility, and support. Includes primary source and information literacy as well as methods of promoting the value of archives to the public and other audiences. This component should also articulate the benefits the profession provides to society beyond competent management of the organizational records and personal collections in archivists' care."[40]

In museum studies, one of the components of the curricula guidelines for museum professional development is "Public programming competencies: Knowledge of and skills in serving the museum's communities."[41] These competencies include knowledge of:

Communications (communication theory, signage, etc.)

Exhibitions (exhibition theory, lighting, virtual exhibitions, website creation and management, etc.)

Education and interpretation (learning theory, use of text, objects, graphics, manipulative materials and media, etc.)

Publications and products

Visitor service and public relationships (visitor characteristics, non-visitor characteristics, local, national, international and regional situations, issues, etc.)

Some of the museum collections or management software programs offer diverse capabilities for accessibility, use, programming, and exhibitions. For an additional fee, for example, smaller institutions and collections can create virtual exhibitions in PastPerfect. And larger collections can use a program such as Explorer Systems Museum Software to manage their inventory and content, as well as expand their online presence and programming, just as the Cosmosphere Science Education Center and Space Museum in Kansas did.[42] To be sure, features for access and use of collections—for example, viewing of digital collections, viewing of finding aids online, and viewing of online exhibitions are integrated in robust collections and archival management programs.

Other tools expand the way users can access collections. Archivists and museum curators and managers can use tools and technology that are affordable and not necessarily part of an integrated system. For example, an institution may want to expand access to a collection by creating an online exhibit or a digital collection. One tool for the creation of digital collections is Omeka, an open source web publishing for research, collections, and exhibitions. Many institutions have used Omeka to create basic digital collections—that is, with the "bells and whistles," and so have individuals, families, and small groups.[43] As a matter of fact, as of the time of this writing, many libraries are offering workshops in which they provide to anyone who signs up instructions for creating digital collections.[44]

Archives and museums can expand access to collections and exhibits by creating a timeline of topics, events, and people. Timeline technology such as EDMStudio's Timeline allows archives and museums to insert images, audio, video, and text over a timeline and allows users to read, view, and hear about the topic, event, people, and so on with a touch of the screen. EDMStudio's Timeline was created for museums and other cultural heritage institutions, but there is also timeline technology created for other purposes, such as project management. Such technology, such as Aeon Timeline, may be used by cultural heritage institutions as well.

Cultural heritage institutions can make the user or visitor experience via mobile apps that they develop. Tools such as OnCell and Vamonde provide a digital storytelling platform that are particularly propitious when the user is visiting a cultural heritage site, landmark, and the like.

Besides accessing and viewing records and collections, cultural heritage institutions, particularly museums seek to facilitate an environment in which their users interact with their collections. With tools and technology, institutions can facilitate an environment in which users not only view a collection, but can become co-create collections. A participatory cultural heritage institution has been the call of many, such as Nina Simon, who wrote,

> How can cultural institutions use participatory techniques not just to give visitors a voice, but to develop experiences that are more valuable and compelling for everyone? This is not a question of intention or desire; it's a question of design. Whether the goal is to promote dialogue or creative expression, shared learning or co-creative work, the design process starts with a simple question: which tool or technique will produce the desired participatory experience?[45]

In Chicago, Illinois, the Field Museum of Natural History is expanding the concept of co-creation to co-curation, which "engages communities outside the Museum in the stewardship, documentation, and interpretation of heritage objects in . . . collections." One example of this is the Philippine Collection Co-curation Partnership, "which engages Chicago's Filipino-American community in the stewardship of the Museum's 10,000 Philippine artifacts, including the digitization of collections data and images, creation of an interactive web portal, collections tours for academic and community groups, and public conversations on heritage topics."[46]

Users and visitors can co-curate with cultural heritage institutions using other technology. They can co-curate using basic social media technology. A cultural heritage institution's Facebook page, for example, can welcome comments and tags about objects and artifacts. Users' and other stakeholders' tags can form a folksonomy for the institution. Or they can co-curate using technology, such as HistoryPin. For example, using HistoryPin, the National Archives (United States) encouraged its audience to "upload . . . digital files, add descriptive information and personal narratives to these items, and experience how familiar environments have changed over time."[47] HistoryPin "allows users to overlay photographs, videos and audio recordings on Google maps." Users are encouraged to share their memories and stories related to the photographs, videos, and audio recordings.

While tools that provide a storytelling platform, such as the ones mentioned here, are useful and favorable, the standby tool—that is, the regular audio recording tool—is useful and favorable as well. Cultural heritage institutions can engage users by conducting an oral history project, in which staff use digital recorders to digitally record history as told by users or in which users use the recorders with each other.

Oral history, as a tool in cultural heritage institutions, deserves more space than we have in this chapter. Thus, we will not focus on it here.

FINAL COMMENTS

In this chapter, I describe some of the diverse tools and technology that are favorable to cultural heritage institutions. I describe these tools and technology within the early framework of technology as posited in the sub-discipline of organization theory. Technology is changing and it is now high or advanced technology. That too will change. In the process, my hope is that cultural heritage institutions will continue to benefit from it.

Note: scanning and replication and printing technology is one of the most gratifying technology in archives and museums. Furthermore, it is being enthusiastically developed and advanced. There are various levels of 3D and replication technology use and implications. The discussion of this technology is too important and warrants more space than available in this chapter.

NOTES

1. Scott, W. Richard. "Organizational Structure." *Annual Review of Sociology*, 1 (1975): 5–6.
2. Society of American Archivists. Glossary of Archival and Records Terminology. http://archivists .org/glossary/terms/a/archives.
3. ICOM: International Council of Museums. Museum definition. http://icom.museum/the-vision/ museum-definition/.
4. Jessop, Martyn. "The Application of a Geographical Information System to the Creation of a Cultural Heritage Digital Resource." *Literary & Linguistic Computing* 20, no. 1 (March 2005): 71–90.
5. Salvatore, Cecilia Lizama and Lizama, John T. "Cultural Heritage Components." In Salvatore, Cecilia, ed. *Cultural Heritage Care and Management: Theory and Practice*. Lanham, MD: Rowman & Littlefield, 2018.
6. Logothetis, Sotiris, and Efstratios Stylianidis. "BIM Open Source Software (OSS) for the Documentation of Cultural Heritage." *Virtual Archaeology Review* 7, no. 15 (2016): 28–35. http://polipapers .upv.es/index.php/var/article/view/5864.
7. Megahed, Naglaa A. "Towards a Theoretical Framework for HBIM Approach in Historic Preservation and Management." *Archneet-IJAR* 9, no. 3 (November 2015): 130–147.
8. Riley, Jenn. *Understanding Metadata: What Is Metadata, and What Is It For?* National Information Standards Organization, 2017.
9. Dublin Core Metadata Initiative. DCMI Metadata Terms. http://dublincore.org/documents/dcmi-terms/
10. Gill, Tony (Revised by Murtha Baca, with assistance from Joan Cobb, Nathaniel Deines, and Moon Kim.) "Metadata and the Web." In *Intoduction to Metadata, third edition*. Murtha Baca, ed. Los Angeles: Getty Research Institute, 2016.
11. Library of Congress. Standards at the Library of Congress. https://www.loc.gov/standards/.
12. Digital Curation Centre. Disciplinary Metadata. http://www.dcc.ac.uk/resources/metadata-standards.
13. Ibid.
14. Ibid.
15. The International Council on Archives. http://www.ica.org/en/international-council-archives-0.
16. International Council on Archives. *ISAD(G): General International Standard Archival Description, Second Edition.* http://www.ica.org/en/isadg-general-international-standard-archival-description -second-edition.
17. Society of American Archivists. *Describing Archives: A Content Standard (DACS), Second Edition.* http://www2.archivists.org/groups/technical-subcommittee-on-describing-archives-a-content -standard-dacs/dacs.
18. Society of American Archivists. Encoded Archival Description (EAD). http://www2.archivists .org/groups/technical-subcommittee-on-encoded-archival-description-ead/encoded-archival-description -ead.
19. The Library of Congress. *Thesauri & Controlled Vocabularies.* https://www.loc.gov/library/ libarch-thesauri.html.
20. *American Folklore Society Ethnographic Thesaurus.* http://id.loc.gov/vocabulary/ethnographic Terms.html.
21. The Getty Research Institute. *Getty Vocabularies.* http://www.getty.edu/research/tools/vocabularies/.
22. Ibid.

23. Chenhall, Robert G. *Nomenclature for Museum Cataloging*. Nashville: American Association for State and Local History, 1978.

24. *Nomenclature 4.0 for Museum Cataloging*. Edited by Paul Bourcier, Heather Dunn, and the Nomenclature Task Force. Lanham, MD: Rowman & Littlefield/AASLH, 2015.

25. International Council of Museums International Committee for Documentation. *LIDO*. http://network.icom.museum/cidoc/working-groups/lido/.

26. Gill, Ibid.

27. Ibid.

28. Spiro, Lisa. *Archival Management Software: A Report for the Council on Library and Information Resources*. Washington, DC, Council on Library and Information Resources, January 2009. https://www.clir.org/pubs/reports/spiro/spiro/spiro_Jan13.pdf.

29. Ibid.

30. Ibid.

31. Ibid, 13.

32. Ibid, 82.

33. ArchivesSpace. http://archivesspace.org/about/mission-and-history/.

34. Ibid.

35. Capterra. PastPerfect. http://www.capterra.com/museum-software/spotlight/121813/PastPerfect/PastPerfect.

36. Capterra. Explorer. http://www.capterra.com/museum-software/spotlight/121532/Explorer/Explorer%20Systems.

37. Capterra. Lucidea: Argus. http://www.capterra.com/museum-software/spotlight/147166/Argus/Lucidea.

38. Council on Library and Information Resources. *Digital Library of the Middle East*. https://www.clir.org/initiatives-partnerships/DLME.

39. Council on Library and Information Resources. "CLIR and Axiell Partner to Create the Digital Library of the Middle East." https://www.clir.org/about/news/pressrelease/clir-axiell-partnership.

40. Society of American Archivists. Guidelines for a Graduate Program in Archival Studies (2016). http://archivists.org/prof-education/graduate/gpas.

41. ICOM Curricula Guidelines for Museum Professional Development. http://icom.museum/fileadmin/user_upload/pdf/professions/curricula_eng.pdf.

42. Cosmosphere. Outreach Programs. http://cosmo.org/explore/outreach-programs.

43. See for example: http://www.ardenkirkland.com/work/portfolio/inside-a-digital-collection/; http://herstories.prattinfoschool.nyc/omeka/.

44. See for example: http://newsonline.library.vanderbilt.edu/2016/02/build-digital-collections-with-omeka/, http://calendar.cal.msu.edu/?ai1ec_event=digital-collections-with-omeka-workshop.

45. Simon, Nina. The Participatory Museum. http://www.participatorymuseum.org/chapter1/.

46. The Field Museum. "What is Co-curation?" http://philippines.fieldmuseum.org/heritage/narrative/4166.

47. The National Archives on HistoryPin. https://www.archives.gov/social-media/historypin.html.

11

Curating Digital Cultural Heritage Materials

Stacy Kowalczyk

"Cultural Heritage is an expression of the ways of living developed by a community and passed on from generation to generation, including customs, practices, places, objects, artistic expressions and values" (CID, 2016). The artifacts of current cultural heritage are digital— photographs, documents, personal histories, recipes, letters, journals, games, are captured and saved as digital things. Because social media has become a routine manner for recording daily life, it has become an important primary source of cultural and historical information.

> As society turns to social media as a primary method of communication and creative expression, social media is supplementing and in some cases supplanting letters, journals, serial publications and other sources routinely collected by research libraries. Archiving and preserving outlets such as Twitter will enable future researchers access to a fuller picture of today's cultural norms, dialogue, trends and events to inform scholarship, the legislative process, new works of authorship, education and other purposes. (Osterberg, 2013, para. 6)

Thus, preserving cultural heritage is becoming a digital endeavor. In addition to the born digital cultural heritage materials being created daily, archives, libraries, museums, and other cultural memory institutions are using digital technologies to produce digital surrogates of their holdings to reduce the wear and tear of the physical object and to increase the visibility of and access to their holdings. The digital surrogates need to be managed and preserved as well.

Preserving cultural heritage is a complex multidisciplinary endeavor that includes history, science, anthropology, archival science, and other disciplines. Digital curation, the process by which digital materials are managed and preserved, is also a complex multidisciplinary endeavor; in addition to the traditional cultural heritage studies, digital curation requires library science, information science, and computer science. The goals of cultural heritage preservation are generally accepted to be "conservation and protection on the one hand and enhancement on the other hand" (Barile & Saviano, 2014, p. 80). Digital curation shares these goals: to protect the materials and to enhance meaning through context and experience. "With common issues and concerns, a growing convergence of institutions—libraries, archives, museums and historic houses—face the same challenges for cultural heritage preservation. These include storage, display, research and exhibition areas that meet the needs of preservation" (France, 2009, para 1). Whether digital or physical, storage, access, and display of materials are key issues.

DEFINING DIGITAL CURATION

Digital curation includes preservation, management, context, and access. One of the earliest definitions focuses on preservation: "the planning, resource allocation, and application of preservation methods and technologies necessary to ensure that digital information of continuing value remains accessible and usable" (Hedstrom, 1997, p. 190). Another widely used definition is "the managed activities necessary for ensuring both the long-term maintenance of a byte stream and continued accessibility of its contents" (Research Libraries Group & OCLC, 2002, p. 11). Digital curation "is concerned with 'communication across time'" and endeavors to provide "interoperability with the future" (Rusbridge et al., 2005, p. 31) for uninterrupted access to the intellectual content for future generations.

THE NATURE OF DIGITAL MATERIALS

It might be helpful to first define the difference between digital and physical things. Digital things are defined as intellectual expressions that exist *in silico*, in a computer. A digital thing is generally referred to as a digital object, which can be defined as "an information object, of any type of information or any format that is expressed in digital form" (Thibodeau, 2002, p. 6).

DIGITAL OBJECTS ARE FRAGILE

Digital things are inherently fragile. The fragility of digital things is at multiple levels: access, fixity, and obsolescence. Access to digital things can break easily because links break as data is moved. Digital things rarely describe themselves. Often context of a digital thing is external to its instantiation; that is, the description, the metadata for that thing exists as different digital thing in a separate system. Context for a digital thing can be visible as when it exists within a webpage, a library or archival system, or publicly available database; context can be hidden as when it exists within another digital document such as a Word file or PDF or in a secured, off-line database.

Digital things are easy to copy, move, and manipulate. These are features that make digital content so appealing but also cause issues when curating these materials. Because digital things can be copied and manipulated so easily, it is difficult to know whether the digital object "in hand" is an exact replica of the original.

Digital things can be changed either inadvertently or maliciously. As digital things are copied and moved via software over networks, data can be corrupted or lost. Digital things can be corrupted by an inadvertent error in software or by an intended function designed to do damage such as a virus. Digital things can be corrupted by hardware technologies both computational and storage. The instability of data is often referred to as the problem of fixity. Unlike books and other analog things, digital things are not fixed in a physical medium. Curators must be able to ensure that the digital things they have are exact copies of the original.

While digital objects are fragile, digital curators have multiple tools and techniques to fortify digital materials. To combat fragility, digital curators can implement several simple options that help solve fixity, broken links, and lost context.

Fixity can be insured by implementing a checksum feature. A checksum is a mathematical algorithm that calculates a sum based on the contents of the file. This checksum can be stored as an element in the technical or administrative metadata for the file and can be recalculated and compared the stored value. If the checksum is identical, the file has not changed; if the checksum is different, the file has been changed. Changed files need to be investigated to determine the cause and to find the last best copy. Many curation programs use a simple checksum such as the MD5 algorithm.

To combat the problem of fragile Internet links, digital curators can implement a more robust linking mechanism known as Persistent Identifiers. There are four leading persistent identification technologies: Digital Object Identifiers (DOI), Persistent URLs (PURL), Handles, and Archival Resource Keys (ARK). Traditional Internet links use URLs. The full name for the URL technology is Uniform Resource Locators. The reason that URLs are fragile is that they combine two functions: location of the object and the name of the object. URLs generally have a path to the object, basically a set of directions to find the object; if a file is moved, that path in the URL is no longer an accurate description of the location. All four of the persistent identification technologies listed above separate the name of the object from its location. The persistent identifier looks like a URL; but rather than being a path to the object, it is an object name that links to a separate system that stores the location of the object. This name "resolves" to a URL via a resolution service, a program that looks up the location of the persistent identifier. This resolution happens behind the scene and is nearly instantaneous. Because it provides better and more sustainable access to materials, persistent identification is an important component the digital curation program.

DIGITAL OBJECTS ARE TECHNOLOGY DEPENDENT

To fulfill their functionality, digital objects require electricity and equipment to render on a screen in order to be perceived. It is difficult to see the digital object outside of its technology. *Digital things are opaque.* It is possible to hold a disk drive; it is possible to hold the display screen; it is possible to hold the printed version of the digital thing; but it is not possible to touch the digital thing itself.

Digital objects are tied to a specific technology environment. This technology environment requires computational, display, and storage hardware. Some digital things may require very specific additional peripheral equipment. Each component of this hardware environment needs to communicate with the other; thus operating systems, device drivers, communication buses, and file systems must be included in this technology environment. Digital things are tied to specific formant, an organization scheme with a specific syntax that allows a computer program to interpret, process, and to render; thus, in addition to hardware, digital things require software—software that can access the digital thing, display or render the digital thing, or manipulate, modify, or use the digital thing.

Technology Obsolescence

Technology changes quickly. Digital curators need to monitor both software and hardware and have plans to replace technology in a three-to-five-year rotating schedule. Server technology and operating systems change regularly. These changes can have an impact the operations of a digital archive. When storage technologies become obsolete, that is the technologies are no longer being supported, contents upon those storage devices are imperiled. Not only does technology change, it also often fails; the mechanics within a hard drive can break and shred the digital media; sections of the magnetic media can be corrupted; environmental factors such as heat, water, and smoke can also impact the media causing damage and impacting the integrity of the digital files.

Over the past fifty years, a body of best practice has been developed for long-term data storage. Many organizations, such as businesses and academic and research organizations, have implemented data center best practices. Data Center best practice dictates a minimum of three copies of any file or record: one on active media, one on a near-line backup media, and one on a remote backup media. Krogh (2009) has summarized this best practice in a catchy phrase: 3, 2, 1: keep 3 copies of all files—1 primary and 2 backups; keep the files on 2 different media types to protect against different types of failures; store 1 copy offsite (e.g., outside your organization or business facility) (Krogh, 2009).

Unfortunately, creating copies is not sufficient. These files need to be managed. The media needs to be rotated and refreshed based on the manufacturer's most conservative lifetime estimates. Media reliability degrades with the number of writes. Backup tapes or other removable media need to be rotated off the backup schedule after a certain number of uses. Offsite media need to be refreshed on a regular schedule. After some number of years (again, based on the manufacturer's recommendation), the offsite media need to be rewritten. But this schedule also needs to be managed. Technology needs to be monitored to reduce the risk of obsolescence.

File Formats

Data is stored in files. But in order to use that data, software needs to understand the layout of that data. In other words, the format of the data must be known. *Format is defined as the internal structure, the arrangement of bits and bytes, that allows software to read, process, and render the data in meaningful ways.* Since the primary goal in digital curation is to make data accessible and usable to the future, understanding file formats is a key component of digital curation. Abrams contends that "the concept of representation format permeates all technical aspects of digital repository architecture and is, therefore, the foundation of many, if not all, digital preservation activities" (2004). The technical format of a file determines its probability of being preserved. The more open, accessible, widely used a format is, the easier it will be to maintain that format and support the underlying content.

File Format Standards

File formats can be either proprietary or open standards. Proprietary file formats are defined as being owned by one or more organizations or individuals with legal restrictions of use. Open standard formats are defined as being in the public domain or owned by an organization that makes the format available with no legal restrictions and has publicly available documentation and software for processing and/or rendering. Proprietary formats are often developed by and used in application software created by for-profit organizations. Some of the world's most popular and ubiquitous file formats are proprietary. Many other formats, however, are open: JPEG, TIFF, PNG, and many others are available to use without restrictions. Open standards are often controlled by national and international organizations such as NISO and ISO. These organizations control and maintain the formal descriptions of these file formats. Changes are vetted and approved by communities.

Best Practice in File Formats by Level of Use

Formats need to be discussed within the context of the "levels of use." Digital objects can be stored in different formats for different uses. In order to keep a file useable for the longest period of time, a digital object should be created in the format with the most information, in the most open format with the least risk of failure. This high-quality object is often referred to as an archival master file. Some materials need to be "digitally repaired." When the customized digital manipulations are completed, these files can be saved as production masters in an archival format to preserve the effort and expense expended on the repair. Archival formats are usually not network- or web browser–friendly, so smaller files are created from either the archival or production master for end-user delivery. These files are often referred to as derivative or delivery files.

Choosing an archival file format may seem to be a complex, technical, and somewhat daunting process. Documentation for many file formats is densely technical and quite difficult to read. Understanding the details of a file format may seem to be a difficult challenge. Digital curators are not required to understand those technical details of different file formats. It is unnecessary for a curator to understand the TIFF directory structure or the offsets of the tags. It is, however, important for a digital curator to know that TIFF is an open, transparent, widely used archival format for images. Digital curators do not need to make decisions about archival formats by themselves. Fortunately, digital curation professionals can rely on a large network of both practitioners and researchers for advice. Organizations such as the Digital Library Federation,[1] the Library of Congress,[2] and the Digital Curation Centre[3] can provide digital curators with access to network of practitioners for support and guidance.

It is not always possible for curators to control the file formats of the data in their archives. Born digital material is created, saved, and archived in a format chosen by their creators. Many software applications, including word processing applications, accounting software, statistical analysis tools, and scientific instrumentation, create proprietary formats. There may be millions of files that will be difficult to preserve. However, because of the ubiquity of these formats, solutions may be available in the future to help preserve them. Keeping these files safe will be the first step to long-term preservation.

Best Practice for Archival File Formats

As with many other technical fields, digital curation best practice changes as technologies evolve. What was best practice in 1993, when the digital revolution began, is significantly different from current best practice. As best practice changes, digital curators need to keep current by monitoring authoritative resources. Digital curators can verify current practice with reliable sources such as the Library of Congress, the Digital Library Federation, and the Digital Curation Centre.

Photographic Images

Cultural heritage preservation organizations often have large holdings of photographic images as film negatives (and occasionally positives), prints, and increasingly as born digital files. Many organizations are actively digitizing their paper-based materials. Best practice for digitized analog photographs is uncompressed TIFF. The best case scenario for digital photography is to digitize to the native raw file and save as TIFF. Just as in the past as they received boxes of photographs from contributors, cultural heritage organizations should expect to receive digital photographs. Many of these photographs will be in lossy compressed[4] file formats such as JPEG. Because these files have already lost data, it is impossible to recover that data. For files in compressed formats, many libraries and archives are maintaining them in their original format.

- Born digital—Convert raw files to TIFF
- Analog to digital—Digitize directly to TIFF. Some organizations are looking at uncompressed JPEG2000 as an archival format for some materials.
- Derivative files for delivery—JEPG is the most common deliverable format. The use of JPEG2000 is increasing

Documents

Documents, including letters, journals, books, white papers, and so on, are a significant component of archival holdings. Cultural heritage organizations are digitizing many of their unique holdings. Best practice calls for digitizing directly to uncompressed TIFF. Born digital documents present greater challenges to archives as they arrived in a wide variety of formats, many of which are proprietary. Some organizations make a choice to migrate files at the time the data is acquired. The national library of the Netherlands, as an example, chooses to migrate all documents to PDF/a. This simplifies their curation requirements with only one file type to manage. For documents in proprietary formats, best practice would require the archive to maintain the original file in its original format in addition to the converted formats.

- Born digital—maintain the original file. For proprietary formats, convert to PDF/A
- Analog to digital—Digitize directly to TIFF
- Derivative files for delivery—JPEG and/or PDF or PDF/A

Audio

Digitizing audio holdings on tape, lacquer discs, and other vulnerable formats is of increasing importance to cultural heritage organizations as these materials are deteriorating at an alarming rate. Because the original materials can often only support a single read, archival quality of the digital process as well as the format are of the upmost importance; thus, digitizing audio creates very large files. Most audio being generated currently is born digital. The National Archives normalizes born digital audio for long-term preservation.[5]

- Born digital—Normalize to archival formats if possible
- Analog to digital—Broadcast WAV
- Derivative files for delivery—MP3 is a common delivery format

Moving Images

Like audio, digitizing analog film and video is increasingly important for archives and libraries as the media destabilizes. Best practice is to create uncompressed MPEG2 or MPEG4. However, these uncompressed files are huge. An hour of uncompressed video ranges between 70 gigabytes to nearly 1 terabyte depending on the bit-rate, frames per second, and other variables. For many libraries and archives, this is unsustainable; the cost of the uncompressed data is too high (FADGI, 2014). While uncompressed is preferred, lossless compression is acceptable. Born digital video is a mainstay of social media. Once uploaded to a web service such as YouTube, the file has been hyper compressed with lossy algorithms. For digital curators, the only versions may be one of these files. As with born digital photographs, once the data is lost, it is not recoverable.

- Born digital—Capture in archival formats, normalize if possible, or accept as is
- Analog to digital—MPEG2 and MPEG4
- Derivative files for delivery—Compressed streaming formats

DIGITAL OBJECTS ARE COMPLEX

A book is an information object. As a physical object, it has a cover, either soft or hard, and a set of pages in between. The pages could have text, images, or be left intentionally blank. A digital book has digital representations of those same elements—covers and pages with text, images, or left intentionally blank. While a physical book has many component elements, it is generally a single object. However, a digital book is made up of hundreds of individual components, files, that must be coordinated and managed. A small book of 100 pages can comprise over 300 individual digital things: 100 archival images (large files with as much information as possible for future uses), 100 web delivery images (smaller, faster to load, and easier for web browsers to display), 100 files containing the text of the book generated by optical character recognition processing (OCR), and a file with structural metadata (data that indicates which file is page 1, which file is page 2, etc.) that allows the software to display and return the pages. It is likely that more digital things could be part of this digital book—descriptive metadata such as a MARC or Dublin Core record, perhaps a PDF of the entire book, PDFs of each chapter, edited and encoded files for research use, and so on (see figure 11.1).

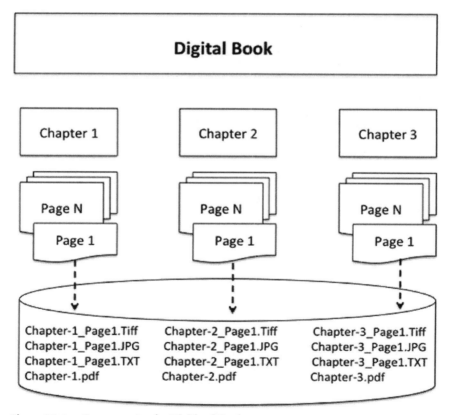

Figure 11.1. Components of a Digitized Book.

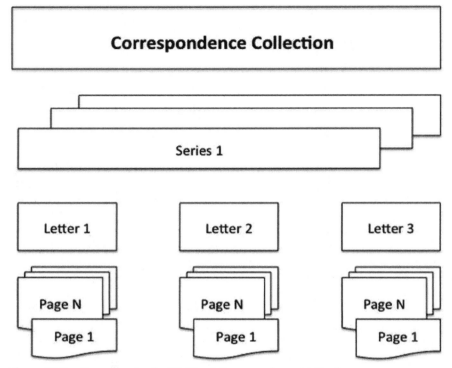

Figure 11.2. Components of a Digitized Correspondence Collection.

When working with digital materials, one must decide the level of the object. Many curators decide that the digital object is the intellectual object. In the case of a book, the digital object should include all of the files that contain the intellectual content of the physical book. A book is a relatively simple example. A curator has more decisions to make with more complex materials such as a collection of letters (see figure 11.2). As with the book, each page will have multiple files—and archival master file, a deliverable file, perhaps a text file either via transcription or OCR. The question is what is the level of the logical object: the letter, the folder, the series, or the entire set?

By their very nature, digital objects are inherently complex. As described above, digital objects comprise many individual files of different file types, each with a specific function. These individual files have relationships to other files. These relationships fall into several categories: master/derivative (is derived from), component (is part of), and sequence (order). These relationships define the structure of the digital object. In order to effectively manage the components of the object, the relationships between the files need to codified. Structural metadata is the means by which the relationships are documented.

Structural metadata can be thought of as a wrapper for the data. Structural metadata can provide information to allow navigation of the object. For a book-like object, structural metadata documents the internal features of a resource such as pages, chapters, indexes, full text, and so on. Structural metadata also describes the relationships between the various files based on use requirements: image A is the archival master; image B is a derivative of the archival master and is used for full-screen display; image C is derived from the archival master and is a thumbnail. Structural metadata can be captured and stored in several ways. Most archival institutions use automated scripts to generate their structural metadata. They may choose to store the information in a database or in a metadata standard developed specifically for structural metadata—the Metadata Encoding Transmission Standard (METS)[6] that was developed and is maintained by the Library of Congress. Structural metadata is important for access and delivery. Systems that deliver digital objects often use structural metadata for display and for user actions such as turning pages interviewing next object. Structural metadata is a vital component for curation. Documenting the components of an object is critical to ensuring its integrity. Without knowing all of the component pieces of the digital object, it is impossible for a curator to know that they are all present and accounted for. Structural metadata can help fortify the fragility of digital objects by creating and maintaining the context of the object.

CURATION CONCEPTS

Open Archival Information System (OAIS) Conceptual Model

The OAIS is a conceptual model, a representation of the relationships within the major components of an archival organization (see figure 11.3). The OAIS is an abstract model, is not an architecture, not a system, not a cookbook for digital preservation success, but a communications vehicle for complex constructs. The OAIS was developed by the Consultative Committee for Space Data Systems (CCSDS). In 1995, the CCSDS held its first international workshop proposing to develop the OAIS. Drafts were circulated in 1997 and 1999; it was published in the draft standard in 2000 and approved as an ISO standard (14721) in 2002. The CCSDS created a collaborative and inclusive environment when developing the standard and included librarians and archivists as well as scientific domain experts to develop this conceptual model. A revised version was published in 2012 and focuses on recommended practice. This conceptual model was designed to help organizations develop systems, both human and technical, to archive and preserve digital materials. An Archival Information System is "an organization of people and systems that has accepted responsibility to preserve information and make it available for a designated community" (CSSDS, 2012, p. 1.1).

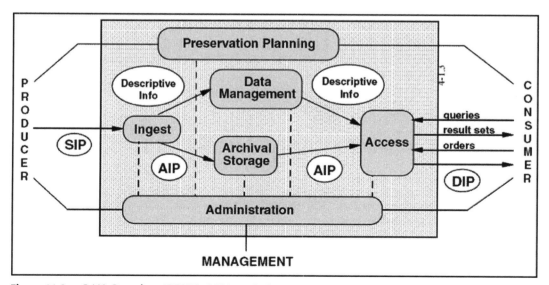

Figure 11.3.   OAIS Overview (CCSDS, 2003, p. 4-1).

An Archival Information System exists in an environment that includes producers of information and consumers of that information. The system itself sits as a mediator between these two sets of information users. The entire Archival Information System needs regular and ongoing management to be successful. An Archival Information System has a number of components to help it fulfill its mandatory responsibilities.

- *Ingest* is the process to accept information from data producers and successfully store the data.
- *Archival Storage* is described as technology, the long-term storage and maintenance of digital objects.
- *Access* describes the processes in which consumers of the data, that is, users, can discover, request, and receive information.
- *Data Management* is the process to maintain and manage data about the digital objects including descriptive and administrative metadata.
- *Preservation Planning* includes developing strategies for the Archival Information System and managing changes in technology, user communities and expectations, and funding.
- *Administration* involves the day-to-day operations of the archive.

An Archival Information System has a number of mandatory responsibilities. It must accept content from producers. It must obtain control over that content including, if necessary, intellectual property rights. The Archival Information System must be able to modify the files and make copies of the files as necessary, hence the requirement for control. The Archival Information System must ensure that the consumers of the information are able to independently understand the information; that is, that the user community can access and render the data. An Archival Information System needs to develop and follow procedures to preserve information and to make the preserved information available by the dissemination of authenticated copies.

The OAIS has had a significant impact on digital curation. It has provided framework for discussion and a vocabulary to define complex concepts so that curators, librarians, technologists, and the research community can communicate and collaborate to develop solutions.

CURATION STRATEGIES

Curating digital materials requires a strategy, a plan of action to accomplish the goals of the organization. Three primary strategies for curating digital materials have been developed: technology preservation, technology emulation, and data migration. Each of these strategies has strengths and weaknesses. Most organizations will have a primary strategy for the majority of their materials but may need to implement other strategies for specific applications or materials.

Technology Preservation

As discussed above, digital materials are bound to a specific technology; that is, digital files need specific software for rendering, manipulation, and/or use. This software requires specific operating systems and hardware in which to function. One strategy for preserving access to objects that require obsolete software and hardware is to preserve the original technology environment. This involves maintaining old computers, old storage devises, old operating systems, and old software. In many ways, this can appear to the reasonable strategy. Keeping the original technologies seems to be straightforward, and the information would be available in its original context. But in actuality, technology preservation is a difficult strategy to implement. Technologies become obsolete so quickly that the number of hardware and software configurations that must be maintained can grow rapidly. Finding resources, both human and technical, to maintain the machines and software, becomes increasingly difficult. Imagine a scenario in which an organization needed to maintain applications and data running in DOS, Windows 3, Windows XP, Windows NT, a variety of UNIX operating systems, and Mac OS from its earliest versions to the current release. Finding or developing staff with expertise in all of these technologies would be difficult.

Providing access to this material for researchers and the general public would also be a significant challenge. Few of these technologies could be made available via the Internet; researchers would need to physically visit the organization to be able to access the information. Not only would researchers need physical access to the computers, they would also need access to detailed documentation. For example, DOS, the Disk Operating System, was the ubiquitous operating system from 1974 through 1995. New generations of computer users have had no experience with MS-DOS and would be completely confused by a blinking cursor on a black screen. Providing detailed instructions on all of the DOS commands, explaining file and directory structure and navigation in order for users to find programs and data would be difficult; in addition, users would need an explanation of the use of function keys as well as the specific functions of each program. Scaling these types of instructions for each program in each operating system would be daunting. Technology preservation is an impractical large-scale solution.

Technology preservation has been referred to as the museum-style approach (UKOLN, 2006). Not surprisingly, this approach has been used by museums specifically for art installations where the look, feel, and functionality of the original, proprietary, and unique hardware are considered by the artist to be significant components of the art itself.

Technology Emulation

Technology emulation is the second of the three digital curation strategies. This strategy involves creating a technical environment that is able to execute existing software. This strategy was considered very controversial when it was introduced in the late 1990s. There were concerns about developing, implementing, and maintaining an emulation engine (Rothenberg, 1999; UKOLN, 2006). However as time has passed, a number of emulation engines have been developed and deployed very successfully.

The computer gaming community is one of the driving forces for the emulation strategy. This community has taken upon itself the task of preserving access to computer-based games. The problems of preserving access to computer-based games are many and complex, the sheer number of game platforms being first among them. Microsoft, Sony, Nintendo, Atari, and more have their own proprietary gaming systems that include hardware, peripherals, operating systems, and of course, games. The second significant problem with preserving access to computer-based games is the primary requirement to exactly replicate the look, feel, and interactive functionality of the original. Because of these issues, emulation is considered to be the best strategy for preserving games. Historically, there has been a close tie between gaming and computer science. One result of that close tie has been the development of a number of emulation engines specifically for gaming platforms. Gaming websites list dozens of emulators. As an example, the FantasyAnime[7] gaming website lists more than fifty emulators.

Data Migration

The data migration strategy acknowledges that technology will change and that data formats will become obsolete. To ensure that data will be accessible over time, the data migration strategy expects to convert data from the obsolete format into new formats. This is the prevalent strategy in place in most organizations with digital curation programs. This strategy requires organizations to be able to recognize format obsolescence and to have sufficient management control of their objects and adequate technical metadata to identify the objects that require migration.

Data migration strategy has two approaches: one is preemptive; that is, data is migrated when it is accepted into the repository; the second is a just-in-time strategy that expects plans to migrate data at time of format obsolescence. Using a preemptive data migration strategy means that data is migrated upon accession. This process is often referred to as format normalization. In general, an archivist would choose several optimal preservation formats. An archivist could expect to receive documents in a number of different formats including a variety of Microsoft Word formats (.doc, docx), plain text (.txt), rich text (.rtf), Apple compressed/encrypted format (.dmg), and many others. To implement the preemptive data migration strategy, the archive would convert all of these files to a more preservable format such as PDF/a. To follow best archival practice, this archive would save and commit to ongoing to bit-level maintenance of the original documents. But the normalized version would be the file that would be preserved for access.

Using the just-in-time data migration strategy means that the archiving organization needs to be aware of the file formats in its repository and must monitor for obsolescence of these formats. When the organization recognizes the need to migrate, the resources needed to plan and implement a migration project must be marshaled. These resources could include systems analysts, programmers, project managers, format experts, systems administrators, as well as the collection owners and other organizational stakeholders.

In order to migrate data, software to read the existing file, modify the data to the new format, and write the new file out must be created. In order to write such a program, the file format must be knowable; that is, there must be sufficient documentation for programmers to be able to deconstruct the current file, map the existing data into the new format, and validate the data transfer. This means that format becomes a significant indicator of preservability.

Data migration is a well-understood phenomenon. It is a regular practice of any organization that deals with information systems. Whenever a system is modified and requires new data elements, data must be migrated. New data formats, whether for long-term data preservation or for transactional systems, require migration. Many organizations choose the migration strategy because they have had successfully migrated data in other situations.

While data migration is the most common primary strategy, it is not without issues. Unlike the technology preservation and emulation strategies, data migration does not allow for the preservation of the original "look and feel" of the interface. For some applications, such as games, this is an unacceptable loss. However, for documents, photographs, and other types of materials, the content is more important than the experience. Again unlike technology preservation and emulation strategies, data migration can introduce error into the preservation process by actually changing the format of the data. Errors can be introduced during the mapping process either by misidentifying fields, by misunderstanding the meanings of fields, or by the inability to find an appropriate new format for one that is obsolete. Errors could be introduced through bugs in the programs that read, transform, and write the files.

DIGITAL REPOSITORY SYSTEMS

Repository systems have been developed to solve the problems managing the vast amount of information generated by digitizing and the collection of born digital materials including describing the materials, providing access to the materials, and preserving the materials. Applying curatorial functions such as file integrity checking, storage management, and so on can be centralized. Digital repository systems provide uniformity to user interfaces that help patrons remember functionality.

REPOSITORY FUNCTIONS

The OAIS provides a framework to discuss digital repository software functions. Using the language of OAIS functions—ingest, data management, archival storage, and access—the primary features and structure of a digital repository will be examined (see figure 11.3).

Ingest

Ingest is a set of functions to prepare to bring data into the repository system. The data comes to the repository as a Submission Information Package (SIP). This SIP comes from the data producer and contains the files that comprise the digital object and information such as the relationships between the files and some type of description of the logical object. The data provided by the producer is rarely sufficient for curating the data over time. The data must be enhanced. During ingest, the data is evaluated and processed. The descriptive, structural, and administrative information is transformed into metadata. Files are validated and verified.

Data Management

After the ingest process, the data and metadata are ready to be accepted into the repository system. The digital repository's data management functions provide services that store the files, generate indexes for searching and retrieving data, populate database tables, and create relationships between files and objects. The digital repository must ensure that it has sufficient administrative, structural, and descriptive metadata before it can fully commit to archiving the object. All of the component data files and elements are considered to be an Archival Information Package (AIP).

The data management functions extend beyond the initial deposit of objects. Data management is an ongoing process. Management reports, ongoing data integrity checks, referential integrity monitoring are ongoing data management functions that the repository can provide. The repository also needs ongoing maintenance in order to ensure its ongoing data management functions. The repository's database needs to be maintained. Schemas need to be maintained; software needs to be updated; indexes need to be regenerated; hardware must be maintained and upgraded as needed.

Archival Storage

Archival storage is more than just hardware; a repository needs to monitor hardware for capacity, use, and integrity. The repository needs to warn administrators when errors are detected when reading or writing files, when fixed city checks fail, and when a capacity threshold is passed. Repositories need to provide services for migrating data to new storage hardware that would include efficient and fast transfer, efficient use of storage, and integrity checks to the files as they are moved. The archival storage function maintains an inventory of files and objects in order to detect and report any issues. The archival storage function manages the multiple copies of files (that 3-2-1 rule discussed earlier).

Access

Providing access to data is one of the key aims of curation. OAIS considers access to be an important function of the repository. Accessing data in the repository requires one final data transformation; the Archival Information Package is changed into a Dissemination Information Package (DIP). The intellectual metadata that has been stored within the system needs to be searchable by end users. Objects and their contextual information need to be delivered to the end user's computer. Certainly one would expect the intellectual metadata to be delivered to the end user; but additional information is often needed. Many access systems need structural metadata in order to support the behavior users need, such as turning a page in a book-like object, picking between different sizes of a photograph, and choosing the best version of the document for reading. And rendering information may also be necessary; a system may want to present two options to a user for a JPEG2000 file—the fully interactive version that allows panning and zooming or a straight JPEG version. To provide access to digital content, a digital repository system needs an interface to format and render the results of queries.

POPULAR REPOSITORY SYSTEMS

Digital curators have a number of digital repository systems to choose from. These systems have been developed to meet a specific set of needs. Some are highly customizable and require development staff while others have fix functionality but are easy to install and run. The functions, features, flexibility, and sustainability need to be evaluated carefully to match the needs of the organization.

CONTENTdm is a product developed, maintained, and sold by OCLC. CONTENTdm can be implemented either in the OCLC cloud or in the organization's infrastructure. CONTENTdm supports a number of file formats and media types, uses commonly accepted metadata standards, and provides interfaces for both content administration and public access by patrons. The system is relatively flexible and allows libraries and archives some measure of customization.

Integrated library systems vendors also offer digital library management systems with repository functions. These can be standalone or fully integrated with the bibliographic application. There are advantages to using a single vendor, such as a long-term investment, relationship with the support staff, and an integrated interface for researchers and patrons. An example is the Rosetta from Ex Libris.

Some digital archives management systems have repository functions. Two of the best of these systems are ArchiveSpace[8] and Archivematica.[9] Both of these systems are open source, and both have multiple implementation options including on-site and hosted services. Both systems have good governance structures, active user communities, and significant install bases.

The term "Institutional Repository" refers to a category of repository system designed to manage the intellectual output of organizations. Libraries and archives have a number of software options for their institutional repository. DSpace[10] is the primary package in this niche. DSpace is an open source system supported by an active, committed, and well-funded foundation and user community. The software is nearly turnkey—easy to install and configure. The functionality is straightforward for patrons with traditional features such as search, display, and access; the staff functions allow for customized ingest and approval workflows.

The Integrated Rule-Oriented Data System (iRODS) and the Flexibile Extensible Digital Object Repository Architecture (Fedora) are two major digital repository systems that have a very different model from the others discussed thus far. These systems are not ready for use upon installation; each of these systems requires software development before they can be used. They require programmer support for implementation and ongoing support. Both are open source projects with robust governance organizations and a committed and active development community. They both scale well to support very large digital collections. iRODS is used by pharmaceutical and chemical companies, federal agencies with large research data sets, and academic institutions. Fedora is used by many large academic libraries, research centers, and national libraries to manage their digital contents. Fedora has a number of add-on applications to extend its functionality: Islandora provides a Drupal front and to a Fedora repository; Hydra provides workflows and user front ends to a Fedora repository.

Each repository system has a specific functional focus. Many digital archives find that a single repository system does not meet all of their needs. Organizations can have multiple instances of a single repository software package or have several different repository systems. For example, an organization may use a repository system such as CONENTdm for their digital photographic images, a system such as DSpace for their archival documents, and a system such as Fedora for complex digital content such as research data or digital video. Or an organization may have three separate instances of DSpace—one for their institutional repository, one for their archival documents, and one for research data.

SUMMARY

Cultural heritage preservation and digital curation share many concerns including long-term, safe storage of materials, and enhancing access via improved context. Digital materials can be more complex than their physical counterparts; while the book is a single object, a digital book may have hundreds of individual files that need to be understood in a sequence. The context of digital objects includes not only its intellectual meaning, but also its structure and its technical environment. Digital objects are dependent on technology; they require a specific technology in which to be rendered in order to be accessed and understood. Technology becomes obsolete on a relatively fast cycle; digital curators need to monitor technology and make changes accordingly to preserve access to their objects. Digital repositories are systems that manage digital content; a wide variety of systems are available to help organizations preserve their digital objects. Archivists, librarians, and researchers continue to study and enhance our understanding of digital curation; best practice will continue to evolve. Digital curators have a wide variety of resources available to them, including the Library of Congress in the digital correction center. Keeping current on new trends in digital curation is very important.

NOTES

1. https://www.diglib.org/.
2. http://www.digitalpreservation.gov/.
3. http://www.dcc.ac.uk/.
4. Lossy compression reduces the file size and complexity by permanently removing data.
5. https://www.archives.gov/preservation/products/products/aud-p3.html.
6. http://www.loc.gov/standards/mets/.
7. http://fantasyanime.com/emulators as of November 30, 2016.
8. http://www.archivesspace.org/.
9. https://www.archivematica.org/en/.
10. http://dspace.org/.

BIBLIOGRAPHY

Abrams, S. A. (2004). The Role of Format in Digital Preservation. *Vine*, *34*(2), 49–55.

Barile, S., and Saviano, M. (2014). From the Management of Cultural Heritage to the Governance of the Cultural Heritage System. *Cultural Heritage and Value Creation: Towards New Pathways*. Springer International Publishing, 71.

Consultative Committee for Space Data Systems (2003). *Reference Model for an Open Archival Information System (OAIS), Recommendation for Space Data System Standards, CCSDS 650.0-B-1*. Blue Book. Washington, DC. Found at http://public.ccsds.org/publications/archive/650x0b1.pdf.

Consultative Committee for Space Data Systems [CCSDS] (2012). *Reference Model for an Open Archival Information System (OAIS)*. Issue 2. Recommendation for Space Data System Standards (Magenta Book), CCSDS 650.0-M-2. Washington, DC: ISO 14721:2012. Found at http://public.ccsds.org/publications/archive/650x0m2.pdf.

Culture in Development [CID] (2016). What is Cultural Heritage. Found at http://www.cultureindevelopment.nl/cultural_heritage/what_is_cultural_heritage.

Federal Agencies Digitizing Guidelines Initiative [FADGI] (2014). Creating and Archiving Born Digital Video: Part I. Introduction. Found at http://www.digitizationguidelines.gov/guidelines/FADGI_BDV_p1_20141202.pdf

France, F. G. (2009). Best Practice and Standards in Environmental Preservation for Cultural Heritage Institutions: Goals, Knowledge, Gaps. *Advances in Paper Conservation Research*, 16. Found at https://www.loc.gov/preservation/resources/staffpubs/France%20Best%20Practices.pdf.

Hedstrom, M (1997). Digital Preservation: A Time Bomb for Digital Libraries. *Computers and the Humanities*, *31*(3), 189–202. doi:10.1023/A:1000676723815.

Krogh, Peter (2009). *The DAM Book: Digital Asset Management for Photographers*, 2nd Edition, p. 207. O'Reilly Media.

Osterberg, G. (2013, January). Update on the Twitter Archive at the Library of Congress. In *Library of Congress* (Vol. 1). Found at https://blogs.loc.gov/loc/2013/01/update-on-the-twitter-archive-at-the-library-of-congress/.

Research Libraries Group & OCLC (2002). *Trusted Digital Repositories: Attributes and Responsibilities: An RLG-OCLC Report*. Mountain View, CA: Research Libraries Group and OCLC. Retrieved from http://www.oclc.org/research/activities/past/rlg/trustedrep/repositories.pdf.

Rothenberg, J. (1999). *Avoiding Technological Quicksand: Finding a Viable Technical Foundation for Digital Preservation*. Washington, DC: Council on Library and Information Resources. ISBN 1-887334-63-7. Found at http://www.clir.org/pubs/reports/rothenberg/contents.html.

Rusbridge, C., Burnhill, P., Ross, S., Buneman, P., Giaretta, D., Lyon, L., and Atkinson, M. (2005, June). The Digital Curation Centre: A Vision for Digital Curation. In 2005 IEEE International Symposium on Mass Storage Systems and Technology (pp. 31–41). IEEE. Found at doi:10.1109/LGDI.2005.1612461.

Thibodeau, K. (2002). Overview of Technological Approaches to Digital Preservation and Challenges in Coming Years. *The State of Digital Preservation: An International Perspective*, 4–31. Found at http://www.clir.org/pubs/reports/reports/pub107/pub107.pdf.

UKOLN. (2006). *Good Practice Guide for Developers of Cultural Heritage Web Services.* Retrieved July 15, 2006 from http://www.ukoln.ac.uk/interop-focus/gpg/.

12

Cultural Heritage, Audiovisual Archives, and Digital Return

The Twenty-First-Century Mandate

Diane Thram

INTRODUCTION

Cultural heritage is commonly divided in two categories: tangible heritage and intangible heritage. Tangible heritage is physical objects made by humans that you can pick up, touch, and hold. This includes artifacts and art objects such as relics, sculptures, objects of adornment, jewelry, musical instruments, folk art carvings and paintings, regalia, traditional clothing and costumes, and indigenous technological tools such as scrapers and carving tools. Intangible heritage is the ephemeral manifestations of culture created in the moment through performance. It includes music, ritual practices, cultural ceremonies, and indigenous knowledge in general, such as healing practices. Historically, cultural heritage of both forms was passed down from generation to generation through oral transmission by learning directly from someone knowledgeable in the particular cultural art form, be it tangible or intangible. With the advent of the printing press, audio recording devices, and still and moving image cameras, it became possible not only to document and preserve cultural heritage but also to learn about cultural heritage—your own and foreign cultures—in ways other than aural transmission, such as looking at images, reading, and listening to recordings.

It is important to realize, however, as Hugh Tracey pointed out back in 1955, that the images, recordings, and what authors write about cultural art forms are only representations of the real thing. In an article titled "Recording African Music in the Field," Tracey wrote:

> When you are presented with a musical situation which has to be recorded you must first face the fact that any sound recording is only a partial statement of the whole event. The apparatus is mono-aural, and therefore can give only one sense of direction, nearness and farness, spatial, but not lateral. The microphone, therefore, must be focussed like a camera to select salient features of the music and to present them in such a way as to suggest a complete representation of the occasion. In other words, recording is an art form operating within the limitations of a frame which demands its own set of rules. The very success of a good recording is perhaps inclined to hide the fact that it is an art which conceals art. A recording, however good, is never the real thing, but a representation of the original. (1955: 7)

At the turn from the nineteenth century to the twentieth century, with the invention of the wax cylinder in the 1890s, a device capable of recording and replaying sound, the Vienna Phonogramm-Archiv (established 1899) and Berlin Phonogramm-Archiv (established 1900)[1] were founded in Europe as repositories for conservation and comparative study of collections of field recordings of the music and languages of the various cultures of the world. The impetus of the founders of these institutions, who sent recordists out on expeditions to collect recordings from throughout the world, was preservation of cultural heritage feared to be vanishing due to the forces of modernity and urbanization for future generations. When the recordings and images were deposited in these audiovisual archives, comparative, "armchair" study of them was undertaken by linguists, ethnologists, and comparative musicologists of the time who were seeking to determine language types and music types and create classification systems for the various cultural forms being documented. This was in accordance with the "collect and classify" paradigm of that era.

With these two early archives setting the example, deposit of field recordings in archives for preservation and further study was standard practice among music scholars in the early to mid-1900s, as comparative musicology developed and later on, in 1955, officially took ethnomusicology as the name for the discipline. This is evidenced by the fact that George Herzog (1901–1983)[2] established what was to become the Archives of Traditional Music (ATM) at Indiana University in 1948, when he joined the faculty there as professor of anthropology. Herzog's collection of his own wax cylinder field recordings and others he brought from Germany to the United States comprised the archive's initial holdings (Reed 1993: 70–71). The pioneering work of Hugh Tracey (1903–1977), who from the late 1920s to early 1970s amassed and disseminated one of the most significant African music collections consisting of an estimated 12,000 audio recordings from throughout sub-Saharan Africa, was in tandem with the "collect and classify" paradigm described above. Although Tracey did not have a university degree or post at a university, a Nuffield Foundation grant matched with funds donated from the South African mining industry gave him the means to establish the International Library of African Music (ILAM) in Roodeport, South Africa, in 1954 as an independent research institute and repository for his field recordings. His vision was to also archive the recordings of other researchers in order to document and create regionally specific educational materials for the music of the entire continent.[3]

In a letter to the Rockefeller Foundation in 1958, Hugh Tracey stated the purpose of his work as follows:

> to circulate recordings of the best and most representative items of contemporary African music for immediate use in radio programmes and in industrial or municipal localities where facilities exist for transmission, thus enabling a large proportion of the African community to experience the music of their own race, of which they would otherwise be almost totally ignorant, living as they do in small circumscribed communities.[4]

After extensive research of Hugh Tracey's documents and publications for his PhD thesis, Noel Lobley concludes of Tracey's intentions for his recordings:

> As well as intending to archive and preserve styles of music, his recordings were meant to remain alive and useful, being reflective of a living and evolving art form . . . In 1966 the *New York Times* reported how keen Tracey had been to stress that he was interested in the continuity and vitality of African musical expression, and not merely in the preservation of a receding or decaying form. (2010: 110–111)

> Tracey ultimately wanted his musical examples to be used as the basic data for textbooks to help ensure the future transmission of indigenous music, but in the short term he wanted his records to be used, firstly by African audiences, and secondarily by world audiences. (2010: 220)

Tracey was appalled that the schools managed by colonial governments and Christian mission stations throughout sub-Saharan Africa were teaching only European music to their African pupils and often forbade performance on African instruments, the singing of African songs, and African dancing. Because of this he saw an urgent need to develop material for teaching African music in the schools of Africa as a method to assure its retention and continued performance by future generations (*cf* Thram 2010, 2015).

In the foregoing I have shown that Hugh Tracey's vision for his work at the International Library of African Music, his independent research center and archive, always had sustainability of African musical heritage at its core. In what follows I use the International Library of African Music (ILAM) as a case study for music archive practice that promotes music sustainability, after a brief discussion of paradigm shifts and present-day issues faced by music archives.

Twentieth-Century Paradigm Shift

At the height of Hugh Tracey's career in the mid-twentieth century, the "collect and classify" paradigm of comparative musicology was transforming with the realization that extended field research was required to understand cultural forms. This was concomitant with the emergence of anthropology and ethnomusicology as disciplines whose practitioners conducted in-depth, situated field research in particular cultures as their prime methodology. Although many ethnomusicologists continued to archive their field recording collections in established archives, the practice has waned as the twentieth-century research methodology of fieldwork with extended residence/presence of the researcher in the culture being researched has softened and at the same time it has become more common for researchers to expect to create recordings for their own research purposes only and no longer feel any ethical responsibility to deposit them in established archives. This suggests a need for standards for research methodology in ethnomusicology to be established that reflect twenty-first-century conditions for researchers and the researched and that consider the implications of this shift for disciplinary ethics (*cf* Topp-Fargion 2009, 2012).[5]

In addition, with the turn of the twentieth century to the twenty-first century, postmodern discourse has brought broad and nuanced meanings to the word archive(s) with scholars using it as a metaphor for larger social phenomena in publications such as the collection *Refiguring the Archive* (2002). In what follows I do not engage with that literature, but rather focus on actual practices in sound/audiovisual archives (hereafter referred to as music archives) as on-the-ground places that maintain collections of audio and audiovisual recordings, photographic images, and musical instruments that constitute cultural heritage in need of conservation, dissemination, and repatriation (*cf* Thram 2014). Nor do I engage in the postmodern critique of ILAM's founder, Hugh Tracey; suffice it to say that his career spanned the colonial era and, as a man of his time, he displayed attitudes prevalent in colonial discourse in his publications.[6] That the recordings and documentation Tracey created had value while he was actively creating them in the mid-twentieth century and that they hold great value for music sustainability now among the descendants of the many musicians of varied African cultural origins he recorded is unquestioned, regardless of the colonial, evolutionary paradigm under which he worked and the ideology of the time in which he lived. Regarding the colonial legacy and the postmodern critique of it, I argue that repatriation of historic recordings such as the Hugh Tracey Collection and numerous others preserved in archives throughout the world provides an opportunity for ethnomusicology as a discipline and music archives that house historic collections of field recordings to begin, in a concrete way, to redress ethnomusicology's colonial legacy and address the postmodern critique of the same.

Issues in Twenty-First-Century Archival Practice

The role of audiovisual archives in the twenty-first century has been rapidly transforming due to present day realities of analog to digital conversion and preservation in digital format that offer new and varied options for dissemination. However, although digital conversion may ensure preservation of historic recordings, it does not ensure the sustainability of the music culture preserved on those recordings. It is possible that the music heritage will be preserved for posterity (provided the digital carriers withstand the test of time) and true that it is more easily accessible to all in digital format, most often via the Internet. But the reality of low bandwidth and sparse Internet accessibility for many in the southern hemisphere dictates that to achieve continuity and retention of the music heritage, dissemination needs to take place in ways other than the Internet as well.

Present day realities of the digital age that endanger the sustainability of cultural heritage and therefore musical traditions throughout the world (such as mass migration, dislocation, and effects of global popular culture on younger generations) make it urgent for archives to return historic recordings directly to their communities of origin for the sake of revitalization, renewal, and sustainability of the music traditions that are now, due to deterioration of their original analog carriers, preserved in digital format. Although the costs are often prohibitive, the possibilities for dissemination afforded by digital carriers have given rise to the twenty-first-century mandate for music archives to find workable ways to carry out digital return of their holdings to their communities of origin.

I support Topp-Fargion's argument that, since ethnomusicologists are largely responsible for creating the many collections of music heritage recordings preserved in music archives, ethnomusicology as a discipline needs to adopt a commitment to a broad range of activities that assure the sustainability of music heritage grounded in Titon's argument that the discipline needs to treat music as a sustainable cultural resource that we have the capacity to maintain (see Titon 2009 and http://sustainablemusic.blogspot.com). Topp-Fargion calls for ethnomusicologists and music archives to adopt an expanded understanding of preservation and undertake concomitant activities to promote music sustainability as follows:

> I suggest a much broader definition of preservation, namely, to describe it as the facilitation of the continuation of tradition. Continuation is facilitated through a range of activities including: research—fieldwork to gather data and knowledge; education—teaching in schools and universities; dissemination—publication, media journalism, books, internet, exhibitions; and archiving—engaging in all of the above and ensuring it does not all disappear and that it is available to all. These activities create an environment in which performance of tradition can continue to thrive. Such an holistic preservation, I argue, equates with Titon's sustainable music, sustainable carrying the definition "capable of being maintained." Through our activities as ethnomusicologists (in researching, teaching, publishing and archiving), we are all engaged in holistic preservation. We are all engaged, therefore, theoretically at least, in promoting a sustainable music. (2012: 76)

As shown in the earlier discussion of Hugh Tracey's intentions for his recordings, a precedent to this broader definition of preservation exists in Tracey's vision for the International Library of African Music in that he carried out exactly the type of activities advocated by Topp-Fargion. As I have pointed out elsewhere (2010), Tracey's seminal achievements—research, documentation, preservation, dissemination (via audio, *Sound of Africa* and *Music of Africa* LP Series and print publications, *African Music*—ILAM's scholarly journal devoted to research on African music founded by Tracey in 1954); and community outreach and education—became and remain to this day the mission of the International Library of African Music. Tracey's work has served as a model for dissemination of field recordings since the release of his monumental *Sound of Africa Series* consisting of 210 LPs produced from his field recordings between 1958 and 1962, with eight LPs of his son Andrew Tracey's field recordings added later for a total of 218 LPs.[7] Intended for use by researchers and educators, it remains the largest collection of field recordings of African music ever published. The *SOA Series* was given to sixty university libraries in 1962, under the auspices of the Ford Foundation grant that supported its creation, publication, and dissemination.

As Hugh Tracey's accomplishments and as ILAM projects in research, publication, outreach, and education over the past decade (2007–2016) show, archives with collections of music heritage recordings are well positioned to promote music sustainability through creation of access to and dissemination of their holdings, especially to the cultures from which they originated where the heritage may be endangered. With digital conversion and various options for dissemination via the Internet having become the status quo, a challenge remains for music archives to bridge the digital divide through creative outreach, education, and repatriation (digital return) initiatives that make their collections accessible, not only to the world at large through the Internet, but also through return directly to the communities where the recordings were created. Unfortunately source communities are often located in underdeveloped rural settings where there is no Internet access; or if there is access, the bandwidth is insufficient to allow download of large audio and/or video files. What's more, for efforts in music sustainability to be effective, it is critical that repatriation projects find ways to engage community youth with the recordings of their music heritage being returned because far too often younger generations no longer know their music heritage due to rapid change in lifeways, worldviews, and mass media proliferation, to name a few reasons.

Issues in Music Archives Management

An urgent issue facing archives in general, and a music heritage archive and research institute such as ILAM in particular, is how to generate income and external grant funding without compromising professional ethics in regard to archival practice. Professional ethics pertain to all areas of an archive's operations, from the basic functions of accessioning collections to the securing of funds—whether institutional, external grants, or from sales—for ongoing operations, for research projects, for outreach and education projects and for repatriation projects, all crucial to the functions of archives in the twenty-first century.

The perpetual issue faced by ILAM and most archives, depending on how much government and/or institutional support they are given, is how to source and maintain adequate funding for operating expenses. ILAM generates some income from its publications and ILAM Studio Services, which is managed by ILAM's qualified sound engineer, who provides analog to digital conversion and CD and DVD replication services to the general public for set fees. This income doesn't begin to cover ongoing needs for basic operations such as accession and preservation of additional collections being deposited, dissemination via online access and costs of producing audio, audiovisual, and print publications. Research projects and research publications, outreach, and education projects, and projects to carry out repatriation/digital return to source communities are, in ILAM's case, simply not possible without external funding. In general, institutional support from national governments and/or universities that house archives is never enough. Project funding most often has to be sourced from external sources such as government funding agencies and independent foundations. Writing project proposals to secure outside funding is necessary and part of the archive director's responsibilities.

Cataloguing and digitizing the Hugh Tracey audio, film, and photo collections and cataloguing and preservation of the Tracey African musical instrument collection was accomplished through fund-raising from government, corporate, and international sources including the National Research Foundation (NRF), the National Heritage Council, the Rand Merchant Bank Expressions Programme, the Mellon Foundation, and the US Ambassador's Fund for Cultural Preservation. After five years of committed effort (2007–2011), the Hugh Tracey Collection, Andrew Tracey Collection, and Dave Dargie Collection were catalogued, digitized, and made accessible via the Internet from the ILAM website online catalogue. The processing of these collections and purchase of an expandable storage server capable of storing the digital files created was made possible with funding from the Andrew Mellon Foundation. That storage server, purchased in 2008, was obsolete and unstable by 2015. Storage servers are a substantial ongoing expense for audiovisual archives. The necessary infrastructure for digital conversion and preservation is costly and in need of frequent updating, which causes an additional fund-raising issue for archive managers.[8]

With online access to the Hugh Tracey Collection accomplished late in 2008, the question arose, what are the ethical implications of providing Internet access globally, while countless descendants of the musicians Hugh Tracey recorded not only do not have Internet access, they often have no idea the recordings of their music heritage even exist? With this came the realization that, now that we have the Collection catalogued and know what we have, it's time to give it back to descendants of the musicians and the communities the recordings came from. But what is the best way to do this? And what are the ethical considerations? ILAM was already involved in reproduction and sale of digital heritage via its CD series, sale of digital audio files and images through Internet vendors, and was aiming to repatriate recordings in whatever ways possible. Guidelines for this work were needed. With sponsorship from the University of Michigan Ann Arbor African Studies Center, a Digital Heritage Workshop was held at ILAM in December 2008. Workshop participants from heritage institutions in South Africa, Ghana, and the United States, in a three-day workshop, produced Guidelines for Reproduction and Sale of Digital Heritage and Guidelines for Repatriation of Digital Heritage. These guidelines, in very succinct, accessible language, were published in the 2009 issue of ILAM's journal *African Music* 9(3), as an appendix in Thram 2015, and are available for download from the ILAM website www.ru.ac.za/ilam. In 2010, as director of ILAM, I presented both sets of guidelines at the annual conferences of the International Association of Sound and Audiovisual Archives (IASA) and the Society for Ethnomusicology (SEM).

Our aim at ILAM after completion of cataloguing, digitizing, and creation of online access to our holdings, was to disseminate and "give back" Tracey's audio recordings, still images and films through outreach and education projects that create materials designed to educate and inform about ILAM's legacy for African music while exposing the general public, and youth in particular, to their music heritage. This work began in 2010 with two projects for this purpose, the "ILAM Music Heritage Project SA" and the *For Future Generations—Hugh Tracey and the International Library of African Music* traveling exhibition, which has been moving biannually and installed at museums throughout South Africa. It has reached countless school groups and the public at large since its launch at the Origins Centre Museum at WITS University in October 2010.[9] The "ILAM Music Heritage Project, SA" was conceived as an attempt to fulfill Tracey's desire to publish textbooks from his field recordings and as a way to get the recordings out of the archive and into the hands of educators and the youth in the schools, where there remains to this day a serious lack of materials to teach African music. Under the auspices of the "ILAM Music Heritage Project, SA," ILAM published two music education textbooks,[10] each with a media disc loaded with many audio tracks of Tracey's recordings and several video clips to illustrate the lessons. Each of these unique textbooks is richly illustrated with photographs from his field excursions that form the bulk of ILAM's 8,000+ image photo collection. Digitization of the Hugh Tracey audio, photo, and film collections made creation of the traveling exhibition and the project textbooks possible. Concurrently, the ILAM oral history research project on South African jazz titled "ILAM-Red Location Music History Project," which ran from 2009–2013, has served as a model for engaged ethnomusicology and the ethic of reciprocity it embraces in that project data was returned to the community through creation of the *Generations of Jazz* permanent exhibition at the Red Location Museum and publication by ILAM of the exhibit catalogue that accompanies the exhibition (see Thram 2014).

Repatriation of ILAM's Historic Hugh Tracey Collection

Initially, the "ILAM Music Heritage Project, SA" was thought of as a method to repatriate Hugh Tracey's music heritage recordings through the schools. It then became clear that the music provided through the textbooks did not necessarily reach the cultures and communities from which it originated; thus the textbook project was actually a project in outreach and education, and strictly speaking did not accomplish repatriation. Return of Hugh Tracey's recordings to their counties of origin began in 2009. To date all of Hugh Tracey's Tanzania, Kenya, Uganda, Swaziland, Zambia, Zimbabwe, and Malawi field recordings have been digitally returned to universities and/or national archives in those countries. In Zimbabwe and Zambia, Shona recordings have been returned through a postdoctoral project that returned recordings to several universities and to communities of origin in 2016. Xhosa, Pedi, and Tswana recordings have been returned through two ethnomusicology MMUS thesis projects in South Africa and Botswana in 2015–2016. Tracey's Chopi xylophone recordings were returned to *timbila* composers and musicians in Mozambique through a PhD student from SOAS in 2015–2016.

The first opportunity to actually return Tracey recordings directly to several surviving musicians well up in their eighties, whom he recorded, and descendants of many others in source communities, came in July 2014 with support from the Abubillah Music Foundation and Singing Wells Project (www.singingwells.org), based in the United Kingdom and Tabu Osusa, founding Director of Ketebul Music, an NGO recording studio in Nairobi. It needs to be noted that returning recordings to source communities cannot happen without support and preliminary ground work to locate the communities and make contacts there. To view a brief YouTube video titled *Lost Songbooks* that gives a glimpse of how this project was executed go to https://www.youtube.com/watch?v=Gi8xeDrsQTs&feature=youtu.be.

ILAM's Pilot Project in Repatriation and Re-study of Hugh Tracey's Field Recordings was launched late July 2014 with return of Tracey's Wagogo recordings to the Chamwino Arts Centre during the annual Wagogo Music Festival in Chamwino, Tanzania. This was immediately followed with return of his Zanzibari recordings to the Dhow Countries Music Academy in Zanzibar at a Music Education Symposium 1–2 August 2014. Kipsigis and Luo recordings were returned in the Rift Valley and Lake Victoria regions of Kenya the first two weeks of August 2014, which was only possible due to funding and staff support from Abubillah Foundation who covered expenses and Ketebul Music who provided a videographer, sound engineer, and "fixers" (first language Kipsigis and Luo speakers who made local contacts, set up village visits, and served as translators) for each location.

Follow-up return of the Zanzibari recordings to descendants of musicians and a local taraab orchestra took place in June 2015 when I had the opportunity to do the fieldwork several days before and after a conference I attended at the Dhow Countries Music Academy. Tracey's recordings made in 1950 and 1952 in Mombasa and Malindi were returned in February 2016 to descendants of the musicians he recorded and the island's only surviving taarab orchestra in a second collaboration with Ketebul Music possible due a modest research grant from the International Association of Sound and Audiovisual Archives (IASA).

In May 2016, Tracey's recordings made in Port Herald (now Nsanje), Salima, Kasungu, and Chikwakwa Districts in Malawi on three tours in 1949, 1950, and 1958 were returned to the Malawi National Archive and to musicians' descendants in the villages where the recordings were made in southern and central Malawi, at ILAM's expense. This return was made possible by Malawian ethnomusicologist Dr. Moya Malamusi, who facilitated the entire project and served as my translator everywhere we went. Most recently, in early November 2016 Andrew Tracey and I returned copies of Hugh Tracey's recordings of Zulu music, photographs, and films made at various times between 1939 and 1972 in South Africa's former Zululand, now Natal Province. Digital copies of recordings of Shembe Church hymns and images were returned to Shembe Church leaders (including a documentary film of the Shembe annual pilgrimage to their sacred mountain made by Hugh Tracey in the 1950s). Tracey's Zulu recordings, images, and films were given to prominent Zulu leader, Prince Mangosuthu Buthelezi (b. 1928, eighty-eight years old at the time of this event), son of Princess Constance Magogo KaDinuzulu, whose Zulu *Ugubu* mouth bow and vocal music recorded by Tracey in 1972 was released as the last album [MOA 37] in Tracey's *Music of Africa Series*. The return included Tracey's 1939 film of Zulu village life and recordings of Prince Buthelezi himself singing on some of Tracey's Zulu recordings made in 1955 in Chief Mhlolutini's kraal when he was twenty-eight years old. At the same event, all of this Zulu material was returned to the present Chief Mhlolutini, a grandson of the Chief Mhlolutini with whom Hugh Tracey worked.

CONCLUSION

From the above account of the ways ILAM has managed to give back digital copies of Hugh Tracey's field recordings, and in some cases also images and films, it may seem like substantial in-roads have been made. However, the work done so far has returned only a small portion of his many recordings. Return to source communities remains to be done in Kenya, Malawi, Mozambique, Namibia, Rwanda, South Africa, Tanzania, Uganda, Zimbabwe, and Zambia.

Lessons learned from ILAM's Pilot Project in re-study and return of Hugh Tracey recordings include: return of the recordings to musicians Tracey recorded still alive, to descendants of musicians he recorded, schools, and culture organizations in the various communities where contact made was deeply appreciated; the cost of doing this work is prohibitive and impossible for ILAM without external funding; not enough time was available for re-study of the original field recordings, although corrections to Tracey's metadata were discovered and new metadata was collected; not anticipating the lack of electricity in the rural villages and/or portable playback devices and bringing the music in CD format was a problem. To correct this, return of recordings in Malawi (May 2016) was also on USB memory sticks with inexpensive radios with rechargeable batteries and USB ports given to recipients without CD players, to assure they could listen to the music. CDs were still given to those who had access to CD players. In general, CD technology is being replaced by listening from cell phones and MP3s played from portable devices.

Of great concern is the lack of a method to gauge how effective return of the recordings is in getting the music to community youth in order to expose them to it and stimulate interest in their music heritage, much less assure its continued performance. It is encouraging that there is a groundswell of interest in promotion of music sustainability and that in some quarters funding is being secured for this work. In 2017 ILAM will be collaborating with ethnomusicologist Andrea Emberly on her project, "Connecting culture and childhood: implications of the repatriation of archival recordings for children and young people," funded by the Canadian Social Science and Humanities Research Council (SSHRC) for return of John Blacking field recordings of Venda music in South Africa dating from the late 1950s, some of which are archived at ILAM. This project seeks to determine ways to effectively engage the youth in their music heritage.

Clearly, there is an ethical imperative for digital return of collections of field recordings to their communities of origin to continue for the sake of sustainability of the music heritage. On a very immediate level for ILAM, because Hugh Tracey realized the importance of his recordings for future generations of Africans, and to honor his legacy, it is imperative that ILAM makes every effort to get his recordings OUT of the archive and into the hands of those future generations who now, in the twenty-first century, often have little contact with or knowledge of the music of their forebearers. I advocate for an ethic of reciprocity (*cf* A. Fox 2013) to be established among ethnomusicologists carrying out field research and among music archives preserving collections of field recordings that extend not only to researchers responsibly depositing their field recordings in established archives for posterity and research purposes, but also to giving them back to researched communities at the time the research is being done. The work of returning historic collections to their source communities is daunting. Discovering ways to do it effectively is the urgent challenge.

NOTES

1. For a more detailed account of the origins and work of the Vienna and Berlin Phonogramm Archivs and their relationship to comparative musicology, see D. Christensen, 1991; Thram, 2014 and the Vienna and Berlin Phonogram-Archiv websites.

2. George Herzog studied comparative musicology at the Berlin Phonogram-Archiv and emigrated to the United States to study anthropology at Columbia University under Franz Boas. See D. Reed, 1993, for a detailed account of Herzog's career and its importance to professionalization of music archiving and ethnomusicology.

3. In the mid-1960s Tracey formulated his "Codification and Textbook Project," an ambitious design for the recording, classification, transcription, and publication of teaching materials of indigenous music from the entire African continent, to be accomplished over a ten-year period. He traveled to various universities in Africa in 1966 and began to garner support for the project. He envisioned research centers at cooperating universities throughout the continent from which teams of trained researchers would fan out and record indigenous forms to then classify and analyze. The International Library of African Music was to be the clearing house, repository, and publisher of outcomes of the project to include textbooks specific to each region. In 1969 he published, with Gerhard Kubik and Andrew Tracey, an extensive guide to the project in which he proposed two series of recordings, a limited edition for scientific study and educational purposes and the other for general release featuring selections of outstanding musical merit. It was a major disappointment to Tracey that this project never came to fruition because of the apartheid regime in South Africa, which meant potential funding from foreign foundations did not materialize due to sanctions against South Africa.

4. Letter from Hugh Tracey to Robert W. July, Assistant Director, the Rockefeller Foundation, New York, 1 October 1958.

5. For discussions of ethical issues in audio-visual archives practice, repatriation of field recording collections, and how these issues extend to applied (advocacy and/or engaged) ethnomusicology and

practice in the discipline in general see the collections, *Music Archiving in the World* (2002) and *Archives for the Future* (2004) and the following: G. Averill 2003; R. Dirkson 2012; A. Fox 2013; K. Harrison 2012; R. Lancefield 1993, 1998; S. Mills, 1996; A. Seeger 1996, 2008; D. Thram 2010, 2011, 2014, 2015; J. Titon 2009; J. Topp-Fargion 2009, 2012 to name a few.

6. For a postmodern analysis of Tracey's written traces and publications see P. Coetzee, 2014.

7. In 1958, Tracey began production of his *Sound of Africa* LP Series, compiled from his field recordings. By 1960 the first 100 LPs of the series were published. Tracey then undertook a lecture tour of twenty universities in the United States and approached the Ford Foundation for funding to continue with the project. He was initially granted funds to cover the cost of producing the next 100 LPs of the *Sound of Africa* Series. A second Ford Foundation grant allowed him to give the full set of 210 LPs to sixty selected universities throughout the world.

8. Additional holdings digitized and catalogued at ILAM after completion of the Hugh Tracey Collection include John Blacking's recordings of Venda music made while affiliated at ILAM in the 1950s; the Ian Huntley Collection of Cape Town jazz recordings and photographs from the late 1960s; Jaco Kruger Collection of Venda recordings from 1980s–1990s; and Michael Drewett Collection of South African music censorship interview recordings from 1990s–2000s. Collections presently being processed include the Singing Wells East Africa Projects Collection of still images, interview and performance videos from 2011–present; ILAM-Red Location Music History Project still images, interview, and performances videos from 2009–present; Keiskammahoek Xhosa Music and Community Engagement Project still images, interview, and performance videos from 2013–present; the Erich Bigalake Collection and the Derek Worman Collection. All ILAM collections are catalogued and digitized, for purposes of preservation and access, in accord with standards set by the International Association of Sound and Audiovisual Archives (IASA).

9. For a more in-depth description and images of the *For Future Generations* traveling exhibition see the exhibition catalogue of the same title, D. Thram, ed. 2010, Thram 2014, 2015, and the ILAM website www.ru.ac.za/ilam.

10. For a more in-depth description of the "ILAM Music Heritage Project, SA" and the two textbooks published through it—*Understanding African Music* (2012) and *Listen and Learn—Music Made Easy* (2013)—see Thram 2014, 2015; Thram and Carver 2011; and the ILAM website www.ru.1ac.za/ilam.

BIBLIOGRAPHY

Averill, Gage. "Ethnomusicologists as Public Intellectuals: Engaged Ethnomusicology in the University." *Folklore Forum* 34 (2003): 49–59.

Berlin, Gabriele and Artur Simon, eds. *Music Archiving in the World.* Berlin: Verlag für Wissenshaft und Bildung, 2002.

Carver, Mandy. *Understanding African Music*, edited by Diane Thram. Grahamstown: International Library of African Music, 2012.

Christensen, Dieter. "Erich M. von Hornbostel, Carl Stumpf, and the Institutionalization of Comparative Musicology." In *Comparative Musicology and the Anthropology of Music*, Bruno Nettl and Philip Bohlman, eds. Chicago: University of Chicago Press, 1991. 201–209.

Coetzee, Paulette. Performing Whiteness; Representing Otherness: Hugh Tracey and African Music. PhD dissertation. Rhodes University, 2014.

Digital Heritage Workshop Participants. "Guidelines for Reproduction and Sale of Digital Heritage" and "Guidelines for Repatriation of Digital Heritage." Digital Heritage Workshop, International Library of African Music, December 2008. *African Music* 9 no. 3 (2009): 179–81.

Dirksen, Rebecca. "Reconsidering Theory and Practice in Ethnomusicology: Applying, Advocating, and Engaging Beyond Academia." *Ethnomusicology Review* 17. (2012) http://ethnomusicologyreview.ucla.edu.

Fox, Aaron A. "Repatriation as Reanimation through Reciprocity." In *The Cambridge History of World Music*, Philip Bohlman, ed. Cambridge: Cambridge University Press, 2013: 522–554.

Grant, Catherine. "Rethinking Safeguarding: Objections and Responses to Protecting and Promoting Endangered Musical Heritage." *Ethnomusicology Forum* 21, no. 1 (2012): 31–51.

Hamilton, Carolyn, V. Harris, M. Pickover, G. Reid, R. Saleh, and J. Taylor, eds. *Refiguring the Archive*. Cape Town: David Philip, 2002.

Harrison, Klisala. "Epistemologies of Applied Ethnomusicology." *Ethnomusicology* 36 (2012): 505–529.

Lancefield, Robert C. "'Musical Traces' Retraceable Paths: The Repatriation of Recorded Sound." *Journal of Folklore Research* 35, no.1 (1998): 47–68.

———. On the Repatriation of Recorded Sound from Ethnomusicological Archives. MA thesis. Wesleyan University, 1993.

Lobley, Noel. The Social Biography of Ethnomusicological Field Recordings: Eliciting Responses to Hugh Tracey's *The Sound of Africa* Series. DPhil. dissertation. Oxford University, 2010.

McConnachie, Boudina. *Listen and Learn: Music Made Easy*, edited by Diane Thram. Grahamstown: International Library of African Music, 2013.

Mills, Sherylle. "Indigenous Music and the Law: An Analysis of National and International Legislation." *Yearbook for Traditional Music* 28 (1996): 57–86.

Reed, Daniel. "The Innovator and the Primitives: George Herzog in Historical Perspective." *Folklore Forum* 26 (1993): 69–92.

Seeger, Anthony. "Theories Forged in the Crucible of Action. The Joys, Dangers, and Potentials of Advocacy and Fieldwork." In *Shadows in the Field: New Perspectives for Fieldwork in Ethnomusicology*, Gregory Barz and Timothy J. Cooley, eds. Oxford: Oxford University Press, 2008. 271–288.

———. "Ethnomusicologists, Archives, Professional Organizations, and the Shifting Ethics of Intellectual Property." *Yearbook for Traditional Music* 28 (1996): 87–105.

Seeger, Anthony and Shubha Chaudhuri, eds. *Archives for the Future: Global Perspectives on Audiovisual Archives in the 21st Century*. Calcutta: Seagull Books, 2004.

Thram, Diane. "Performing the Archive: Repatriation of Digital Heritage and the ILAM Music Heritage Project SA." In *African Musics in Context: Institutions, Culture, Identity*, T. Solomon, ed. Kampala, Uganda: Fountain Publishers, 2015. 67–85.

———. "The Legacy of Music Archives in Historical Ethnomusicology: A Model for Engaged Ethnomusicology." In *Theory and Method in Historical Ethnomusicology*, D. Hebert and J. McCollum, eds. Lanham, MD: Rowman & Littlefield, 2014. 283–310.

Thram, Diane and Mandy Carver. "African Music for Schools: Repatriating ILAM Field Recordings through Music Education Textbooks." In *Readings in Ethnomusicology: a Collection of Papers Presented at Ethnomusicology Symposium*. Dar es Salaam: University of Dar es Salaam, 2011. 87–91.

Thram, Diane, ed. *For Future Generations Hugh Tracey and the International Library of African Music*. Grahamstown: International Library of African Music, 2010.

Titon, Jeff Todd. "Music and Sustainability: An Ecological Viewpoint." *The World of Music* 51, no. 1 (2009): 119–137.

———. http://sustainablemusic.blogspot.co.uk (last accessed 12 December 2016).

Topp-Fargion, Janet. "Connecting with Communities: Building Sustainable Models for Audiovisual Archiving into the Future." In *Ethnomusicology in East Africa: Perspectives from Uganda and Beyond*, Sylvia Nannyonga-Tamusuza and Thomas Solomon, eds. Kampala, Uganda: Fountain Publishers, 2012. 49–59.

———. "'For My Own Research Purposes': Examining Ethnomusicology Field Methods for a Sustainable Music." *World of Music* 51 no.1 (2009): 75–93.

Tracey, Hugh. "Recording African Music in the Field." *African Music* 1, no. 2 (1955): 6–11.

———. *African Music Codification and Textbook Project*. [with G. Kubik and A. Tracey]. Roodeport, South Africa: International Library of African Music, 1969.

———. *Catalogue The Sound of Africa Series. Vol. 1*. Roodeport: International Library of African Music, 1973.

13

Toward Community Engaged Archiving

Building a Digi-Rasquache Archives

Janet Ceja Alcalá and Desiree Alaniz

There has been a "community turn" in archival studies. The discourse generally regards community archives as unconventional documentation projects that encompass collecting and preserving records of marginalized community experience. The novelty is that archivists recognize community authority as a principle to be reckoned with, and thus seek to understand how and why communities exercise control over their records (Bastian 2009, Stevens, Flinn et al. 2010, Cook 2013, Sheffield 2017). Traditionally, mainstream heritage organizations—archives, libraries, and museums—have held the authority to select, preserve, and provide access to cultural heritage resources. Community archives invert this power dynamic by documenting experience at a communal level. Community authority can range from a group working autonomously and retaining physical control over their material collections, or donating them to a cultural heritage organization and formally taking part in decision-making processes that inform how the group is represented. Community archives also are the result of legacy collection development practices that have failed to systematically and collaboratively examine gaps in the historical record (Ham 1975, 1981, Samuels 1986, Erickson 1991, Caswell 2014). Therefore, community archives challenge the exclusions and misrepresentations of marginalized groups by addressing those unacknowledged gaps.

In this chapter, we build on community archives discourse by proposing that the contributions of mainstream organizations to community archiving are within a spectrum of practice and engagement that must be further dimensionalized. We refer to these contributions as *community engaged archiving* and we define it as those who consciously work alongside and partner with communities to give voice to their collections, whether the collections are in heritage organizations or in autonomous environments. We take inspiration from community engaged scholarship, where academic expertise is applied to a community setting through partnerships that garner reciprocity among scholars and those outside of the academy. Much like the scholarship of engagement, we view community engaged archiving situated on a continuum that can move from low to high activity depending on the type of interaction, need, and comfort level that community members have with archivists (figure 13.1).

To illustrate community engaged archiving, we present a digital archives project titled *Recuerdos de Antes y Ahora* (Memories of Before and Now) (http://recuerdos.omeka.net). The project was started by the first author with the goal of documenting and engaging a diasporic community through a website built in Omeka.net. The project is an experiment in archiving

More intensive

Complete collaboration in all aspects

Example: Los Angeles Latino Arts Survey Project conducted by the UCLA Chicano Studies Research Center, http://www.chicano.ucla.edu/research/csrc-latino-art-survey

Embeddedness; two-way communication

Example: Student service-learning project at Pratt Institute led by Professor Anthony Cocciolo on digitizing audiovisual collections at the Lesbian Herstory Archives, http://www.lesbianherstoryarchives.org/digital.html

Medium

Access; one-way communication

Example: Creating finding aids, minimal involvement from community in describing and arranging collections.

Less intensive

Figure 13.1.   Community engaged archiving continuum can range from low to high activity.

done *a lo rasquache*, what Tomas Ybarra-Frausto describes as those *movidas* or "coping strategies you use to gain time, to make options, and to retain hope" when a person's material realities are far too tangled up in survival (Ybarra-Frausto 1991). This stitching together of possibilities means that rasquache work is done with great creativity and skill to make do with what is at hand. The outcomes of such labor also lend themselves to a rasquache aesthetic that favors hybridity over purist forms. Recuerdos de Antes y Ahora is fueled by this do-it-yourself philosophy.

We begin by discussing how this project grew from the findings and records gathered by the first author while investigating a religious fiesta in a small town in Mexico and the sociocultural practices that preserve the fiesta in the absence of a formal archives. We then go on to describe how the objectives for engagement of Recuerdos de Antes y Ahora are aligned with Omeka.net's built-in functionalities. Finally, we propose that the community's archives is a distributed community of records with important implications for other community-engaged archiving projects.

DOCUMENTING IDENTITY IN LA PLAZA DEL LIMÓN

Every year, the residents of La Plaza del Limón, an agricultural town in Michoacán, Mexico, and members of the town's diaspora in the United States, come together to celebrate Our Lady of Guadalupe's religious fiesta for nine days. Our Lady of Guadalupe is a Marian figure who embodies the syncretism of indigenous and European heritages, though some scholars are suspicious of her story of origin (Ricard 1966). She is said to have appeared to the Christianized Aztec–Náhua peasant Juan Diego three times in 1531. Each time she asked him to speak to the

Catholic bishop about building a place of worship in her name on Mount Tepeyac (present day Mexico City). However, it was not until after her third apparition that the Catholic authorities believed Juan Diego. Our Lady of Guadalupe had finally given him the evidence to prove her existence, fresh flowers that were not native to the area. This miracle story is now a source of popular piety for people all over the world, including La Plaza del Limón.

On each day of Our Lady of Guadalupe's fiesta, members of the community assemble two processions celebrating her apparition. Then at night, concerts with *banda* musicians and dancing take over the town square. As seen in figures 13.2 and 13.3, La Plaza del Limon's fiesta is documented through video and photography captured on portable devices. Moreover, the rendering of the fiesta through websites like YouTube ensures that the town's ritualistic memory is always available for invocation.

Archival records documenting other areas of the community's daily life were encountered in neighboring towns as seen in figures 13.4–13.6. Some of these locations include the homes of local videographers, the archives of the region's Catholic diocese, and the more intimate archives of a nearby local parish. For instance, one community member born during the the *Cristero War*, which took place roughly during the years 1926–1929, went most of her life believing she was four or five years younger than her actual age (Ceja 2013). It was not until she found her baptismal record at the nearby parish archives that she learned otherwise. At the center of the Cristero War insurgency was the power of the Catholic Church and its zealous followers against the secular government expropriating the Church's land after the Mexican Revolution. As a result of the Cristero War uprising, religious rituals and recordkeeping within the Catholic Church went underground. Many of these records now live outside of their actual place of origin. To this day, the Cristero War period continues to affect people's ability to officially authenticate their identities. By developing Recuerdos de Antes y Ahora, we are making the existence of such records visible to the local and diasporic community of La Plaza del Limón.

Figure 13.2. A woman video recording the fiesta's evening banda event in the town square (2012).
Photo by Janet Ceja Alcalá.

Figure 13.3. A man using a portable video camera with a video light to enhance image quality during the fiesta's evening banda event in the town square (2012).

Photo by Janet Ceja Alcalá.

Figure 13.4. Audiovisual records and supplies on a bookshelf inside the home office and workroom of a local videographer in Ixtlán de los Hervores.

Photo by Janet Ceja Alcalá.

Figure 13.5. Various historical documents in a folder from the archives of the Diocese of Zamora in Zamora, Michoacán.
Photo by Janet Ceja Alcalá.

Figure 13.6. Once clandestine baptismal records from the archives of the San Francisco de Asís Parish in Ixtlán de los Hervores.
Photo by Janet Ceja Alcalá.

Recuerdos de Antes y Ahora

Our first step in developing this project was to give it a name. Recuerdos de Antes y Ahora was chosen because it represents a local vernacular rooted in how members of La Plaza del Limón reference the past. For example, when referring to elders it is not uncommon to hear people use the phrases *la gente de antes* (people of the past) and *la gente de más antes* (people of the more distant past).[1] As such, temporality and memory are used to ground the project's mission: to preserve the history, memory, and culture of this region by documenting religious fiestas, agriculture, migration, and women's stories "of before and now." With this mission in hand, our next step demanded that we study the ways in which the community interacted with each other through a hometown website created in the 2000s and through Facebook more recently. It was important for us to understand the existing virtual communities and the type of interaction taking place in those spaces to design Recuerdos de Antes y Ahora.

Bienvenidos al portal de La Plaza del Limón.net

La Plaza del Limón's hometown website, though now defunct, is one of the earliest records of the community's presence on the Internet. The site was designed and managed by a member of the community from approximately the mid-2000s until the early 2010s. A good portion of the content posted by the webmaster was user-generated. Some user-contributions were enabled by the technical features of the website, such as discussion boards, a comments form, and the site guest book. Other user contributions were emailed directly to the webmaster to be posted on the website. Examples of contributions included photographs displayed as photo albums as seen in figure 13.7. To give an idea of the reach and interest in this website, from 2006 to 2012,

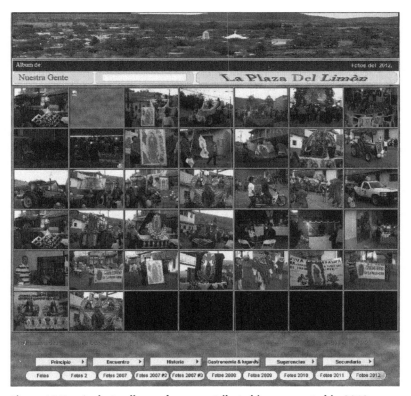

Figure 13.7. A photo album of user-contributed images posted in 2012.
https://web.archive.org/web/20131225104239/http:/laplazadellimon.net/Fotos2012.html.

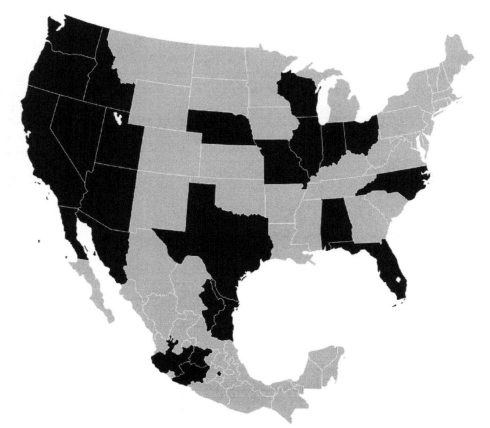

Figure 13.8.   A U.S.–Mexico map with gray highlights identifying the locations from which website visitors from La Plaza del Limón self-identified; the red region is the state of Michoacán.

visitors who left comments self-identified as writing from locations as far as Alabama, Arizona, Baja California, California, Florida, Guanajuato, Idaho, Illinois, Indiana, Jalisco, Mexico City, Missouri, Nebraska, Nevada, North Carolina, Nuevo León, Ohio, Oregon, Sonora, Tamaulipas, Texas, Utah, Washington, Wisconsin, and locally from the state of Michoacán (https:// web.archive.org/web/20120906015723/http:/www.laplazadellimon.net/contactus.html). When rendered visually as in figure 13.8, the mapping of these localities demonstrates the distributed nature of the diaspora and the geography of the community's records universe. The website is historically significant because it was once a major communication node that brought together early Internet adopters on both sides of the U.S.–Mexico border.

Ixtlán. Página informativa del Grupo Voluntario de Estudios Municipales

On the last day of the fiesta in 2016, a photograph exhibit was held in the town square titled: "La Plaza en el Norte. Un Siglo de Presencia" (La Plaza in the North. A Century of Presence). As seen in figures 13.9–13.11, the event highlighted the historical presence of the community in the United States through the personal photographs of locals and the diaspora, referred to as "hijos ausentes" (absent children). The oldest photograph displayed, dating back to the year 1935, showcased a well-dressed migrant worker named Jesús Salcedo Cervantes in the state

Figure 13.9.   The photo exhibit, "La Plaza en el Norte. Un Siglo de Presencia" held on January 31, 2016, in La Plaza del Limón's town square.
Photo by Janet Ceja Alcalá.

Figure 13.10.   A poster from the exhibit "La Plaza en el Norte. Un Siglo de Presencia."
Photo by Janet Ceja Alcalá.

Figure 13.11.   The Facebook album documenting the photo exhibit in La Plaza del Limón on the "Ixtlán. Página informativa del Grupo Voluntario de Estudios Municipales" group page.
Image capture from the Group's Facebook page.

of Indiana. The photograph's description claims he was one of the earliest migrants to the United States. This exhibition revealed that family archives are critical in documenting the townspeople's story of migration.

A local volunteer interest group organized the event and subsequently published it on their Facebook group—"Ixtlán. Página informativa del Grupo Voluntario de Estudios Municipales" (Ixtlán. Information page of the Volunteer Group on Municipal Studies). The site has over 700 members from different parts of Mexico and the United States. The platform, moreover, reinforces the image and text-based interaction used in LaPlazadelLimon.net. What is new here is that Facebook is being used as a storytelling tool to collectively remember the past with an audience that can be much more clearly identified and traced back to this region.

Given LaPlazadelLimon.net's user-generated data and interactivity, it is no surprise that the community continues to enact some of the same communication and documentation activities on Facebook. With Facebook, however, communication has become even more distributed and visually interconnected. From LaPlazadelLimon.net and Ixtlán. Página informativa del Grupo Voluntario de Estudios Municipales we learned that the website features most likely to be utilized by the community include exhibiting collections of images as "albums" and having the ability to comment through simple text messaging.

OMEKA AND COMMUNITY ENGAGEMENT

With a better understanding of how members of the community were leveraging websites to build and sustain connections, we identified Omeka.net, an open source platform for managing digital collections, as a space that could build upon this existing network while offering tools tailored to our desired outcomes. Omeka.net was developed by the Roy Rosenzweig Center for History and New Media at George Mason University as a platform for the display and exhibition of digital collections. This strong visual emphasis fit perfectly with our design goals.

There are two versions of the platform, Omeka.net and Omeka.org. The latter requires that developers install the software on a server, whereas the former is a web-based version supported through different levels of membership. We chose Omeka.net because it requires minimal ongoing maintenance by providing the technical infrastructure to support the features we identified in LaPlazadelLimon.net and Ixtlán. Página informativa del Grupo Voluntario de Estudios Municipales. In Omeka.net we found a platform that would allow us to create and track information adhering to professional standards.

The Omeka platform has become popular with those developing digital collections and exhibitions in libraries, archives, and museums both because of its low barriers to access and the minimal coding knowledge required to build a sophisticated and customizable site (Kucsma, Reiss, and Sidman 2010, L. Hardesty 2014, Rath 2016). One of the most versatile features of Omeka is the wide selection of "plugins," which are optional add-ons that enhance the site with more complex features. For instance, as seen in figure 13.12, by adopting the social

Figure 13.12. Screen shot of social bookmarking plugin linking collection item to social media networks.

bookmarking plugin, users can link collection items to various social media networks. Because Omeka is an open-source tool, it also allows for users with the requisite coding knowledge to build additional plugins for versatility and greater levels of customization as needed.

A recent assessment of Omeka noted six functional strengths of the platform that inform our project design: collection-building, media formats, collaboration, metadata, social media, and user contributions (Rath 2016). All of these functions are important in helping us to construct an archives that is flexible and decentralized. It also allows us to reflect on how the community may be able to use features beyond those originally identified. In this manner, our project could follow other digital collection projects utilizing Omeka.

For instance, the John Cage archives, hosted by the New York Public Library (NYPL) for the Performing Arts, includes digitized images and manuscripts from the library's John Cage Music Manuscript Collection (http://exhibitions.nypl.org/johncage). Until October 2016, the archives also accepted audiovisual submissions for works inspired by John Cage's work and philosophy. The curation in the assembly of these videos involved adapting information provided through the submission form to fit a template for these submitted "records." The primary theme guiding the collection and exhibition of submissions was connection to the work and spirit of the composer John Cage, while also promoting the existing collection of John Cage materials at the NYPL.

The Bracero History Archives, a joint project of several universities and cultural organizations, is another example. Its archives provides digital access to "oral histories and artifacts" about the Bracero guest worker initiative implemented in the United States from 1942–1964 (http://braceroarchive.org). In addition to the collected holdings of the various institutional partners, the project allows users to submit their own stories, many of which are visible to the public without any curation on the part of the project historian. The project also permits users to register an account to assemble records into their own collection with the ability to add annotations.

Two areas where the Omeka platform presents both opportunities and challenges are in imposing descriptive standards, and organizing submissions to ensure the greatest level of accessibility.

A key distinction of archival projects is the use of descriptive standards, which create pathways for users to retrieve records, thereby making them "findable" and accessible. Simply digitizing materials provides a minimal level of access. Descriptive standards are important to understanding the way that archivists approach cultural work and Omeka helps users to participate in this social world. In Omeka, items are described by using the Dublin Core standard, which requires that specific fields like "title," "creator," and "format" be filled out to describe an item. If we should also intend for the site to function as an archive for user submitted media, the first step in our design would be to ensure that our submission form is customizable for a variety of formats, including images, text, and oral histories (see figure 13.13).

The platform also offers a plugin tool called Simple Vocab, which could help us to develop an internal, locally controlled vocabulary based on tags added by users through the user submission form. Controlled vocabulary is an important tool in developing information about records because it establishes a set of standard terms to describe a record. These standard terms in turn allow users to see connections between records with, for instance, the same keywords or formats. In line with our commitment to centering community practices in the archives, our objective is to eventually develop a system using tagging and a site vocabulary based on user submitted data that honors our rasquache ethos through the use of hybrid descriptive standards.

CONTRIBUTE

What type of item do you want to contribute? | Imagen / Image ▼ |

CONTRIBUTE A IMAGEN / IMAGE

Upload a file | Choose File | No file chosen

Descripción de la Imagen / Image Description

An account of the resource

Personal Information
Name

Email Address

Please include any tags that describe the content/subject your submission:

Figure 13.13. Screen shot of how Omeka's media submission form can be customized.

FINAL THOUGHTS: A COMMUNITY OF RECORDS

The community turn in archival discourse motivated us to bridge these analyses with praxis-oriented work we defined as community engaged archiving. Our experience in developing Recuerdos de Antes y Ahora has allowed us to reflect on how community engagement will vary from project to project, be contingent upon different circumstances, and require different sets of commitments and competencies. In some cases, we may be called upon to be involved technically with community archiving projects, while in others we may have to be advocates in promoting and making archival tools legible to communities. In our case, community engaged archiving represents our circumstances in developing a digital archives *a lo rasquache*, that is, with the archiving resources that were freely available to us. As the website continues to evolve, we will conduct outreach to better understand the type of participation people are willing to take part in. More research is needed to test and develop community engaged archiving as a concept that is theoretically viable and helpful to the archival profession. We hope that our example will motivate archivists to experiment with this idea.

La Plaza del Limón's historical representation on the web creates what Jeannette A. Bastian calls a *community of records* because these websites exist as a network in which the community is both the "record-creating entity and memory frame that contextualizes the records it creates" (Bastian 2003). Moreover, because these websites have a logic oriented toward the shaping of community memory rather than their description and long-term preservation, we believe our rasquache approach helps to connect these different, though not mutually exclusive, logics. In this sense, our work is no different from what Chicanx archivists and librarians have been doing for years: building bridges between our communities and archives, library, and museum cultures (García-Ayvens and Chabran 1984, Güereña 1988, Luévano-Molina 2000, Güereña 2012). Recuerdos de Antes y Ahora is a continuation of this community engaged tradition.

NOTE

1. Anthropologist Oscar Muñoz Morán found that the Purhépecha community of Sevina, Michoacán, not too far from La Plaza del Limón, organized their worldview into similar narrative timeframes: "now" (*ahora*), "in the past" (*antes*), and "in the most distant past" (*el más antes*). See Muñoz Morán, Ó. (2009). Muñoz Morán, Ó. (2009). *Permanencia en el tiempo: Antropología de la historia en la comunidad Purhépecha de Sevina*. Zamora, Colegio de Michoacán.

BIBLIOGRAPHY

Bastian, J. A. (2003). *Owning memory how a Caribbean community lost its archives and found its history*. Westport, Conn.: Libraries Unlimited.

Bastian, J. A. (2009). "'Play mas': Carnival in the archives and the archives in carnival: Records and community identity in the US Virgin Islands." *Archival Science* 9(1): 113–125.

Caswell, M. (2014). "Report from the field: Seeing yourself in history: Community archives and the fight against symbolic annihilation." *Public Historian* 36(4): 26–37.

Ceja, J. (2013). Informal records and the autochthonous preservation of the fiesta of Our Lady of Guadalupe in rural Mexico. Doctor of Philosophy Dissertation, University of Pittsburgh.

Cook, T. (2013). "Evidence, memory, identity, and community: Four shifting archival paradigms." *Archival Science* 13(2–3): 95–120.

Erickson, T. L. (1991). "At the "Rim of Creative Dissatisfaction": Archivists and acquisition development." *Archivaria* 33: 66–77.

García-Ayvens, F. and R. F. Chabran (1984). *Biblio-politica Chicano perspectives on library service in the United States*. Berkeley: University of California.

Güereña, S. (1988). "Archives and manuscripts: Historical antecedents to contemporary Chicano collections." *Collection Building* 8(4): 3–11.

Güereña, S. (2012). An archival call to action. *Pathways to progress issues and advances in Latino librarianship*. J. L. Ayala and S. Güereña. Santa Barbara, Calif.: Libraries Unlimited, 161–168.

Ham, G. F. (1975). "The archival edge." *The American Archivist* 38(1): 5–13.

Ham, G. F. (1981). "Archival strategies for the post-custodial era." *The American Archivist* 44(3): 207–216.

Kucsma, J., K. Reiss and A. Sidman (2010). "Using Omeka to build digital collections: The METRO case study." *D-Lib Magazine* 16(3/4).

L. Hardesty, J. (2014). "Exhibiting library collections online: Omeka in context." *New Library World* 115(3/4): 75–86.

Luévano-Molina, S. (2000). Ethnographic perspectives on trans-national Mexican immigrant library users. *Library services to Latinos : an anthology*. S. Güereña. Jefferson, N.C.: McFarland, 169–181.

Muñoz Morán, Ó. (2009). *Permanencia en el tiempo : antropología de la historia en la comunidad Purhépecha de Sevina.* Zamora: Colegio de Michoacán.

Rath, L. (2016). "Omeka.net as a librarian-led digital humanities meeting place." *New Library World* 117(3/4): 158–172.

Ricard, Robert. (1996) *The spiritual conquest of Mexico an essay on the apostolate and the evangelizing methods of the Mendicant Orders in New Spain, 1523–1572.* Berkeley: University of California Press.

Samuels, H. W. (1986). "Who controls the past." *The American Archivist* 49(2): 109–124.

Sheffield, R. (2017). Community archives. *Currents of archival thinking.* H. MacNeil and T. Eastwood. Santa Barbara: Libraries Unlimited, 351–376.

Stevens, M., A. Flinn and E. Shepherd (2010). "New frameworks for community engagement in the archive sector: From handing over to handing on." *International Journal of Heritage Studies* 16(1–2): 59–76.

Ybarra-Frausto, T. (1991). Rasquachismo: A Chicano sensibility. *Chicano art: Resistance and affirmation, 1965–1985.* R. Griswold del Castillo, T. McKenna, Y. Yarbro-Bejarano, S. W. A. G. Frederick and C. N. A. Committee. Los Angeles: Wight Art Gallery, University of California, Los Angeles, 155–162.

14

The Power of Lists
World Heritage through Its Information System

Marta Severo

INTRODUCTION

A list keeps together, in one way or another, items or materials that are somehow related. This chapter explores the recent transformation of the list in response to the emergence of new complex, disperse, and interconnected heritage objects. Our analysis focuses on the case of the UNESCO World Heritage (WH) List. Although WH sites far exceed the physical and conceptual dimensions of the typical objects of inventories, their identification and documentation proves increasingly necessary for their conservation. The WH List can undoubtedly be considered a success in coping with these challenges. In recent years, the UNESCO World Heritage Centre, which manages the list, has emerged as a key actor in the selection process of cultural heritage.

POWER AND THE CRISIS OF LISTS

First introduced into the cultural field by the cabinets of curiosities (Impey and MacGregor 1985), the technique of inventorying[1] has proved to be extremely successful in many different institutions, such as museums, archives, and libraries. Thanks to its guarantee of a massive and effective organization of information, the inventory has become the standard tool for the classification and management of material objects.

Much of the history of the inventory has been lost over the centuries. If we consider the inventory as a list that will keep in its memory what cannot be kept in the mind (Leroi-Gourhan 1964), its origins can be traced back to the first writing systems (Goody 1977). It was then rapidly adopted in a variety of contexts to store and classify information. In scientific practice, the list "is both a hierarchical ordering and a practical tool for organizing work and the division of labor" (Bowker and Leigh Star 2000, 137). A scientific list not only identifies the characteristics of a phenomenon, but also defines its very nature by giving it a new form (Latour 1987, 96). Throughout the centuries, lists have helped to organize species, diseases, books, monuments, and knowledge in general. Whether as a catalog, an inventory, a directory, a dictionary, or an encyclopedia, the classificatory power of lists shapes knowledge in numerous fields (Bowker and Leigh Star 2000).

Although its origins go back a long way, the inventory has become even more crucial in the era of digitization (Geser and Pereira 2004). In recent years, more and more institutions have relied on new digital technologies to catalog their collections (Cameron and Robinson 2007). Information systems have been built to digitize lists of objects and to facilitate their management. These systems not only ensure the permanence of the data, but even more interestingly, they contribute to the construction of the list by formalizing and standardizing the action of selection (Fraysse 2008).

The list has emerged as a tool that is particularly appropriate to cultural heritage. In fact, there is a strong affinity between cultural heritage objects such as monuments and lists: "both depend on selection, both decontextualise their objects from their immediate surroundings and recontextualise them with reference to other things designated or listed" (Hafstein 2009, 93). That is why the list has been often used in the governance of cultural sites, both in the management of information and in the process of "heritagization" (the use of the word "heritagization" to refer to the process of how culture is constructed or cultural heritage selection is gaining wide acceptance).[2] Regarding the management of information, the first private collections had catalogs. Following the model of naturalistic collections, inventories allowed the unambiguous identification of objects, the consistent organization of data, and the monitoring of objects over time. Regarding the process of cultural heritage selection, we can observe that no state can disregard the necessity of inventories of national treasures in order to preserve them for future generations (Francioni and Lenzerini 2006, 35).

Yet, after its glorious past, the cultural heritage list is currently experiencing a difficult phase. The process of heritagization has recently undergone massive expansion. The category of "heritage," employed since the Middle Ages for private properties, has been extended to public sites recognized as meaningful for the collective identity. In recent years, the word "heritage" has been used far beyond its original contexts, ranging from the ordinary to the extraordinary, from the sacred to the profane, from the tangible to the intangible, from objects to places, from culture to nature (Di Meo 2008) up until "all heritage" (Guillaume 1980, 11, our translation). As noticed by Nathalie Heinich in the French cultural context, the lack of stability in the definition of heritage undermines "the scientific image of the function of the Inventory" (2009, 97, our translation).

Undoubtedly, the recent enlargement of the category of heritage has had a profound impact on the function of the list, both as a technical tool for data management and as an interpretative tool that shapes cultural heritage. While historical monuments—the heritage object par excellence—have distinctive features and specific borders that fit the classification power of lists well, new heritage objects—landscapes, eco-museums, intangible cultural heritage, digital heritage, and so on—are difficult to capture, identify, and classify. How can we inventory an eco-museum[3] in a way that records its ties with the community and its territory (Desvallées and Mairesse 2007, 147–148)? How can we document the interconnection between heterogeneous and dispersed elements that compose a landscape (Severo 2009)?

Yet, paradoxically, the expansion of the category of cultural heritage makes inventories even more necessary. Because of its varied and changing nature, cultural heritage needs to be identified and listed to be safeguarded. As Françoise Benhamou (2010, 128) emphasizes, the rhetoric of emergency is one of the main elements that drives the creation of lists. The threat of disappearance calls for tools for its identification, documentation, and conservation. And in this field, nothing is as successful as the list. With its power of selection and its capacity to organize information, the list remains the most effective tool to safeguard heritage properties (Schuster 2002).

This chapter aims to study the process of transformation of the list through the case of the World Heritage List. Not without controversy and failures,[4] the WH List offers protection for more than a thousand properties in 165 countries. To study this case, we use an innovative methodology called "reverse knowledge engineering." Through analysis of the information system related to WH, we identify the mechanisms that underlie the selection of these cultural objects and the solutions that the WH list implements to deal with the enlargement of cultural heritage. The following paragraphs will introduce our case study and methodology. We will then present the results of our analysis by following the trajectory of a site from its "inscription"[5] on the list through its administration once listed.

THE WORLD HERITAGE LISTS

The category of "world heritage"[6] was created in 1972 by UNESCO through the Convention Concerning the Protection of the World Cultural and Natural Heritage (UNESCO 1972). Faced with threats of degradation and loss during and after the Second World War, the convention aimed to safeguard cultural and natural heritage of "outstanding universal value."[7]

In order to achieve this objective, the convention established two lists: the World Heritage List and the List of World Heritage in Danger. Both lists are compiled by the WH Committee. The Committee is composed of fifteen representatives elected by the General Assembly of States that have ratified the Convention. These lists are the inventory of World Heritage. Their management has been controversial from the beginning, and States Parties[8] were far from sharing a common position on it. In the first version of the Convention, the lists did not exist and the safeguarding action was based mainly on the distribution of financial support from the WH Fund. Under pressure from the American delegation, lists were established as a further protection tool (Schuster 2002). Today not only do lists exist, but they are the most well-known of all UNESCO's activities.[9]

Although the authority and reputation of WH is indisputable, the UNESCO lists are not free from the threats to all types of inventory today. In recent years, the WH list has faced many political (wars and tensions between countries), economic (mass tourism), social (conflicts between local interests and the universal value of the site), and natural (climate change) challenges. Several measures have been put in place to react to these challenges. On the one hand, the Committee, assisted by experts, has carried out an in-depth consideration of how the Convention should be amended. Working groups have been set up and some changes have been made to deal with increasingly complex and varied heritage. This is, for example, the case concerning the introduction of the category of "cultural landscape" into the Convention (Rössler 2006). On the other hand, the WH Centre, which guarantees the maintenance of lists and assists the Committee in its activities (Vrdoljak 2008), has modified its management routines on a day-to-day basis to meet the needs of the new heritage context. While corrections to the Convention are slow and controversial, the practices of the WH Centre change faster and more informally. It is therefore interesting to focus an analysis on them.

The Centre is responsible for the implementation of the Committee's decisions and for the daily interpretation of the Convention. This role is crucial because the Convention does not provide detailed guidance for practical action (Vrdoljak 2008, 250). For example, while the Convention provides definitions of natural (art. 2) and cultural heritage (art. 1), it gives no detailed explanation of what "outstanding universal value" means, thus leaving the Committee with the task of defining more precise criteria. These criteria are provided by the Operational

Guidelines for the Implementation of the World Heritage Convention.[10] Unlike the Convention, these guidelines fall down because of their abundance of new terms, strategic objectives, additional definitions, and detailed tasks. Although this abundance is the basis of the Committee's activities, it complicates the Centre's implementation of the Convention. The Centre staff are asked to interpret the official texts with a certain amount of freedom and to translate them into practice. Through its actions in the management of the WH List, the Centre has thereby established itself as a key actor in the selection process of heritage.

METHODOLOGY

What makes management of the WH lists particularly interesting is the role played by the digital information system. Not only have new technologies been introduced heavily into the activities of the WH Centre, but the WH Committee also devotes considerable attention to the regulation of these tools in official documents. In them, the WH Centre is identified as responsible for data management—documents, decisions, information on properties, and so on—and it is obliged to make all these data available on its website (UNESCO 2008, art. 280–295). Consequently, the Center is the repository of all information about the properties, and manager of all data flows, including digital data, which constitute the backbone of the website.[11]

Indeed, the WH inventory is stored in the database of the WH Centre's website. All data managed by the Centre are centralized in this database: we could therefore say that all knowledge concerning UNESCO World Heritage is archived there. This is the reason why an investigation of the WH information system is expected to be so interesting.

Our analysis of this inventory was conducted through a "reverse knowledge engineering"[12] approach. Such an approach integrates the advantages of "reverse engineering" with the objectives of "knowledge engineering." To explain it, we will briefly summarize these two concepts. Reverse engineering is a method of analysis that consists in the study of a technical object to deduce its functions and internal structure (Chikofsky and Cross 1990). It is traditionally used to infer the intentions of the object's designers, when not accessible because they are lost—as in the case of the archaeology of techniques—or protected owing to a trade secret. In our case study, the method of reverse engineering is useful because the WH information system has been developed in a completely unsystematic way. Many people contributed to the design of these information tools, and numerous corrections and changes have been made over the years. Therefore so many debates, discussions, and compromises have influenced the database structure that it is impossible to trace them. Of course, this does not imply that the system is meaningless. But it is the result of a long and complex negotiation that has involved different types of actors (Dalbin and Guyot 2007; Courbières and Régimbeau 2006): the Centre's staff members, but also Committee members, managers of sites, and several experts. Through this negotiation, UNESCO's practices of heritagization have been written in the Centre's information system.

Knowledge engineering can be defined as the work necessary to write the practices of an organization within a computer system, as "a technique of manipulating digital entries to be interpreted as knowledge—offering machines that make us think not thinking machines" (Charlet 2005, our translation).[13] Knowledge engineering has certainly played a major role in the digitization of heritage inventories, especially in the case of the WH Centre.[14] For this reason, we decided to define our approach as "reverse knowledge engineering" (Severo 2011).

In our study, we consider the Centre's information system as "inscription [. . .] of knowledge,"[15] that is to say, traces that can reveal how the institution considers heritage and its selection process. Far from being neutral, such systems embody the explicit and implicit knowledge of the institution and reflect the practices by which the WH Convention is implemented. Choices relating to information management, and notably to the database structure, cannot be reduced to purely technical issues: they are indicative of the Centre's management of knowledge about cultural heritage.

The analysis presented in these pages is derived from long-term research: nine months of participant observation at the WH Centre headquarters in Paris—March to December 2007—and dozens of interviews with stakeholders of the Centre. Through this fieldwork, we were able to identify the criteria at work in the selection of information concerning properties recognized as world heritage. The analysis took into account the data archives of all lists and the information-gathering process related to the Centre's various activities. In this chapter, we present the most interesting phenomena that this analysis identified.[16] First, we present the IT management of the process of listing a site; we then analyze the data structure related to sites included on the WH lists; and finally we focus on one of the most controversial features, the link between sites and states.

THE TRAJECTORY OF A SITE ON THE WORLD HERITAGE LIST

Analysis of the WH Centre's information system will be presented following the life of a site, from inscription proposal to follow-up procedures—and in rare cases, exclusion from the list. The next few paragraphs will show the main issues that emerged at each stage.

Inscription of a Site

Information systems play a very important role in the process of inscription of a WH site. Interestingly, the process of adding a new site to the website[17] follows a certain administrative procedure workflow. First, a state includes the site on its tentative list. The tentative list of each state lists sites that could be added to the WH List. Tentative lists of all States Parties are published on the WH website. As a second step, the state may apply to nominate the site for the WH List. Usually nominations are preceded by informal discussion with the Centre. The nomination can be approved, not approved, or deferred and returned to the state to be completed. Finally, when the Committee approves inscription, the site is moved from the webpage of the tentative list to the page of the official list where it is listed under the name of the state that requested the inscription.

It is interesting to note that all data relating to a site are uploaded into the database from the moment the site is included on the tentative list. There is a unique data repository that includes information on properties included on the tentative lists and on the official list. So, the upgrade of a site from the tentative to the official list implies a change in the status of the site from "tentative" to "inscribed." Such a change is simply made by ticking a checkbox that triggers the automatic update of all sections of the website. Similarly, if the Committee decides to exclude an item from the list (Buzzini and Condorelli 2008), from an IT perspective this action corresponds to a change of status of the item from "inscribed" to "delisted." So, the item remains published on the WH website and its information remains in the database. Exclusion from the list is marked by a graphic expedient: the site name is crossed out to indicate its exclusion from the list.

In short, this means that the database includes not only data related to official lists, but also to sites proposed by states—before approval by UNESCO—and sites removed from the official list by the Committee. If the decision to "delist" a site is deemed appropriate by the

Committee, the Centre establishes how to implement such a decision, which has a critical effect on the public perception of heritage. In a similar way, the inclusion of data from the tentative lists in the database and on the website is not without consequences. Properties that are included gain some visibility and political recognition—even if only implicitly—by UNESCO before being submitted for the Committee's evaluation. This can provoke significant misunderstandings, as in the case of properties related to Jerusalem.

Jerusalem appears three times on the WH website: on the pages of the official WH list, the World Heritage in Danger List, and on the page of the State of Israel's tentative list. On the one hand, there are two sites included on the official lists. The "Old City of Jerusalem and its Walls," proposed by Jordan, has been included on the WH list since 1981 and on the List of World Heritage in Danger since 1982 and, therefore, appears on the pages corresponding to both official lists. This site does not appear under "Jordan," but under the text "Jerusalem (Site proposed by Jordan)," which obviously does not correspond to a state in the list of States Parties. Moreover, while all properties are also displayed on the page of the state that submitted the nomination, the site "Old City of Jerusalem and its Walls" does not appear on any state's page, not even that of Jordan. On the other hand, in 2000, Israel added a proposal called "Jerusalem" to its tentative list (a proposal which has not yet been recognized by UNESCO) in order to include the area of Mount Zion.[18] Israel has not yet submitted this proposal to the Committee because informal negotiations have taken place between the Committee—by means of the Centre—and the state in order to delay the submission. In this example, the information system is required to provide empirical solutions to some very delicate political issues (notably the question of the relationship between Jerusalem and a state), to which the Committee has not yet given an official response. And such solutions can be highly controversial. For example, in early July 2011, *Gulf News* accused UNESCO of recognizing Jerusalem as Israel's capital and of neglecting the existence of the occupied Palestinian territories.

This controversy over Jerusalem is obviously the result of a misunderstanding in a reading of the website, yet in fact it reveals a much more sensitive issue. It illustrates clearly the influence of the information system on the implementation of the WH principles and, finally, on the heritage selection process. While the inscription of a site may appear to be the crucial stage of selection, analysis of the information system helps to highlight the importance of the stages that precede final inscription on the official list, that is to say inclusion on the tentative list, application for nomination and, notably, informal political exchanges related to the passage from the tentative list to nomination.

Administration of a Site

Once included on the WH list, a site is subject to numerous activities of monitoring, management, and evaluation. All information regarding these activities is stored in the database as news, decisions, documents, missions, partnership agreements, publications, and other forms. Analysis of the information system highlights the fact that the dynamic life of a site, often marked by several milestones and significant changes, does not translate into a similar dynamism in the data management.

The main feature of the WH data repository is the absolute centrality of the WH List. All data concerning listed sites are organized in a data table. Most of the other tables in the database are related this table: States Parties' data, but also events, decisions, documents, themes, threats, users, and so forth. All nominations are stored in the database directly in the inscribed properties' table and an identification number is assigned to them. This number plays a very important role in the management of information: it is the element that ensures links with the data of all other tables. All nominations withdrawn, postponed, or revised by the Committee or by the State Party are identified by the same number followed by a three-letter suffix (rev, bis, ter) according to their status in the registration process (revised, deferred, inscribed). For example, "Ferrara: a city of the Renaissance (Italy)" was included on the list in 1995, identified by the reference 733. When, in 1999, the nomination file underwent significant changes (criteria extension and change of name "Ferrara, City of the Renaissance, and its Po Delta"), a suffix was added to the number identification (733bis).

It is important to emphasize the stability of the identification number, which uniquely identifies a site despite nomination changes.[19] A change in the criteria for inscription, which can strongly affect how cultural heritage is selected and collected (Di Giovine 2009), does not affect identification of the object in the database, or, therefore, the connection between the site and other information contained in the database. The stability of the information system is also established by managing the data procedures related to monitoring activities such as periodic reporting. States are required to prepare regular reports on the state of conservation of their properties. These reports allow the Committee to assess the situation of the site and possibly take corrective measures. The report consists of two sections: Section I on the legislative and administrative provisions and Section II on the conservation status of each site.

Since the second cycle of periodic reporting—begun in 2009 with the Arab States region—the report must be completed online via a questionnaire on the Centre's website. Data obtained through this questionnaire are not stored in the Centre's database, but in a standalone database. The only link to the Centre's database is the site's identification number. Moreover, some data obtained in Section II of the report—on the state of conservation—are not even saved. For example, this section includes questions about factors affecting the site—such as pollution, natural disasters, and the impact of tourism. Based on data provided by the site manager, the tool generates an automatic evaluation of the state of conservation of the site by highlighting dangerous situations. These data are used by the Centre to assess intervention needs, but they are not saved in the database. Therefore, no information collected by the periodic report is published on the official webpage of the site. Although this online form allows updated data on properties to be collected, the Centre, through the definition of its information system, decides not to mix conservation data with nomination data. The result of this technical choice is that the UNESCO website displays a static image of properties, neglecting to reflect changes, threats, and discussions involved in the experience of cultural heritage.

The fact that all monitoring data are excluded from the website is coherent with the typical approach to WH conservation (Schmitt 2009, 119). It is generally recognized that the WH Convention encourages site management oriented toward maintenance of its outstanding universal value, and in particular of the integrity and authenticity of the site (Francioni 2007). Our analysis of the information system highlights how this approach to cultural heritage is still very much at work in WH routines, even facing the emergence of cultural heritage properties' more dynamic and varied nature.

The Relationship between Sites and States

One of the most controversial aspects highlighted by the reverse knowledge engineering analysis is the IT management of the relationship between sites and states. The structure of the database shows the centrality of this link (Francioni and Lenzerini 2008a), and its management has raised important controversies on several occasions. Three examples can be mentioned.

First, the system prevents the creation of sites without a state. Yet the previous example "Old City of Jerusalem and its Walls" clearly shows that this relationship is not trivial. This site has been proposed by Jordan and is linked to that country in the database, but the connection is not clearly visible on the website for political reasons. As we have seen, displaying a link between Jerusalem and a country (whether this be Israel, Palestine, or Jordan) raised immediate reactions in the media. Yet while the highly sensitive issue of the relationship between Jerusalem and a state can remain open and controversial in terms of political management, the information system must find a clear and unambiguous technical solution to it.

Second, transboundary properties (which are managed by several states) also pose considerable technical problems: for example, how to display them in the list (considering the list is organized by country, these properties would appear several times). And how should they be counted within statistical data (they may be counted more than once)? And how should related follow-up procedures be managed (one single periodic report or one for each concerned country)?

Third, properties in series, that is to say, objects with multiple locations—often transnational—have also raised many difficulties. As described in the previous paragraph, the site is the basic unit of the database. The Centre's information system is not designed to handle networks of sites. So, the management of serial sites necessitated the creation of an external table to manage multiple geographical coordinates. In recent years, discussion on this type of site has been lively,[20] and the Committee has made various decisions[21] to support and clarify this type of inscription. It is interesting to note that items in a series can be considered to be either a new proposal or an extension of an existing proposal. Indeed, the IT system does not provide for the combination of several already inscribed sites because this would require the recognition of lower units of the site in the database.

These information management problems related to the relationship between site and state can be interpreted in the context of a more general reflection on the World Heritage Convention. Notably, we can recall the tension between the notion of cultural heritage as a universal value and the principle of national sovereignty[22] that underlines the Convention. The link between site and state is increasingly challenged by the increase of cross-border properties and by the Committee's recent Strategic Policy aiming to encourage reform of the nomination process by facilitating international cooperation.[23] However, the resistance of the IT system demonstrates the difficulty of overcoming the role of the state even in a context of increasing globalization.

CONCLUSION

The list has been the preferred tool for cultural heritage administration over the centuries, and remains so today. With its power of classifying and archiving information, the list remains the backbone of conservation and the heritage selection process. The recent emergence of new heritage objects—which are more complex, interconnected, and scattered—which appeared to threaten the list's function, has ultimately rendered it more central than ever. For these complex heritage objects that escape categorization and ignite debate, lists can provide a tool of factual selection that is difficult to achieve through theoretical reflection and political debate. World heritage is certainly a good example. Composed of different elements, geographically dispersed, administered by several institutions and sometimes several countries, subject to media and business attention, world heritage has a networked nature (Severo 2009), which makes it difficult not only to administrate in practical terms, but also to understand theoretically. Through analysis of the WH Centre's information system, we identified the main issues relating to such heritage sites.

First, the analysis has shown that documentation and classification of this type of heritage opens up several practical controversies: how to manage the relationship between data concerning listed and unlisted properties (those on tentative lists or delisted); how to manage the relationship between data on the site's outstanding universal value and those on the state of its conservation (for example periodic reports); and how to manage the relationship between data related to multiple states (for example transnational and serial sites). Behind these technical problems, we find significant theoretical questions: the impact of the WH Centre's informal negotiations on the inscription process; the balance between the sustainability of outstanding universal value and the inevitability of changes in management; and the ambiguity of the universality of world heritage in the definition of the relationship between states and sites.

Second, this study leads us to a more general reflection on the role of information systems within an organization. As we have seen, information systems are forced to respond in practice and in daily routines to complex and often controversial situations generated by the dynamic nature of sites. Far from being merely technical choices that an institution sets up in building its information system, they have a strong political component. Through the construction of its database, for example, the WH Centre defines practices that have undeniable effects on the heritagization process.

In conclusion, this study highlights the importance of the list as a technical tool that can influence the process of documentation and interpretation of cultural objects. The inclusion of a site on a list, such as a traditional inventory or an online database, is never a neutral action, yet it is always a political choice. It is not only the result of the use of legal or technological tools, but—in particular—of the interaction between social actors. In the words of Michel Rautemberg, "There are two very different approaches in the construction of heritage. The first . . . is to determine a category of objects that are both unique and universal [. . .] the other is social and ordinary, starting with the recognition of actors" (Rautemberg 2003, 21, our translation). Analysis of the World Heritage case—which by definition should be based on the first approach—makes it clear that the definition of a heritage object is always at the intersection of these two approaches.

NOTES

1. In this chapter, we use the word "list," "inventory," "catalog," "directory," "register" as synonyms. Indeed, all these tools share the feature of selecting, organizing, and classifying a series of elements.

2. See, for example, *Science and Technology for the Conservation of Cultural Heritage*, Miguel Angel Rogeria-Candelera, Massimo Lazzari, and Emilio Cando, editors. New York: Routledge, 2013.

3. The term eco-museum was established at the ninth conference of ICOM (1971) to cover the idea of a heritage linked to a community and an environment.

4. See for example Francioni and Lezenrini 2006.

5. The term used by UNESCO to refer to a site's inclusion on the list.

6. On the origins of the concept of World Heritage see Gamboni 2001. For a detailed analysis of the Convention see Francioni and Lenzerini 2008b.

7. The concept of "outstanding universal value" is still controversial. This concept was introduced in the Guidelines, but Ben Boer (2008, 88) emphasizes the vagueness of its definition. The Committee intervened on its definition in various documents (see WHC.09/33.COM/9 decisions WHC.08/32.COM/9, WHC. 07/31.COM/9, WHC.05/29.COM/INF.9A, WHC.11/35.COM/13).

8. Term used by UNESCO to denote states that have ratified the Convention.

9. For a review of the extensive literature on the WH list see Frey and Steiner 2010.

10. The Guidelines are written by the Committee to establish clear criteria for listing properties and for managing international assistance of the World Heritage fund. They are revised periodically to include new concepts, knowledge, or experience.

11. An audit report of the Centre conducted in 1997 noted: "The World Heritage Centre is located at the confluence of several major information flows. Documents circulate between the Advisory Bodies and States Parties and are addressed primarily to the Committee. The Centre is also a focal point for information and media requests" (WHC-97/CONF.208/CONF.5, Annex B, para. 180). The following audit report, produced in 2007 at the request of the Committee, notes the same phenomenon and highlights its problematic nature, notably, "the workload has also grown in response to the increase in the volume of information requested by the Committee (format of state of conservation reports, reports on Committee proceedings, etc.)" (WHC.07/31.COM/19A.Rev, 20). The report also notes the importance of information systems, especially the website: "the quality of the Centre's work was stressed regarding the management of its website, which made available a wealth of easily accessible up-to-date information. Development of the Center's website, once the CEP office had been set up, provided an important tool of communication and information with regard to both the general public and partners" (WHC.07/31.COM/19A.Rev, 56).

12. This term is used by Quintas and Demaid 2000.

13. Jean Charlet also notes: "These digital entries must be valid with a double perspective: a) from the perspective of IT and formal techniques that allow them to be manipulated, and b) in relation to the context of use of the tool, that is to say in relation to a system of norms and conventions of the context in which the tool is included. Knowledge engineering is a technique of formal inscriptions and critical interpretation of them." See also Bachimont 2004.

14. We can mention the fact that for years an information system advisor assisted the Director of the Centre.

15. On the interpretation of digital traces as inscriptions of knowledge, see Laflaquière, Settouti, Prié and Mille 2007.

16. For a more comprehensive description of the activities of the Centre and of its information systems see Severo 2009.

17. http://whc.unesco.org/.

18. There is a note on the website that explains: "This concerns the property entitled 'Jerusalem–the Old City and Ramparts to include Mount Zion' proposed by Israel as an extension to the 'Old City of Jerusalem and its Walls' inscribed on the World Heritage List in 1981, upon proposal by Jordan." The Committee at its 25th Session (Helsinki, 2001) endorsed the recommendation of the 25th session of its Bureau (Paris, June 2001) "to postpone further consideration of this nomination proposal until an agreement on the status of the City of Jerusalem in conformity with International Law is reached, or until the parties concerned submit a joint nomination. It should be noted that, the UNESCO General Conference in its Resolutions 32C/39 and 33C/50, affirmed that: '(. . .) nothing in the present decision, which is aimed at the safeguarding of the cultural heritage of the Old City of Jerusalem, shall in any way affect the relevant United Nations resolutions and decisions, in particular the relevant Security Council resolutions on the legal status of Jerusalem.'"

19. It is interesting to note that data management concerning the Convention on Intangible Cultural Heritage (2003) is completely different. A new number identifies each amendment to the inscription files.

20. See documents WHC-08/32.COM/10B, WHC-09/33.COM/10A, and WHC-10/ 34.COM/9B.

21. See decisions 32.COM 10B, 33.COM 10A, and 34 COM 9B.

22. Helen Hazen (2008) analyzes the ambivalent relationship between (international) heritage and national sovereignty and stresses the importance of the dimension of the state in the management of heritage conservation. Buergin (2001) gives an example of the relationship between world heritage and state. In describing the case of the protected area of Thung Yai in Thailand, she shows the importance of the national dimension (especially at the legal and community levels) in the context of a global approach to heritage.

23. On the Committee's new policies, see Kishore 2010 and the document WHC-10/34.COM/12A.

BIBLIOGRAPHY

Bachimont, Bruno. "Pourquoi n'y a-t-il pas d'expérience en ingénierie des connaissances?" *15èmes Journées francophones d'ingénierie des Connaissances* (Lyon: France, 2004).

Benhamou, Francoise. "L'inscription au patrimoine mondial de l'humanité. La force d'un langage à l'appui d'une promesse de développement," in *Revue Tiers Monde* 202 (2010): 113–130.

Boer, Ben. "Identification and Delineation of World Heritage Properties," in *The 1972 World Heritage Convention: A Commentary*. Ed. Francesco Francioni and Federico Lenzerini (Oxford: Oxford University Press, 2008), 85–102.

Bowker, Geoffrey C., and Susan Leigh Star. *Sorting Things Out: Classification and Its Consequences* (Cambridge, MA: MIT Press, 2000).

Buergin, Reiner. Contested Heritages: Disputes on People, Forests, and a World Heritage Site in Globalizing Thailand. Thesis, Working Group Socio-Economics of Forest Use in The Tropics and Subtropics, (Albert-Ludwigs-Universität Freiburg, 2001).

Buzzini, Gionata P., and Luigi Condorelli. "Article 11 List of World Heritage in Danger and Deletion of a Property from the World Heritage List," in *The 1972 World Heritage Convention: A Commentary*, ed. Francesco Francioni and Federico Lenzerini (Oxford: Oxford University Press, 2008), 175–200.

Cameron, F. and Robinson, H. 2007, "Digital Knowledgescapes: Cultural, Theoretical, Practical, and Usage Issues Facing Museum Collection Databases in a Digital Epoch," in F. Cameron and S. Kenderdine (eds), *Theorizing Digital Cultural Heritage: A Critical Discourse* (opens in a new window), MIT Press, Cambridge, pp. 165–191.

Charlet, Jean. *L'ingénierie des connaissances, entre science de l'information et science de la gestion*, accessed 31 March 2014 http://archivesic.ccsd.cnrs.fr (2005).

Chikofsky, Elliot J., and James H. Cross II. "Reverse Engineering and Design Recovery: A Taxonomy," in *IEEE Software* 1 (1990): 13–17.

Courbières, Caroline, and Gérard Régimbeau. "Entrées pour le document: praxis, matières et formes sociales," in *Sciences de la société*, 68 (2006): 3–9.

Dalbin, Sylvie, and Brigitte Guyot. "Documents en action dans une organisation: des négociations à plusieurs niveaux," in *Études de communication*, 30 (2007): 55–70.

Desvallées, Andre, and François Mairesse. "Sur la muséologie," in *Culture et Musées*, 6 (2007): 131–155.

Di Giovine, Michael A. *The Heritage-scape: UNESCO, World Heritage, and Tourism* (Lanham, MD: Lexington Books, 2009).

Di Méo, Guy. "Processus de patrimonialisation et construction des territoires," in *hal*, 99–100 (2008): 1–19, accessed 31 March 2014, http://hal.archives-ouvertes.fr/halshs-00281934/.

Francioni, Francesco. "Des Biens culturels au patrimoine culturel: l'évolution dynamique d'un concept et de son extension," in *L'Action normative à l'UNESCO*, ed. Yusuf (2007): 221–236.

Francioni, Francesco, and Federico Lezenrini. "The Future of the World Heritage Convention: Problems and Prospects," in *The 1972 World Heritage Convention: A Commentary*, ed. Francesco Francioni and Federico Lenzerini (Oxford: Oxford University Press, 2008a), 401–410.

Francioni, Francesco, and Federico Lezenrini. *The 1972 World Heritage Convention: A Commentary* (Oxford: Oxford University Press, 2008b).

Francioni, Francesco, and Federico Lezenrini. "The Obligation to Prevent and Avoid Destruction of Cultural Heritage: From Biniyan to Iraq," in *Art and Cultural Heritage: Law, Policy, and Practice*, ed. Barbara T. Hoffman (Cambridge: Cambridge University Press, 2006), 28–41.

Fraysse, Patrick. "Effets du système d'information sur l'évolution de la notion de patrimoine," in *L'information dans les organisations: dynamique et complexité,* ed. Christiane Volant (Tours: Presses Universitaires François-Rabelais, 2008), 303–314.

Frey, Bruno S., and Lasse Steiner. "World Heritage List: Does it make sense?" in *Working Paper Series*, 484 (Institute for Empirical Research in Economics, University of Zurich, 2010): 1–20, accessed 31 March 2014, http://ssrn.com/abstract=1600052.

Gamboni, Dario. "World Heritage: Shield or Target?" in *Newsletter Getty Conservation Institute*, 16.2 (2001).

Geser, Guntram, and John Pereira. *The Future Digital Heritage Space: An Expedition Report, 2004, Digicult Thematic Issue* (2004), accessed 31 March 2014, http://www.digicult.info/downloads/dc_the matic_issue7.pdf.

Goody, Jack. *The Domestication of the Savage Mind* (Cambridge: Cambridge University Press, 1977).

Guillaume, Marc. *La politique du patrimoine*. Paris, Galilée, 1980.

Hafstein, imar Tr. "Intangible Heritage as a List: From Masterpieces to Representation," in *Intangible Heritage*, ed. Ed. L. Smith and N. Akagawa (London: Routledge, 2009).

Hazen, Helen. "'Of Outstanding Universal Value': The Challenge of Scale in Applying the World Heritage Convention at National Parks in the US," in *Geoforum*, 1 (2008): 252–264.

Heinich, Nathalie. *La fabrique du patrimoine. De la cathédrale à la petite cuillère* (Paris: Maison des Sciences de l'Homme, 2009).

Impey, Oliver, and Arthur MacGregor. *The Origins of Museums. The Cabinet of Curiosities in Sixteenth- and Seventeenth-Century Europe* (Oxford: Clarendon Press, 1985).

Kishore, Rao. "A New Paradigm for the Identification, Nomination and Inscription of Properties on the World Heritage List," in *International Journal of Heritage Studies*, 3 (2010): 161–172.

Laflaquière, Julien, Lotfi-Sofiane Settouti, Yannick Prié and Alain Mille. *Un environnement pour gérer des traces comme inscriptions de connaissances*, Rapport de recherche de LIRIS UMR 5205 CNRS/ INSA de Lyon (Lyon: Université Claude Bernard Lyon 1, 2007).

Latour, Bruno. *Science in Action: How to Follow Scientists and Engineers through Society* (Milton Keynes, UK: Open University Press, 1987).

Leroi-Gourhan, André. *Le geste et la parole* (Paris: Albin Michel, 1964).

Quintas, Paul, and Adrian Demaid. "Reverse Knowledge Engineering," in *Management of Innovation and Technology. ICMIT 2000. Proceedings of the 2000 IEEE International Conference*, 2 (2000): 702–707.

Rautemberg, Michel. *La rupture patrimoniale* (Bernin: A la croisée, 2003).

Rössler, Mechtild. "World Heritage cultural landscapes: A UNESCO Flagship Programme 1992–2006." *Landscape Research* 31, 4 (2006): 333–353.

Schmitt, Thomas M. *Global Cultural Governance: Decision-Making Concerning World Heritage between Politics and Science* (Bonn: University of Bonn, 2009).

Schuster, J. Mark. "Making a List and Checking it Twice: The List as a Tool of Historic Preservation," in *Biannual Conference of the Association for Cultural Economics International Rotterdam*, the Netherlands, June 13–15, 2002.

Severo, Marta. *Heritage Networks. Managing Network Cultural Heritage with the Web* (Saarbrucken: VDM Verlag Dr. Muller, 2009).

Severo, Marta. "La sélection du patrimoine mondial: une analyse des systèmes d'information de l'UNESCO," in *Cahier de l'Institut du patrimoine* (Québec: Editions MultiMonde, 2011).

UNESCO. Convention Concerning the Protection of the World Cultural and Natural Heritage, 1972.

UNESCO. Operational Guidelines for the Implementation of the World Heritage Convention, 2008.

Vrdoljak, Ana Filipa. "Article 14, The Secretariat and Support of the World Heritage Committee," in *The 1972 World Heritage Convention: A Commentary*, ed. Francesco Francioni and Federico Lenzerini (Oxford: Oxford University Press, 2008), 243–269.

15

Tools and Methods for Georeferencing Library Heritage

Agata Maggio and Maurizio Lazzari

INTRODUCTION

In the age of digital archives and online data consultation, libraries in the world integrate standardized bibliographic description and unified computer language. Consequently, an online library can be a tool for more ambitious and global interest aims, particularly for studies, research, and applications across different professional fields. In spite of this, however, a library online catalogue still cannot insert all representative geographic locations contained in a document to its catalogue record—that is, to georeference the catalogue record.

Library cataloguing software and systems allow the access of bibliographic information relating to an item or specimen by querying the catalogue using specific data, such as author, title, subject, keyword, ISBN (International Standard Book Number), or the computer code of the bibliographic record (BID or Book Identification) that is assigned to the record during the development of the card catalogue. Research has shown, however, that there is the need to highlight and extract spatial data from the information contained in the printed or digital form of an item or specimen. Because of this need, there are a lot of experimental projects, software programs, and theories that deal with procedures for applying manual and/or automatic extraction of spatial data and on how to share the procedures and organize and display them[1] (Humphrey and Prindal, 2012). Even with the attendant possibilities of and added values in cataloguing, the world of research still copes with the impossibility of finding library material when searching for the geographic information that is linked to that material. Geographic information can be overcome only by querying the catalogue using the specific geographic location itself as subject or keyword(s). Thus, one has to know the specific geographic territory in order to track the name of a place and specific areas of interest. The identification of a library material in a language or using an alphabet system other than one's own is an added challenge in the search process.

The need for geographic information searching was highlighted by Bin Zhu et al. (1999). The authors stressed the problem of the inability to retrieve geographic information in digital contents and in digital archives, and suggested translating the textual analysis of the elaboration of maps. Nearly eighteen years after Bin Zhu et al., we ask whether the evolution of the web and high technology now allow not only the geographic display of text or images and contents but also the direct query of geographic data, and whether this is made possible through the interconnection of bibliographical data through advanced cataloguing structures and systems.

These new bibliographical data could make use of Geographic Information Systems (GISs) in order to georeference and make the query results visible through the instant construction of a spatial distribution map of the data.

In this chapter we offer an overview of the tools and methods for searching documents of study and different territorial aspects through the official channels of OPAC cataloguing. We address the need to consult not only map data but also related territorial research, such as from old and modern printed texts, scientific papers, archival documents, and so on. Different categories of people who may have this need could include researchers, scholars, and professionals coming from various disciplines, such as geology, health sciences, history, archaeology, sociology, legal and economic sciences, who might not know the toponyms of a specific geographic area linked to, for example, field-survey missions, theses, or any other research activity. The tools that we discuss, when used properly, are not implemented to encroach on the work of specialized staff, such as library and archives staff, but to solve a problem so as to optimize the work of the staff themselves and respond to the needs of "sophisticated" library and archives users as in the case of researchers and scholars (Maggio et al., 2016).

STATE OF THE ART OF CATALOGUING AND
GEOREFERENCING BIBLIOGRAPHIC DATA

At present, the inclusion of specific georeferenced data together with geographical coordinates during the cataloguing phase is carried out only in the cartography field. The inclusion of places/localities deduced from books, articles, and magazines is not undertaken. The georeferencing of the places included in the catalogued library material has not been taken into consideration in international standards. The recent need for georeferenced maps, documents, and bibliographic records has favored the start of some specific studies and initiatives applied to specific geographical areas, thus placing important elements for future developments alongside developments in computers. Among the initiatives is the creation of a georeferenced database at the University of Oregon (United States) and the production of a map at the Institute of Marine Biology (OIMB) that, considering the importance of the coastal area of Coos Bay and the consequences of industrial development there, used Google Earth and GeoCommons to accurately locate the geographic content of documents such as theses, peer-reviewed articles, and technical reports (figure 15.1).

In this way it is possible to develop a real georeferenced bibliography (Butler and Schmitt, 2012) that can become a visible online map. In this case, the researchers can collect and process data from state and federal agencies, universities, and nonprofit organizations, and then submit their work through the network as a tool for future researchers. This project, like others, is based on the idea that it is possible to create spatial or georeferenced bibliographies through free or open source software such as Google Earth or GeoNetwork or GIS.[2]

The list of projects that aim at experimenting with and creating georeferenced databases and new techniques that could then be shared includes important attempts, undertaken primarily in the United States, such as those by Bond Lamberty and Thomson (2010), the Papahanaumokuakea Information Management System (2012),[3] the USGS Coastal and Marine Geology Program (2012),[4] Watterson and Topper (2007), the Geo-referenced database for Coastal Cutthroat Trout Oncorhynchus Clarki of Washington and Oregon,[5] Webstey and Hiveley (2006) and the Galvveston Bay Information Center (1997),[6] JournalMap[7] with the addition of a georeferenced map,[8] ScienceBase,[9] DPLA,[10] GeoRef,[11] and ThisWormyWorld.[12] Additionally, pub-

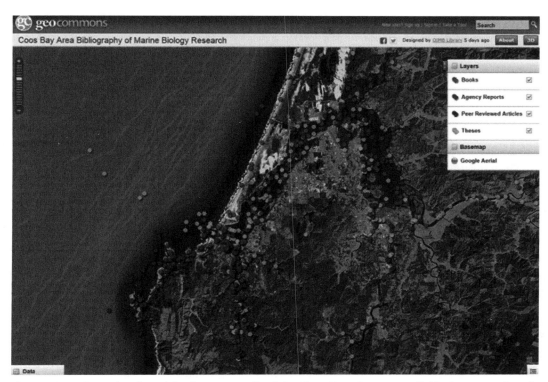

Figure 15.1. Example of spatial references realized for Coos Bay, Oregon, available for researchers in marine biology, through the possibility of observation on the GeoCommons framework.

lishers like Pensoft and Elsevier allow for the entry or submission of geographic information at the time of article submission. These resources contain the most significant cases, of which many are experimental and independent of the specific discipline involved.

In order to better understand how a search engine for georeferenced bibliography works it is worth considering, first, the interesting works that provide evidence of the fact that the search tools for thematic literature do not take into consideration the geographic location of the research (Karl et al. 2013a). In particular, we would like to show that geographic research would enhance productivity, relevance, and value (Karl et al. 2013b). The following two projects are worth describing:

1. A project by Harvard University, the aim of which is to improve searching by catalogue through geospatial technologies. By using an interactive map, the project shows that the geocoding of catalogue data allows the identification of spatial relations between catalogue resources, thus showing relations that otherwise would not be evident;[13]
2. A project designed by the Biodiversity Heritage Library, a consortium of ten international libraries (natural history museum, libraries of botanical gardens, and associate technology partners) with the aim of digitalizing the corpus of historical literature on biodiversity and also georeferencing data.[14]

Among the most important European projects is the Digimap project, a UK archive of maps and cartographic data developed by the National Data Centre Edina, which acquires and makes geodata available for those in the field of education. The data entered are derived from the analyses of material and documents relating to different disciplines (archaeology, geology, architecture, design, planning, engineering, geography, ecology, hydrology, zoology, forestry, health and medical sciences, epidemiology, history, literature, and languages).[15] The data are arranged so that they are downloadable and favor the use of GIS or CAD software or the view of online maps generated by Digimap.

The creation of a global portal of georeferenced[16] historical maps is an ambitious but extremely important aim. The project, supported by a partnership between the University of Portsmouth (UK) and the Klokan Technologies Gmbh (Switzerland), aims to develop software for the management, manipulation, and visualization of historical maps on the web, as well as including developments in 3D visualization for the benefit of libraries, archives, and museums. The idea is to identify the maps by utilizing geographic research, extrapolating through free tutorials and open source or free software to publish scanned maps online.

The retrieval and the collection of items for the construction of thematic bibliographies in well-defined geographical areas are a necessary library service, particularly for specific types of study and research. The following three examples of georeferenced bibliographic research illustrate this. The first example focused on the Basilicata region in southern Italy, in which the Italian National Research Council focused on the close relationship between literature/scientific production and the need for georeferencing any single element of this production. A census of the bibliographic sources on paleontology in Basilicata was conducted, with the aim of taking a census of the paleontological sites and georeference the bibliographic data collected in order to enhance the sites and make them usable. The data, collected from libraries and entered into tables organized in chronological order, have been restated in graphical form and maps (GIS and Google Earth) and used for the design of a PaleoBas geo-application (Lazzari et al., 2014) for Smartphone and tablets (figure 15.2).[17]

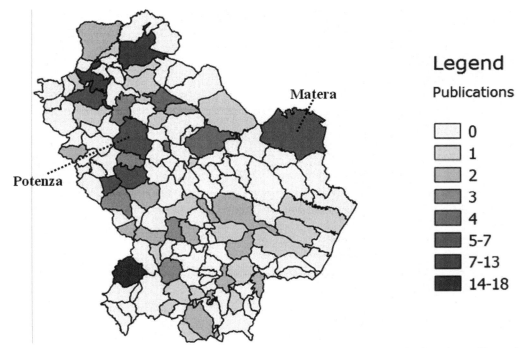

Figure 15.2. Statistic distribution of publications relating to palaeontological findings in Basilicata for each municipality.

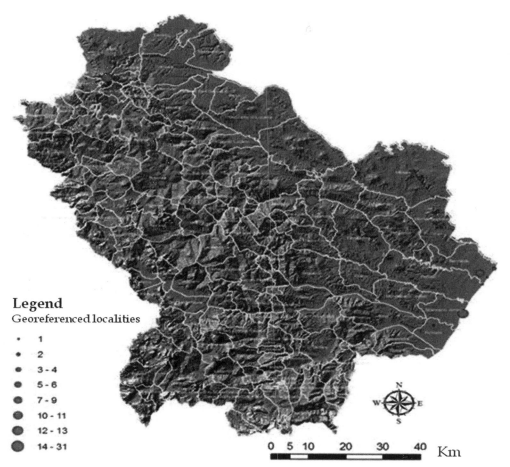

Figure 15.3. Geographic distribution and frequency of citation of the sites located in Basilicata region (southern Italy) cited in the works of poets and writers (Lazzari and Maggio, 2014).

The second example was research of literacy sources of the Basilicata region (Lazzari and Maggio, 2014), for the period of time between the sixteenth and twentieth centuries. This work aimed to identify, select, and analyze poetry and/or prose that described the geomorphological outlines of the landscape, as well as the specific locations mentioned by the authors. After an extensive investigation, conducted by time period and geographical area, the selection was carried out through a reasoned reading of the texts analyzed. The georeferenced locations identified in the works of each author have permitted the graphical display, the frequency of citations, and their geographical distribution (figure 15.3) through the use of a GIS platform.

The third example was concerned with the georeferencing of places mentioned in the bibliography of the Basilicata geological literature (Lazzari et al., 2013). The georeferenced bibliography allowed the identification of the most and the least studied areas in Basilicata over time, thus highlighting the need for possible future studies on lesser-known areas (figure 15.4).

In agreement with Haas et al. (2002), according to which "geography is an intrinsic factor in many fields of research," even the bibliographic field could not be excluded in a specific numeric field within the construction of the bibliographic record, such as the MARC 651 or 034[18] (corresponding to 607 and 123 fields of UNIMARC,[19] the latter used exclusively for car-

Figure 15.4. Shows the citation frequency of the sites (toponyms) cited in the geological literature of Basilicata. The recognition of the localities has been designed with respect to the cartographic base in scale 1:25000 of the Italian Military Geographic Institute (Lazzari et al., 2013).

tographic material), in which the longitude and latitude coordinates are included to get a specific location. Therefore, the indexing of the information by inserting geographic coordinates is not commonly done for non-cartographic data. Nebert and Fullton (1995) propose the use of flexible, freely available software that uses the Z39.50 search and retrieves the standards, making such indexing possible. As more digital spatial information, reports, and reconnaissance data are put online, it is necessary to provide a reliable means of accessing them without being restricted to a geographic place-name hierarchy.

Technological advances and the creation of GISs have shown the limit that the single insertion of a datum presents with respect to the possibility of developing data from a geospatial perspective. Haas et al. (2002) tried to overcome this limitation by exploiting the functionality of the Z39.50 protocol, removing data from some fields (including those mentioned above) and reworking them with ArcView software for the construction of a geodatabase. This approach, which proved to be valid, represents a further step in the relationship between bibliography and the georeferenced, also including online catalogues to be considered as an important component in the construction of databases and maps. All this is evidenced in the work on the geospatial bibliographies of Oahu and the Honolulu islands[20] (Coleman et al., 2002), which was structured to facilitate the work of the persons responsible for the environment at the US Fish and Wildlife Service (USFWS) office. It is managed through the same data removal process in ArcView, by cutting and pasting the selected data from an online catalogue and exporting them to an Access database.

In light of all this, our work has mainly aimed at identifying the projects concerning the georeferencing of library material. After highlighting these projects we are going to create a process that is able to act directly through the software used in the library and also used during the cataloguing phase. This would expand the network of data sharing and visualization within a worldwide interaction supported by standardized criteria such as those for the cataloguing of library material.

BiblioGeoreTe: A New Italian Project for Georeferencing Bibliographic Geological Data

Among the different examples of projects aimed at processing the bibliographic data as a geographic datum, we should cite the BIBLIOGEORETE or in Italian referred to as *BIBLIOgrafie GEOREferenziate Tematiche* or Georeferenced Temathic Bibliographies. It is a project that started in 2015 and is sponsored by the Italian National Research Council (CNR), the Italian National Institute for Environmental Protection and Research (ISPRA, Istituto Superiore per la Protezione e la Ricerca Ambientale), the Italian Association of Libraries (AIB), and the Rovereto Museum Fondation (MCR or Fondazione Museo Civico di Rovereto). The aim of the project is the recovery or reinstatement of an older national project supported by CNR tra gli anni '60 ed '80, which was finalized to realize a series of Regional Geological Bibliographies, supporting the Geological Map of Italy 1:100000 and subsequent finalized projects. The recent project, which is realized with modern research criteria and with the support of new technologies, serves as a first stage in a larger project on the geological theme already started by the CNR, and will be extended to other environmental and cultural themes at the regional level. It is expected to have a positive and useful impact on many areas of knowledge, such as basic research, education, self-employment, and spatial planning.

The objectives of the project and its work phases can be summarized in the following points (see figure 15.5):

- Establishment of a working group and national coordination with representatives of the Proponent Bodies, which, as a first stage, will prepare the text of the institutional memorandum of understanding;
- Provision of a prototype project to define the guidelines to be used in bibliographic research, the protocols to be used in citations, the georeferencing of bibliographic data—following the example already made in Basilicata (Lazzari et al., 2013; figure 15.4), and for inserting into a specific online web platform (national database) so as to make data available even in real time;
- Defining a project financial support plan;
- Establishment of regional working groups coordinated by the national committee; and
- Digitization of rare volumes.

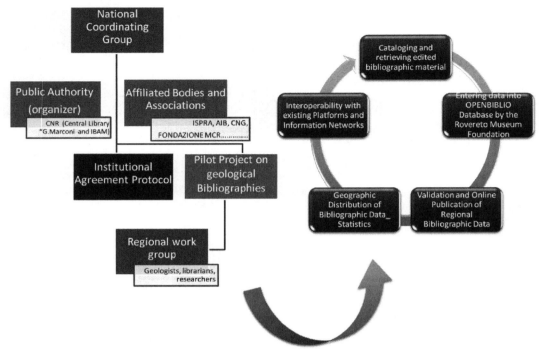

Figure 15.5.   Flowchart summarizing the conceptual structure of the Bibliogeorete project and the relationships in the operational phase.

The BIBLIOGEORETE project represents a modern form of bibliographic (environmental) data processing as a geographic datum (Maggio et al., 2016) in order to verify the regional and territorial distribution of the results of the studies carried out over time and the consistency and frequency of citation for municipalities and studied places (see example of Basilicata in Southern Italy, Lazzari et al., 2013). This will allow one to see which areas of the territory have been studied the most and which areas need further study, thus enabling better management of economic and human resources in the latter areas. Such a project will enhance the bibliographic and documentary resources available in numerous libraries and not only of CNR, but also of all those within the national territory, thus forming a network of information publicly available on a dedicated platform.

ADVANTAGES AND CRITICISM

As Mitidieri and Ridi (2006) remind us, the Internet has become much more convenient, faster, and more complete than the traditional model of the library, with billions and billions of web pages serving as catalogues and archives and thus as an essential tool for any type of study. In the Internet era, information can be accessed at any time and from any location through a computer, a smartphone, or a tablet; however, accessing the information is not always the result of an instant search, and likewise, is not always the most accurate and satisfactory answer. Sometimes, the work of intermediaries, such as librarians, bibliographers, references, information brokers, and so on, is necessary. These intermediaries make effective use of tools, like catalogues, in less time and with better results, such as the retrieval of diverse types of documents, such as texts, graphics, video, or audio.

It is inevitable that the evolution of cataloguing, with the inclusion of a new application for georeferencing the places contained in the books, such as software and other online tools for cataloguing, in accordance with the international regulation for their use, would allow an advanced search that preserves the traditional cataloguing data, but to which is added the capability to optimize the specific needs of the researcher.

The georeferencing of the places mentioned in bibliographical sources will be carried out during the cataloguing phase by using validated geographic dictionaries, which meets two needs: (1) adherence to the logic of bibliographic cataloguing, which sets its application on the basis of shared and approved international standards; and (2) the use of a global common vocabulary.

The research projects show, in most cases, a close link between topic, theme, location, and georeferenced maps through the identification of works and the construction of bibliographies. However, the use and construction of georeferenced maps, in addition to bibliographies, have the added advantage of sharing, graphically, either the territorial origin of a field survey/research or their geographic distribution, from which it is possible to stimulate further reflection.

What is the advantage of georeferencing the works of catalogues with respect to traditional bibliographies? The major advantage is encompassed by the same distinction between a bibliography and a catalogue. Both contain the main data useful for identifying the work; however, the former is useful for bringing together works that share a common theme, is a list of documents that are selected based on the catalogue, and is a complete identification or ID card of the work which includes the "address" of each specimen in the library, so that it is possible to consult it, borrow it via interlibrary loan, or copy or view it.

An epidemiologist, for example, who is doing research on rare clinical cases on a global scale will map the temporal distribution of the disease by reading the historical record and, in addition to identifying the document, s/he will also need to access the content by consulting the document itself. S/he will be able to do so on the basis of this proposal, performing a single search directly in OPAC that is compatible with the specific requirements imposed by the libraries concerned. The epidemiologist, however, may also wish to search from a different perspective—that is, according to a specific territorial or geographical specification. In this way, the query of a georeferenced map to identify the works for a specific geographic area would allow her/him to achieve the same results as the previous search in a single operation, but from a different perspective. Some improvements to the search facility have been planned, and have already been made to the traditional OPAC research, through the use of appropriate filters as subjects or keywords. All this will be possible only by building a map that is able to transfer data from an online catalogue to the network. From a technical point of view, the advantage is closely linked to computer and web diffusion.

OPAC and MetaOPAC offer, in fact, the advantage of using secure, controlled, and regulated data, thus making this application a tool for easy and immediate use, so as to ensure the retrieval of data both through the traditional search (title, author, subject) and georeferenced data. A georeferenced map that locates places of interest of a work represents an added value for both the user (it is possible to use an additional search path) and the library (which will show the areas from its collection that are most analyzed, and thus be equipped to plan for future purchases that will fill the gaps in the collection). This map represents a tool within a structure and is able to benefit from it and enhance it, but in turn can become a digital document to integrate and maintain and, as such, respond to the future, as discussed by IFLA.

The evolution of Opal (Open Public Access Library), to access local and remote digital resources, was already discussed by IFLA in 2005. It goes without saying that such an instrument, which takes advantage of OPAC and MetaOPAC rather than the single bibliographies, involves the need to focus on the definition of standards accepted and spread on a global scale, as well as the selection of words and the standardization of procedures to share.

FIELD OF APPLICATION ON BIBLIOGRAPHIC SOURCES

Each work catalogued on the basis of rules and standards, however, can contain the topics of one or more disciplines identified both by navigating with the help of the subject and Dewey Decimal Classification and making a direct analysis of the document from the title (remembering that sometimes it may be misleading and may not correspond to the content), table of contents, index, introduction, as well by opening some sentences of chapters and conclusions. The concept of completeness, in this way, will correspond to the cataloguer's capacity to indicate accurately the discipline or disciplines involved in the content of the work, while specificity represents the exact ratio between each discipline concerned and the specific place of reference involved in georeferencing. In this context it will be essential to conduct a literature search through a georeferenced location flanked by the subject (used as a filter), in order to define only the works of interest.

The above-cited example, proposed by Lazzari and Maggio (2014), which focused on landscape analysis and landscape changes (natural and anthropic) through research carried out on prose and poetry texts published over the centuries, shows that it is not possible, at least at the moment, to make a precise selections of place names.

HOW TO STANDARDIZE THE PROPOSAL

In order to standardize the georeferencing procedure of bibliographic data, Maggio et al. (2016) proposed—besides the possibility of displaying the map with georeferenced points—to add new information that, in fact, will be part of the bibliographic record. As such, from a processing point of view, the work will not be limited to structure and the addition of a string, in which to insert the information, but it will be necessary to establish and suggest the rules to be adopted. The standards, on which the cataloguing rules and global standards for the bibliographic description are based, are designed for any library regardless of the type, size, and nature of the preserved heritage and are in line with Svenonius's principles and sub principles, especially that of "standardization: [on the basis of which] the descriptions must be standardized as far as possible, in extent and level" and that of "integration: [on the basis of which] the descriptions for all types of material should be based, as far as possible, on common rules" (Svenonius, 2000). The rules, by definition, take into account the needs of a detailed, rigorous, and uniform cataloguing that allows the sharing of catalogues in cooperation systems and networks.

TECHNOLOGICAL AND INFORMATION SOLUTION

The technological solutions proposed take into account that the aim is to provide the user with an overview of the geographical places mentioned in the publications contained in a library, museum, archives, or another cultural institution. Among the several management software and services of cataloguing adopted by libraries, the following features, which is a characteristic of almost all the most popular systems, are worth considering:

- The client-server system, a network architecture in which a client computer connects to a server to make use of a service, such as the sharing of a software resource with other clients, by using standard protocols (HTTP, etc.);
- Compliance with the standard Z39.50, as the client-server IT communication protocol, which is necessary for web search database information and/or catalogues;
- The implementation of the UNICODE standard, which is the coding system that assigns unique number to each font used for writing texts, regardless of the language of the cataloguing, the computing platform, or the program used;
- The introduction of FSX, a device for managing link citations in open mode, which is useful to provide the users with contextual links to full-text articles as well as to other resources as defined by the library;
- The operator of *metasearching*, which is a device developed to allow the user to query many electronic resources simultaneously through a single interface in order to get results organized according to criteria appropriate to the research purposes;
- International electronic formats for bibliographic records, UNIMARC (adopted in several European countries, including Italy, and with specifications established by IFLA) and MARC 21 (developed in the United States, in Anglo-Saxon countries, and in many other countries), as the standard for data exchange between different applications for cataloguing purposes;
- Use of the semantic web for the concept of data transformation, from simple published documents to linking information, and shared data (metadata) that specify the context (Bianchini and Guerrini, 2014).

This list of IT or information technology features allows the support of the hypothesis to develop the application through online catalogues, while offering at the same time some useful applicability extensions (in terms of quantity and quality). The inclusion of a "field," on the basis of an initial cognitive analysis that is carried out while considering both UNIMARC and MARC 21 formats, is suggested for the fields defined by numbers and coded information—that is, language and country of publication and/or production. The field length should be varied and repeatable within the rules already adopted in other fields.

A structure built for fields and subfields must enable the insertion of a term for the locality that will be georeferenced without neglecting the information inherent in the territory (region and country) in which it is included. For example, if the operator wants to georeference the city of Naples, the field and subfields should report sequentially each of the data as shown in figure 15.6.

Figure 15.6.   Example of a first level form to input the georeferenced geographic data.

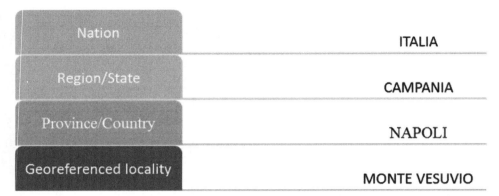

Figure 15.7.   Example of a subgroup form to input the georeferenced geographic data.

These subfields would allow the GIS software to locate data precisely and georeference them, using a routine procedure that collects the data from the subfield "georeferenced locations." The GIS software can process the data and return them in a map attached to OPAC as a digital product that is always available and upgradable by the library cataloguer. The scale of representation and visualization of results could vary depending on the graphic management system of online data. So for example, in case the structure *Region/State—Country/Province—georeferenced locality* is not sufficient to identify the location, a further subgroup should be assumed so as to obtain the sequence shown in figure 15.7.

This type of spatial subdivision applies the same procedure adopted for structuring the subject in the presence of places, where the generic areas precede the single territory. The advantage of a hierarchical structure in entering and displaying georeferenced geographic data is immediately useful. In fact, the user, by reading the data and viewing the map, will be able to trace the corresponding bibliographic material more easily even without having a direct knowledge of places and toponyms (figure 15.8).

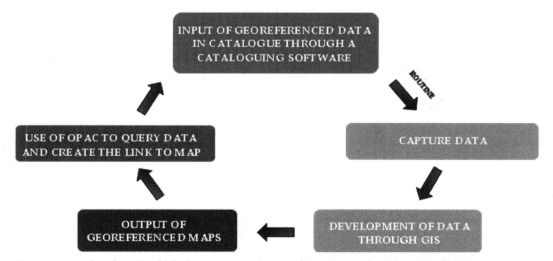

Figure 15.8.   Flowchart in which the sequence of steps of insertion and cataloguing of bibliographic data, generating a map and query via OPAC of external users with the display of the map of the spatial distribution of bibliographic data are shown.

For the field and subfield in question, it is desirable to provide the ability to enter data by clicking a series of choices on the list from a drop-down menu, which has the advantage of standardizing the items mentioned and reducing the possibility of error. For the subfield "georeferenced locality," considering the need to achieve the highest accuracy possible and the multitude of possible items to be included on the list, it is desirable to think about the possibility of a double-entry procedure:

- By clicking the drop-down menu (in the case of terms known as "Naples");
- Reporting the location manually (in the case of lesser known terms, "Mount Vesuvius").

However, it is worth considering that since georeferenced data refer to places, accuracy cannot be defined because locations do not have defined perimeters and, consequently, they will be represented through points placed in central areas.

An Alternative Entry Procedure by Using a Map

Another way of inserting georeferenced localities into a form (the cataloguing procedure), discussed by Maggio et al. (2016), could be that of determining the coordinates or the georeferenced locality by clicking directly on a map. In order to show how this might work, this process can be divided into two steps: (1) the identification of the georeferenced locality on the map by clicking on it, and (2) the information transfer on to a form. Examples of these can be found on the world wide web. For example, in order to identify the georeferenced locality by clicking on a map, the map application, visible on http://geoportal.bayern.de/bayernatlas/ and referred to as the Landesamt für Digitalisierung, Breitband und Vermessung (formerly Bayerische Vermessungsverwaltung), should be considered. By clicking on the map (inside the Bavarian borders), an information window pops up, showing, among other things, the municipality (Germeinde, *comune* in Italian) and the parish (Gemarkung, *frazione* in Italian). In the same way, the BayernAtlas is aware of the administrative division of Bavaria, and a GIS module attached to the catalogue could identify all the territories whose boundaries are known by the atlas.

In the case of the second step—the information transfer to a form, the alpinist site (http://www.deine-berge.de) supplies an auxiliary function by converting geographical coordinates into other geographical projections (http://www.deine-berge.de/umrechner_koordinaten.php). It is possible to either enter a pair of coordinates manually into the form or trigger them by clicking on the included map. In this way the coordinates are transferred to the fields of the form. Such methods could be adopted to facilitate librarians in the enrichment of catalogues with geographical data.

SEMANTIC WEB, LINKED DATA, AND RDA

It is useful to contextualize the above within the concept of the semantic web, intended to overcome the simple and pure publication of documents on the web and to create a link with data and information (as in, metadata). As Guerrini and Possemato (2015) state, "The semantic web is intended to convert the current web, characterized by unstructured and semi-structured documents, into a data web by encouraging the inclusion of semantic content on web pages. The idea of semantic web can be addressed first and foremost as a linguistic phenomenon: the method that allows the coherent integration of different data."

The semantic web is therefore the evolution of the web of documents through qualified links between objects in different data sources. In this context, the semantic web changes the nature of the links as they acquire a meaning that can be interpreted by a machine (semantics of data). Linked data represent the tool to create qualified links between objects in different sources. Further evolution of the semantic web is represented by RDA (Resource Description Access), based on shared international principles and applicable to any resource.

The semantic web with RDA provides a further result: the coordinated integration of data from various cultural institutions such as libraries, museums, and archives. It is above all in this context that it is possible to insert links that would allow the georeferencing of sites contained inside of bibliographic specimens for the purpose of increasing and improving the possibilities of research and access to resources.

Nomenclature

In full respect of the rules and standards of cataloguing diffused on a global scale and applied by various countries, it is important that data entry should meet the criteria of standardization and the sharing of the adopted nomenclature, so as to overcome any language and alpha barriers. For this reason, the use of a universal atlas of recognized value, such as the *New Concise World Atlas*, published by Oxford University Press,[21] should be suggested. The shared use of terms and data management, as is the case for the subject, for example, allows a clearer reading of the data regardless of the alphabet of the language used. The language used, of course, for the input of these data respects the rules and national needs (Humphrey, 2012; 2014).

FINAL REMARKS

The proposal presented in this paper makes explicit a new and innovative practice to manage the library heritage, based on georeferencing the places recalled in the bibliographic sources. This approach is useful for several professional groups, such as researchers, scholars, and professionals. The professional categories, the disciplines involved, and the material examined cover a wide range of research and do not leave out aspects generally considered superficial or marginal. Given the close relationship between locations and georeferenced catalogues, when formulating and articulating the proposal it was decided to attach the same weight and respect to the technical sector and information technology (practical realization) and to librarianship (for the compliance with the rules and standard procedures).

The Web confers a big advantage in terms of amount of information and reduction of geographical distances, but at the same time, it requires organization, control, and sharing in order to ensure reliable, usable, and recognizable information. The librarian sector, in this logic, is privileged compared to other areas of cultural heritage, because it takes advantage of shared, regulated channels for the description and retrieval of individual items. For this reason we propose a new procedure through this sector and the above-described instruments, with the aim of extending the applicability to museums, archives, and all the cultural centers. In addition, as far as research activity is concerned, it will be possible to extract georeferenced data and further develop them also by using graphic supports and thematic maps (Tufte, 2011).

NOTES

1. *Geocoding versus Spatial Metadata for large Text Archives: Toward a Geographically Enriched Wikipedia.* http://www.dlib.org/dlib/september12/leetaru/09leetaru.html. Automatic georeferencing of web-pages: Old Maps online. http://help.oldmapsonline.org/metadata Gogeo. http://www.gogeo.ac.uk/gogeo/metadata/geodoc.htm. Opengeoportal.http://opengeoportal.org/geoblacklight/. Harvard Geospatial Library. http://calvert.hul.harvard.edu: 8080/opengeoportal/.

2. GeoNetwork Opensource. http://geonetwork-opensource.rg/.

3. Papahanaumokuakea Marine National Monument Spatial Bibliography.

4. USGS Coastal and Marine Geology Program. http://cmgds.marine.usgs.gov/gsearch.html.

5. Geo-reference for coastal cutthroat trout Oncorhynchus clarki of Washington and Oregon. http://ocid.nacse.org/nbii/cutbib/index.php.

6. Galveston Bay Bibliography. http://www.tamug.edu/gbic/gbb.html.

7. JournalMap. https://journalmap.org/.

8. Sage Grouse georeferenced bibliography. http://blog.journalmap.org/sage-grouse-georeferenced-bibliography/.

9. ScienceBase. https://www.sciencebase.gov/catalog/.

10. DPLA /Digital Public Library of America). http://dp.la/.

11. GeoRef. http://www.americangeosciences.rg/georef/georef-information-services.

12. This Wormy World. http://thiswormyworld.org.

13. *Enhancing Catalog Searching with Geospatial Technology.* https://osc.hul.harvard.edu/liblab/projects/enhancing-catalog-searching-geospatial-technology.

14. *Geocoding LCSH in the Biodiversity Heritage Library.* http://journal.code4lib.org/articles/52.

15. *Digimap Resource Centre.* http://digimap.edina.ac.uk/web-help/resources/index.html.

16. project.oldmapsonline.org.

17. http://www.paleobas.it/index.html.

18. *Marc 21. Formato Conciso per Dati Bibliografici*, 343 (contessi and Gadea Rega, 2007).

19. Unimarc bibliographic in Italian. http://unimarc-it.wikidot.com/#blocco0.

20. Northwestern Hawaiian Islands Bibliography is a publicly available spatial search engine for bibliographic references, geographic data, and gray literature for the NWHI region. The Spatial Bibliogaphy presently contains over 30 subject categories and can be sorted by over 20 bibliographic or location categories. Of the 1995 references currently available in the database, 930 have some level of geographic location information. These 930 spatially linked geographic location using ArcMap. The remaining 1065 references can be found using MS Access' database query functions (See Taylor and Nelson, 2006).

21. *New Concise World Atlas* (Keyith, 2009). Other good reference databases from which to draw the correct geographical classification may be GeoNames, OpenStreetMap, Library of Congress Authorities and Vocabularies Service, National Historical GIS (NHGIS), Natural Earth, NPS Historic Places Register, Tigerline and the Historical Place Marker Database (HMDB). One example among many is the dictionary of the Library of Congress: http://github.com/LibraryOfCongress/gazetteer;hhttp://loc.gaetteer.us; http://nypl.gazetter.us.

BIBLIOGRAPHY

Bianchini Carlo and Mauro Guerrini. *Introduzione a RDA*. Milano: Bibliografica, 2014.

Butler, Barbara A. and Jennifer Schmitt J. *Coos Bay Bibliography*. University of Oregon Libraries, 2012, http://ddlhandle.net/1794/12309.

Coleman, David E., Paul Jokiel, Eric Hill, et al. "Better document management though georeferencing." *ArcUser Online*. 2012. http://www.esri.com/news/arcuser/0402/docmanage1of3.html.

Guerrini, Mauro and Tiziana Possemato. Linked data per biblioteche, archivi e musei. Milano: Bibliografica, 2015.

Haas, Stephanie C., Joe Aufmuth, David E. Coleman, et al. "Marc and Arc: Geospatially Enabling Bibliographic Records." In *Bridging the Digital Divide: Proceedings of the 28th Annual Conference of the International Association of Aquatic and Marine Science Libraries and Information Centers (IAMSLIC)*, Maatlan, Sinaloa, Mexico, 6-11 October 2002. IAMSLIC, 2003. pp. 119–126.

Humphrey, Southall. "Rebuilding the Great Britain Historical GIS, Part 2: A Geospatial Ontology of Administrative Units." *Historical Methods: A Journal of Quantitative and Interdisciplinary History* 45, no. 3 (2012): 119–134.

Humphrey, Southall. "Rebuilding the Great Britain Historical GIS, Part 3: Integrating Qualitative Content for a Sense of Place." *Historical Methods: A Journal of Quantitative and Interdisciplinary History* 47, no. 1 (2014): 31–44.

Humprey, Southall and Petr Prindal P. "Old Maps Online: Enabling Global Access to Historical Mapping." *ePerimetron* 7, no. 2 (2012): 73–81.

Karl, Jason W., et al. "Geo-Semantic Searching: Discovering Ecologically Relevant Knowledge from Published Studies." *BioScience* 63, no. 8 (2013a): 674–682. DOI: 10.1525/bio.2013.63.8.10.

Karl, Jason W., Jeffrey K. Gillen, and Jeffrey E. Herrick. "Geographic Searching for Ecological Studies: A New Frontier." *Trends in Ecology & Evolution* 28 no. 7 (2013b): 383–384. DOI: 10.1016/j.tree.2013.05.001.

Lazzari, Maurizio, Agostino Lecci, and Nicola Lecci. PaleoBas: A Geoapplication for Mobile Phone. A New Method of Knowledge and Public Protection of the Paleontological Heritage of Basilicata (Southern Italy). In *Computational Science and its Applications:* ICCSA 2014 (Part II), Lecture Notes in Computer Science. v. 8580, 2014: pp. 663–676.

Lazzari, Maurizio and Agata Maggio. "La lettura geomorfologica del paesaggio letterario in Basilicata tra XVI e XX secolo." In Atti del Convegno Dialogo intorno al Paesaggio-percezione, interpretazione, rappresentazione, Perugia, Italy, 19–22 Febrary 2013. Università degli Studi di Perugia, 2014: pp. 211–225, http://www.ctl.unipg.it/issues/DIP2013_TOMO_I.pdf 1.

Lazzari, Maurizio, Giuseppe Zafarone, and Maria Danese. Fonti bibliografiche della Letteratura geologica. Basilicata (1551–2011). Lagonegro: Editore Grafiche Zaccara, 2013.

Maggio Agata, Lazzari Maurizio, and Kuffer Josef. "Advances and Trends in Bibliographic Research: Examples of New Technological Applications for the Cataloguing of the Georeferenced Library Heritage." *Journal of Librarianship and Information Science*, 2016: 1–14. DOI: 10.1177/0961000616652134.

Mitidieri, Fabio and Riccardo Ridi. Biblioteche in Rete: Istruzioni per l'uso. Roma-Bari: Laterza, 2006.

Nebert, Douglas D. and James Fullton. "Use of the ISite Z39.50 Software to Search and Retrieve Spatially-Referenced Data." In Second annual conference on the theory and practice of digital libraries, DL 1995, Austin, Texas, 11–13 June 1995.

Svenonius, Elaine. *The Intellectual Foundation of Information Organization.* Cambridge, MA: MIT Press, 2000.

Taylor, Christine and David Moe Nelson. "Northwestern Hawaiian Islands spatial bibliography: a science-planning tool." Atoll Research Bulletin, no. 543 (2006): 51–62.

Tufte, Edward. *The Visual Display of Quantitative Information*, 2nd ed. Cheshire.

Tufte, Edward. *The Visual Display of Quantitative Information,* 2nd ed. Cheshire, CT: Graphic Press, 2001.

Zhu, Bin, Tobun D. Ng, Bruce Schatz, et al. "Creating a Large-Scale Digital Library for Georeferenced Information." *D-Lib Magazine* 5 no. 7/8 (1999). http://www.dlib.org/dlib/july99/zhu/07zhu.html.

16

Visual Environment for Cultural Heritage (VECH)

Arantza Respaldiza and Monica Wachowicz

INTRODUCTION

Cultural heritage is a complex and diverse concept, which brings together a wide number of resources such as physical objects, books, works of art, pictures, historical maps, aerial photographs, archaeological surveys, and 3D models. Moreover, all these resources are listed and described in the digital environment by a variety of metadata specifications that allow their online search, retrieval, and consultation. Some examples include *Art & Architecture Thesaurus* (AAT); *Dublin Core Metadata Element Set* (Dublin Core); *Categories for the Description of Works of Art* (CDWA); *CIDOC Conceptual Reference Model* (CIDOC-CRM); the *Getty Thesaurus of Geographic Names* (TGN); the *Keyhole Markup Language* (KML); *MuseumDat*; *Describing Archives: A Content Standard* (DACS); *Machine Readable Cataloging* (MARC);[1] *Metadata Object Description Schema* (MODS); *Preservation Metadata* (PREMIS); VRA Core (the data standard for the description of works of visual culture); *Extensible Markup Language* (XML); the UK Museum Collection Management Standard, *SPECTRUM*; *Cataloging Cultural Object* (CCO); the geographic information metadata, ISO 19115, and the information retrieval protocol, Z39.50.

Gateways are in place to integrate these metadata standards with those used in a Spatial Data Infrastructure, such as *ISO 19115*[2] or *INSPIRE*,[3] the infrastructure for spatial information in Europe, but substantial work still remains to be done for a comprehensive incorporation of cultural heritage metadata. Toward this challenge, this research aims to implement what we refer to as *Visual Environment for Cultural Heritage* (VECH) for making metadata accessible to a community of users. With VECH, the complexity of cultural heritage resources can be dealt with by a visual exploration of their metadata within a visual environment. Our prototype implementation is a promising tool that represents a new frontier of our capacity of learning, understanding, communicating, and transmitting culture.

The human aspects of asynchronous collaboration at a distance have been the focus of those who seek to build visual environments for supporting access and interaction with cultural heritage information. A starting point for supporting collaboration across different places has been provided by the development of web technologies and distributed databases. Many have reviewed these developments, including Bucciero and Mainetti (2013), Bustillo et al. (2015), Carrozzino et al. (2013), and Fernández-Palacios, Morabito, and Remondino (2016). In all the previous research work, metadata visualization and interface issues have been investigated mainly by those concerned with how to visually represent the metadata to users. However, metadata visualization plays a more important role because it represents the spatial-temporal, semantic, symbolic, and interpretative relations between different cultural heritages in order to support a multi-user interpretation process.

The ArchaeoLandscapes Europe project (ArcLand) is a particular effort toward making a better use of existing archaeological, LIDAR (light detection and ranging), and photogrammetric survey data and their respective metadata specifications for sharing cultural heritage information that is scattered all over Europe.[4] Another commendable effort is the ARIADNE portal, which gathers and allows for the search and retrieval of digital resources and services for archaeological research, learning, and teaching across Europe.[5] The ARIADNE portal superseded the ARENA portal, which was running since 2004.[6] One effort has sought to create domain specific standards, such as the "3D conform consortium," which aims to "establish 3D documentation as an affordable, practical and effective mechanism for long term documentation of tangible cultural heritage."[7] It "proposes an ambitious program of technical research, coupled with practical exercises and research in the business of 3D to inform and accelerate the deployment of these technologies to good effect." And still another—EPOCH—has gathered research, publications, and tools useful for the visualization of cultural heritage.[8]

Our overall research goal is to design a visual environment where a multidisciplinary scientific community (e.g., historians, archivist, archaeologists, experts in human and social sciences, and communication experts) can meet and interact in real-time, exchange and test their hypothesis, share data and simulate different scenarios in order to discuss possible interpretations and methods. It is designed to be an interactive and dynamic environment for supporting continuous updating with new metadata information. This chapter proposes a metadata visualization approach for creating a visual structure for understanding connections and voids between current domain-specific standards in cultural heritage. We implemented a prototype in Tossa de Mar (Girona, Spain) because of the area's vulnerability and territorial diffusion of historical, cultural, and environmental values. Thus, the Tossa de Mar is our case study. We describe this case study in this chapter.

METHODOLOGY

Our visual environment is based on a visual map of the metadata landscape previously proposed by Riley (2010) and Fairbairn (2001). As a result, our visual representations are designed for creating hierarchies among the metadata specifications of cultural heritage resources and their different interpretations, as well as their relationships.

The standards represented in the VECH are among those most heavily used or publicized in the cultural heritage community such as DACS, Dublin Core, MARC, MODS, PREMIS, and VRA Core. The sheer number of metadata standards in the cultural heritage sector is overwhelming, and their interrelationships further complicate the situation. The strength of a standard in a given category is determined by a mixture of its adoption in that category, its design intent, and its overall appropriateness for use in that category. This visual map of the metadata landscape is intended to assist planners with the selection and implementation of metadata standards. Each of the 105 standards listed here is evaluated on its strength of application to defined categories in each of four axes: community, domain, function, and purpose.

- Community refers to the groups that currently or potentially use the standard. Those that originated a standard or who are the primary audiences are stronger matches, while those that could use the standard effectively but do not frequently do so are weaker matches. Libraries refer to those organizations that collect and preserve both primary and secondary material in support of research, scholarship, teaching, and leisure (MARC, MODS, PREMIS, XML, and VRA Core). Academic, public, special, and corporate libraries are included here. Archives refer to those organizations that collect and preserve the natural outputs of the daily work of individuals and other organizational entities, including traditional records management processes (DACS). Their emphasis is frequently on the context of the creation of the materials and their relationship to one another. Museums refer to those organizations that collect and preserve artifacts from a given field with an emphasis on their curation and interpretation (AAT, CCO, CDWA, CIDOC-CRM, MuseumDat, SPECTRUM, and TGN). Art, science, natural history, and many other types of museums are included here. Information Industry refers to the diverse organizations that make up both the public and the commercial Web (KML and XML). Technologies that support inventory and knowledge management, e-commerce, and the workings of the Internet are included here.

- Domain refers to the types of materials the standard is intended to be used with or could potentially be useful for. The specific categories represented here are not intended to be exhaustive, nor are they mutually exclusive; rather, they are focused on some common material types that are managed by cultural heritage and other information organizations. Cultural Objects refers to works of art, architecture, and other creative endeavors (AAT, CCO, CDWA, CIDOC/CRM, MuseumDat, SPECTRUM, TGN, XML, and VRA Core). Data sets refer to collections of primary data, largely before interpretive activities have taken place (Dublin Core). They may be collected by scientific instruments, or through research activities in the sciences, social sciences, humanities, or other disciplines. Geospatial Data refers to information relevant to geographic location, either as the data about geographic places themselves or the relationship of a resource to a specific location (Dublin Core, ISO 19115, and XML). Moving Images refers to resources expressed as film, video, or digital moving images (Dublin Core, XML, and Z39.50). Musical Materials refers to resources expressing music in any form, including as audio, notation, and moving image (Dublin Core, XML, and Z39.50). Scholarly Texts refers to resources produced as part of a research or scholastic process, and includes both book-length and article-length material (Dublin Core, XML, and Z39.50). Visual Resources refers to material presented in fixed visual form (AAT, CCO, CDWA, Dublin Core, VRA Core, XML, and Z39.50). These materials may be either artistic or documentary in nature.

- Function refers to the role a standard plays in the creation and storage of metadata. Some functions define the basic entities to be described, others define specific fields, others give guidance on how to record a specific data element, and still others define concrete data structures for the storage of information. Conceptual Models provide a high-level approach to resource description in a certain domain (CIDOC/CRM). They typically define the entities of description and their relationship to one another. Metadata structure standards typically use terminology found in conceptual model in their domain (CCO and DACS). Content Standards provide specific guidance on the creation of data for certain fields or metadata elements, sometimes defining what the source of a given data element should be (AAT, MARC, and TGN). They may or may not be designed for use with a specific metadata structure standard. Controlled Vocabularies are enumerated, either fully or by stated patterns, lists of allowable values for elements for a specific use or domain (AAT, MARC, and TGN). Classification schemes that use codes for values are included here. Framework/Technology is a general term encompassing models and protocols for the encoding and/or transmission of information, regardless of its specific format (XML and Z39.50). Markup Languages are formats that allow the featuring of specific aspects of a resource, typically in XML. They are unlike other "metadata" formats in that they provide not a surrogate for or other representation of a resource, but rather an enhanced version of the full resource itself. Record Formats are specific encodings for a set of data elements (MARC, MuseumDat, KML, and PREMIS). Many structure standards are defined together with a record format that implements them. Structure Standards are those that define at a conceptual level the data elements applicable for a certain purpose or for a certain type of material (CDWA, Dublin Core, ISO 19115, KML, MODS, MuseumDat, PREMIS, and VRA Core). These may be defined anew or borrowed from other standards. This category includes formal data dictionaries. Structure standards do not necessarily define specific record formats.

• Purpose refers to the general type of metadata the standard is designed to record. Typically a standard will be strongly focused on one purpose but include a few data elements for other purposes considered especially important. Data here refers to standards whose purpose is to enclose the resource itself, possibly together with metadata or with added value such as markup. Descriptive Metadata standards include information to facilitate the discovery, via search or browse, of resources, or provide contextual information useful in the understanding or interpretation of a resource (AAT, CCO, CDWA, CIDOC/CRM, DACS, ISO 19115, MARC, MODS, MuseumDat, SPECTRUM, VRA Core, and Z39.50). Metadata Wrappers package together metadata of different forms, or metadata together with the resource itself. Preservation Metadata is broadly the information needed to preserve, keep readable, and keep useful a digital or physical resource over time (PREMIS). Technical Metadata is one type of preservation metadata, but preservation metadata also includes information about actions taken on a resource over time and the actors who take these actions. Rights Metadata is the information a human or machine needs to provide appropriate access to a resource, provide appropriate notification and compensation to rights holders, and to inform end users of any use restrictions that may exist. Structural Metadata makes connections between different versions of the same resource, makes connections between hierarchical parts of a resource, records necessary sequences of resources, and flags important points within a resource. Technical Metadata documents the digital and physical features of a resource necessary to use it and understand when it is necessary to migrate it to a new format.

The aspects of visualization research are mutually interrelated as: data, purpose, technology, impact, and form. The five sections identify multiple aspects of the relationship between representation and visualization:

• Data: The nature of what kind of data and phenomena are to be represented, the form of representation chosen, for example, conceptual model or database representation.

- Purpose: The purpose for which representation is undertaken and used, the users for whom representation is undertaken, and the methods and the technologies that enable representation to be accomplished.
- Technology: The changing technology to support new forms of representation, how representations can be accessed and enhanced.
- Form: The representation purpose includes matching the representation with generic or specific data handling tasks as well as appearance and form of representation, visual design, and the user interface. The issues of concern in visualization research include characteristics of data to be visualized, purpose and form of representation, impact of form on understanding and task outcomes, and technology to support new form of representation. To reiterate, we consider the most critical issues to be those concerned with the characteristics of the data to be handled, including issues of its generalization, organization, and its inherent attributes.
- Impact: The impact of representation form on both understanding and task outcomes, in particular, user interaction with dynamic representations and with other users.

IMPLEMENTATION

The case study was conceived, designed, and built for the heritage of Tossa de Mar (Girona, Spain). The implementation was carried out in *Improvise* (Weaver 2006). *Improvise* is a fully implemented Java software architecture and user interface that enables users to build and browse highly coordinated visualizations interactively. Users gain precise control over how navigation and selection affects the appearance of data across multiple views by coupling a shared-object coordination model with a declarative visual query language, and using a potentially infinite number of variations on well-known coordination patterns such as synchronized scrolling, overview and detail, brushing, drill down, and semantic zoom. In the interface implementation attention has been directed, particularly, toward making the cultural heritage information accessible to a community of users with the metadata. Other components of this work will involve supporting the collection of locally generated information and comparing public use of a virtual decision making environment.

How Does the User Characterize the Metadata?

The catalog of heritage consists of items from the Tossa del Mar. CCO, MARC (figure 16.1) and CDWA is the standard catalog used. And the controlled vocabularies used are based on AAT and TGN. In *Improvise* the relational metadata model consists of several schemes that describe the columns of tabular data sets by name and type of object. The schemes are used for two different purposes: to validate access to content metadata sets and define the characteristics of both input and output of query expressions.

```
001      .b35890691

008      060912s1888 sp |||||| | o| 0 ||spa d

009      Lligam001CCUC. 01/20100315

035      C299590360|9ES-BaBNC001

035      0877-54660|9ES-BaBNC035

040      ES-BaBC|bcat|cES-BaBC

043       e-sp---|be-spcsl|2catmarc

080      912(467.1 Sl Tossa de Mar)

110      1 Espanya.|bDirección de Hidrografía

245      10 Plano del surgidero de Tossa|h[Document cartogràfic] : |blevantado en 1885 por la Comisión
         Hidrográfica al mando del capitán de fragata Rafael Pardo de Figueroa /|cL. G. Llanos y Cobos lo
         dibujó ; I. Tubau lo grabó ; P. Bacot grabó la letra

250      Ed. corr.

255      Escala 1: 5 000

260      Madrid :|bDirección de Hidrografía,|c1888

300      1 mapa :|blitografia ;|c30 x 49 cm

500      Correcciones: VIII, 917, II, 946, IV, 953

500      Precedeix al títol: Mar Mediterráneo, costa oriental de España

505      8 Inclou finestra: Faro de Tossa de Mar visto desde el E.

530      Reproducció digital disponible a: Memòria Digital de Catalunya

650      7 Costes|zMediterrània, Mar|xMapes|2lemac

650      7 Cartes nàutiques|zMediterrània, Mar|2lemac

651      7 Tossa de Mar|xMapes|2lemac

655      7 Mapes|zMadrid (Comunitat autònoma)|zMadrid|y1880-1890 |2gmgpc//cat

700      1 Bacot, P.

700      1 Tubau, I.,|egrav.

700      1 Llanos y Cobos, L. G.,|ds. XIX,|eil.

700      1 Pardo de Figueroa, Rafael

710      2 Fons Ignasi M. Colomer i Preses (Biblioteca de Catalunya)|5ES-BaBC

730      0 Memòria Digital de Catalunya

740      0 Mar Mediterráneo, costa oriental de España

856      41 |zAccés lliure|uhttp://mdc.cbuc.cat/u/?/mapesBC,247

935       0877-54660

993      0101|bM.Col 1089|ctampó: "Corregida por avisos a los navegantes hasta el 15 ene. grupo 1 de 1957"|dXV
         A 238|e01 |j8-Donatiu|kColomer i Preses|pIgnasi M.

999      VTLSFF1065 080326 0065
```

Figure 16.1. Plano del surgidero de Tossa.

How Does the User Personalize the Purposes?

The user personalizes the purposes in *Improvise* by using visual variables and reusable expressions that can be invoked by using multiple projections, filters, and classifiers (figure 16.2).

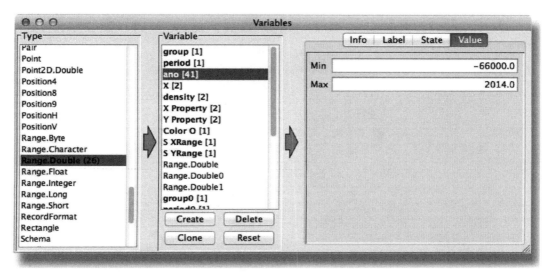

Figure 16.2. Creating variables and editing their values.

How Does the User Identify Technology?

The user identifies the technology and creates, edits, and coordinates different variables that materialize in the visual representations (figure 16.3).

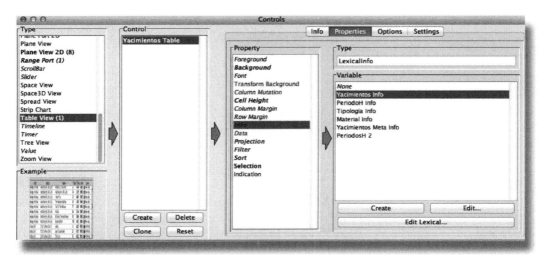

Figure 16.3. Creating views and other controls.

How Does the User Propose the Form?

The user creates and sets the parameters for a visual representation from the information available in the metadata in *Improvise*. The user develops the interface, creating pages, parameter frames, and panel views. The results are shown in figure 16.4.

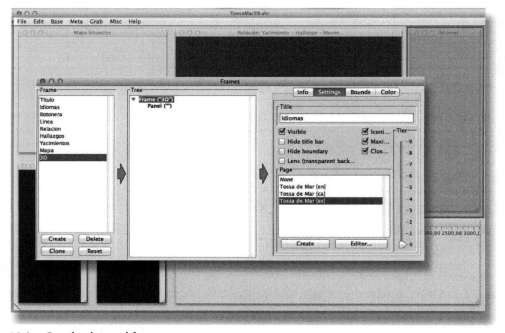

Figure 16.4.   Creating internal frames.

How Does the User Understand the Form?

The user makes a query and evaluates the results, and finally selects the best one for an intended use. The main stages of the process are shown in figure 16.5. The process is highly iterative as users refine the requirements while gaining more insight of available information.

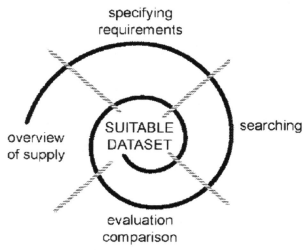

Figure 16.5.   The iterative process of geographic datasets (Ahonen-Rainio 2005).

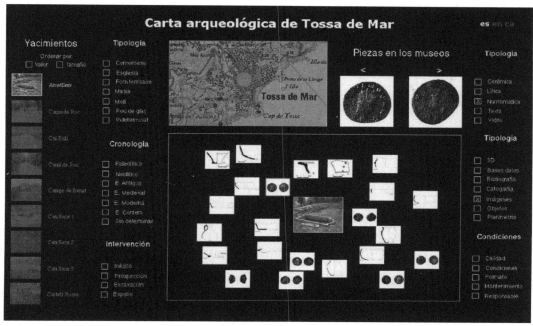

Figure 16.6. Interface.

Finally, figure 16.6 is the interface that the user can explore patrimonial resources, properties, and relations.

CONCLUSION AND FUTURE WORK

Visual environments have a profound impact on society since they represent a new way of improving user engagement in sharing cultural heritage information. This research work has shown the need for the development of search interfaces that are tailored to the visualization of metadata information according to the different levels of perceptions among users. Moreover, visual environments are promising tools that represent the new frontier of our capacity of learning, understanding, communicating, and transmitting culture. Further research is needed to study the social collaboration of users that can emerge from visual environments because they allow an interaction with cultural heritage information, constructing cyber maps, and landscapes. VECH is a visual environment where users can interact, discussing about key features of the information, interpretations, and general overviews. Therefore, our future research work will be focused on paradata.

The notion of paradata is defined as information about human processes of understanding and interpretation of heritage (Bentkowska-Kafel, Denard, and Baker 2012). It is closely related to "contextual metadata," which tend to communicate interpretations of an object or collection, rather than the process through which one or more objects were processed or interpreted. Examples of paradata include descriptions stored within a structured dataset of how evidence was used to interpret an object, or a comment on methodological premises within a research publication. The origins of the ongoing paradata discussion date back to the 1990s, and to a certain extent also to earlier discussions on the representation of heritage, that is, illustration using primarily pen and paper and other non-digital means for representing the past (Adkins and Adkins 1989). Later on in the 1990s, the cultural heritage professionals and scholars began to express increasingly critical comments on the prevailing technology driven practices of computer based heritage visualizations (Durand 2002; Roussou and Drettakis 2003). Subsequently, different methods of non-photorealistic rendering (Klein et al. 2000) were proposed as a remedy to the challenge of communicating uncertainties and the different phases of the process of interpretation that were often impossible to discern in a photo-realistic rendering of a heritage object or historic landscape. Since then, the discussion on heritage paradata has continued and several authors including Forte (e.g., Forte 2010; Forte and Kurillo 2010; Forte and Pescarin 2007), Niccolucci (Niccolucci and Cantone 2003), and Hermon (e.g., Hermon and Kalisperis 2011) have proposed various approaches to address the challenge of representing the process of interpretation. But nevertheless, the advances have been relatively few. And the London and Seville charters are a significant step on the level of establishing principles and acknowledging the significance of paradata, but as the contributing authors in the *Paradata and Transparency in Virtual Heritage* anthology underline, the charter needs to be complemented with practical guidelines and techniques to realize its potential.

NOTES

1. Note: MARC is set to be replaced by *Bibliographic Framework* (BIBFRAME).
2. https://www.iso.org/standard/26020.html.
3. http://inspire.ec.europa.eu/.
4. http://www.arcland.eu/.
5. http://ariadne-portal.dcu.gr/.
6. http://ads.ahds.ac.uk/arena/.
7. http://vi-mm.eu/2016/09/27/3d-conform-tools-and-expertise-for-3d-collection-formation/.
8. http://epoch-net.org/site/.

BIBLIOGRAPHY

Adkins, Lesley, and Roy Adkins. *Archaeological Illustration.* Cambridge: Cambridge University Press, 1989.

Bentkowska-Kafel, Anna, Hugh Denard, and Drew Baker. *Paradata and Transparency in Virtual Heritage.* New York: Routledge, 2012.

Bucciero, Alberto, and Luca Mainetti. "Model-Driven Generation of Collaborative Virtual Environments for Cultural Heritage." In *International Conference on Image Analysis and Processing*, 268–277. Springer, 2013.

Bustillo, Andres, Mario Alaguero, Ines Migual, Jose M. Saize, and Lena S. Iglesias. "A Flexible Platform for the Creation of 3D Semi-Immersive Environments to Teach Cultural Heritage." *Digital Applications in Archaeology and Cultural Heritage* 2, no. 4 (2015): 248–259.

Carrozzino, Marcello, Alexandra Angeletaki, Chiara Evangelista, Cristian Lorenzini, Franco Tecchia, and Massimo Bergamasco. "Virtual Technologies to Enable Novel Methods of Access to Library Archives." *SCIRES-IT* 3, no. 1 (2013): 25–34.

Carrozzino, Marcello, and Massimo Bergamasco. "Beyond Virtual Museums: Experiencing Immersive Virtual Reality in Real Museums." *Journal of Cultural Heritage* 11, no. 4 (2010): 452–458.

Durand, Frédo. "An Invitation to Discuss Computer Depiction." In *Proceedings of the 2nd International Symposium on Non-Photorealistic Animation and Rendering*, 111–124. NPAR '02. Annecy, France: ACM, 2002.

Fairbairn, D., G. Andrienko, N. Andrienko, G. Buziek, and J. Dykes. "Representation and Its Relationship with Cartographic Visualization." *Cartography and Geographic Information Science* 28, no. 1 (2001): 13–28. doi:10.1559/152304001782174005.

Fernández-Palacios, Belen Jiménez, Daniele Morabito, and Fabio Remondino. "Access to Complex Reality-Based 3D Models Using Virtual Reality Solutions." *Journal of Cultural Heritage* (2016).

Forte, Maurizio. *Cyber-Archaeology*. Oxford: Archaeopress, 2010.

Forte, Maurizio, and Gregorij Kurillo. "Cyber-Archaeology and Metaverse Collaborative Systems." *Metaverse Creativity* 1, no. 1 (2010): 7–19.

Forte, Maurizio, and Sofia Pescarin. "XXX Behaviors, Interactions and Affordance in Virtual Archaeology." *Making 3D Visual Research Outcomes Transparent: Advanced ICT Methods Guide*, 189–202. Ed. Lorna Hughes. London, 2007.

Garagnani, Simone, and Anna Maria Manferdini. "Parametric Accuracy: Building Information Modeling Process Applied to the Cultural Heritage Preservation." In *3DArch2013, Conference Proceedings of the International Archives of the Photogrammetry, Remote Sensing and Spatial Information Sciences* 87–92, Trento, Italy, 2013.

Hermon, Sorin, and Loukas Kalisperis. "Between the Real and the Virtual: 3D Visualization in the Cultural Heritage Domain-Expectations and Prospects." *Arqueologica* 2 (2011): 99–103.

Klein, Allison W., Wilmot Li, Michael M. Kazhdan, Wagner T. Corrêa, Adam Finkelstein, and Thomas A. Funkhouser. "Non-Photorealistic Virtual Environments." In *Proceedings of the 27th Annual Conference on Computer Graphics and Interactive Techniques*, 527–534. SIGGRAPH '00. New York: ACM Press/Addison-Wesley Publishing Co., 2000.

Lewis, Andrew, Sandra Woolley, Eugene Ch'ng, and Erlend Gehlken. "Observed Methods of Cuneiform Tablet Reconstruction in Virtual and Real World Environments." *Journal of Archaeological Science* 53 (2015): 156–165.

Mortara, Michela, Chiara Eva Catalano, Francesco Bellotti, Giusy Fiucci, Minica Houry-Panchetti, and Panagiotis Petridis. "Learning Cultural Heritage by Serious Games." *Journal of Cultural Heritage* 15, no. 3 (2014): 318–325.

Moscato, Vincenzo, Antonio Picariello, and V. S. Subrahmanian. "Multimedia Social Networks for Cultural Heritage Applications: The GIVAS Project." In *Data Management in Pervasive Systems*, 169–182. New York: Springer, 2015.

Niccolucci, Franco, and Francesca Cantone. "Legend and Virtual Reconstruction: Porsenna's Mausoleum in X3D," 57–62. Martin Doerr, Apostolos Sarris, 2003.

Parry, Ross. *Museums in a Digital Age*. London: Routledge, 2013.

Riley, Jenn. "Seeing Standards: A Visualization of the Metadata Universe." 2010. http://www.dlib.indiana.edu/~jenlrile/metadatamap/.

Roussou, Maria, and George Drettakis. "Photorealism and Non-Photorealism in Virtual Heritage Representation." In *The 4th International Symposium on Virtual Reality, Archaeology and Intelligent Cultural Heritage*, 51–60. 2003.

Styliani, Sylaiou, Liarokapis Fotis, Kotsakis Kostas, and Patias Petros. "Virtual Museums, a Survey and Some Issues for Consideration." *Journal of Cultural Heritage* 10, no. 4 (2009): 520–528.

Weaver, Christopher Eric. "Improvise: A User Interface for Interactive Construction of Highly-Coordinated Visualizations." Doctoral dissertation, University of Wisconsin at Madison, 2006.

Zhao, Pei, Sara Sintonen, and Heikki Kynäslahti. "The Pedagogical Functions of Arts and Cultural-Heritage Education with ICTs in Museums: A Case Study of FINNA and Google Art Project." *Instructional Technology* 3 (2015).

17

Architecture, Heritage, and Tourism in Nicaragua and Morocco

Using Cataloguing Tools to Strengthen Cultural Identities and Heritage

Guido Cimadomo

INTRODUCTION

The 1968 UNESCO "Recommendation Concerning the Preservation of Cultural Property Endangered by Public or Private Works" (UNESCO 1968) and the 1972 "Convention Concerning the Protection of the World Cultural and Natural Heritage" (UNESCO 1972) make clear the aim of the United Nations to identify and conserve the achievements of the past in order to protect and to transmit it to future generations. "Cultural heritage" has to be seen as a fundamental part of the development and self-identification of different civilizations. As Kamenka explained, "the importance to human beings of the sense of identity, given not so much by material improvement, but by customs and traditions, by historical identification, by religion" (1988, 134). Hence the improvement of cultural identity is pivotal to the development of communities. Until recently, the identification of cultural heritage—tangible and intangible—was strictly the responsibility of state authorities or intergovernmental organizations even as they worked under the assumption that any community should be able to outline its cultural identity through its identification of what was worth protecting and leaving for future generations (Blake 2000, 68).

The role of communities in the protection of cultural heritage is slightly envisioned in UNESCO's 1976 "Recommendation on the Safeguarding and Contemporary Role of Historic Areas," (UNESCO 1976). Article 21 states:

After the survey . . . has been completed and before the safeguarding plans and specifications are drawn up, there should in principle be a programming operation in which due account is taken both of town-planning, architectural, economic and social considerations and of the ability of the urban and rural fabric to assimilate functions that are compatible with its specific character. The programming operation should aim at bringing the density of settlement to the desired level and should provide for the work to be carried out in stages as well as for the temporary accommodation needed while it is proceeding, and premises for the permanent rehousing of those inhabitants who cannot return to their previous dwellings. This programming operation should be undertaken with the closest possible participation of the communities and groups of people concerned. Because the social, economic and physical context of historic areas and their surroundings may be expected to change over time, survey and analysis should be a continuing process. It is accordingly essential that the preparation of safeguarding plans and their execution be undertaken on the basis of studies available, rather than being postponed while the planning process is refined.

In essence, this UNESCO document is related to the need for temporary or permanent accommodation of local inhabitants, who might not have had the power to decide on the restoration of architectural heritage or the power to determine the criteria for conservation. Nevertheless, the debate about the suitability of the Western approach to heritage has evolved from these early experiences, where local people were frequently excluded in decisions related to their own heritage. Fairly recently, the point of view of other cultures, different from the Western dominant precolonial approach, has been heard, starting with the "Nara Document on Authenticity" of 1994 (Nara, Japan),[1] which recognizes the conservation process relative to context (Winter 2014, 124). This point from the document demonstrates best the central focus of the Nara document: "All judgements about values attributed to cultural properties as well as the credibility of related information sources may differ from culture to culture, and even within the same culture. It is thus not possible to base judgements of values and authenticity within fixed criteria. On the contrary, the respect due to all cultures requires that heritage properties must be considered and judged within the cultural contexts to which they belong."[2]

Since then, the notion of heritage has been evolving and can now be considered extremely wide, including almost all elements of culture and nature. More pertinent to this chapter is the recognition of the value that landscapes have in the understanding of heritage in a wider sense. The "Council of Europe Framework Convention on the Value of Cultural Heritage for Society," signed in 2005 in Faro, Portugal—while it was limited to the European Region—could be considered a turning point in the participation of communities in the protection of cultural heritage, as it aimed to emphasize the value and potential of cultural heritage when used as a resource for sustainable development and quality of life in a constantly evolving society, and to reinforce social cohesion by fostering a sense of shared responsibility toward the places where people live. At the council, the concept of *heritage community* was officially defined as a group that valued specific aspects of cultural heritage they wished to sustain and transmit to future generations. The need for open public participation in discussions related to cultural heritage was also emphasized. The idea of *heritage by appropriation* was noted highly for it considered all kinds of cultural, social, and ethnological heritage, including non-exceptional landscapes. In fact, these elements are recognized by citizens as significant in their everyday lives, and therefore meaningful to be transmitted to future generations (Dupagne et al. 2004, 11). All this is what Tweed et al. (2007, 63) refer to as underlining the growing democratization of culture and the active role communities can assume as they are put in charge of recognizing heritage values.

MOVING FROM HERITAGE AS A CHARGE TO HERITAGE AS AN ASSET

Besides *heritage by appropriation*, Dupagne et al. (2004) mentioned a second category, *heritage by designation*. This is still the most common form of identification, when heritage is considered as a label or a qualifying attribute, listed and institutionalized by experts, and usually imposed on communities. This kind of heritage has significant drawbacks. For example, when it is assigned to monuments, then national or international funds would be allotted to preserve them. But then, the preservation and conservation of second level heritage—heritage that is at a regional or local scale, is left up to their owners. This separation between legislative entities and the local or regional community creates many disagreements, harming the same heritage and, in a direct way, the community itself. If we move these considerations to underdeveloped countries with scarce resources, the situation becomes more gripping and impels a solution.

The protection of cultural heritage is a value that if correctly administered, can be a detonator for social and economic development. But as pointed out in the UNESCO "Periodic Report and Regional Programme Arab States 2000–2003" the preservation of cultural heritage recognized as part of local human activity with a collective having its own identity is more important than the development of tourism. This perspective encourages the implementation of community participation in order to create activities and knowledge about the opportunities that can be created for the development of the community itself. Tourism dynamics can create the need for new necessities that can be easily hosted in second level heritage buildings, a solution less expensive than abandoning them—a common trend recognized in several contexts—considering the social, historical, and heritage issues related. These activities can also be considered a detonator for social and economic development that can have positive effects when correctly managed.

Linking tourism with architectural heritage is relevant because it demonstrates the threats to and opportunities of heritage within the concept of heritage as economic resource. Tourism-related and recreational activities are the common conditions for the use of cultural or natural heritage resources. However, it is much more important to assume the idea that heritage is not a sum of recognized objects worth protecting, but a territorial system in which the relationship between heritage and human actions create a sense of wholeness (Feria 2012, 7). Tourism has to be sustainable tourism, which develops the tourism economy, as well as the local community whose heritage—whether it is a building, a landscape, or an intangible asset—the tourists come to see. This is referred to as *social sustainability*. To reach this target, analysis methodologies and development proposals for sustainable tourism models have to be established for the appreciation and protection of heritage that would satisfy the economic, social, and aesthetic needs of the community (Pié Ninot et al. 2012). Tourism can be considered as one of the most transforming and dynamic activities, and has to be addressed together with local human actions in a short period of time in order to protect their integrity and identity. It is therefore necessary to understand threats and opportunities in context with scarce economic resources, in order to maintain the identity of the inhabitants, and to offer alternative responsible models that can protect the existing architectural and landscape values (Cimadomo et al. 2012).

There is a dichotomy between *heritage by appropriation* and *heritage by assignation,* which is nevertheless evolving into a new model where communities have real participation in heritage development. Information technologies offer wide new opportunities to this engagement, and several cases can be found all over the world. For example, the Scottish Coastal Heritage Risk Project (SCHARP) mobilized volunteers from local communities to track the state of known coastal archaeology at risk. Volunteers were asked to visit sites that were identified to be at risk by the Scottish Coastal Archaeology and the Problem of Erosion Trust (SCAPE) and to update information and images that describe the conditions of these vulnerable assets. In this way SCAPE can reduce the number of times it would need to visit all the assets on the more than nine thousand kilometers of Scottish coast, where erosion is a fast evolving threat for the preservation of heritage assets. SCAPE can more efficiently set priorities preserving the most endangered archaeological sites (Dawson et al. 2013). The works of excavation to document the most endangered sites that are at risk of disappearing have also been realized with the help of local communities, volunteers, and associations. This creates empowerment of local groups and associations in the knowledge and transmission of their cultural heritage. A similar project can be found in Lesotho, where archaeological works in the Metolong Dam Catchment made great efforts to involve local communities to build capacity in archaeology and cultural heritage through training for Lesotho's National University teachers and students (Mitchell and Arthur 2010). In Hermopolis (Greece) GIS software, information technology platforms, and crowd-funding have been developed in order to save private buildings recognized to be of cultural interest in communities with an impelling economic situation. This reduced the possibilities of direct intervention of municipalities (Chatzigrigoriou et al. 2013).

If the experiences presented here are related to heritage items already identified, it is important to remember that there are a lot of situations where these values are still hidden and not identified by authorities or by the same communities that inhabit the place. It is then important to conduct surveys and documentation in the areas where social tendencies are changing and pressures are growing, in order to offer guidelines and models that would be adopted. Cataloguing heritage buildings means, first, giving subjective value to some of them, comparing them with other buildings located in the same place. In this chapter, I will discuss two experiences related to the documentation of building heritage in Nicaragua and Morocco—two countries where tourism pressures are increasing—so as to demonstrate the benefits of early heritage recognition in the strengthening and development of communities.

CASE STUDIES FROM NICARAGUA AND MOROCCO

The colonial town of Granada, Nicaragua, built in 1524 by Francisco Hernández de Córdoba, is one of the most attractive cultural attractions of Nicaragua, and together with several other colonial cities of Central America, is at the center of a heritage program given impulse by the Spanish Agency for International Development (AECI-D). The architectural interest of the city is due, paradoxically, to its destruction at the end of the nineteenth century in the hands of the pirate William Walker. Two building typologies were used to rebuild the city after this event: courtyard houses, following the same solutions used in the period preceding the fire, and diverse solutions built by the new dominant classes based on neoclassical or neo-baroque tendencies from Europe and North America. This twofold character defines the character and history of the city. Under the AECI-D funded program many public buildings have been rehabilitated in order to protect the heritage and to promote a program of integral development. In Granada, Colón Square and the train station were renewed in the 1990s, which facilitated new interest in the city, and soon transformed it as a national and international target for tourism. Together with these specific interventions, a wider program for the protection and development of the Granada historic center was developed in collaboration with the municipality, which included survey and typological studies of the built environment (henceforth referred to as the "Plan"). The scope of this program, which was active for more than ten years, was the dissemination of and education about the Plan and the public recognition of the importance of the protection of cultural heritage. The specific objectives of the program were framed with the notion that there should be an understanding of heritage as a social capital for the community, to enjoy and protect, so it could be transmitted to future generations. These objectives were:

1. Maintain cultural heritage as the basis of the community's social memory.
2. Rescue heritage as an economic development factor.
3. Build capacity in all the specializations of heritage protection and management.
4. Strengthen local administration capacity for the protection of cultural heritage.
5. Participate in the cultural enrichment through participative work and sharing technical and cultural capacities.

A program at the Oficina del Centro Histórico de Granada (OCHG) was developed, including implementing an urban plan and developing a building code to define the most common aspects of construction to be observed by the citizens. According to Reyes (1999), the phases to accomplish this were:

1. Realize a detailed survey of the 1.742 plots of the historic center, and several sectoral analysis in order to prepare a general diagnostic of urban issues founded on the needs of the community, configuring the first phase of the Plan.
2. Develop an urban plan for the protection and development of the historic center.
3. Define and approve an urban regulation for the historic center.
4. Update the heritage catalogue, including new elements detected in the survey.
5. Define a general and economic strategy that would make possible the realization of the Plan.

The realization of the fourth objective above—that is, to update the heritage catalogue—came in the year 2000, and what at the beginning was thought to be just an upgrade of the previous catalogue developed by UNESCO in 1996. The new document took into account all data obtained during the survey phase, and the new protection grades to be applied through the building code. Three main grades were defined:

1. *Integral*—the protection of all the elements and aspects that make the building significant in the city and the way the building occupies urban space.
2. *Estructural*—the protection of the basic ornamental and structural elements of the building that need to articulate and occupy urban space.
3. *Ambiental*—the protection of the exterior of buildings in order to keep volumetric relations, composition, and homogeneity of materials for the maintenance of a coherent image of the city. This included all the buildings in the historic center area.

Buildings were given a subjective value that included *high heritage value, heritage value,* and *high stylistic values.*

The real possibilities that these buildings—most of which were owned by private citizens—would get some level of protection generated excitement about other possibilities that would effectively maintain the built environment. Despite the scarce possibility that funds would be received from the municipality or other public bodies to preserve these buildings, the Catalogue of Heritage Buildings realized by the author had a positive effect. It helped to convert all the buildings into properties that were in high demand from the growing number of foreigners who were moving to the city who looked at these buildings as possible investments (Cimadomo 2008, 259). The inclusion of buildings in the catalogue was not seen as bureaucratic

Table 17.1.   Grade of Protection and Items Affected

Classification	Number of Buildings Declared	Grade of Protection
Items with High Heritage Value	47	Integral, Estructural
Items with Heritage Value	25	Estructural
Items with High Stylistic Value Facades	299	Ambiental
Buildings in the Historic Center	597	Ambiental
Items in the Buffer Zone	775	Ambiental
Public Urban Spaces	5	Ambiental

intrusion on the owners, but as a positive act, as property prices rose. Since the publication of the catalogue, there was a growth in the real estate market and transactions increased—a positive trend for the local economy. New facilities were built to support the growing tourism industry that targeted the city of Granada. The protection levels also provided the possibility to change how a building would be used, as new activities, often related with the requirements of tourism, were allowed and implemented in these historic buildings. In this sense, some restaurants, hotels, and hostels could fit into the traditional typology of *casa colonial*. Without all this, many of the buildings would not have been restored and preserved, because of the community's economic difficulties.

There were other aspects of the process that could be evaluated more deeply in this chapter. For example, there were gentrification issues as well as real benefits for the community, in the long run. But from a heritage conservation point of view, we can consider that the catalogue, and the whole program implemented in the city, had a positive outcome on the conservation of the built heritage, and on the social and economic welfare of the community involved.

A second experience related to the documentation of cultural heritage as a way to boost the economic activities of a community took place in the preSaharian M'goun Valley of Morocco, where the beauty of the landscape and the rural environment together with earthen architectures offer a great opportunity to test relations between the protection and development policies and tourism activities. Tourism in the preSaharian M'goun Valley has to be addressed together with local human activities in a short period of time, in order to protect the valley's identity and its cultural heritage (Cimadomo et al. 2012). The first conclusions realized after the field survey was to consider the valley and its earthen architecture as a living cultural landscape in order to foster its enhancement and guarantee its survival and development (Nogueira Bernárdez et al. 2012, 545).

Documentation of earthen historical buildings in the valley, together with classification of landscape units and the analysis of development patterns of the urban centers, was carried out during two workshops held in 2011 and 2012 by the School of Architecture at the University of Malaga, in a wider project targeting new responsible tourism models. We consider this act as a first step that let the owners come to realize the exceptional value of their buildings and to recognize them as something to be protected and maintained, and eventually as a possible source of new incomes. There were threats to these cultural heritage resources, such as in the lack of state or city norms about conserving properly the buildings that were recognized to have cultural value and the lack of institutional aids dedicated to the conservation and rehabilitation of these buildings. The economic subsistence situation of many of the owners also made it difficult to carry out the proper conservation of this heritage. Thus, the proposal to impulse new trends that were related to cultural tourism and being respectful of the habitat of the region was considered an acceptable way to generate incomes for the inhabitants. They were obliged to invest in the conservation of the buildings, in order to maintain good economic flow.

Protecting and maintaining heritage and landscape values in contexts like the one found in the M'goun Valley was only possible, from my personal point of view, if they were recognized as relevant aspects that could foster the living conditions of their inhabitants. Incomes from the correct use of these assets can generate pride in their owners, just like they did centuries ago when they were first built. Finding a way to increase inhabitants' economic status was good, but only if the people of the valley were actively involved in decision making.

This project combined heritage, landscape, and tourism and could produce a new understanding of heritage among the local population, leading to the acknowledgment of the values of earth architecture. We look with great expectations for the effects of the catalogue without any regulations imposed on it. We look to it showing in a tangible way the most interesting buildings of the valley. We think that if properly recognized, renewing these buildings to recover their use or to adapt to new ones can be less expensive than abandoning them, considering the social, historical, and heritage issues associated with them. Tourism can offer the need for new facilities that can easily fit into these buildings, being the transformation of ancient Kasbah into Riads—sort of local hotels—as the easiest and more common option.

In this scenario, much has still to be done, starting with the need to find general trends for the protection of the cultural heritage, a value that if correctly administered, can be a detonator for social and economic development. Lack of maintenance and abandonment are origins of the deterioration of rammed-earth buildings, which within a short period of time become prone to collapse and disappear in the community (Bui et al. 2009). I consider these buildings as providing a great opportunity to preserve and value the heritage that is the priceless cultural architecture. I reject the crucial trend neglecting these buildings for new typologies based on contemporary constructive solutions and materials.

Ultimately the aim of the heritage cataloguing project and the Heritage Catalogue was not just to catalogue and disseminate earth architecture, but to create original proposals for sustainable tourism through the analysis of landscape, urban development, and society. The publication of a Heritage Catalogue is the first step in the involvement of the local community to realize the opportunities of the architecture in their midst.

CONCLUSION

The work realized by the author in Granada (Nicaragua) and the field works realized in the M'goun Valley (Morocco) have been used to show how the process of identifying and cataloguing architectural heritage can have positive effects on local communities. It can be the first step to realizing the exceptional value of the buildings in the community, and to recognize these buildings as something worth protecting and maintaining, and eventually as possible sources of new income. The threats identified in these regions can overpower opportunities if there is lack of state or city codes that obliges people to conserve properly the buildings that are recognized to have cultural value and the lack of institutional aids that are focused on the conservation and rehabilitation of these buildings, together with the subsistent economic situation many of the owners are in (Cimadomo et al. 2012).

Finally, new information and communications technologies offer the possibility to actively engage communities from the first steps, such as in the survey and identification of cultural heritage. The effects of this are, in turn, highly positive as they strengthen cultural identity (Cimadomo 2013). When communities realize the value of their built heritage from the very beginning of the process, it is much easier to agree to the need to preserve it for future generations, when they are faced with the combination of *heritage by appropriation* and *heritage by assignation*, which I described early in this chapter. Moving from simply looking at cultural heritage protection as the act of finding a single item to protect to thinking about the development of the whole landscape and finding the most relevant buildings to preserve is also offering new opportunities to communities. Understanding buildings as live systems where social dynamics develop is moving the attention to the searching of sustainable development activities that offer payback to communities, as well as the built heritage.

We know that tourism is a strong force in the process of economic development. But it is also one of the riskiest activities to take when you want to keep cultural identities. Hence, it is important to focus on local human activities first. It is at a later time that you integrate tourism development activities. It is possible to protect the local cultural heritage with the participation of local associations and communities in several activities and give great relevance to program administrators and specific on-site conditions.

As a final consideration it could be stressed that each landscape territory should be understood as a "place capital" that should be promoted and should be treated as having great potential and as providing the identity of the region. All stakeholders in the region should realize or should be made aware of this potential in order to incite them to begin to find ways to develop it without losing their identity (Parente 2012, 58). The soul of a "place" is strongly affected and transformed when tourism pressures are not well controlled, and threats like erosion, overcrowding, and damage become real risks.

NOTES

1. "Nara Document on Authenticity," accessed November 1, 2016, https://www.icomos.org/charters/nara-e.pdf.

2. Ibid, 47.

BIBLIOGRAPHY

Agencia Española de Cooperación Internacional (AECI-D). *Programa de preservación del patrimonio cultural en iberoamérica*. Madrid, 2000.

Blake, Janet. "On defining the cultural heritage." *International and Comparative Law Quarterly* 49 (2000): 61–85. doi: 10.1017/S002058930006396X.

Bui, Quoc-Bao, Jean-Claude Morel, B. V. Venkatarama Reddy, and W. Ghayad. "Durability of rammed earth walls exposed for 20 years to natural weathering." *Building and Environment* 44, no. 5 (2009): 912–919. doi: 10.1016/j.buildenv.2008.07.001.

Cimadomo, Guido. "La intervención patrimonial en Nicaragua: El éxito del catálogo de bienes patrimoniales de la ciudad de Granada." In *Libro de Actas IX Congreso Internacional de Rehabilitación del Patrimonio Arquitectónico y Edificación. Patrimonio cultural e innovación*, 259–264. Gran Canaria-Sevilla: Centro Internacional de Conservación del Patrimonio, 2008.

Cimadomo, Guido. "Threats and opportunities in the documentation and typological study of Mgoun Valley's traditional rammed-earth architecture, High Atlas, Morocco." Paper presented at 3rd International Architectural Conservation Conference and Exhibition (IACCE), Dubai, U.A.E., December 17–19, 2012.

Cimadomo, Guido, José Alberto Simón Montesinos, and Amor Vacas Álvarez. "Cataloging and typological study of Mgoun Valley's traditional fortified architecture, Morocco." In *Rammed earth conservation*, edited by Camilla Mileto, Fernando Vegas, and Valentina Cristini, 493–498. London: Taylor & Francis Group, 2012.

Cimadomo, Guido. "Documentation and dissemination of cultural heritage: Current solutions and considerations about its digital implementation." In *Proceedings of the 2013 Digital Heritage international conference (DigitalHeritage)*, edited by Alonzo C. Addison, Gabriele Guidi, Livio De Luca, and Sofia Pescarin, 555–562. Marsella: IEEE, 2013. doi: 10.1109/DigitalHeritage.2013.6743796.

Council of Europe (CoE). *Council of Europe framework convention on the value of cultural heritage for society*. Faro, 2005.

Dawson, Tom, Anna Vermehren, Alan Miller, Iain Oliver, and Sarah Kennedy. "Digitally enhanced community rescue archaeology." In *Proceedings of 2013 Digital Heritage International Congress*

(DigitalHeritage), edited by Alonzo C: Addison, Gabriele Guidi, Livio de Luca, and Sofia Pescarin, 29–36. Marseille: IEEE, 2013. doi: 10.1109/DigitalHeritage.2013.6744726.

Dupagne, A., C. Ruelle, and J. Teller. *SUIT. Sustainable Development of Urban Historical Areas through an Active Integration Within Towns*. Luxembourg: European Commission, 2004.

Feria, José M., ed. *Territorial heritage and development: Proceedings of the international workshop on territorial heritage and sustainable development*. Boca Raton, FL: CRC Press, 2012.

Kamenka, Eugene. "Human rights and people's rights." In *The rights of peoples*, edited by J. Crawford, 127–139. Oxford: Clarendon Press, 1988.

Kent, Ethan. "Place capital: The shared wealth that drives thriving communities." Accessed April 14, 2014. http://www.pps.org/reference/place-capital-the-shared-wealth-that-drives-thriving-communities/.

Mitchell, Peter, and Peter Arthur. "Archaeological fieldwork in the Metolong dam catchment, Lesotho, 2008–2010." *Nyame Akuma* 74 (December 2010): 51–62.

Nogueira Bernárdez, Belén, Jorge Asencio Juncal, García Ruiz de Mier, Teófilo, and Ignacio Álvarez-Ossorio Martínez. "Earthen architecture landscapes as identity items in Southern Morocco: Studies in M'goun Valley, High Atlas." In *Rammed earth conservation*, edited by Camilla Mileto, Fernando Vegas, and Valentina Cristini, 545–550. London: Taylor & Francis Group, 2012.

Oficina del Centro Histórico de la ciudad de Granada (OCHCG). *Propuesta del Plan de Revitalización del Centro Histórico de la ciudad de Granada*. Granada, Nicaragua, 2000.

Parente, M. Affermare l'identità dei territori. *Ottagono*, 249 (April 2012): 58–65.

Pié Ninot, Ricard, Carlos J. Rosa Jiménez, Guido Cimadomo, Jorge Asencio Juncal, Belén Nogueira Bernárdez, and Úrsula Martín Codes. "Del turismo sostenible al turismo de base comunitaria. Intenciones y alternativas de cooperación en el sur de marruecos basado en el turismo responsible." In *Cooperación y turismo: Intenciones y olvidos. experiencias de investigación a debate*, edited by Enrique Navarro Jurado, and Yolanda Romero Padilla, 77–102. Malaga: Universidad de Malaga, 2012.

Reyes, Auxiliadora. "La ciudad de Granada y el Plan de Revitalización de su Centro Histórico," *Nuestro Patrimonio Cultural*, no. 4 (January–June 1999).

Tweed, Christopher, and Margaret Sutherland. "Built cultural heritage and sustainable urban development." *Landscape and Urban Planning* 83 (2007): 62–69. doi: 10.1016/j.landurbplan.2007.05.008.

UNESCO. *Recommendation concerning the preservation of cultural property endangered by public or private works*. Paris: United Nations Educational, Scientific and Cultural Organization, 1968.

———. *Convention concerning the protection of the world cultural and natural heritage*. Paris: United Nations Educational, Scientific and Cultural Organization, *1972*.

———. *Recommendation on the safeguarding and contemporary role of historic areas*. Paris: United Nations Educational, Scientific and Cultural Organization, 1976.

———. *Periodic report and regional programme: Arab states 2000–2003*. Paris: United Nations Educational, Scientific and Cultural Organization, 2004.

Winter, Tim. 2014. "Beyond Eurocentrism? Heritage conservation and the politics of difference." *International Journal of Heritage Studies* 20, no. 2 (02/17; 2014/04): 123–37. doi: 10.1080/1352 7258.2012.736403.

18

"Memovoice"

Approaches to Participative Identification of (Ladin) Heritage in the Dolomites

Emanuel Valentin

INTRODUCTION

"Cultural heritage" discourse in the nineteenth century and the construction of "cultural heritage" have played a fundamental role in the process of national formation (Handler, 1988; Macdonald, 2013). Cultural forms of expression, ranging from language to tradition, have been used to legitimize a common cultural lineage and thus, a political coherence of a nation (Hafstein, 2004). But according to Anderson (1991), nations represent "imagined communities." These communities are invented and devised, and they consist of a crowd whose members are not personally acquainted with each other but which celebrate and constantly reimagine themselves as a community through symbols, such as monuments, landmarks, and foodways. He states, "communities are to be distinguished not by their falsity/genuineness, but by the style in which they are imagined" (p. 6). Hence, the construction of heritage goes hand in hand with the construction of communities.

Communities were for a long time excluded from the "UNESCO heritage apparatus" (Adell et al., 2015b, p. 8) and were only gradually integrated into the UNESCO conventions (Adell et al., 2015a). With the 1989 UNESCO Recommendation on the Safeguarding of Traditional Culture and Folklore, however, other experts, such as ethnologists, folklorists, and museum staff were entrusted with the documentation and cataloguing of cultural elements. As Adell et al. state, "while this strategy inserts different levels of reflexivity and/or alienation among practitioners of tradition, it safeguards, at best, representations of culture, but not the practices themselves" (Adell et al., 2015b, p. 8).

Adell et al. (2015a) further argue that this recommendation saw a strong link between cultural identity and the preservation of traditions, although sociological and ethnological studies had long recognized that identity—both ethnic and national—is a construct, and as such based on imagination (Anderson, 1991; Barth, 1969), and is a powerful instrument of group formation. The UNESCO Convention for the Safeguarding of Intangible Cultural Heritage of 2003 excluded also the fact that there are often problematic relationships between culture and identity, that communities can be divided and that individuals are using multiple identities in an increasingly mobile, globalized and uncertain world. The fact that there are often problematic relationships between culture and identity, that communities can be divided and that individuals are using multiple identities in an increasingly mobile, globalized, and uncertain world, was also excluded from the UNESCO Convention for the Safeguarding of

Intangible Cultural Heritage of 2003. The convention introduced the concept of "intangible heritage" and developed the link between tradition, community and identity further (Adell et al., 2015b, p. 8ff.), "as if this were a natural, harmonious and good union between three things that, in themselves, are natural and good" (Brumann, 2015, p. 273).

UNESCO conventions seem to have largely ignored discussions in anthropology and social sciences about the concept of community, especially those discussions that have appeared since the end of the 1960s. As a result, the combination of heritage and community produces a redundancy, which is aptly pointed to by Crooke (2011). As he states, "the community group is defined and justified because of its heritage and that heritage is fostered and sustained by the creation of community" (Crooke, 2011, p. 25).

Nevertheless—or maybe because of this—participative approaches involving communities have increasingly become important in heritagization processes. These are the processes of transforming objects, places, and practices into heritage by placing value on them. Participation and community involvement seem to have become necessary conditions for the preservation and management of heritage. Theoretically, the participation of the social actors is not limited anymore to the conservation measures of elements selected by external experts only. Rather, participation should already be applied where the attribution and identification of heritage itself is concerned. More precisely, the participation of communities should be implemented at different levels—identification, documentation, research, conservation, protection, promotion, transfer, and revitalization—as stated by Articles 2 and 15 of UNESCO's 2003 Convention. Consequently, it is no longer purely scientific criteria that attribute elements to the heritage status but theoretically "indigenous" criteria as well, which are determined by the social actors themselves (Bortolotto, 2011, p. 67f).

The participatory turn of the 2003 Convention has been indeed a massive paradigm shift in the international cultural policies of UNESCO. However, case studies have shown that because of the problems connected to the term community, the difficulty of its definition, and the multiple and heterogeneous interests existing within communities, the term "community participation" ultimately shows a problematic ambiguity which makes it almost unusable (Adell et al., 2015a; Albro, 2007; Balen & Vandesande, 2015; Chirikure, Manyanga, Ndoro, & Pwiti, 2010; Chirikure & Pwiti, 2008; Deacon & Smeets, 2013; Waterton & Watson, 2011).

The threefold interplay between heritage, communities, and participation—while seemingly anything but easy to solve—was the starting point of my PhD research in which I raised—among others—the question: is it possible to identify and document "cultural heritage" in a participative way, so that emic conceptions of heritage can be revealed without being filtered by expert opinions? Is a democratization of heritage and the eradication of the "authorized heritage discourse" paradigm (Smith, 2006) feasible? Do intangible heritage and digital heritage bear new potentials for eliminating and overcoming the dichotomy between experts and so-called laymen—that is, for a deinstitutionalization of the heritage discourse and a shift of its focus towards civil society? In trying to find not only theoretical but also practical answers to these questions, I developed and tested a methodological tool, which I called "Memovoice." In this chapter, I will describe this tool and make some preliminary reflections on the insights gained from this research process.

RESEARCH FIELD

The Dolomites, an alpine mountain landscape in the northeast of Italy, is particularly suitable for exploring my research questions. On the one hand, the Dolomites were registered as a World

Natural Heritage Site in UNESCO's World Heritage List in 2009. On the other hand, we find there one of those rare cases in which a UNESCO Natural Heritage coincides precisely with the settlement area of an ethnic minority, the Ladins, a Raeto-Romance language minority to which I personally belong. One of my starting hypotheses was that UNESCO, during the inscription process of the Dolomites as a world natural heritage, had largely ignored the particular "cultural heritage" existing in this specific environment. During my research, this is revealed to be true. The "UNESCOification" of the Dolomites appears as a continuation of the historic colonization of this territory, which now presents itself in the form of international heritage rhetoric.

In this research I followed the proposal of Alonso Gonzalez (2013), who says that analysis of "cultural heritage," should be carried out on two levels in order to avoid a simplifying reduction of this concept and to promote a processual definition. The first level refers to Kirshenblatt-Gimblett's analysis of "cultural heritage" as "metacultural production" (Kirshenblatt-Gimblett, 2004), which relates especially to institutional and academic constructions and practices, and to which I would add Smith's notion of "authorized heritage discourse." The focus of the second level of analysis lies on an emic approach that understands "cultural heritage" as follows: "something that somebody or some people consider to be worthy of being valued, preserved, catalogued, exhibited, restored, admired (etc.); and others share that election—freely or by various mechanisms of imposition—so that an identification takes place and that 'something' is considered ours" (Novelo in Alonso Gonzalez, 2013, p. 3).

Applied to my research, the first level of analysis ("metacultural production" and "authorized heritage discourse") corresponds to the Dolomites' inscription on the World Heritage List as far as the "natural heritage" aspect is concerned. It also refers, however, to the more historical development of local, regional, and supra-regional institutions and actors who have profoundly shaped today's understanding of "Ladin culture" and of "Ladin cultural heritage."

In this chapter, I will focus only on the second level of my analysis, which is devoted to emic aspects, and in which I present my method that may possibly be a suitable tool for generating processes of participatory identification and community-based management of heritage in other research fields, as well.

MEMOVOICE: OUTLINE OF A METHOD FOR A PARTICIPATIVE IDENTIFICATION OF "CULTURAL HERITAGE"

"Community-based participatory re-search (CBPR) methods,"[1] "participatory action research (PAR)," and "collaborative research" have become important methodological approaches for studies of "cultural heritage." These collaborative research approaches derive from participatory action research, an emancipatory methodology that promotes reciprocal research practices as well as the participation of the "researched" in the phases of design, implementation, evaluation, and use of a research project (Borda, 2001; Reason & Bradbury, 2001b). PAR combines participatory research with action research and aims at "empowerment" of the participants and a social change (Elsen et al., 2015; Freire, 1972; Reason & Bradbury, 2001a; Whyte, 1991). On the other hand, "collaborative research has the potential to reveal important insights into the different value systems relating to 'heritage,' which can contribute to successful heritage management, especially when coupled with an ethnographic approach" (Nicholas & IPinCH Collective, 2012, p. 32).

Cooperation in research makes emic values appear behind "cultural heritage," thus permitting a different interpretation, which may deviate from the usual interpretation by experts, academics, and institutional representatives. However, emic perspectives cannot be collected if the relationship between the researcher and the researched is characterized by mistrust and unequal power relations. Cooperative research starts precisely from this problem. "Such an approach prioritizes community needs, while also fostering relationships that address at least some of the long-standing issues surrounding academic research relating to mistrust, unequal power, and loss of control over the process and products of research" (Nicholas & IPinCH Collective, 2012, p. 30).

Hollowell and Nicholas (2009) see two primary challenges that science must face in undermining scientific colonialism, and even if their statement refers to archaeology, it certainly applies also to other branches of science. These are, "respect for alternative ways of interpreting and knowing the past, and greater equity in the relations of power and privilege that mark differential access to decision-making, and the ability to have one's decisions count." They state, "as we see it, community-based heritage management is founded on these principles (Hollowell & Nicholas, 2009, p. 143), and the taking back of control over what others have defined as a community's relationship to the past in the present—i.e., its 'heritage'—and the representation, interpretation, and caretaking of this heritage—i.e., its 'management'—is the work of decolonization" (Hollowell & Nicholas, 2009, p. 143).

The methods presented here are part of an action-oriented research culture, which tries to articulate emic conceptions of "cultural heritage" and to develop a sustainable management of heritage. This is, however, not a simple endeavor, because, as Alonso Gonzalez (2013) describes, there is a constant epistemological problem that must be overcome. "In attempting to produce ever more radical and alternative heritage knowledge, many scholars reproduce these epistemic schemas whereby studies about the subaltern are carried out rather than studies with and from the subaltern" (Alonso Gonzalez, 2013, p. 9).

So how must such a heritage research "with" and "from" and not "about" communities be designed? How can such a research be carried out in a participatory way without reverting ourselves to the epistemological schemes and taxonomies of UNESCO? Are ethnographic methods enough for documenting the articulation of community-based conceptions of "cultural heritage," as suggested by the title of the article by Hollowell and Nicholas (Hollowell & Nicholas, 2009)?

Even though ethnographic methods are certainly suitable for documenting emic conceptions of "cultural heritage" and that they are more participative than many other scientific methods, I have my doubts as to whether they can be regarded as true "participatory methods." Numerous other scientific disciplines outside anthropology have long recognized the value of ethnographic methods for their research work, but these have increasingly been equated with participatory methods in recent decades. While ethnographic methods absolutely have participatory facets, they do in no way exhaust the potential of participation. In my opinion, the equation of ethnographic and participatory methods is a missed opportunity in the development of specialized tools to ensure participation as comprehensively as possible.

In the development of a suitable methodological instrument, I have been strongly oriented toward participatory visual and digital methods, which I would like to briefly outline next. After that, I will describe my methodological approach, which emerges from a synthesis of these methods and could be useful as a tool for a participatory identification of "cultural heritage."

PHOTOVOICE

Photovoice is a participatory visual method that has its roots in visual anthropology, sociology, and educational research. In this method, community members use photo-cameras to take pictures of a certain topic (community-generated photography). The intention is to generate multiple perspectives that emerge from the lifeworld of individuals, point out concerns within a community, and produce local knowledge. The photographers themselves choose the photos, which are then used in a group to stimulate comments and discussions ("elicited narratives" and "participant voice") and to make background stories visible. This method is not only used for data collection. It increases the awareness within a community on a certain topic and serves also the communication with decision-makers and institutions, which are not always accessible to members of the community, especially if they belong to disadvantaged groups (Gubrium & Harper, 2013, pp. 69–89).

CROWDSOURCING

"Crowdsourcing" refers to a concept that connects world famous platforms like YouTube or Wikipedia with increasing problem-solving strategies of companies or the systematic data enrichment of some scientific projects (Oomen & Aroyo, 2011; Showers, 2010). "Various organizations are currently exploring ways of engaging the wisdom of the crowd for creating and editing of content, solving problems or the organization of knowledge structures" (Oomen & Aroyo, 2011, p. 139).

Crowdsourcing has reached a whole new dimension at the dawn of the digital era and with Web 2.0. Galleries, libraries, and museums worldwide have begun to explore its potential.

GLAMs [Galleries, Libraries, Archives and Museums; remark of author] and their users are now beginning to inhabit the same, shared information space. New services are being launched that explore this fundamentally new paradigm of participation in the GLAM domain. Participation can have a thorough impact on the workflows of heritage institutions, for instance, by inviting users to assist in the selection, cataloguing, contextualization, and curation of collections. These activities can be carried out by end users remotely and can reduce operational costs. These new forms of usage of collections (beyond access) can also lead to a deeper level of involvement with the collections. (Oomen & Aroyo, 2011, p. 139)

Once cultural artifacts are digitized and integrated into an open network, they can be shared, recommended, mixed, and cited in many different ways. In this way, even objects that were previously so "hidden" can get new attention.

PARTICIPATIVE DIGITAL ARCHIVES

Archives are significant "containers of collective memory," "spaces of memory practice" (Ketelaar in Cook, 2012, p. 99), and actors in the process of remembrance. However, the problematic nature of related concepts such as identity and, above all, the dichotomy between evidence and memory have been stated. As Cook states, "beyond evidence, archives also preserve memory. And they create memory" (2012, p. 101). Archives preserve and construct the "collective memory" of nations, groups, institutions and individuals (Blouin & Rosenberg, 2011; Ernst, 2013; Foote, 1990).

From this perspective, then, archives are constructed memories about the past, about history, heritage, and culture, about personal roots and familial connections, and about who we are as human beings [. . .]. Yet memory is notoriously selective—in individuals, in societies, and, yes, in archives. With memory comes forgetting. With memory comes the inevitable privileging of certain records and records creators, certain functions, activities, and groups in society, and the marginalizing or silencing of others. Memory, and forgetting, can serve a whole range of practical, cultural, political, symbolic, emotional and ethical imperatives and is central to power, identity, and privilege" (Cook, 2012, p. 101).

Cook (2012) describes various phases in the archival practices of the last 150 years. Not only did the roles of the archives in the processes of remembrance and identity construction change with each phase, but also the specific function of the archivist. Cook (2012) distinguish four phases and thus four archival paradigms: evidence, memory, identity, and community. The last two more recent archive paradigms are especially interesting for us as far as the aspect of participation is concerned.

From the 1970s onward, the figure of the archivist within the postmodern archives emerged as a professional expert who pursued an increasingly interdisciplinary approach which went beyond the reliance of history. The pluralism and the diversity of society found their way into the archives. "There was no 'Truth' to be found or protected in archives, but many truths, many voices, many perspectives, many stories" (Cook, 2012, p. 110). Administrative reforms of the state apparatus also fundamentally altered archivists' thinking. Description models became more flexible and allowed multiple interpretations. In the context of the demand for more government transparency, archives increasingly became supporters of justice and human rights and were increasingly concerned about the prevention of potential abuse. Public access was facilitated by various measures, including the release of archives in the form of Internet pages. According to this third paradigm, the archive is considered a resource of society, assembled by archivists with a certain sensitivity for the postmodern and digital epoch. Archives no longer served the academic elite alone, but were increasingly used to serve society as a whole. This third paradigm was based on identity: the archivist as a conscious mediator saw himself as a supporter of society in the formation of its multiple identities by using archival memory and trying at the same time to protect the evidence in the face of rapid social and technological transformations (Cook, 2012, pp. 109–113).

According to Cook, we are now in the development phase of a new archival paradigm that incorporates new social and technological realities by giving a new significance to communities and by operating with the concept of the "participatory archive." Participative archives can be found both in the form of so-called community archives—i.e., archives founded by individuals or a collective, as well as in the form of "institutional" archives, which allow manifold ways of participation on the part of the population. Digital technologies and the Internet, especially since the implementation of Web 2.0 (Jimerson, 2011), allow everyone to create his or her own online archives and to share own interpretations side by side with those of experts from the heritage sector (Heimo & Hänninen, 2015; King & Rivett, 2015).

> Archivists thus have the exciting prospect of being able to document human and societal experience with a richness and relevance never before attainable, and with it the opportunity to blend our past foci on evidence, memory, and identity into a more holistic and vibrant "total archive." Some prominent archival voices are accordingly calling on archivists to give up their recently hard-won mantras of expert, of control, of power, and, instead, to share archiving with communities. (Cook, 2012, p. 113)

Hence, the involvement of communities could be seen also as a strategy against capitulation in the face of an immeasurable quantity of evidence, memories, and identities.

The advent of "community archives" was due and inevitable. Today, there is a wide range of such archives: large and small, semi-professional or entirely honorary, long established and more recent ones, and those completely independent or developed in collaboration with heritage experts. As the "Community Archives and Research Group" writes, "[Community archives] seek to document the history of all manner of local, occupational, ethnic, faith and other diverse communities" (cited in Heimo & Hänninen, 2015, p. 6).

The old archives paradigms are no longer sustainable in the face of independent "community archives," which often refuse to surrender their archives to the state or state-financed institutions, as they may feel excluded or even discriminated by them. "Community archives," as they emerge from the communities, are strong identity-forming factors and thus have a strong "vernacular authority" (Howard, 2012).[2]

According to Cook, the archivist has to assume a new role in the context of the "Community Archive": "from elite experts behind institutional walls to becoming mentors, facilitators, coaches, who work in the community to encourage archiving as a participatory process shared with many in society" (Cook, 2012, p. 114). With respect to indigenous communities, Cook argues that a lack of sensitivity for such alternative forms of archiving entails the danger of neo-colonization.

This fourth paradigm does not only imply a special support of communities in the development and maintenance of their own archives. Rather, archivists can now involve interested members of a community into their own work in institutional archives, and arrange acquisition, description, and preservation cooperatively. "Online tagging" and transcription, translation, commenting, or contributing own pictures, videos, or documents by the archives' users are only a few of the manifold possible forms that have been experimented so far (Huvila, 2008; Theimer, 2011). Therein lies a twofold potential: first, archival stocks are experiencing a polyphonic data enrichment that, with the available resources, could never be done by archivists themselves. Second, this involvement promotes the identification of the communities with the archive itself. The implications, however, are far more far-reaching, as Cook argues:

> Community-based archiving involves [. . .] a shift in core principles, from exclusive custodianship and ownership of archives to shared stewardship and collaboration; from dominant-culture language, terminology, and definitions to sensitivity to the "other" and as keen an awareness of the emotional, religious, symbolic, and cultural values that records have to their communities [. . .]. Community archiving, as concept and reality, evidently makes us think differently about ownership of records, replevin, oral and written traditions, the localism-globalism and margins-centre nexus, multiple viewpoints and multiple realities about recordkeeping, [. . .] including evidence, memory, and obviously identity, and, depending on our responses, around deeper ethical issues of control, status, power, and neo-colonialism. (Cook, 2012, pp. 115–116)

Cook therefore pleads for more democratic, inclusive, and holistic archives, which must listen more to the citizens and must be open to "indigenous forms of knowledge, evidence, and memory" (Cook, 2012, p. 116). Thus, the boundaries between "official" and "unofficial cultural heritage"—as suggested by Heimo and Hänninen (2015)—should be examined more closely. They asked, "who has the right to decide what is cultural heritage and what is not? Does it have to be an archive, museum or other expert who makes the decision and has control over it?" (Heimo & Hänninen, 2015, pp. 9–10). Thus, participatory archives can be important educational tools to lever out hegemonic relations and fight against discrimination and injustice. If individuals and groups begin to document their own history, this implies a political and subversive act, especially if it is a suppressed or marginalized story which is at stake (Flinn, 2011; Flinn, Stevens, & Shepherd, 2009). "These 'recast' histories and their making challenge and seek to undermine both the distortions and omissions of orthodox historical narratives, as well as the archive and heritage collections that sustain them" (Flinn & Stevens cited in Cook, 2012, p. 113). Hence, some "community archives" cannot be reduced to pure leisure activities or antiquarianism, but can be understood as proper "social movement archival activism" (Flinn, 2011). "Community archives" thus bear the potential to act as a counter-measure against Smith's "authorized heritage discourse," but this does not mean that there are not even those "community archives" who support this authorized discourse or operate completely outside of it (Heimo & Hänninen, 2015, p. 9).

In the digital era, an ever-increasing number of collections and archives has begun to digitize their holdings and make these "digital archives" accessible to the public on the Internet. This technological development has opened up entirely new possibilities, not only for the digital continuity of the collections, but also for public participation. "The mass digitisation of analogue holdings is key to heritage organizations becoming an integral part of the Web. In the case of fragile carriers (magnetic tapes and chemical film for instance) digitisation is a means to ensure long-term preservation of the information. Digitisation is also a precondition for creating new access routes to collections (Oomen & Aroyo, 2011, p. 139). Furthermore, "ecomuseum," "indigenous curators," "participatory archives," "virtual museums," "participatory museology," "democratization of archives," "decolonization of museums," and so forth are a series of terms, which increasingly question the idea, the understanding, and the traditional role of museums, collections, and archives (Alivizatou, 2012; Gubrium & Harper, 2013, p. 169ff.). "Digital archives" and in particular "participatory digital archives" are a step in this direction.

Participatory digital archives (PDA) are containers of historical documents, images, media files, such as audio, video, or text files, which are accessible online and which involve members of a community into the curation of the collection. PDAs contain not only digital reproductions of objects (artifacts), but also their interpretations (meta-data). But unlike the traditional archive, it is not only the archivist who interprets and categorizes objects. PDAs are rather participatory digital methods that encourage members of a community to collect and interpret. "The turn toward participatory digital archives and virtual museums means that nonprofessional users are encouraged to contribute both artifacts (in the form of digital files) and interpretive meanings of the materials presented" (Gubrium & Harper, 2013, p. 170). Meta-data can result from group discussions in which it is decided how to present and interpret the objects, a process that can also lead to a greater reflection on how knowledge is produced (Gubrium & Harper, 2013, p. 169).

MEMOVOICE: A METHODOLOGICAL SYNTHESIS BETWEEN PHOTOVOICE, CROWDSOURCING, AND PARTICIPATORY DIGITAL ARCHIVE

Inspired by Photovoice, the participative digital archive and crowdsourcing, I have developed a method that, inspired by the term Photovoice, I called "Memovoice." Compared to the Photovoice method, Memovoice is not confined to photos, but leaves the participant completely free in deciding what types of objects are chosen in order to evoke and openly discuss memories.

In short, Memovoice works like this: people are called to identify objects they associate with a certain topic. Collection events are organized during which these objects are digitized and the related knowledge is documented in the format of a semi-structured qualitative interview. The digital reproductions of the objects are fed into a participatory digital archive that is publicly accessible. Here, other users can comment on existing meta-data and supplement further meta-data, interact differently with the contents of the archive and upload their own content. The principle of crowdsourcing is thus implemented on two levels: on the one hand through the collection inputs of single individuals; on the other through interactive functions in the digital archive itself.

Elsewhere, I describe in detail the pilot project, which I carried out in the time period between 2013 and 2015 in one specific valley in the Dolomites, the Val Badia, during which I tested the Memovoice method, and its results (Valentin, 2017 forthcoming). In every municipality of Val Badia information events (in total five) took place through which a total of forty project participants have been recruited. In the same amount of collection events (in total five with a duration of two to three days each) a total of 275 objects have been digitized and documented. A complete description of each project phase—the delimitation of the research field, the involvement of institutions and their representatives, the financial question, the organization of information events, the realization of proper information and collection events, the digitization and documentation of heritage, and finally the restitution of research results—would be too long to discuss here. It is suffice to say that all of these phases had a fundamental impact on the progress of the research, and the critical evaluation of each led to interesting insights.

CONCLUSION

The results obtained so far are not products of a concluded research. Rather they consist of preliminary results of an ongoing participatory process and a long-term project, which will reveal its potential only in the course of several years. The Memovoice method allowed an assessment of emic conceptions of "Ladin culture" on the basis of qualitative and activating research methods and with direct involvement of the population in the Dolomites. Hence, Memovoice turned out to be a useful method for the participative documentation of objects and related knowledge, which are regarded by individuals in Val Badia as "Ladin heritage."

A large share of project participants was from the older population. This is a positive outcome in fact, because older people are the bearers of historical knowledge. Thus far, the project has not been able to attract sufficient members of the younger generation. It will be interesting in the future to start targeted information events, awareness-rising measures and recruiting actions in order to include the younger generation's understanding of "Ladin culture" or "culture in the Dolomites." I especially hope to reach these "digital natives" through the digital archives. Projects in schools or with youth could turn the young population of the Dolomites into co-researchers for the digital archives. Furthermore, future measures could also address non-Ladins in order to allow some space to multiculturalism in the Dolomitic area and to generate data not only about internal ascriptions (Ladins on themselves) but also on external ascriptions (non-Ladins on Ladins).

A detailed analysis of all collected objects and narrations still has to be done. A first rather superficial evaluation shows, however, that each participant interpreted "Ladin culture" in very different ways. The collected objects are very often linked to their own life history, to their own working life, and to family, religious conviction, or private property in the widest sense. Particularly striking is the fact that most of the collected objects were "old things," antique objects which stand emblematically for a life in the past (ancestors, extinct practices) and evoke memories about a "past culture" that is contrasted with "modern life." The social, cultural, and economic change was a recurring theme in the narrations of the research participants.

On the other hand, research participants did not always associate "Ladin culture" with a "past culture." A musicologist, for example, brought a modern Mini Disc recorder to the collection that she used for her research on songs and music in Ladin valleys. In this person's conception, the Mini Disc recorder represented "Ladin culture" in an emblematic way, which in this case contained music culture in the Dolomites. This example shows that the method Memovoice is definitely able to reveal emic conceptions of "cultural heritage" that would not be admissible in "traditional" expert discourses. Even if this person was a musicologist—hence belonging to the category "expert"—she nevertheless counteracts the "traditional" opinion of experts. I doubt that it would be easy to find any expert who would declare a Mini Disc recorder made in Japan as "Ladin heritage." A deeper semantic analysis of the collected objects will certainly provide further interesting insights.

The Memovoice method can represent a possible answer to the question of how tangible and intangible heritage can be identified and documented by using participatory approaches. Certainly, participation has to be developed further through future actions. The preparation of the preliminary results in the form of traveling expositions, publications, presentations, workshops, and focus groups will offer manifold possibilities for the generation of creative participative processes. So far the project has given too little attention to the collective recognition of the identified heritage, and remains until now on the level of individual valorization of objects as heritage. Considering the described problems with the term "community," this methodological approach can help to avoid a priori definitions of community by being centered on single individuals. But the interesting question—which should be deepened in the future—is, to which degree things interpreted as heritage by a single person are regarded as such by a larger collective as well? And more importantly, *who* shares the same opinion? This collective aspect has to be addressed more in future actions.

The Memovoice actions have certainly created some degree of public awareness regarding the understanding of "Ladin culture" or "Ladin heritage." Persons who participated actively in the collection events have, no doubt, reached the highest degree of confrontation. But there is a large majority of the population that remains untouched by the project and I hope that larger involvement can be reached through a continuation of the project in the next years.

As mentioned above, the older people who participated in the project selected "old things," which represented their conceptions of "Ladin culture." But these "old things" also represent a romanticization of the past agricultural life in Val Badia. Hence, these objects seem to refer to certain images of "Ladin culture" which exist in the population and which are fundamentally determined by museal representations. By this I mean the kind of representations of "Ladin culture" in expositions of museums but also the representations of "Ladin culture" in publications by museums, cultural institutes, and other institutions. A great part of the publications on "Ladin culture" are of historical nature and reconstruct "Ladin culture" as it once was, often evoking an association of these past, extinguished, and forgotten aspects of "Ladin culture" with a certain aura of authenticity. On the other side, the situation nowadays—which is not determined anymore by the agricultural calendar but by seasonal tourism—is associated with a modern and non-authentic loss, as something artificial and not original, as a homogenizing process imposed from outside and not as an internal strategy of adaptation in order to guarantee economic survival of the cultural system. A historical analysis could bear interesting insights on how "the Ladins" and "the Ladin culture" have been constructed discursively on an institutional level. In my dissertation I touched this topic only marginally; hence I am not able to present results of a deeper analysis of this issue. But I assume that such cultural construction processes initiated by institutions and experts could be the explanation for the fact that a great part of the collected objects have such an antiquarian character and for being associated so strongly with the notion of a "Ladin culture" which is imagined as being localized in the past and which today exists only in the memories of the older representatives. Certainly, it should not be ignored that even this research project itself and the symbolic valorization of objects which went along with it was definitely an important player in the construction of "cultural heritage," maybe more than the project participants themselves.

At this point, it would be too early to answer the question of how to develop a sustainable management of "cultural heritage" which is sustained by both civil society and institutions. Up until now, the concept for the participative digital archives has been developed but its functionality has still to be tested empirically. The digital archives and the method of crowdsourcing bear in my opinion a big potential for the institutional work with "cultural heritage." The archive and the Memovoice method are useful as collection tools in order to make "invisible heritage" visible—that is, make visible those objects, photographs, videos, and documents of historical value and collective interest which are privately owned and which have not been documented by institutions. Memovoice maps "cultural heritage" on the territory which was not known to institutions before and which could be a useful resource for research, publications, and expositions.

Heritage management is not limited to identification and documentation alone but implicates many additional facets. Hence, measures for a sustainable development (I avoid consciously such a term as "conservation") or actions for intergenerational transmission will be of fundamental importance. Additionally, measures for the valorization of cultural elements— which have been identified through participative actions and implemented by institutions, will be necessary in supporting the bearers of heritage and in keeping it alive. Such aspects cannot be covered by a participative digital archive alone. Rather raising awareness, which promotes a consciousness for the topic of "heritage" among the population, should be a contributing factor. Hence, civic and institutional consciousness should influence each other and represent the basis for the birth of sustainable measures of development, transmission, and valorization.

The project I have presented here could be a valuable contribution especially for historical minorities who ask the question, which concrete possibilities exist if dealing with the interplay between heritage, digitization and participation? At the very least, it challenges the notion of "authorized heritage discourse" and raises awareness of the need for a more civic society and impartial institutions.

NOTES

1. Due to the problematic nature of the term "community" as described above, the use of the term "community-based" may seem just as critical. A good discussion on this, which shows that "community" in conjunction with participation always implies exclusion and not just inclusion, can be found in (Cornwall, 2008).

2. "Vernacular authority emerges when an individual makes appeals that rely on trust specifically because they are *not* institutional. [. . .] 'vernacular' can best be defined dialectically as that which is opposed to its alternate term 'institutional'" (Howard, 2012, p. 81).

BIBLIOGRAPHY

Adell, Nicolas, Bendix, Regina F., Bortolotto, Chiara, & Tauschek, Markus (Eds.). *Between Imagined Communities and Communities of Practice: Participation, Territoritory and the Making of Heritage* (Vol. 8). Göttingen: Universitätsverlag Göttingen, 2015a.

Adell, Nicolas, Bendix, Regina F., Bortolotto, Chiara, & Tauschek, Markus. "Introduction." In *Between Imagined Communities and Communities of Practice: Participation, Territory and the Making of Heritage* (Vol. 8). Göttingen: Universitätsverlag Göttingen, 2015b. pp. 7–21.

Albro, Robert. "The Terms of Participation in Recent UNESCO Cultural Policy Making." In J. Blake (Ed.), *Safeguarding Intangible Cultural Heritage: Challenges and Approaches*. Builth Wells Wales: Institute of Art and Law, 2007.

Alivizatou, Marilena. *Intangible Heritage and the Museum: New Perspectives on Cultural Preservation*. Walnut Creek: Left Coast Press, 2012.

Alonso Gonzalez, Pablo. "From a Given to a Construct: Heritage as a Commons." *Cultural Studies*, 1–32 (2013). https://doi.org/10.1080/09502386.2013.789067.

Anderson, Benedict. *Imagined Communities: Reflections on the Origin and Spread of Nationalism*. London: Verso, 1991.

Balen, Koen Van & Vandesande, Aziliz (Eds.). *Community Involvement in Heritage*. Antwerp: Garant, 2015.

Barth, Fredrik. *Ethnic Groups and Boundaries: The Social Organization of Culture Difference*. Boston: Little, Brown, 1969.

Blouin, Francis X. and Rosenberg, William G. *Processing the Past: Contesting Authority in History and the Archives*. New York: Oxford University Press. 2011.

Borda, Orlando Fals. "Participatory (Action) Research in Social Theory: Origins and Challenges." In P. Reason & H. Bradbury (Eds.), *Handbook of Action Research: Participative Inquiry and Practice* (pp. 27–37). Thousand Oaks, CA: SAGE, 2001.

Bortolotto, Chiara. "Partecipazione e patrimonio culturale immateriale." In ASPACI Associazione per la salvaguardia del patrimonio culturale immateriale (Ed.), *Identificazione partecipativa del patrimonio immateriale*. Milano: Centro Stampa BCS, 2011. pp. 66–72. Retrieved from http://www.echi-interreg .eu/assets/uploads/Identificazione_partecipativa_Patrimonio_Immateriale_dossier.pdf.

Brumann, Christoph. "Community as Myth and Reality in the UNESCO World Heritage Convention." In C. Bortolotto, N. Adell, M. Tauschek, & R. F. Bendix (Eds.), *Between Imagined Communities and Communities of Practice: Participation, Territoritory and the Making of Heritage* (pp. 273–289). Göttingen: Universitätsverlag Göttingen, 2015.

Chirikure, Shadreck, Manyanga, Munyaradzi, Ndoro, Webber, & Pwiti, Gilbert. "Unfulfilled Promises? Heritage Management and Community Participation at Some of Africa's Cultural Heritage Sites." *International Journal of Heritage Studies*, 16, nos. 1–2 (2010): 30–44. https://doi .org/10.1080/13527250903441739.

Chirikure, Shadreck & Pwiti, Gilbert. "Community Involvement in Archaeology and Cultural Heritage Management: An Assessment from Case Studies in Southern Africa and Elsewhere." *Current Anthropology*, 49, no. 3 (2008): 467–485. https://doi.org/10.1086/588496.

Cornwall, Andrea. "Unpacking 'Participation': Models, Meanings and Practices." *Community Development Journal*, 43, no. 3 (2008): 269–283. https://doi.org/10.1093/cdj/bsn010

Crooke, Elizabeth. "The Politics of Community Heritage: Motivations, Authority and Control." In E. Waterton & S. Watson (Eds.), *Heritage and Community Engagement: Collaboration or Contestation?* New York: Routledge (pp. 24–37). 2011.

Deacon, Harriet & Smeets, Rieks. "Authenticity, Value and Community Involvement in Heritage Management Under the World Heritage and Intangible Heritage Conventions." *Heritage and Society*, 6, no. 2 (2013): 1–15.

Elsen, Susanne, Oberleiter, Evelyn, Reifer, Gunther, & Wild, Andreas (Eds.). *Die Kunst des Wandels: Ansätze für die ökosoziale Transformation*. München: Oekom Verlag, 2015.

Ernst, Wolfgang. *Digital Memory and the Archive*. Minneapolis: University of Minnesota Press, 2013.

Flinn, Andrew. 2011. Archival Activism: Independent and Community-Led Archives, Radical Public History and the Heritage Professions. *InterActions: UCLA Journal of Education and Information Studies* 7(2): 1–21.

Flinn, Andrew. Stevens, Mary & Shepherd, Elizabeth. "Whose Memories, Whose Archives? Independent Community Archives, Autonomy and the Mainstream." *Archival Science* (2009) 9: 71.

Kenneth Foote. "To Remember and Forget: Archives, Memory, and Culture." *The American Archivist* 53, 3 (Summer 1990): 378–392.

Freire, Paulo. *Cultural Action for Freedom*. Harmondsworth: Penguin, 1972.

Gubrium, Aline & Harper, Krista. *Participatory Visual and Digital Methods*. Walnut Creek, CA: Left Coast Press. 2013.

Hafstein, Vladimar. Tr. "The Politics of Origins: Collective Creation Revisited." *The Journal of American Folklore*, 117, no. 465 (2004): 300–315.

Handler, Richard. *Nationalism and the Politics of Culture in Quebec*. Madison: University of Wisconsin Press, 1988.

Heimo, Anne, and Kirsi Hänninen. 2015. Participatory, Community and Spontaneous Archives and Digitally Born Cultural Heritage. *Folklore Fellows Network* 47: 4–11.

Huvila, Isto. 2008. "Participatory Archive: Towards Decentralised Curation, Radical User Orientation, and Broader Contextualisation of Records Management." *Archival Science* 8(1): 15–36.

Hollowell, Julie & Nicholas, George. "Using Ethnographic Methods to Articulate Community-Based Conceptions of Cultural Heritage Management." *Public Archaeology*, 8, no. 2 (2009): 141–160. https://doi.org/10.1179/175355309X457196.

Jimerson, Randall C. "Archives 101 in a 2.0 World: The Continuing Need for Parallel Systems." In Kate Theimer (Ed.), *A Different Kind of Web: New Connections Between Archives and Our Users* (pp. 304–333). Chicago: Society of American Archivists, 2011.

King, Laura, and Gary Rivett. 2015. "Engaging People in Making History: Impact, Public Engagement and the World Beyond the Campus." *History Workshop Journal* 80(1): 218–233.

Kirshenblatt-Gimblett, Barbara. "Intangible Heritage as Metacultural Production." *Museum International*, 56, no. 1–2 (2004): 52–65. https://doi.org/10.1111/j.1350-0775.2004.00458.x.

Macdonald, Sharon. *Memorylands: Heritage and Identity in Europe Today*. London: Routledge Chapman & Hall, 2013.

Nicholas, George & IPinCH Collective. "Collaborative, Community-Based Heritage Research, and the IPINCH Project." *The SAA Archaeological Record* 12, no. 4 (2012): 30–32.

Oomen, Johan & Aroyo, Lora. "Crowdsourcing in the Cultural Heritage Domain: Opportunities and Challenges." In *Proceedings of the 5th International Conference on Communities and Technologies/* (pp. 138–149). New York: ACM Press, 2011. Retrieved from http://dl.acm.org/citation.cfm?doid=2103354.2103373.

Reason, Peter & Bradbury-Huang, Hillary (Eds.). *Handbook of Action Research: Participative Inquiry and Practice*. Thousand Oaks, CA: SAGE, 2001a.

Reason, Peter & Bradbury-Huang, Hillary. "Introduction: Inquiry and Participation in Search of a World Worthy of Human Aspiration." In P. Reason & H. Bradbury (Eds.), *Handbook of Action Research: Participative Inquiry and Practice* (pp. 1–14). Thousand Oaks, CA: SAGE, 2001b.

Showers, Ben. Capturing the Power of the Crowd and the Challenge of Community Collections. 2010. JISC. Retrieved from http://www.jisc.ac.uk/publications/programmerelated/2010/communitycollections.aspx.

Smith, Laurajane. *Uses of Heritage*. New York: Routledge, 2006.

Valentin, Emanuel. *Memoria Ladina: Heritage, Community und Partizipation in den Dolomiten*. Bozen-Bolzano: Bozen Bolzano University Press, 2017.

Waterton, Emma., & Watson, Steve (Eds.). *Heritage and Community Engagement: Collaboration or Contestation?* New York: Routledge, 2011.

Whyte, William Foote. *Participatory Action Research*. Newbury Park, CA: Sage Publications, 1991.

Index

About the Contributors

Desiree Alaniz is a graduate student at Simmons College pursuing a dual master's degree in history and archives management. Her research interests include community and participatory archives and social movement history.

Janet Ceja Alcalá is assistant professor in library and information science at Simmons College. She teaches courses in the archives management concentration and cultural heritage concentration. Her research interests are in the areas of moving-image preservation, cultural archives, and community engagement.

Alexandru Chiselev is curator at the Museum of Ethnography and Folk Art, part of the Eco-Museum Research Institute in Tulcea, Romania. Chiselev is a PhD student in cultural studies at Bucharest University, where he is focusing on "Magic Thinking of Ethnic Groups from Northern Dobruja." His research interests also include crafts, sustainable development, rural spaces, museology, organization of exhibitions, and the preservation of the ethnographic heritage of Northern Dobruja, Romania.

Sandra Chung is Distinguished Professor of Linguistics at the University of California, Santa Cruz. A syntactician who specializes in Austronesian languages, she began research on the Chamorro language some forty years ago. She is now the consulting linguist on the *Chamorro–English Dictionary*, and is writing a reference grammar of Chamorro.

Guido Cimadomo is lecturer in the Department of Architectural Composition and Coordinator for International Mobility at the School of Architecture, University of Malaga, since 2010. Guido Cimadomo is an architect from the Politecnico di Milano and holds a PhD from the Seville School of Architecture and conducted research on how landscape and urban territories are transformed by contemporary borders. Cimadomo combines his practice of architecture with his interest and work on the documentation, rehabilitation, and dissemination of cultural heritage and the building of cultural and sport facilities while being mindful of (1) industrial heritage; (2) border and transnational transformations; (3) landscape, heritage, and tourism relations; and (4) heritage rehabilitation processes.

Brian Diettrich (PhD, University of Hawaii at Manoa) is senior lecturer in ethnomusicology at Victoria University of Wellington, New Zealand. His research focuses on the Pacific Islands, and especially on music and dance in the Federated States of Micronesia. His publications include "Music in Pacific Island Culture: Experiencing Music, Expressing Culture" (Oxford University Press, 2011), of which he is a coauthor. Brian is currently chair of the study group on music and dance of Oceania, of the International Council for Traditional Music.

Patty Gerstenblith is Distinguished Research Professor of Law at DePaul University College of Law and Director of its Center for Art, Museum & Cultural Heritage Law. She is founding president of the Lawyers Committee for Cultural Heritage Preservation (2005–2011) and Secretary of the U.S. Committee of the Blue Shield. She served as a member of the president's Cultural Property Advisory Committee in the U.S. Department of State in both the Clinton and Obama administrations. From 1995 to 2002, she was editor-in-chief of the *International Journal of Cultural Property*. Her recent publications include the casebook, *Art, Cultural Heritage and the Law* (now in its third edition). Gerstenblith received her AB from Bryn Mawr College, PhD in art history and anthropology from Harvard University, and JD from Northwestern University. Before joining the DePaul faculty, she clerked for the Honorable Richard D. Cudahy of the Seventh Circuit Court of Appeals.

Gregory Hansen is professor of folklore and English at Arkansas State University. He has worked as a public sector folklorist and a consultant with a number of organizations, including the Smithsonian Institution, the Florida Folklife Program, and the Danish Immigrant Museum. His research and publications focus primarily on folklore and language, fiddle traditions in the southeastern United States, and public presentations of traditional culture. He currently is teaching in the doctoral program in heritage studies at Arkansas State University. Dr. Hansen also is the author of *A Florida Fiddler: The Life and Times of Richard Seaman*.

Stacy Kowalczyk is associate professor and director of the Information Management Master's program in the School of Information Studies at Dominican University. Her research focuses on the problems of research data, big data, and curation, specifically looking at the intersection of social and technical issues. In her current work, she is investigating the research practices of scholars, the lifecycle of research data including data reuse, and the antecedents, barriers, and threats to preservation of research data. She teaches courses on digital libraries, library systems, digital curation, information architecture, systems analysis, and human computer interaction. She has an MLIS from Dominican University and a PhD from Indiana University and a postdoctorate appointment at the Data to Insight Center of the Indiana University Pervasive Technology Institute. She has worked in software development in fortune 100 companies, entrepreneurial startups, and large academic libraries.

Maurizio Lazzari was awarded a bachelor's degree with honors in geological sciences in 1993 and the title of Doctor of Philosophy in earth sciences in 1999. He won a two-year postdoctoral scholarship at the University of Bari (2001) and a Socrates/Erasmus scholarship at the University of Portsmouth (UK). He was adjunct professor of physical geography and geomorphology, paleontology, and paleoecology courses from 2007 to 2012 at the University of Basilicata. He is a researcher in geomorphology and engineering geology at CNR-IBAM (Italian National Research Council—Institute for Cultural Heritage and Monuments), specializing in geological survey (1994). His scientific and research activity is evidenced by more than 100 national and international publications on journals, book chapters and monographies, inherent the natural and anthropic risks, geomorphology, engineering geology, applied geomorphology, geoarchaeology, geological bibliography, and georeferencing of bibliographic data, climatology, stratigraphy, and sedimentology.

John T. Lizama has a successful law practice in the Commonwealth of the Northern Mariana Islands (CNMI). He also served as associate judge for the Commonwealth Superior Court from July 1998, until his retirement in July 2010. Judge Lizama presided over many cases in which traditional or indigenous cultural heritage was involved, sustaining his appreciation for the central place of cultural heritage in a community. Over many years, Judge Lizama had a membership in various associations and organizations in the CNMI. Most recently, he served on and chaired the Board of Regents of the Northern Marianas College.

Agata Maggio holds a degree in modern literature and a master's degree in management of cultural heritage for the management of museums and picture galleries. She has worked in various projects in Europe, such as the Digital Preservation Europe project. She attended a postgraduate specialization course in library science. She is an expert in cataloging using the Sebina software. She is a teacher of the cataloging of modern, as well as old and rare books. She is the reference professional for cataloging at the Leonardo Sinisgalli Foundation (Basilicata region, southern Italy) and is a research authority and technical collaborator at the Institute for Archaeological and Monumental Heritage of CNR (Italian National Research Council). She is the president of the Basilicata Section of the Italian Library Association and author of popular and scientific publications in the field of library science.

Elizabeth Rechebei served as education administrator in the Pacific Islands region, represented her islands in regional organizations in various capacities, led in the development of public institutions, such as the first public library in the CNMI, and the planning of the CNMI museum of history and culture, and coauthored a Palau history book. She is currently coediting the *Chamorro–English Dictionary*. She is also involved in various program evaluations and has a membership on various boards, including the CNMI Historic Preservation Review Board and the Traditional Medicine and Culture Association.

Arantza Respaldiza is a postdoctoral independent researcher, GIS scientist, and data artist. Her interests focus on visual reasoning, theories of visualization, and metadata and heritage. Her research work proposes a visual reasoning process for heritage valuation, which she developed for her thesis. In her proposal, she integrates the process for valuation of heritage with the multifaceted dimension of heritage, exploiting the potential of visual reasoning. She has a strong background in the humanities, arts, and geomatics. She has experience in graphic design, editorial work, and multimedia and web design. Her personal brand is "marh.es," and she has worked for communication agencies, publishing companies, and as a freelancer.

Loriene Roy is Anishinabe, enrolled on the White Earth Reservation (Pembina Band), a member of the Minnesota Chippewa Tribe. Roy received an MLS from the University of Arizona and a PhD from the University of Illinois at Urbana–Champaign. She is currently professor in the School of Information at the University of Texas at Austin where she teaches graduate courses in reference, library instruction, and access and care of indigenous cultural knowledge. She is also an adjunct instructor for the Library & Information Science Program at the University of Hawai'i at Manoa. She served as 1997–1998 president of the American Indian Library Association and the 2007–2008 president of the American Library Association. She is a member of the Library of Congress Literacy Awards Advisory Board, StoryCorps Tribal Library Advisory Group, Design4Learning: 21st Century Online Learning for Library Workers Leadership Team, and the Libraries Without Borders Advisory Committee. She has received numerous professional awards, most recently the 2015 Distinguished Service Award, American Indian Library Association; 2014 Library School Alumni Association Distinguished Alumnus Award, Graduate School of Library and Information Science, the University of Illinois at Urbana–Champaign; and the 2014 Sarah Vann Award, ALA Hawai'i Student Chapter at the University of Hawai'i Manoa Library & Information Science Program.

Marta Severo is associate professor in communication at the University of Paris Ouest Nanterre. Her research focuses on digital methods for social sciences and representations of spatial objects through web-based data. Her current studies concern the Intangible Cultural Heritage and the European cultural routes. She was a postdoctoral fellow at the Politecnico of Milan, at Sciences Po Paris and at the International College for Territorial Sciences (CIST) in Paris. She has also been involved in several UNESCO projects, notably at the World Heritage Centre. Since 2012, she coordinates the research program "media and territories" of the International College of Territorial Sciences (Paris).

Diane Thram (PhD in ethnomusicology, Indiana University, 1999), is Professor Emeritus at Rhodes University where she served as director of the International Library of African Music (ILAM) and edited its annual journal, *African Music*, from 2006–2016. She managed ILAM's cataloging and digitizing project (2007–2011) that made online access possible; directed research, outreach and education, and repatriation initiatives; and launched ILAM's Pilot Project in Restudy and Repatriation of Hugh Tracey Field Recordings in Kenya in 2014. She curated exhibitions and edited exhibit catalogs for the "For Future Generations—Hugh Tracey and the International Library of African Music" traveling museum exhibit (2010) and the "Generations of Jazz" permanent exhibit (2013) at the Red Location Museum in New Brighton, a township of Port Elizabeth. She has published numerous articles and book chapters from her research on music and indigenous religion in Southern Africa, media control in Zimbabwe, and music heritage archives ethics.

Juliana Titov is Department Head at the Museum of Ethnography and Folk Art, part of the Eco-Museum Research Institute in Tulcea, Romania. She earned her doctorate in history with her thesis titled, "Relationship between majority-minority ethnics in Northern Dobruja." She conducts research and writes on ethnology, communication sciences, museum marketing, and the organization of exhibitions. She has a strong research interest on the preservation of the ethnographic heritage of Northern Dobruja, Romania.

Ciaran Trace is associate professor at the School of Information at the University of Texas at Austin where she teaches courses on archives and records management. Her research interests flow across the areas of archives and material cultural. An ongoing research focus is the study of the nature, meaning, and function of everyday writing, recording, and recordkeeping (with a particular focus on organizational document creation and use, and the role of written literacies in the lives of children and young adults). Another research strand looks at how and why individuals and institutions collect material culture, the intersection of material culture and information behavior, and digital materiality including the study of the artifactual nature of computers, computer systems, and digital objects. Ciaran also studies the nature of archival work and work practices (including how technology can help support the work of curating and providing access to archival collections). Drawing from the mentorship of Dr. Loriene Roy, the professional debates surrounding the Protocols for Native American Archival Materials, and the initiatives being developed as part of the IMLS funded Archival Education and Research Institute, Ciaran is seeking to integrate national conversations on traditional cultural expressions into the archival curriculum.

Emanuel Valentin graduated with a magister artium degree in social and cultural anthropology at Eberhard-Karls-University Tübingen (Germany) and holds a PhD in education from the Free University of Bozen-Bolzano (Italy). Currently he is lecturer in cultural anthropology at the Faculty of Education of the same university.

Tasha Vorderstrasse is research associate at the Oriental Institute of the University of Chicago. She received her PhD from the University of Chicago in Near Eastern Archaeology. She works on the material culture of the Near East, the Caucasus and Central Asia, and the interactions between those areas and China.

Monica Wachowicz is associate professor and the NSERC/Cisco Industrial Research Chair in Real-Time Mobility Analytics at the University of New Brunswick, Canada. She is also the Director of the People in Motion Laboratory, a center of expertise in the application of Internet of Things (IoT) to smart cities. Her research work is directly related to the vision of a constellation of interconnected devices in the future that will contain information about the context and mobility of things across several geographical and temporal scales. She works at the intersection of (1) *Streaming Analytics* for analyzing massive IoT data in search of valuable spatiotemporal patterns in real-time; and (2) *Art, Cartography, and Representations* of mobility for making the maps of the future that will be culturally and linguistically designed to provide a greater "sense of people" in motion. Founding member of the IEEE Big Data Initiative and the International Journal of Big Data Intelligence, she is also joint editor-in-chief of the *Cartographica* journal. Her pioneering work in multidisciplinary teams from government, industry, and research organizations is fostering the next generation of data scientists for innovation.

About the Editor

Cecilia Lizama Salvatore is professor at the School of Information Studies at Dominican University in River Forest, Illinois, where she is also coordinator of the Archives and Cultural Heritage Certificate program. She previously developed a certificate program in archives studies at Emporia State University. Prior to obtaining her doctorate from the University of Texas, Dr. Salvatore was the Territorial Librarian/Archivist for the U.S. Territory of Guam and a librarian at the Micronesian Area Research Center at the University of Guam.

Cecilia Lizama Salvatore has served as program evaluator of various federally funded (U.S.) projects and a juror for the Illinois Arts Council. She serves on the Illinois State Archives Advisory Board and on the Genealogy and Local History Collection Standing Committee of IFLA, the International Federation of Library Associations and Institutions. She serves on the board of the Association for Library and Information Education and was chair of the Archival Educators Roundtable and the Oral History Section of the Society of American Archivists. She also served on a committee of the International Relations Roundtable of the American Library Association.

In 2000, she was honored by the Northern Marianas Commonwealth Legislature for being the first female from the Commonwealth of the Northern Mariana Islands (CNMI) to earn a PhD.